HISTORICAL RECORDS OF

BISLEY

WITH LYPIATT

MARY A. RUDD

AMBERLEY

First published privately by Mary A. Rudd, 1937,
Reprinted in facsimile by Alan Sutton, 1977
This facsimile edition published 2008

Amberley Publishing
Cirencester Road, Chalford,
Stroud, Gloucestershire, GL6 8PE

British Library Cataloguing in Publication Data.
A catalogue record for this book is available from the British Library.

ISBN 978-1-84868-154-5

Printed in Great Britain by Amberley Publishing

FOREWORD

by Geoffrey Sanders

Historical Records of Bisley with Lypiatt by Miss Mary Rudd (1863-1945) was published in 1937. One cannot do better than use the author's own prospectus, a copy of which, together with correspondence by her, I have retained over the years.

"It is proposed (she wrote) to print and issue by private subscription a limited edition of a History of Bisley, upon which I have been engaged for several years. No pains have been spared to make it as complete as possible and in addition to searching National and Local Records I have been fortunate in having permission to consult many documents which are not accessible to the general Public. Full advantage has been taken of this special favour, and of other sources, with the result that the History will be found packed with information, presented in a condensed but readable form.

"The History covers the whole of the ancient parish of Bisley, with the exception of Stroud and Paganhill, both of which are fully dealt with in Fisher's *Reminiscences of Stroud*.

"The twelve chapters into which my *Historical Records* is divided will be found to present full accounts of the manors of Bisley and of the six independent manors with their ancient mansions, namely Througham, Sydenhams, Sturmye's Court, Tunley, Denway and Ferris Court. The ecclesiastical history is enriched with authentic accounts of every ancient feature of the Church. The Manors of Over, Middle and Nether Lypiatt with the families owning them offer subjects of great import, whilst the tythings of Oakridge, Avenage, Chalford, Bussage, Bidfield and Steanbridge, with their share in the fortunes of the old clothier families, are here revealed in an unexpectedly interesting light, as their links with past centuries are unfolded. Notes on some of the principal old farms, houses, and families are given, and the records of wills of Bisley inhabitants at Somerset House and Gloucester Probate Registry.

"A full index completes the work.

"The illustrations have been selected with the view of commemorating some of Bisley's most ancient relics, many of which are destroyed or not easy of access".

With its ecclesiastical history and manorial background, few parishes in Gloucestershire have had their history so fully presented. Bisley was once distinguished by having two priests, as witnessed by Domesday, a circumstance which does not appear elsewhere in the county, and until 1360 the parish included Stroud. The history and ownership of the manors of Upper Lypiatt, Middle Lypiatt and Nether Lypiatt occupy nearly one third of the book. Miss Rudd was particularly fortunate in having access to the Lypiatt muniments.

No more than 250 copies were printed at a cost of £277 17s 3d ("a most satisfactory amount", Miss Rudd wrote to a friend). The price per copy was £1 and, although she had obtained ninety subscribers (including my father), she must have been out of pocket. This excellent history, however, was her reward.

In the course of forty years Historical Records of *Bisley with Lypiatt* has become extremely scarce and copies have disappeared from the second-hand market. It is most opportune, therefore, that Mr. Alan Sutton should have undertaken the second edition.

When asked to review it by the Vicar of Bisley for his parish magazine Professor R. H. Tawney wrote, "There are a few misprints, or what appear to the reviewer to be misprints". He regarded this matter as a trifle, but Mr. Sutton has been fortunate in getting our well known local historian, Mr. F. T. Hammond to provide corrigenda. He is mentioned in Miss Rudd's preface as one of her helpers.

Geoffrey Sanders
April 1977

" Hug Com Cest Constabloni et dapifero suo Justic Vicecom Baronibus Ministris et Ballivis et omib q Hoibus suis fiduc et Auzt tam futurus qm psentib Sciatis me reddadu Umfrid de Buhun et heredibz suis tenendum de me et de meis heredibus feodum de Bisseleia ut suam hereditatem q serviciu trcim militu de quinq qui recognescunta et si contigerit qd plures milites qaquinq iveniantur in feodo vel p disrocuratione at p recognicioni, ego Hugo et heredes mei habebem servicu dimidm de incremento et Umfrid et heredes sui p hoc tenednt feodum de me et de meis heredibus sine feodo Philippi de Belmis qd Hugo de Aci in capite tenet de me. Testib istis Ric filio com Gloecestr, Johe Constabloe Cestr, Bertram de Verdun, Roger Malfillastyr, Rad Viccom de Abricis, Herveie de Missi exparte Com et Galfrido de Costentin et Rob filio Walti et Ex parte Umfride de Bohun, Engelger de Buhun, Walte filis Rob, Ric de Vehun, Ric de Abenesse, Walte de Asseleia, Willo de Mineres, Olivero de Mara, Ricardo Bigot, Umfrido de Sco Vigor, Rob. de Vernun."

This charter has the Earl's large seal in green wax, depicting a knight on horseback with an impression on the reverse.

A second charter of the time of King John must be considered with that of Earl Hugh as containing the first mention of the connection of the Mortimers with Bisley.

" Sciant psentes et futra qd ego Rogs de Mortuo Mari concedi et dedi Cecilie de Rodberga et hedibz hus in excabm redditu quatior solidoz scilicet de tra Gerardi Lorestarii p redditu quinq solidoz pcipere solebat de tra Sodewigi de Biselee de dono fraton meor Philipp de Belmis et Ranulfo ad tenendu de me et hedibz meis set hedibz suis p serviciu qd erti ad placita mea apd Biselee p raconabite sumoicoem p oi serviuco. Scan hedes mei his excabiu mutare voluerint Volo et firmat pcipio caran reddant pdicta Cecilie et hedibz suis quinqe solidatis tre et eodem Manno sicut Alicia hint morm hoc excamviu fieret. Hoc au excabiu ha carta mea sigillo meo muytta firmam. Hus testibz Dno Rad Abbate de

Wigmora, Ada Salvags, Philipp de Mort Mar, Henr de Bibbeford, Magtro Willo pa de Biselee, Willo de Mortmar, Hug de Ssco Laur, Rogo de Longsb, Robt o Corbet, Osoto Russell, Ernaldo de Belco, et aliie." (Seal of Roger de Mortimer on horseback in red wax.)[1]

The first of these important deeds explains the origin of the connection of the De Bohuns with Bisley manor ; how Earl Hugh in the reign of Henry II assigned to Humphrey de Bohun land in Bisley to be held by him for the service of three knights fees out of the five assigned to the entire fief, and excluding the fee of Philip de Belmis, that Hugh de Aci then held of the Earl in chief. The second charter reveals that Philip de Belmis is brother or brother-in-law to Roger Mortimer, and it speaks of the land of " Sodewigi de Biselee," who probably is ancestor of the de Bisley family whose history will be traced later. This charter also gives us the first name of a parson of Bisley, William, and also the first connection of the Corbets. By this time it is apparent how completely the Normans were in possession of Bisley, revenues from which went to some of the highest families in the land.

The Earls of Chester continued to be chief Lords of the Manor till 1246. Randolph de Blondeville held it from 1181 to 1232, having been created Earl of Lincoln in 1217, and joining in the Crusades with much distinction from 1218 to 1220. He resigned his Earldom of Lincoln to his sister Hawise to whose son John de Lacy it was confirmed in 1292. After the death of Randolph, the Earldom of Chester passed to the Crown in 1246, and with it the manor of Bisley.

Philip de Belmis is in all probablility son of Walter de Belmeis who was younger brother to the first Richard de Belmeis, Bishop of London, and he was heir to the Shropshire estates of his brother Richard who was second Bishop of London of that name,[2] that is to say, if he was brother-in-law of Roger Mortimer.

The portion of the manor of Bisley granted by the Earl of Chester to Humphrey de Bohun is identified in later deeds

---

1 Carta Sloane xxxiii. 4.

2 Dictionary of National Biography.

and covered Lypiatt, Thrupp, Stroud and Paganhill. That mentioned in connection with Philip de Belmis cannot be defined with any certainty.

Whilst the history of Bisley at this period is obscure, there are glimpses of life as lived there to be found in some of the early records of the P. R. O. For instance, in 31, Hen. I 1130-3 Walter de Maisi (a name which is found centuries later at Bisley) renders account of the farm of Biseleia, " In the Treasury £7 10s. and in gifts by King's letters to Hugh Villano 10s."[1]

In Richard I's reign, 1194, Philip de Bisele paid 3s. to the Bishops of Coventry and Hereford for tenths for the Crusade to Jerusalem.[2]

In 1191, 12s. fine; in 1192, 7d. and one Mark; and in 1194 3s. fine paid for murders in the Hundred of Bisley, indicate the wildness of the times. Punishment for crimes was meted out at Painswick, where the Lord of the Manor had the right to gallows, pillory and tumbrel.[3]

The fact that there are four plow-tillages in demesne mentioned in Domesday Book indicates that even at that time there were four lords holding four portions of the manor. The larger portion known as Lypiatt with Stroud, demised to Humphrey de Bohun, became a separate manor. The three remaining parts are spoken of frequently as the fourth parts of the Manor of Bisley and great confusion has arisen in the County Histories because it has not been recognized that the holders of these portions each spoke of " my manor of Bisley," leading one to think the whole manor was indicated when it was merely a part of it. The course of ownership was also greatly complicated by the rebellions of the Mortimers and Despencers, the resumption of one or other portion or the whole into the King's hands, the re-granting of the same for longer or shorter periods, the letting or sub-letting of the whole or parts of the fourth portions of the ancient manor. Our interest lies in trying to identify the extent

---

1 P. R. O. Indices. Rot. Magnus Pipe 31. Hen. I., p. 79.
2 P. R. O. Pipe Rolls, Ric. I., p. 237.
3 P. R. O. Pipe Rolls, Ric. I., p. 234.

of the lands and jurisdictions of these manorial divisions, together with their owners and tenants.

The first is naturally the estate of Overcourt, the "Maner Superius" of the Ministers' Accounts. The second, the "Maner Inferius," now known as Jaynes Court, and the third Stokesend or Stokeland, a name completely lost sight of in Bisley since the Reformation, signifying the end of the town where the Stoke property lies, and I think there is no doubt that this is to be identified with what is now known as the Mansion and its surrounding land, though deeds to prove this either do not exist or are inaccessible. Stoke Clare College, Suffolk, founded by Richard de Clare ancestor of the Mortimers may have had an interest in this estate, but it is certain that Richard, Duke of York, obtained for the College in 1480 the two rectorial portions of Bisley, carrying with the first portion the patronage of the Chantry, the adjoining property to Stokesend. Of the other two parts of the Manor Overcourt would appear to have been in possession of the de Bisley family down to 1415, and Jaynes Court to have belonged to the Mortimers.

CHAPTER III

PART I

OF OVERCOURT AND THE DE BISLEY FAMILY

The De Bisley family whose connection with Bisley has already been indicated, beginning with Philip mentioned in 1194 and Sodwigius, in the reign of King John, is undoubtedly of Norman origin, but who they really were and how they were connected with other Norman families remains a mystery. The arms attributed to the De Bisleys in Burke's General Armoury, namely, Ar. a chevron engrailed (or invecked) sa. between three raven ppr, (if indeed these are correct for the Gloucestershire family), do not throw any light on the subject. But that one can without doubt place them at Overcourt seems clear on account of the fact that they take their name from the place and also that the eldest son was habitually named Le Eyr or The Heir. This was a common practice in Norman families in the time of the Edwards.

In 1240-1 we find that Thomas de Biselegh has died and Hawisia, his widow, had made an agreement with Nicholas of Sancta Brigidia, holding a third part of half a fee (except in 22s. rent which Hawisia claims as of free holding in the middle of the town belonging to Thomas, her late husband), yielding up her rights in the half fee and in return receiving 15s. rent at the quarter days, namely, from the tenement which Henry de la Strode held in the same town 10s. and from that which Robert de Chalkforde held in the same town 5s.[1]

In 1285, 15 Ed. I., Richard le Eyr de Byseleye, who is probably the son of Thomas, with Roesia, his wife, agreed

[1] Feet of Fines, Glos., 273. P. R. O.

to let half a virgate of land in Bisley for 4s. 8d. rent to Henry
le Deboneyr and Laetitia, his wife, this land having been
in the tenancy of Roger of Litteridge, and the agreement
was sealed by the gift of a sparrowhawk by Richard and
Roesia to Henry and Laetitia.[1]

Richard de Biseleye in 1286-7 was holding a fourth part
of the hundred of Bisley, whilst Peter Corbett was holding
two parts and Theobald de Verdun was holding a fourth
part.[2]

Richard de Bisley's life was not confined to Bisley, for it
appears that he was for some years in the service of Sir
Walter Helyun of Co. Hereford. He was witness of a grant
of Sir Walter's to Sir Anselm de Gyse in 1276, an enrolment
of a grant of land to Sir Walter in 1279, and a grant by Sir
Walter to his son in 1300. In 1291 he had been elected
Verderer of the forest of Dean, but an order was sent to the
sheriff of Gloucester to cause another verderer to be elected,
as Richard could not attend to his duties, being in service
to Walter Helyun.[3]

Richard de Bisley had at least four sons, Hugh, his heir,
Thomas, Walter and Richard. The two latter are mentioned
in a charter[4] of John Page, burgess of Cirencester, assigning
to them the rent and service for Penweslond, otherwise the
Pear, in Bisley, then in the tenancy of William de la Pere[5]
and Alice his wife. This charter is not dated, but is witnessed
by William de Reem, John de la Strode, William le Proute,
Richard de Clyveshale, Walter de Stonehenge, Walter de
Paganhull, Henry de Chalford, William Faber of Bysrugge
(Bussage), Robert of Stonehenge, clerk.

The Calendar of the Records of the Corporation of
Gloucester states that there is a deed of release, of about
1300, from Thomas the Heyr, son of Richard the Eyr of
Byseleye and Margaret, wife of the said Thomas, to Brother

1 Feet of Fines, C. P., 35, Glos. P. R. O.

2 Placita de Quo Warranto, Rot. 13.

3 Calendar of Close Rolls.

4 Lypiatt MS. Book.

5 See Abst. of Deeds B. G. A. S. Trans., li., 211.

John of the Oak (del Ok') Prior to the Hospital of St. Bartholomew and the Brethren of the same of all their right in lands and tenements in Herdewyk and Elmore, W. Robert of the Field, William the Fremon of Elmore, John the Veysery', Robert of the Field, jun., William of Pydismor, John Hathimas.

It would seem from the same Records, that this son broke away from Bisley, and made his home at Gloucester, where we find a Thomas of Bisseleye witnessing a document in 1369 and up to 1457. In 1399, August 24, there is a lease for forty years from Brother John, Prior of the Hospital of St. Margaret near Gloucester and the Brethren and Sisters of the same, with the assent of Edward Taverner, Master of the said Hospital, to John Bysseleye, burgess of Gloucester and Emma, his wife, of a barn with a small piece of land adjoining in the suburb of Gloucester in the Newelonde, between the messuage that John Bowyar holds and the lane leading to the field called Hyde.

Walter and Richard de Bisley in a charter[1] dated at Byseleye on the Feast of the Annunciation 21 Ed. III (1347), assigned the Pownesland which they say they had purchased of John Page, but which was at that time in the tenancy and service of Robert de la Pere, to their brother Hugh. This estate is to be traced in Stancombe, on the West side of the Copsgrove ridge, where a field still bears the name of the Pear, and shows signs of foundations and terraces. It was accessible in those days from the highway which ran through Lypiatt Park down into Stancombe and Bismore, and the estate of the Pear was described as a "Messuage in or near the Tything of Over Lypiatt, and six closes of land meadow pasture and wood grounds containing fourteen acres, together with nineteen and a half acres of arable land belonging to the Pear."

And here it is convenient to give in full a charter of William de la Pere copied in the Lypiatt MS. Book, because it presents a valuable picture of people and conditions in the lifetime of Richard de Bisley.

[1] Lypiatt M.S. Book

" Sciant presentes et futuri quod ego Willus de la Pere dedi et concessi et hac presenti carta mea confirmavi Rogero filio Alexandri Capellani pro homagio et Servicio Suo illam terram meam apud la Pere juxta regales viam ex occ de Byseleye versus Bisrugge cum uno curtilagio Et unam Acram terre juxta Tostone in Campo Orientali Scilicet juxta viam que ducit versus Bisrugge cujus una extremitas extendit at Hurhelyate et alia extremitas extendit super terram Hugonis de Lydeneye Et unam culturam terre super Pirleyehulle juxta terram Dni Hugonis de Mortuomar Persone de Bysseleye et extendit Super terram que fuit Willi Cruste Et una Acram terre in Pirleye que jac juxta terram dicti Dni Hugon Psone et terram Walteri de fraxino (ash-tree) Et unam acram terre in eodem Campo que extendit Super viam juxta la Rocwode et jac juxta terram Roberti de Hanestie Et unam Acram que jac juxta viam que ducit versus Lutlerugge juxta qndm terram Alexandri Capellani jac Et unam Acram que jac juxta Gatewode et extendit super terra dicti Alexandri Et in alio Campo unam particulam terre que vocatur Chefrudinge que jac inter terram Magistri Willi vicarij de Byseleye et Croftum Willi de Coppichegrove cujus oriental extremitas extendit super terram Robti de la Purie Et unam Acram apud Tymberhulle que jac juxta terram Thome Forestern Et unam particulam terre apud Halhymediche et extendit super terram predici Dni Hugon Persone Et unam Acram super la Dune que jac juxta terram predici Dni Hugon Persone et extendit ultra Semitum de Sydenhame Et unam Acram super la Dune cujus una extremitas extendit super terram dci Dni Hugon Persone et altera extremitas extendit super terra dci Alexandri Capellani Et unam Acram que jac juxta terram Radulfi de Hanestie cujus una extremitas extendit super terram que fuit Dni Robti quondm Vicarij de Byseleye Et dimidiam Acram que jac juxta regalem viam apud Crockelporne Habendu et tenendu totam predictam terram cum Messuagio et Curtilagio de me et heredibus meis prefato Rogero et hereditibus sui vel cuicumq assignare voluerit libere et quiete hereditarie imperpetuu Reddendo inde annuatim mihi et heredibus meis ipse et heredes sui vel sui assignati tres solidos ad quatuor Anni terminas Scilt ad Natale Domini novem denar Ad festa bte Marie novem dena ad Nativitatem Sci Johis Bapt novem denar et ad festu sci Michaelis novem denar pro omnibus Servcijs et Curie mee Sertis et Secularibus demandis Salvo regali servicio quantu pertinet ad tantum tenementum in Villa de Byseley Et Ego dcus Willus et heredes mei totam dcam terra cum Messagio et curtilagio prefat Rogero et heredibus suis vel suis assignatis contra omnes mortales imperpetuu warrantizabimus aquietabimus et defendemus Et ut hec donaco mea et concessio prefato Rogero et hered suis vel suis assignatis rata et Stabil imperpetuu permaneat Huic presente Carte Sigillum meum apposui Hijs testibus Reginaldo de Trouham Ricardo de Clyveshale Willo de Tonleye Radulfo Ferre Ricardo de Stroda Thoma Forestario Robto de Stroda Capellano et alijs multis."

The Hugh Mortimer mentioned was the second of that name to be rector of Bisley.   William, Vicar of Bisley, was probably William Calf appointed 1302, and Dominus Robert (formerly vicar), had been presented by Richard de Bisleye in 1282. Alexander the chaplain, may have been one of the Chantry chaplains, or perhaps one of the assistant priests of Bisley.

Other relations may possibly be Roger de Byseleye who was ordained sub-deacon on St. Michael's day, 1291, in the parish Church of Campden to title of patrimony, and Thomas de Byseleye who was ordained priest at the same time and place,[1] but as Bisley was often confused with Bushley in the Bishop's registers at Worcester, there is some uncertainty on that point.

The first documentary notice of Hugh le Eyr de Bisley, son of Richard, is to be found in the Feet of Fines of 11 Ed. II (1317-8) when an agreement was entered into between Hugh de Bisley and Reginald Estrick and Matilda his wife, whereby Hugh de Bisley conveyed two acres of wood, and the

---

[1] Bp. Giffard's Reg.

third part of one messuage and of one virgate of land in
Biseley to the latter for their lives, paying to the said Hugh
and his heirs, one rose yearly on the feast of St. John the
Baptist for all service or exaction of the said Hugh or his
heirs and rendering to the chief lord all services which pertain
to the said tenement.[1]

Hugh's son Henry called le Eyr, therefore presumably his
eldest son, was admitted on 6 December, 1317, in London
to the office of parson (or vicar) of the third portion of the
Church of Bisleye on the presentation of his father.   He was
only ordained on 18 February, 1318, to the orders of acolyte
and sub-deacon, and was then allowed a year's leave to study
for the priesthood to which he was admitted at the Trinity
ordination in 1319.[2]

Hugh de Bisley was in the enjoyment of a pension from
Thomas de Berkeley senior, about which a Commission made
inquisition[3] 12 May, 1324, when it appeared that Thomas de
Berkeley had in writing granted to Hugh de Bisley suitable
maintenance for himself, a groom and a horse as for one of
his esquires and two robes yearly or 35s., because Richard
de Byseleie, father of Hugh, whose heir he is, demised to the
said Thomas a messuage and a carucate of land in Morcote
and Hartwine worth six marks per annum.   The aforesaid
charge amounted to £13 4s. 1¾d., and Hugh enjoyed it until
the manor of Berkeley, etc., was taken into the King's
hand by reason of the forfeiture of Maurice his son.

On the occasion of the knighting of Edward the Black
Prince we find the following entry about Bisley in " Feudal
Aids."

" De Ricardo de Denton pro dimidio feodo Militis in
Byseleye quod Johanna Corbet tenuit ibidem.   XXs."

" De Johanne de Alspathe et Hugone Byselye pro dimidio
feodo unius feodi Militis in Byseleye quam Theobaldus de
Verdon quondam tenuit ibidem.   XXs."[4]

1 Feet of Fines, Glouc., 187, P. R. O.

2 Bp. Cobham's Reg.

3 Cal. of Inquisitions, 1307-49.

4 B. G. A. S. Trans., x. 278.

From this it appears that Hugh de Bisley held his part of the manor of Bisley by payment of a quarter of a knight's fee, the remaining three quarters being due from the holders of Jaynes Court and Stokesend.

In the Lypiatt MS. Book a charter of Hugh de Bisley's is recorded, dated Friday, after the feast of St. James the Apostle, 1347, whereby he demises the Perelonde and Peweslonde estate already mentioned, to Henry de Clifford and his heirs. The reason for the transfer of this property is not evident, but, perhaps, may have had some matrimonial alliance behind it, though unfortunately the surnames of the ladies whom the De Bisleys married have not been recorded. The charter was signed and sealed at Bisley and witnessed by Robert Cronste, Thomas Roberd, Henry de Geneworth, Robert de Stonehenge, Thomas Mody and others. Amongst the Court Rolls of Bisley the earliest but one is that of Hugh de Bisley, on Wednesday before St. Philip and St. James, 1349.[1]

The succession of the manor after Hugh is not clear. Richard, son of William Heir of Byseley grants confirmation of a messuage, etc., in Pepcumbe (otherwise Pathcombe, the combe leading down from Frith wood to Chalford) in an undated charter, and a second Hugh witnesses a deed in 1361,[2] and he, we find in the Register of Bishop Reginald Bryan, was son and heir of John de Biseleye, but as he was a minor at that date, the patronage of the second portion of the Church of Bisley was exercised by Humphrey de Bohun, Earl of Hereford as his over-lord.

Hugh (II) de Byseley was holding the appointment of eschaetor in Gloucester, Hereford and the Welsh March adjacent to them in 1381.[3] He was also Bailiff of the Liberty of the Manor of Bisley[4] and for some reason appears to have been very unpopular, as is evident from his petition to the Chancellor of the King in 1398, concerning an inquisition which he and the Sheriff of Gloucester had arranged to be

1 P. R. O. Court Rolls Port. 175-7 Glos.

2 Abst. of Deeds *B. G. A. S. Trans.* li., 212-3.

3 Cal. Pat. Rolls, 1381, Feb. 15.

4 Selden So., vol. 10, Select cases in Chancery, No. 35, 1398.

held at Stroud with jurors, to make an extent of the lands of Sir Richard de Talbot, knt., for a certain sum in which he was bound to Sir William Heron, knt. and others. On this occasion Thomas Walwyn, John Hikcokkes, Richard Monmouth and Thomas Sudgrove and many others came to Stroud armed with swords, bucklers, bows and arrows, and assaulted Hugh Bisley and so threatened the jurors that they dared not proceed. Thomas Walwyn, moreover, threatened Hugh that if he dared to prosecute or sue anything further in that case or prosecute at law one Richard Greenhull " then he had better not be so bold as to live in his own house for he would be killed." Richard Monmouth was summoned by Richard II to appear in Chancery in person to answer the complaint.

A further case in Chancery,[1] without date, is that of Edmund Franceys, grocer and citizen of London, who had livery of lands in Madesden, Glos., for a debt of £58, but by the conspiracy of James de Clifford and Hugh de Byslee, no man or farmer may dare to occupy or till the same lands, so he begs for relief and enablement to enjoy their use.

Hugh de Bisley was holding his manor courts at Bisley on 7 October, 1377, again on 11 January, 1387, and 10 October, 1393.[2]

He was lying ill the month before the battle of Agincourt, and made his will 21 September, 1415, feeling himself near to death. After bequeathing his soul to God he desired to be buried in the churchyard of the church of All Saints of Bysseley, leaving to the Cathedral Church of Worcester seven pence. He leaves to his wife Joan, half of all his goods which remain at Bysseley, and he directs John Gerald and William Moleyns to sell certain things from his feoffment in Sandhurst, Berkshire, so that they may pay his debts and his executor is to dispose of the residue to the best advantage to his soul. He leaves John Gerald as his executor.[3] No mention is made of any children, and the fact that one Thomas Byseley, lived at Newenton and left a will dated 1518, and another Thomas

---

1 Selden So., vol. x, No. 70. Richard Greenhill held Stancombe and Nether Copsgrove.

2 Bisley Court Rolls, No. 8.

3 P. C. C. 2 Luffenam.

PLATE 1

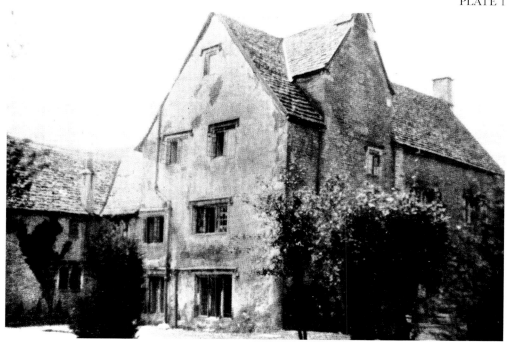

Overcourt—North Side.

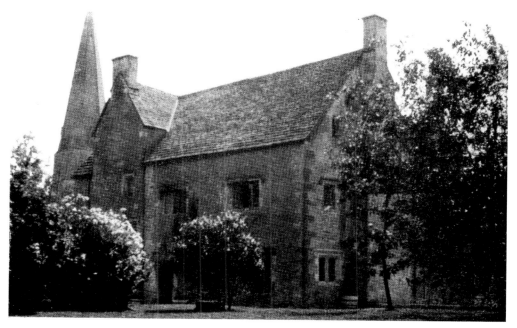

Overcourt—West Front.

PLATE 2

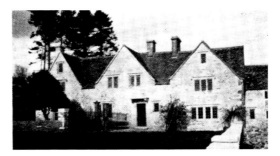

Fig, 1.—Back. (*See* page 71).

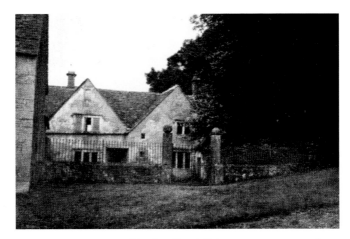

Fig, 2.—Front Entrance.

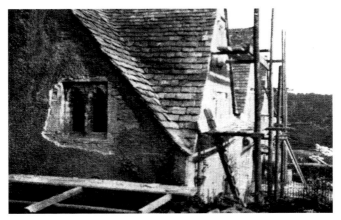

Fig. 3.—Fourteenth Century Window.

THROUGHAM SLAD

PLATE 3

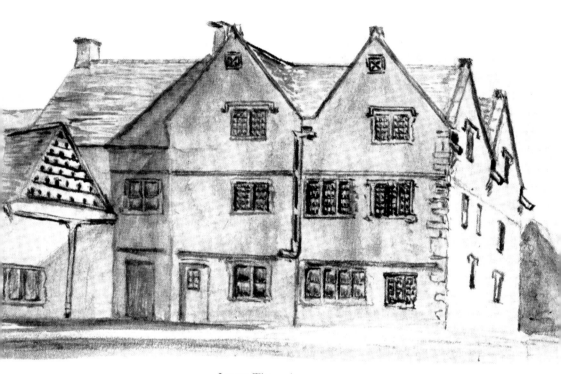

Lower Througham

PLATE 4

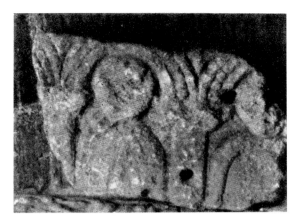

Fig. 2—Portion of Font.

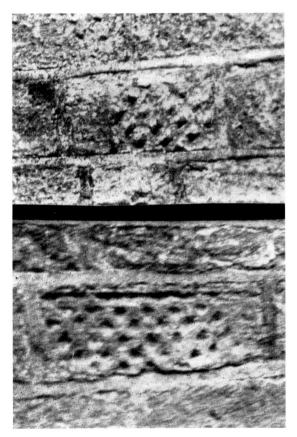

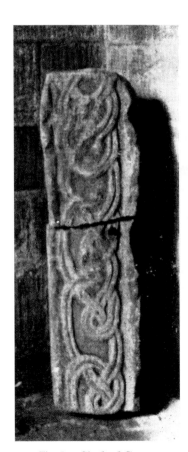

Fig. 1.—Saxon (or Roman?) Stones.   Fig. 3.—Shaft of Cross

SAXON DETAILS OF BISLEY CHURCH.

(By courtesy of The Bristol and Gloucestershire Archaeological Society)

PLATE 5

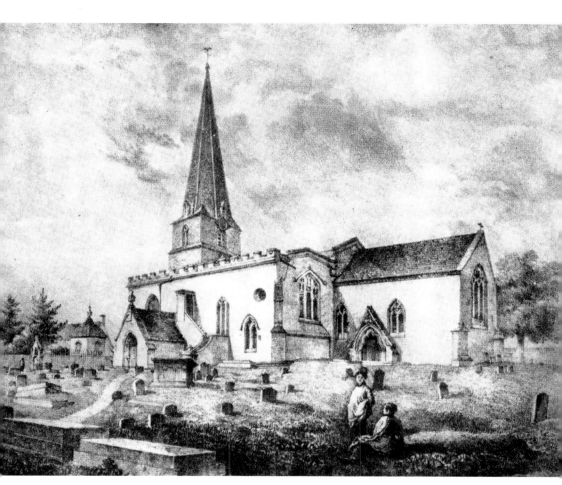

Bisley Church before the Last Restoration.

PLATE 6

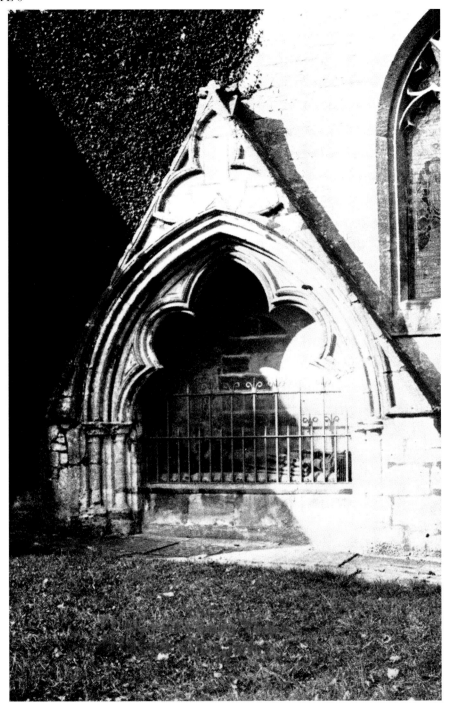

Thirteenth Century Canopy in the Chancel Wall.

PLATE 7

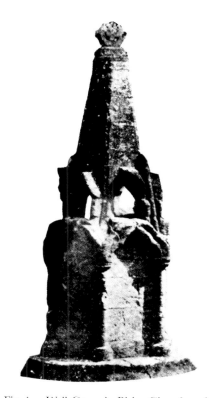

Fig. 1.—Well-Cover in Bisley Churchyard.

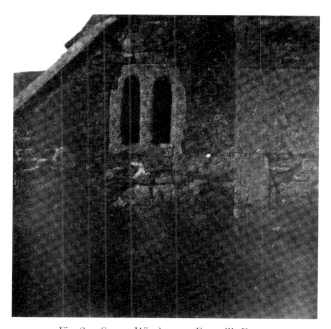

Fig. 2.—Saxon Windows at Fennell's Farm.

PLATE 8

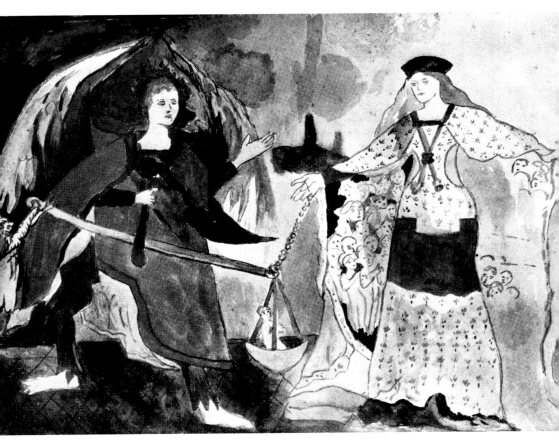

Fresco formely in the North Aisle,
(after the sketch by the Rev. Wm. Lowder.)

PLATE 9

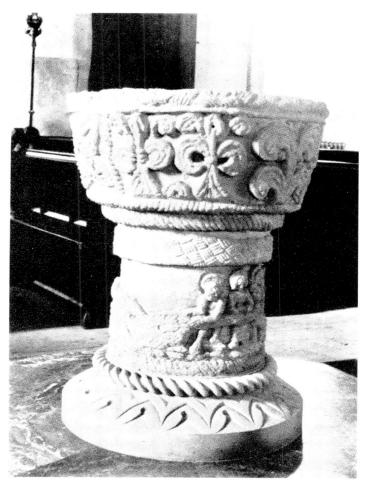

Norman Font.

PLATE 10

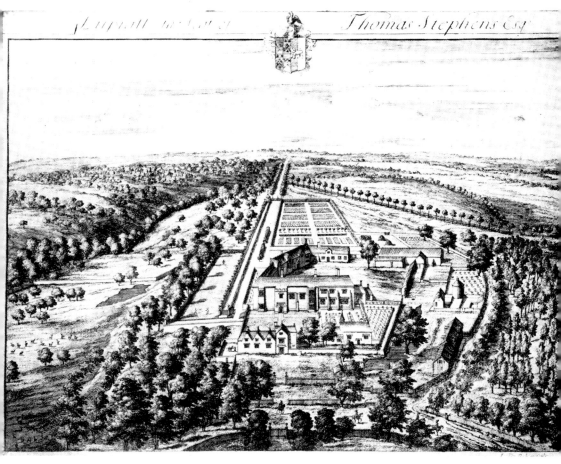

Lypiatt Park after J. Kip's Engraving. 1707.

PLATE 11

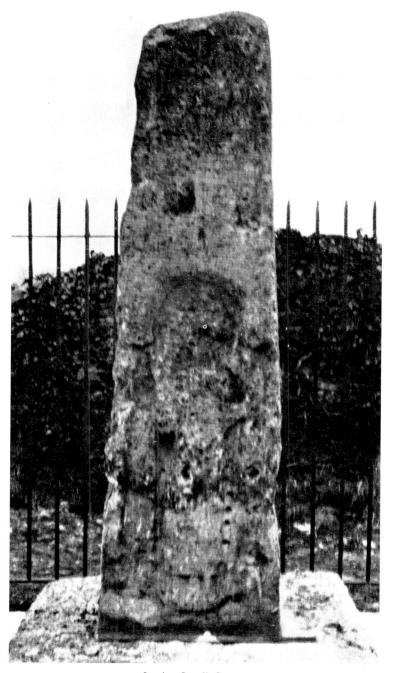

Lypiatt Lord's Stone.

(By courtesy of The Bristol and Gloucesershire Archaeological Society)

PLATE 12

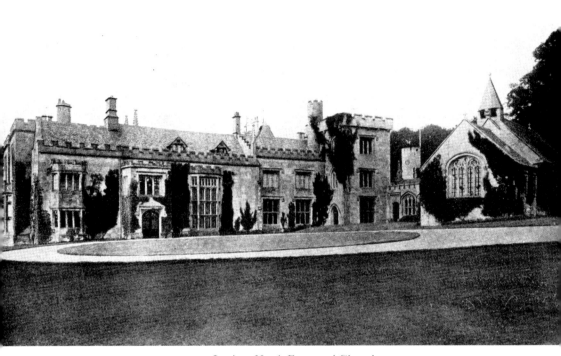

Lypiatt, North Front and Chapel.

PLATE 13

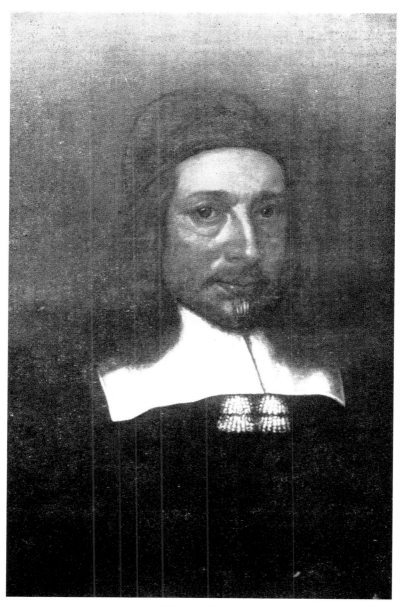

John Stephens.

(From a portrait in the possession of Mrs. Delabere, of Prestbury).

PLATE 14

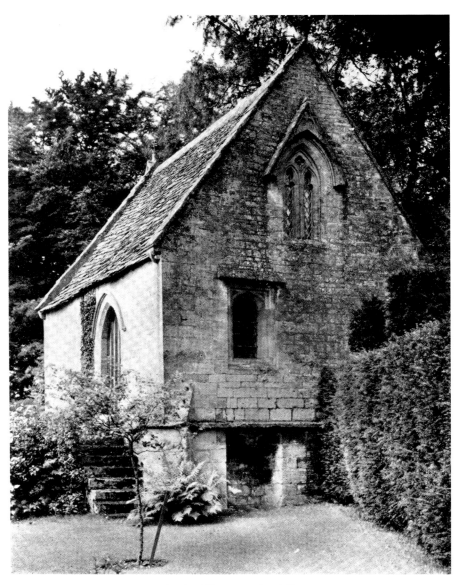

Ancient Granary—Lypiatt.

PLATE 15

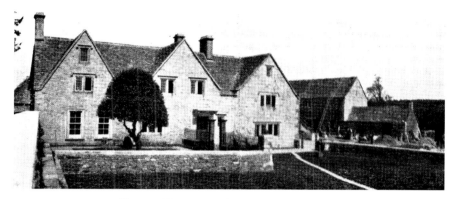

Fig. 1.—Througham Slad, after Restoration.

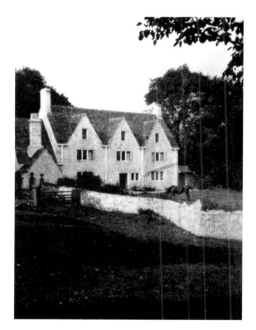

Fig. 2.—Rookwoods.

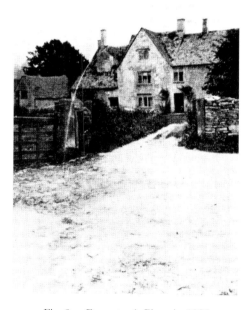

Fig. 3.—Frampton's Place in 1932.

PLATE 16

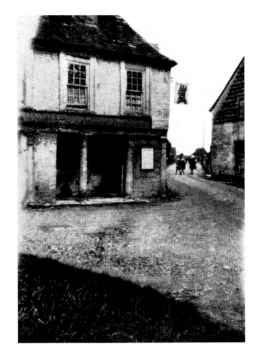

Fig. 1.—Bear Inn, Bisley.

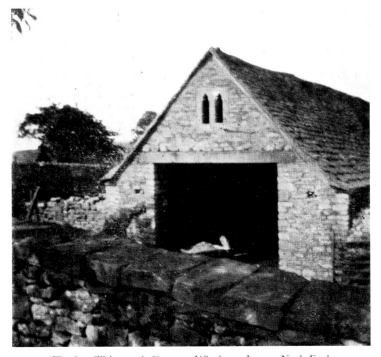

Fig. 2.—Thirteenth Century Windows, Lower Nash End.

PLATE 17

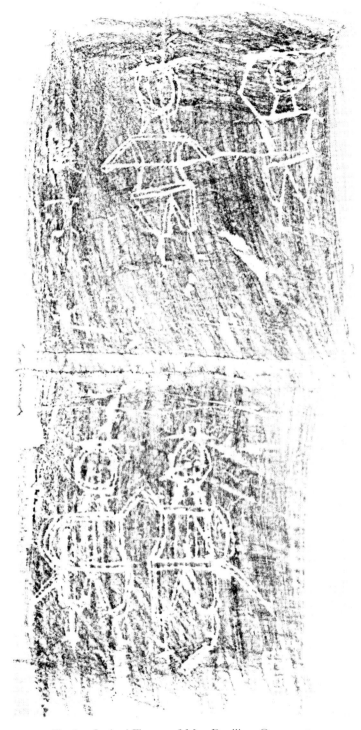

Fig. 1.—Incised Figures of Men Duelling, Overcourt.

PLATE 18

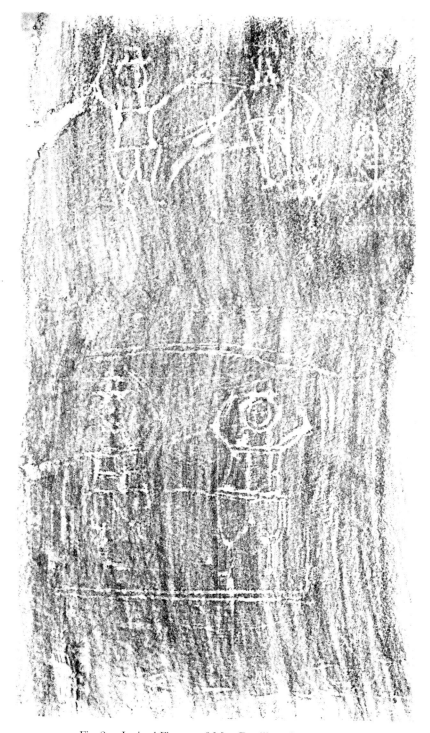

Fig. 2.—Incised Figures of Men Duelling, Overcourt.

PLATE 19

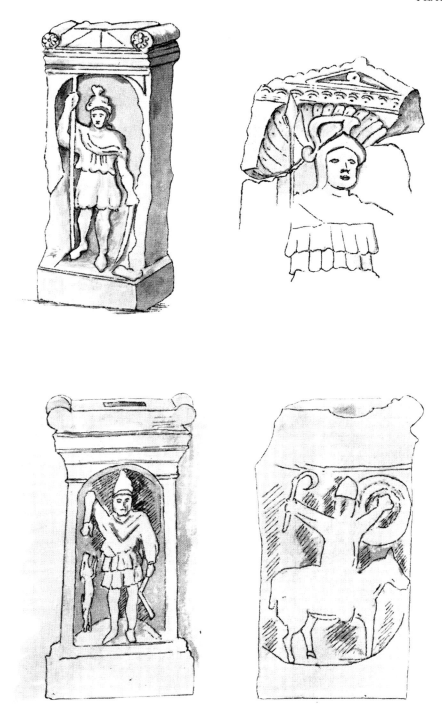

Fig. 1.—Roman Atlas found in a Tumulus on Bisley Common in 1866.

PLATE 20

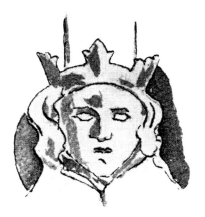

Fig. 1.—King Edward II.

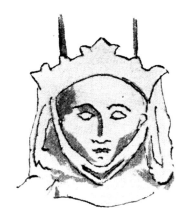

Fig. 2.—Queen Isabella.

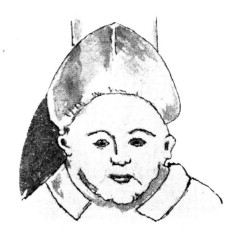

Fig. 3.—Bishop of Worcester.

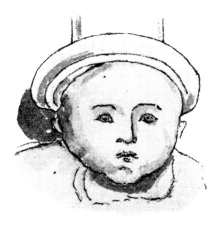

Fig. 4.—Parish Priest of Bisley.

PLATE 21

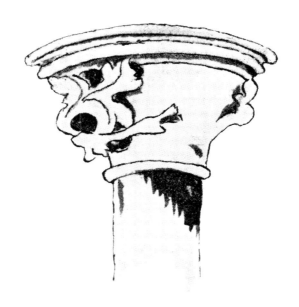

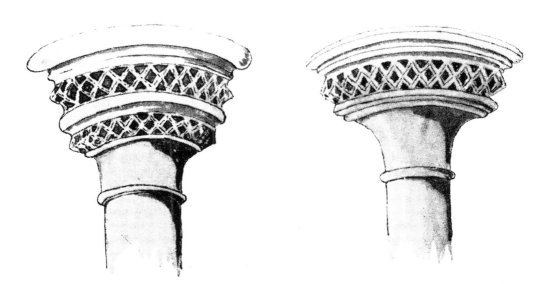

Early English Capitals formely in Bisley Church.
(From sketches by the Rev. Wm. Lowder).

PLATE 22

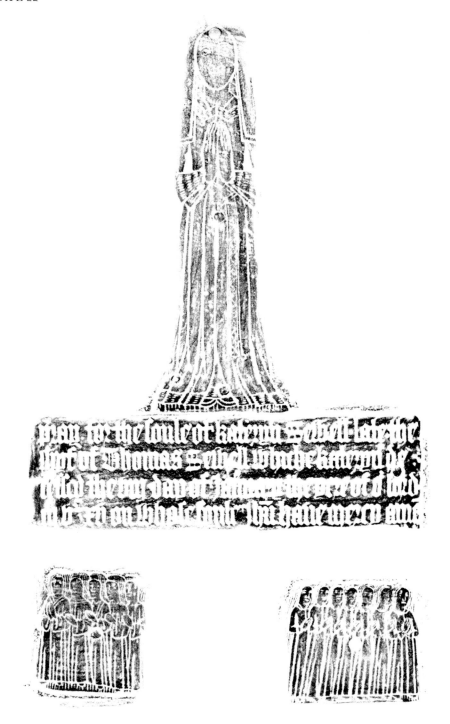

Brass to Kathryn Sewell in Bisley Church.

PLATE 23

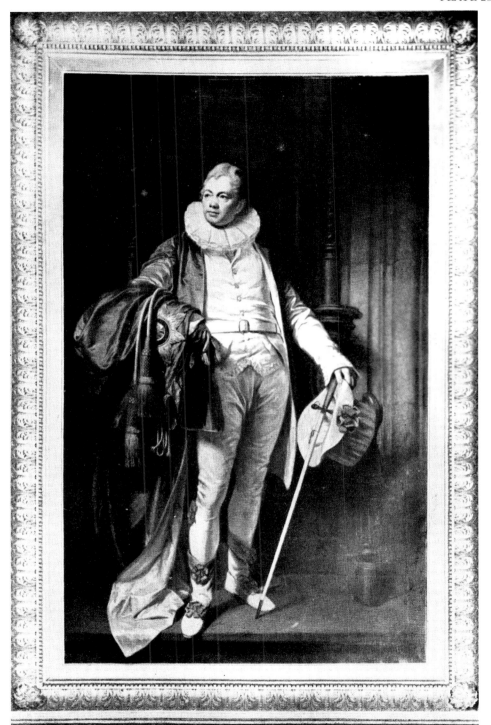

Portrait of Sir Paul Baghott at Lypiatt.

SUGGESTED PEDIGREE OF COMPTON

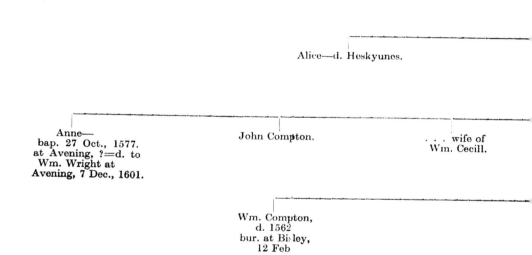

Alice—d. Heskyunes.

Anne—
bap. 27 Oct., 1577.
at Avening, ?=d. to
Wm. Wright at
Avening, 7 Dec., 1601.

John Compton.

. . . wife of
Wm. Cecill.

Wm. Compton,
d. 1562
bur. at Bisley,
12 Feb

John Compton of Wilts.

Wm. Compton =d. Elizabeth, d. of
of Chalford. . . . Showell (? Shewell
Cloth maker. of Ferris Court).
»ur. at Bisley, 1546.

Walter Compton, Esq. =d. Alice, d. of John Lytley   Margery
buried at Bisley   Co. Warwick.   =d. Edmund Webbe.
17 August, 1585.   She=d. 2nd Henry Bridges, Esq.
                        s. of John, Lord Chandos, of
                        Avening, 21 May, 1586.

Francis Compton   Elizabeth   Wm. Compton
Westson=d.   wife of Wm. Smyth.   of Hartpury

Henry Compton=d. Joan, dau. of   John Compton,
bur. at Bisley,   Henry Bridges, Esq., of   bur. at Bisley,
21 April, 1593.   Avening—d. at Bisley,   9 Feb., 1563.
                  1607. bur. there 7 March.

Brydges Compton,   Mary   ? Elizabeth
bap. at Bisley, 26 Feb.,   bap. at Avening,   =d. to Ric. Jeffris,
1587.   10 Jan., 1584.   at Avening, 2 Nov.,
                                                   1607

FREAME OF LYPIATT

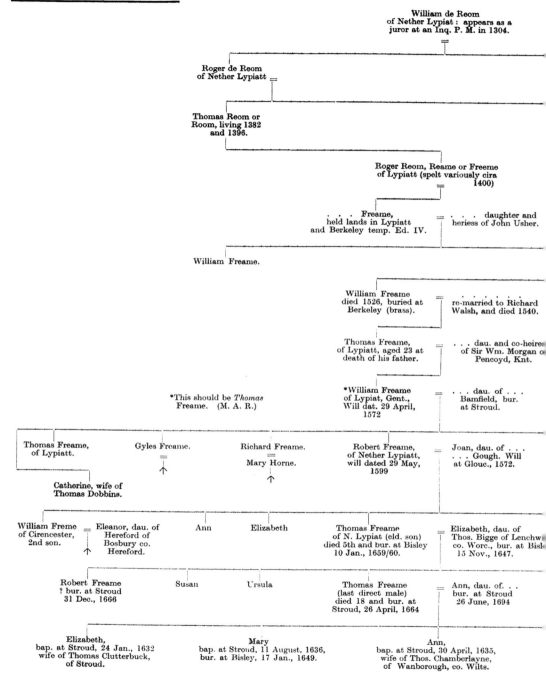

William de Reom
of Nether Lypiat : appears as a
juror at an Inq. P. M. in 1304.

Roger de Reom
of Nether Lypiatt =

Thomas Reom or
Room, living 1382
and 1396.

Roger Reom, Reame or Freeme
of Lypiatt (spelt variously cira
1400)
=

. . . Freame,   = . . . daughter and
held lands in Lypiatt   heriess of John Usher.
and Berkeley temp. Ed. IV.

William Freame.

William Freame   = ...
died 1526, buried at   re-married to Richard
Berkeley (brass).   Walsh, and died 1540.

Thomas Freame,   = . . . dau. and co-heires
of Lypiatt, aged 23 at   of Sir Wm. Morgan o
death of his father.   Pencoyd, Knt.

*This should be *Thomas*   *William Freame   = . . . dau. of . . .
Freame. (M. A. R.)   of Lypiat, Gent.,   Bamfield, bur.
                                 Will dat. 29 April,   at Stroud.
                                 1572

Thomas Freame,   Gyles Freame.   Richard Freame.   Robert Freame,   = Joan, dau. of . . .
of Lypiatt.   =   =   of Nether Lypiatt,   . . . Gough. Will
                       ↑   Mary Horne.   will dated 29 May,   at Glouc., 1572.
    Catherine, wife of   ↑   1599
    Thomas Dobbins.

William Freme   = Eleanor, dau. of   Ann   Elizabeth   Thomas Freame   = Elizabeth, dau. of
of Cirencester,   Hereford of   of N. Lypiat (eld. son)   Thos. Bigge of Lenchwi
2nd son.   Bosbury co.   died 5th and bur. at Bisley   co. Worc., bur. at Bisl
                   Hereford.   10 Jan., 1659/60.   15 Nov., 1647.
                  ↑

    Robert Freame   Susan   Ursula   Thomas Freame   = Ann, dau. of. . .
    ? bur. at Stroud   (last direct male)   bur. at Stroud
    31 Dec., 1666   died 18 and bur. at   26 June, 1694
                                                       Stroud, 26 April, 1664

    Elizabeth,   Mary   Ann,
bap. at Stroud, 24 Jan., 1632   bap. at Stroud, 11 August, 1636,   bap. at Stroud, 30 April, 1635,
wife of Thomas Clutterbuck,   bur. at Bisley, 17 Jan., 1649.   wife of Thos. Chamberlayne,
of Stroud.   of Wanborough, co. Wilts.

John de Reom
living 1349, inherited a
moiety of N. Lypiatt.

Margery
wife of Hugh
de Lasbery.

Thomas Freame═Cecilia de Rodberg.

William Freame.   John Freame.   Walter Freame.
══
↑

Margery.   Edye.

Julian.   Alice,
wife of Joseph
Baynham.   Robert Freame ═ Tacy, dau. of
bur. at Stroud,   Richard Fowler of
6 Feb., 1648.   Brimscombe.

William Freame ═ Mary, dau. of
of, Bisley, gent.   Thos. Pate, of
Cheltenham.   Richard Freame,
of Brimscombe, clothier,
bap. 1639, died 1709.

Thomas
bap. at Bisley, 13 Feb.
1639, and bur. there
Sept., 1645.   Sarah
bap. at Stroud, 19 Oct., 1643,
wife of Henry Windowe,
of Churchdown, Co. Glos.

SMART OF THROUGHAM

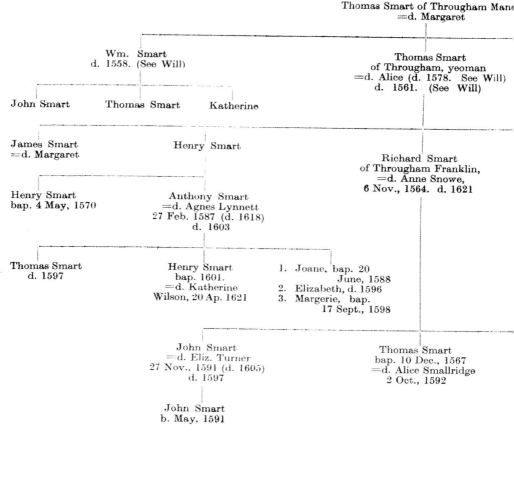

Thomas Smart of Througham Man
=d. Margaret

Wm. Smart
d. 1558. (See Will)

Thomas Smart
of Througham, yeoman
=d. Alice (d. 1578. See Will)
d. 1561. (See Will)

John Smart   Thomas Smart   Katherine

James Smart
=d. Margaret

Henry Smart

Richard Smart
of Througham Franklin,
=d. Anne Snowe,
6 Nov., 1564. d. 1621

Henry Smart
bap. 4 May, 1570

Anthony Smart
=d. Agnes Lynnett
27 Feb. 1587 (d. 1618)
d. 1603

Thomas Smart
d. 1597

Henry Smart
bap. 1601.
=d. Katherine
Wilson, 20 Ap. 1621

1. Joane, bap. 20
   June, 1588
2. Elizabeth, d. 1596
3. Margerie, bap.
   17 Sept., 1598

John Smart
=d. Eliz. Turner
27 Nov., 1591 (d. 1605)
d. 1597

Thomas Smart
bap. 10 Dec., 1567
=d. Alice Smallridge
2 Oct., 1592

John Smart
b. May, 1591

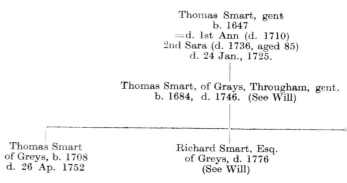

Thomas Smart, gent
b. 1647
=d. 1st Ann (d. 1710)
2nd Sara (d. 1736, aged 85)
d. 24 Jan., 1725.

Thomas Smart, of Grays, Througham, gent.
b. 1684, d. 1746. (See Will)

Thomas Smart
of Greys, b. 1708
d. 26 Ap. 1752

Richard Smart, Esq.
of Greys, d. 1776
(See Will)

James Smart

Wm. Smart
bap. 24 Dec., 1562

Wm. Smart
of Cawdwell

John Smart

Edward Smart, gent.
bap. 7 May, 1578
=d . . . .

1. Ann, bap. 10 Ap.1566
2. Alice, bap. 12 Nov.
   1569
   d. John Turner,
   2 Oct., 1592
3. Jane, bap. 21 June,
   1572
   d. 1573.

Richard Smart
bap. 13 Ap., 1618
? =d. Judith (d. 1637)
d. 1646

1. Helenor,
   bap. 17 Sept., 1605
   d. 1658
2. Brigid,
   bap. 2 July, 1607
3. Elizabeth,
   bap. 4 Ap., 1611
4. Alice,
   bap. 17 Sept., 1615
5. Agnes,
   bap. 11 July, 1624
   d. 1666

? Richard Smart
(" Son of Richard
   of Througham ")
bap. 1 Nov., 1634.

Richard Smart
d. in infancy

Wm. Smart
d. in infancy

PLATE 24

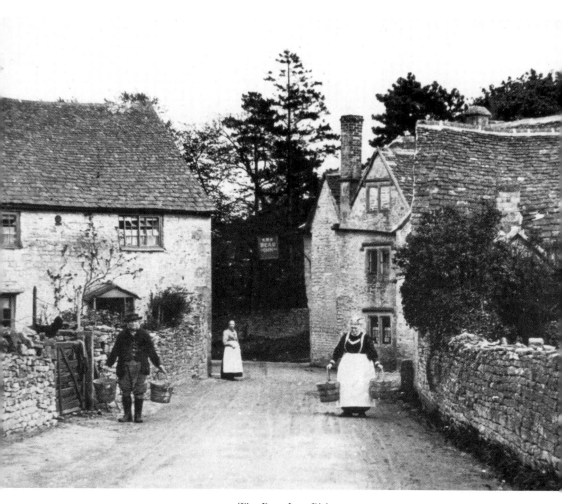

The Bear Inn, Bisley.

PLATE 25

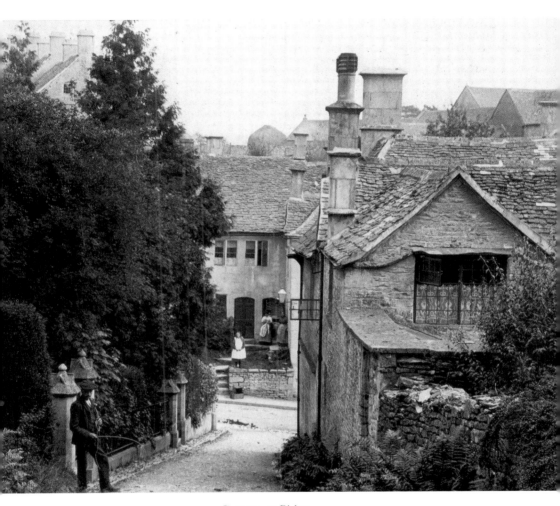

Cottages at Bisley.

PLATE 26

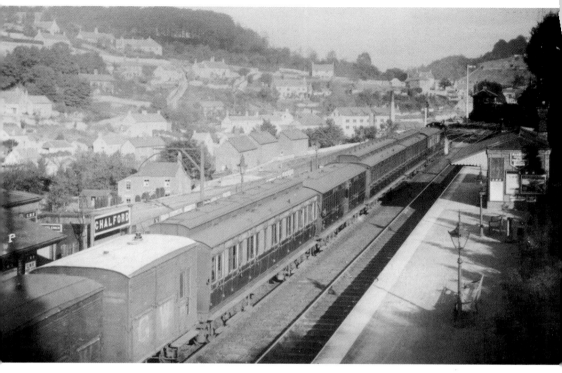

Golden Valley looking Eastward at Chalford Halt.

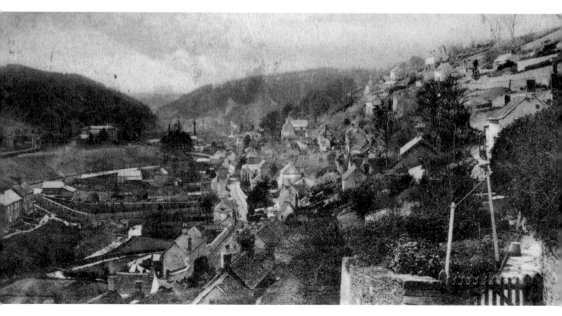

Chalford.

Bisley was of Abingdon and his will is dated 1553 points to the probability that some of the De Bisley family had previously migrated to Berkshire. At any rate there is no trace of any De Bisley at Bisley itself, but that the connection with it was not wholly broken appears likely from the will of Thomas Byseley, clerk, who was priest and sub-warden of the King's "grate College of Gloucester." By his will dated 19 August, 1540, he desired to be buried in the South aisle of the Collegiate Church and he left amongst many bequests twenty marks to Richard Clyssell of the parish of Bisley, who witnesses his will which was proved at Leckhampton, 27 September, in the same year.[1]

Humphrey de Bohun, the last Earl of Hereford, Essex and Northampton, had died in 1373, on 16 January, and at the inquisition taken at Gloucester on the following 2nd of March, it is stated that his daughters, Eleanor aged seven, and Mary, aged five are his next heirs and that amongst other knights fees he held the following in Bisley.[2]—" One fee in Paganhulle, which John Monemouth, John de Seymor, John Do(d)bridge, Thomas Smyth, John Inthefeld, Richard Clerkesson and John Fermor held, worth 100s. : one fee in Lupegate Seupier which John Clifford holds, worth 100s.: one fee in Biselee and Wynston, which Edmund, Earl of March, holds worth 100s : one fourth of a fee in Biselee which Hugh de Biselee holds worth 25s. . . . Half a fee in Lower Lupegate which the abbot of Tewkesbury and the Prior of the Hospital of St. John and Roger Re(em) hold worth 50s. The said Earl held the advowson of . . . Biselee on alternative vacancies, worth 20 marks."

The younger daughter, Mary de Bohun, was Lady of the Manor of Bisley and as such executed two deeds which are extant in the archives of Corpus Christi College, the first granting to William de la Fripe (Frith) of Chalford, the whole field called Fripelond which William of Chalkeford held of Bissleye and which lies in the wood of Bysrugge (Bussage) for rent of 5s., and the second deed is an Indenture of the same.[3]

---

1 P. C. C. 12 Alenger.

2 Index Library, Pt. vi., p. 69. List of Knights' Fees.

3 Abst. of Deeds, *B. G. A. S. Trans.*, li., 211-2.

Mary de Bohun married in 1380 Henry Bolingbroke afterwards Henry IV, conveying to him the manor of Bisley. She died in 1394.

It is in the reign of the grandson of Henry IV, namely 26 Hen. VI, that Ministers' Accounts begin to give interesting details of the manor.[1] From these we learn that the Overcourt estate was in 1446-7 rented at 113s. 4d. per annum to Mr. John Burne, for all lands in demesne and pasture. Tradition says that in mediaeval times a park was attached to Overcourt extending almost to Lypiatt park. In the Accounts of 1450-1, the name of John Burne is crossed out as renting the site of Overcourt with dwellings and buildings existing, and the name of John Butt is inserted in pale ink, and this continues as the name of the tenant in 1452-3. In the accounts of Edward IV's reign no details are given.

In 27 Hen. VI, John King, then bailiff, states that the dovecote was worth nothing being totally waste, neither the farm of the garden because there were no trees or pannage for swine in the wood formed there that year. The sum of 17s. 9d. was received for the sale of faggots in Blackes, Barnhegge, Luteragge, Tymbercombe, Tagonhegge and Peyntonesfryth. The Ministers' Accounts for Henry VI's reign end in 1452-3.

By a deed dated at Coventry in 1459-60, King Henry VI acknowledged that he had promised to Cecily, Duchess of York, one thousand marks yearly for relief of herself and her infants who had not offended against the King, to be raised from certain possessions of her late husband Richard, Duke of York, who had been slain at the battle of Wakefield. Part of this annuity arose from the profits of that portion of the manor and lordship of Bisley and Bisley hundred which had belonged to the Mortimers, to whom the late Duke of York was heir. Through his rebellion he forfeited his possessions and these came to the King's hands by Act of Parliament held at Coventry, 20 November, 1459. The King had committed these lands to the custody of certain knights.[2]

---

  [1] P. R. O. Min. Accts., 850/26-32.

  [2] Cal. Pat. Rolls, 1459-60.

CHAPTER III

PART 2

OF THE NETHER MANOR AND STOKESEND

Having reached the time at which the three parts of Bisley manor became merged into one, it will be convenient to follow the history of the Nether Manor with its capital messuage on the site of Jaynes Court, and Stokesend, where the Mansion marks the site of the capital messuage, up to the time when the king retained the whole manor in his own hands.

The connection of the Mortimers with any part of the manor must have begun at a very early date, judging from the agreement of the time of King John already quoted, between Roger Mortimer and Cecily of Rodburgh. The history of the Mortimers was so interwoven with that of the English nation that in order to understand their connection with Bisley, some allusion must be made to their public life.

Ralph Mortimer was one of the principal commanders at the Battle of Hastings and, having taken prisoner Edrich, Earl of Shrewsbury, he was rewarded with great estates, amongst others the lordship of Wigmore, Herefordshire, where he built the Castle which was the chief residence of the Mortimers on the Marches of Wales. Ralph Mortimer had two sons of whom Hugh the elder, who was hostile to Henry II, founded the Abbey of Wigmore, endowing it largely in 1179 and dying there as a Canon in 1185, at a great age. There had been difficulties for the Canons who had originally been settled at Schobbeden by Oliver de Merlymond, chief Seneschal of the lands of Hugh Mortimer, in the time of King Stephen, but a great dissension having arisen between him and his master, the Canons were much harassed and had to move several times before finally settling at Wigmore.

Sir Roger Mortimer, his son, also behaved very unkindly to these canons at first, so that they again removed to Schobbeden for a time. It is this Roger (I.) after the Conquest, who granted the exchange of land in Bisley to Cecily de Rodburgh, the deed being witnessed by the Abbot of Wigmore, Philip Mortimer his brother, William Mortimer his uncle, and William the first-named parson of Bisley.

Though Sir Roger at first supported the Barons in the reign of Henry III, he afterwards returned to due allegiance to his King. He had suffered imprisonment for two years for the murder of the Welsh prince Cadwallon. He died in 1215-6, having been twice married, his second wife being Isabel de Ferrers. His son, Hugh of Wigmore, by his first wife, married Amora, daughter of William de Braose, and attended the King's army at Cirencester about 1214, so we may surmise that he visited Bisley at that time. He died without issue in 1227, and Ralph Mortimer, his half brother succeeded to the family estates. He was taken prisoner by the King of France in the time of King John, and during his absence, the Abbey of Wigmore was raided and burnt by the Welsh. He married Gladys, daughter of Llewellyn ap Iowerth, Prince of Wales. We find him granting to William de Chalford for his suit and service all lands and Mills pertaining to him in Chalford at the rent of 16s. per annum.[1] This deed is witnessed by his uncle, Philip Mortimer. He died in 1245-6 after a life of great military activity, including building of castles on the Welsh Marches.

Roger (II), son of Ralph Mortimer, succeeded to his father's estates, paying livery of 3000 marks, and he was faithful to his King, Henry III, during the latter's troubles with the Barons.

He married Matilda, daughter of William de Braose, Lord of Brecknock, and had, it would appear, six sons and one daughter, Isabella, married to John Fitzalan. Hugh Mortimer, Rector of Bisley, may be assumed to have been a son, for in 1280 he held a dispensation to dwell with the Lady Matilda in Ireland and meanwhile to let his Church to farm.[2]

1 Abst. of Deeds, *B. G. A. S. Trans.*, li., 212.
2 Bp. Giffard's Reg.

No further dealings of Roger Mortimer (II.) with Bisley are on record. He died 26 October, 1282.

Ralph, the eldest son having died without issue, in 1275, Sir Edmund Mortimer succeeded his father in 1282, though he had been destined for the priesthood. He was born in 1255, and was created Baron Mortimer of Wigmore in 1294. In 1280 he married Margaret, daughter of Sir William de Fendles, or Fiennes, a kinswoman of the Queen Consort Eleanor of Castile, and great estates were bestowed upon him, amongst which were the Manor of Bisley and two parts of the advowson.[1] In 1290[2] he presented Hugh Mortimer (II) as rector to the Church of Bisleya, though it is not recorded what relation he was. Most likely he was a younger son.

Sir Edmund was mortally wounded at Builth and died at his castle of Wigmore in 1304, being laid with his ancestors in the Priory Church they had founded there. The Priory having been destroyed, no monuments remain of the Mortimer family.

At the Inquisition held at Minchinhampton on 10 December, 1404, before the King's eschaetor, enquiry was made into the knights' fees and advowsons of Churches held by Sir Edmund Mortimer in the county of Gloucester at the time of his death, and information was given on oath by William de Reom (Freame), Thomas of Eggeworth, Nicholas of Seymor, Henry the Farmer, William the Pronte, William of Bysrugg (Bussage), John Stormy, Thomas Acchard, Reginald Jurdan, William of Sydenham, William of Tunley, and Robert Selwynne, who say that the said Edmund was seised of two parts of the Church of Byseleye, which are worth, per annum, fifty marks.[3] At an Inquisition made at Aure on October 25, it was stated that Sir Edmund held one knight's fee in Stokes end and Biseleye held by William de Radebrig.[4]

Sir Edmund Mortimer was succeeded by his son Roger (III.) born in 1287, and created Earl of March in 1328.

1 Atkyns.

2 Bp. Giffard's Reg.

3 P. R. O. Chanc. Inq. P. M., Ed. I.

4 P. R. O. Inq. P. M., Hen. III-VII., vol. iv., 164.

In 1305-6 he departed from the King's army in Scotland without leave, in consequence of which the sheriffs of Gloucestershire seized his lands, which, however, were restored to him the following year, 1306-7, in response to a petition in his favour signed by Gilbert de Clare, Henry and Humphry de Bohun, Peter de Gaveston, Theobald de Verdun and others.[1]

In 1322 Roger Mortimer, together with his uncle, Roger of Chirk, joined with Damory, Mowbray, Giffard, Berkeley and others in raiding, burning, and slaying in the lands and manors of Hugh le Despencer the younger, special mention being made of lands in Bisley, Wyshanger, Wynston, and Musardrie (Miserden).[2]   For this offence both uncle and nephew were imprisoned in the Tower where the elder Roger died, but the younger escaped in 1324, through a hole cut in the wall of his cell into the King's kitchen, whence a climb up the chimney led to the roof, and a ward of the castle being gained, a rope ladder enabled him to escape to a boat on the Thames. From there he reached France, and the story of his intrigue with Queen Isabella, his treachery to his King, Edward II, and his struggles with his rivals the Despencers fill the history of this period.   He met the fate he deserved when, after being deprived of all his honours, he was hung at Tyburn, then called the Elms, on 26 May, 1360.   He was the first person to be hung at that spot.

He was buried at the Church of the Grey Friars, though later his family had permission to remove his remains to Wigmore Priory, but if they availed themselves of this concession, the removal did not take place for many years after.   Meanwhile Queen Isabella was laid near him in the same Church.

---

1 Cal. Close Rolls.
2 Cal. Close Rolls.

OF STOKESEND

We must now leave the Mortimers in order to consider a confusing number of names of historic personages who appear seized of this portion of the manor held by the Mortimers, but which was taken into the King's hands from time to time, owing to their lapse from fealty. Most of these families appear to have been connected by marriage, which may account for some of the un-explained sub-infeudations.

On Wednesday before St. Simon and St. Jude in 1278-9, Theobald de Verdun authorised Thomas de Wyanlode to deliver to Sir Hugh le Despencer the elder, for five years, seisin of the manor, advowson of the church and his share of the Hundred of Biselegh.[2] On the same day letters patent were issued by Theobald de Verdun ordering all his tenants doing suit to the manor and Hundred of Byselegh to be intendant to Sir Hugh le Despencer the elder, to whom he had granted the said manor, etc.[1] This was accompanied by letters patent of the same date witnessing that he had sold to Sir Hugh all his goods and chattels and crops in the manor of Byselegh.[3] Letters patent of 27 March of the same year granted to Sir Hugh all the goods and chattels found in the manor of Bysele on the day on which Theobald de Verdun had delivered the said manor to Sir Hugh. In this deed he is named Constable of Ireland, which discloses the reason for these transactions. There is a further Indenture, a memorandum of the agreement made at Lambeth on 25 October, 1278-9 between the same parties, reciting the details as before but adding that Sir Hugh le Despencer is to hold them as completely as the ancestor of the said Theobald had them of the ancestor of the Earl of Hereford.

Further light is thrown on the holding of the fourth part of the Hundred of Bisley, by Theobald, in 15 Ed. I, 1286-7, in the Placita Quo Warranto held apparently at Biseley before the Bailiff of the King, when Peter Corbet, Theobald de Verdun and Richard de Byseley were summoned and made reply as to their claim to inherit the Hundred of Bisley and

---

1 Desc. Cat. of Ancient Deeds, IV., 233.

2 Cal. of Ancient Deeds III., Glouc. A., 5798.

3 Cal. of Ancient Deeds IV., 6792 and 7887.

view of frankpledge there. They said that Peter Corbet had half the profits of the Hundred by right and inheritance of Joan, his wife, by whom Thomas was his heir, then of full age. Richard de Byseley held a quarter part of the said Hundred and Theobald de Verdun held the other quarter part by the inheritance of Margery his wife, by whom he has a son, John, then under age[1].

Sir Peter Corbet was commissioned by the King in 1281, to destroy all the wolves he could find in the Counties of Gloucester, Worcester, Salop, Hereford and Stafford. On 29 April, 1301, his huntsman brought Sir Peter's dogs to the King after his master's death, and received 6s. 8d. for his pains. The Corbets held the manor of Siston near Pucklechurch.

Theobald de Verdun was son of John de Verdun by his wife, Margaret de Lacy whom he married before 1348, she being a co-heiress, with her sister Matilda, to her grandfather Walter de Lacy's estates in Shropshire, the Welsh Marches and Ireland,[2] and also of the Hundred of Bisley. Theobald went to Ireland in 1274 having got possession of his Irish estates the previous year. He was imprisoned in 1291 on not appearing at Abergavenny to answer for divers transgressions and he was deprived of Ewyas Lacy. He was in Ireland in 1292-1301, and his son, Theobald, was by royal permission sent to represent him in the Scottish campaign of 1297-8. Theobald senior had excused himself as being infirm and having lost his eldest son John.[3] He died on Sunday, 24 August, 1309, at Alveton, Staffs., the family seat, and he was buried at Croxden Abbey.

At Theobald de Verdun's Inquisition Post Mortem taken at Biseleye, 12 September, 1309, before the eschaetor, evidence was given by John de la Felde, Nicholas de Seymor, William de Reem, John Stormie, John de Frampton, Walter de Stonhenge, William Faber, Thomas de Paganhull, Nicholas Seburn, Richard son of Peter, Adam de Rokwode and Walter de Sidenham, who said that Theobald held the tenements

---

1 Placita de Quo Warranto, 251. Rot. 13.
2 Dic. Nat. Biography.
3 Cal. Close Rolls, 1297.

underwritten at Byseleye in free marriage of the Earl of Hereford by the service of paying one pound of cummin on the feast of St. Michael yearly.

There is a certain capital messuage which is worth p.a. clear 2s. There are five acres of arable land which are worth p.a. 12s. 6d., price of the acre 3d. There is there half an acre of meadow worth p.a. 2s. There are there fifty acres of wood where there is no underwood, therefore it is worth nothing p.a. There are there twenty free tenants who hold divers tenements and pay p.a. 55s. 5d. at the four terms. Also seven natives, each of whom holds the fourth part of a virgate of land in villeinage, their rents and services being worth p.a. 46s. Pleas and perquisites p.a. 2s., sum of the value of the whole extent p.a. 119s. 11d. Theobald his son and heir is aged 30 and more.[1]

Theobald de Verdun the younger married firstly Matilda, daughter of Edmund Mortimer and sister to Roger first Earl of March, who died in 1312. He married secondly, in 1316, Elizabeth de Clare, the King's niece, sister of the deceased Gilbert, Earl of Gloucester and widow of John de Burgh, heir of Ulster. He died himself that same year, and at his Inquisition P.M. no mention is made of the Bisley estate, because in 1313, on 1 November, he had granted to Hugh le Despencer senior all his rights in the manor, advowson, and Hundred of Bisley.[2]

The Verduns bore for arms—Or. a fret gu.

Hugh le Despencer senior, had married Eleanor, a co-heir of the Earl of Gloucester. On his attainder in 1326, and cruel death at Bristol at the age of 90, (he being buried at Tewkesbury Abbey, where are several tombs of the Despencers), Roger Mortimer had a grant of a messuage and ten librates (520 acres) of land in Bisley as reward for services rendered to Queen Isabella. After Roger Mortimer's execution in 1330 we gather from Letters Patent of Ed. III of 1340, that the King had granted to Gerard de Alspath the same messuage lands and rent in Biseleye and the manor and lands in

---

[1] Chanc. Inq. P. M., 3 Ed., No. 2. See *B. G. A. S. Trans.* Inquisitions I.
[2] Carta Harl. 57c. 25.

Winstone for life,[1] and in 1340, his son, John de Alspath, the King's yeoman, petitions the King for the manor of Winstone and the quarter part of the manor of Bisley and of the Hundred, with the advowson of the Church of Winstone, all which were granted to him. But in 1350, his brother and heir, Edmund de Alspath, obtained licence to enfeoff John de Clinton of his interests in Bissleye and Winstone.[2]

Investigations were made in Parliament in 1355[3] at the suit of Roger de Mortimer then Earl of March, who asserts that Sir John de Clinton had entered one messuage, two carucates of land and £10 rent in Bysele which Gerard de Alspache chev. had held for life by demise of the late Earl of March. The sheriff was bidden to summon Sir John de Clinton to appear before the King at Easter, the notice being given to Clinton by Richard de Clyveshale, bailiff of the liberty of Byseleigh. John de Clifford of Deneway appeared on behalf of John de Clinton and recited the facts as stated above, but Parliament ordained that the Earl of March should have full seisin of the aforesaid messuage, etc. The charter of the King, granting to John of Alspath the tenements by the name of one messuage and the moiety of one carucate of land, etc., in Byseleye for life, as well as a second charter granting the same by the name of a quarter part of the manor of Byseley to John de Alspach and his heirs, were apparently set aside. Sir John de Clinton was of the family of the Earl of Huntingdon, and inherited the manor of Temple Guiting with appurtenances in Frampton, Weston Birt and Foxcote.

To resume the history of the Mortimer family, Sir Edmund Mortimer, son of Roger first Earl of March, did not succeed to his father's honours, but was knighted 1 February, 1328, and was summoned as a Baron to Parliament 20 November, 1331, dying on 17 December following, having married in 1328 Elizabeth, third daughter and co-heiress of Bartholomew de Badlesmere by his wife, Mary, daughter and co-heir of Thomas de Clare (who in 1338 married secondly William le

---

[1] Cal. Pat. Rolls, 1338-40.
[2] Cal. Pat. Rolls, 1350. The arms of Alspath were arg. a bend sa. cotised gu.
[3] Coram Rege Roll 379. m. 69.

Bohun, first Earl of Northampton). Their son, Roger (IV), born 1327, distinguished himself in the war with France, and was knighted by the Black Prince, 13 July, 1346. He was also one of the foundation knights of the Garter. The attainder of his grandfather having been reversed, he became Earl of March in 1354, and married Philippa, daughter of William Montacute, first Earl of Salisbury, dying in 1360. He held his manor court at Bisley, 5 October, 1357.

At his Inquisition P. M. taken at Payneswyke, 25 April, 1360, when John de Bysele, John Dammesel, John of Frampton, William Chalkeford and others, bore witness, it is stated that long before his death he had with the king's license demised the manors of Byseleye and Wynston to William, Bishop of Winchester and others for the terms of their lives, and at a later Inquisition that the late earl held the advowson of two-thirds of the Church of Byslee at each vacancy, worth 20s. a year, and the advowson of Winstone, worth five marks a year. As the heir, Edmund Mortimer, was only aged nine at his father's death, the King held the manor in his own hands, but confirmed the grant to William, Bishop of Winchester, in 1360.[1] The manor court was held in the Bishop's name at Bisley on St. Michael's day 1361, and again in 1364. The court was held in the name of Edmund Mortimer, Earl of March, on 25 October, 1369, he having attained the age of eighteen, and being in possession of the Mortimer inheritance. He married Philippa Plantaganet, daughter and heir of Lionel, Duke of Clarence, second son of Edward III. After her death, he went to Ireland as the King's Lieutenant and died in 1381, being buried at Wigmore. His son Roger (V) succeeded him, but King Richard II held the manor of Bisley in his own hands during his minority, manor courts being held at Bisley in the King's name 13 November, 1382, and in 1388.

On 12 March, 1382, the King granted to Matthew de Swetenham, yeoman of the chamber, for life during the minority of the heir, the lordship of the Hundred of Bisley.[2] By 7 September, 1392, Roger Mortimer had attained his

1 Cal. Pat. Rolls.
2 Cal. Pat. Rolls, 1382.

majority and courts were held at Bisley at that date, and in 1393 in his name. He married Alianora, daughter and co-heir of Thomas Holland, Earl of Kent, and he died in 1398, being slain in Ireland, where he had been left as viceroy by King Richard II, who also had declared him heir-presumptive to the crown. He had in 1394 granted to his brother Sir Edmund Mortimer and his heirs, yearly rents from his manors, including £40 from Bisselee, Brymisfeld and Wynstone. These were confirmed to him on 3 October, 1398.[1]

Alianora, Countess of March, had re-married to Osward Charlton by 29 September, 1400, on which date a Court was held in their joint names at Bisley as also about 15 August, 1401. On 21 November, 1403, the Countess received from the King a grant of £40 yearly from the issues of the manors of Brymefeld and Biselegh, etc. (as previously granted to Sir Edmund) in consideration of the fact that she had had to support two daughters of her late husband, since his death, at no small expense, and all the possessions of her own dower and of the inheritance of the Lord of Powys now her husband, in Wales, whereby these charges should be borne, were now burnt, wasted and destroyed. Recognizing her as his kinswoman, the King made ample provision for her dower.

Edmund, Earl of March, eldest son of Roger (V) and Alianora died without issue in 1424.[2] His only recorded act concerning Bisley is his presentation of Thomas Donecan, M.A., to the second portion in Bisley Church in 1423.

His younger brother, Roger, dying also without issue, the elder sister, Anne Mortimer, who married Richard de Conis-borough, Earl of Cambridge (beheaded in 1415), mother of Richard Plantagenet, Duke of York, appears to have conveyed the Bisley estates to her son. His first court was held at Bisley, 12 April, 1435, and another on 19 April, 1439. On 27 April, 1434, licence was granted to Richard, Duke of York, to grant to John Stonham (or Stonehouse) the manor of Over-sodyngton, Glos., in chief, in exchange for a fourth part of the manor of Bisley, and for the advowson of the

---

[1] Cal. Pat. Rolls, 1398.

[2] He had been taken prisoner by Owen Glendower when only six years of age. (Atkyns).

second portion of Bisley Church.[1]   This exchange is mentioned in Ministers' Accounts of 1446-52 when £4 6s. 10d. rent is paid for the fourth part of the manor formerly of John Stonehouse in exchange for the manor of Sodyngton, and 40s. is paid as rent for the farm of the lands of the Nether manor by Richard Clerke, who also rented the Inhoks (Inacres) pasture for 3s. 4d., formerly also of John Stonehouse. Richard Benett was seneschall during these years.   In these same accounts much detail is preserved of the Stokeland or Stokesend manor, and constant reference is made to each tenement as formerly in the tenure of John Clynton.[1]   As several holdings are accounted for, it points to the conclusion that the Stokesend manor included what is now the Mansion and Paulmead cottage together with the lower part of Bisley on the opposite side of the road from the springs, and running up to the present high road.   Richard le Smyth paid 23d. of new rent for one waste place in " le Strete."

1 Cal. Pat. Rolls, 1434.

D

CHAPTER III

PART 3

THE MANOR RE-UNITED

The whole manor of Bisley, excepting Lypiatt, was now in the King's hands, and the Duchess Cecily became the Lady of the Manor for life. Cecily of Raby, youngest daughter of Ralph Neville, Earl of Westmorland, by Joanna Beaufort, daughter of John of Gaunt, his wife, married Richard, Duke of York, who had been her father's ward. Her beauty was remarkable, as was her excessive pride. In the North she was called the "Rose of Raby," but in the neighbourhood of Fotheringay Castle where she kept almost regal state, "Proud Cis." It was a great trial to her to have to give place to the wife of her son Edward IV, Elizabeth Woodville, but after the many tragedies of her life, as years advanced, she appears to have led a strictly religious life in her old age. It is said that King Edward IV restored Overcourt for his mother, but whether she ever resided there is doubtful. It was only one of many manors in her dower, and remote and inaccessible in those times. The Duchess died 31 May, in 10 Henry VII, 1494-5, at her castle of Berkhampstead, and was buried at Fotheringhay with her husband.

The Manor court rolls of this period have not been preserved, but records of a court leet at Bisley, 8 Ed. IV, 1468-9, refer to the Princess Cecilie, Duchess of York, as Lady of the manor in the matter of John Frampton and his daughter, Agnes Olyff, of Chalford.[2]

On 10 May, 1488, it is recorded that Sir Edward Ralegh, Knt., was holding the office of steward of the Hundred of

[1] P. R. O. Min. Accts. 850/26-32.

[2] Abst. C. C. C. Deeds, *B. G. A. S. Trans.* li. 217.

Bisley and keeper of the parks of Barnesley, Brimsfield and Miserden, which the Duchess held for life. The reversion of the office was granted to Thomas Poyntz, Esquire of the King's Body.[1]

On 1 February, 1492, the office of bailiff of Bislegh and the lordship of the manor of Bysleche were granted to Elizabeth, Queen of Henry VII, which anticipates the death of the Duchess Cecily, for some unexplained reason, by two years. Also the Hundred of Bysley was in 1508 granted to John Yowarde, groom of the ewery, during pleasure, being at the King's disposal through the death of the Duchess of York, with wages of a penny a day with usual profits.[2] Arthur, Prince of Wales, son of Henry VII, held the Manor,[3] and after his death it came to Henry VIII, who assigned it as part of the dower of Katharine of Arragon, then to Sir Thomas Seymour, and later to Princess Elizabeth, afterwards Queen.

Records of Courts held in 1545–46–47, also from 1584 to 1602, are preserved at the Public Record Office. That of the Court of the Hundred, 26 Elizabeth, gives an interesting list of names of those who attended it, namely :—Giles Lord Chandos, Simon Raughley, Knt., John Throgmorton, knt., Giles Codrington, Esq., Robert Freame, gentleman, Anthony Field, gentleman, Richard Payne, gentleman, John Coxwell, gentleman, the President and scholars of the College of Corpus Christi, Oxford, Feoffees, tenants and guardians of the Church of Byseley, John Hallyday, William Fowler, Richard Watts, Thomas Blisse, Richard Smart, Richard Shewell, Robert Gardner, William Pearse, Richard Blackwell, Thomas Aldridge, Thomas Gibbins, Richard Warner, William Shewell, Walter Handcock, Richard Fletcher, Jeronimus Jeoffreys, John Gardener of Tunley.

Sir Henry Poole, who died in 1616, was possessed of the Hundred of Bisley, and all fairs, markets, view of frankpledge, etc., in Painswick, Bisleigh, Througham, Bydfield, Tunley, Strowde, and Pakenhill, held as of the manor of East Greenwich in free socage by fealty only, and worth 2s. 5d. per

1 Cal. Pat. Rolls, 1488.
2 Cal. Pat. Rolls, 1508.
3 MS. Bibl. Reg. 18A, 77.

annum. Also he held lands and tenements in Thrupp and Nether Lypiatt (as well as in Minchinhampton), worth 12d. per annum.[1]

On the accession of James I, he granted the manor of Bisley to his Queen, Anne, and at her death in 1619, it was granted to George, Marquis and Earl of Buckingham, who held it as of the manor of East Greenwich. No Court rolls exist for this period. Amongst the title-deeds of Overcourt is an indenture dated 8 June, 1594, between Hugh George, of London, gentleman, and Thomas Tayloe, of Bisleighe, clothier, in which it is stated that the Queen has let the scite of the Manor of Bisley, called Overcourt, in as full manner as Walter Compton, late tenant, held and occupied parcel of the Manor of Bisley and of lands, etc., granted for Her Majesty's maintenance, to Thomas Tayloe, his wife, Alice, and Thomas, his son, for the rent of £3, reserving all manorial rights and advowsons of the Church and chapels of ease, to Hugh George, which he demises entirely to the Tayloes. The Tayloes do not appear, however, to have been lords of the manor.

The parcel of the manor held by Walter Compton was Jaynes Court, where a small window, of unknown origin, containing some portions of stained glass (one Flemish piece being dated 1535), has a fragment of an inscription to " John —ompton, Presbyter."

The Tayloes, after being tenants of Overcourt, bought it in 1621, from the Marquis of Buckingham, and the Feoffment of 1 March states that the site had been in the tenure of John Snow. Thomas Tayloe was to pay £90, and a yearly rent of £3, the purchase money to be paid in two sums of £45 upon the font stone in the Temple Church, London, and fee-farm rent of £53 16s. 6¾d. was reserved to the King.

The lordship of the manor meanwhile became separated from the demesne, after passing into the hands of the Marquis of Buckingham, who sold it to Thomas Masters, D.D., Master of the Temple, whose descendant, Thomas Master, Esq., of Longhope, sold it to Sir Robert Atkyns, 11 June, 1678, the

---

[1] *B. G. A. S. Trans.*, L., 217.

latter's first court being held 30 October, 1679, his last in 1708, when the manor was sold to Thomas Stephens, Esq., of Lypiatt. Since that time the manor has been held by the successive owners of Lypiatt down to the time of the death of Sir John Dorington, and passing after the death of Lady Dorington to her heir. The lordship of the manor is now practically in abeyance, the heir having failed to find a purchaser for it when the estate of Lypiatt was broken up.

The Court rolls are complete from 1675 to 1838 and are preserved at Lypiatt.

CHAPTER IV

PART 1

THE MANOR HOUSES OF BISLEY, THEIR OWNERS AND TENANTS

OVERCOURT

That the site of the chief manor house of Bisley has been occupied for many centuries, is deduced from the finding of several Roman remains in and about the grounds, but traces of the manor house of the eleventh, twelfth and thirteenth centuries are absent. The earliest date that may be assigned to any part of the present structure, is late fourteenth century, which may be attributed to the entrance hall and rooms on either side of it. The very primitive form of the external remains of the garderobe on the south side, suggest this early estimate and would make this part of the house to be the work of the last Hugh de Bisley. Edward IV is traditionally said to have restored the house for his mother, the Duchess Cecily. The eastern portion of the house was added in the reign of William and Mary, and the inner drawing-room in that part, had, till lately, a fireplace adorned with old Dutch tiles of Scriptural subjects of the same period.

At the restoration of the last century, indications of a hall reaching up to the roof beams were found on the north side of the entrance, and a small room was opened out where certain woodcarving seemed to point to preparations for an important guest,—possibly Queen Elizabeth, who *may* have slept here a night on her way from Berkeley and Frocester to London, on the eve of St. Lawrence, 1595. Failing any record of such a sojourn at Bisley, this conjecture cannot be substantiated.

The house must have been considerably altered during the residence of the Tayloes, and the large hall would then have been divided into rooms. At the restoration of the house by General Gordon, a needlework picture of Charles I and Henrietta Maria was found in a winding staircase which had been walled up, leading from the dining-room to the bedrooms above. This picture which was probably hidden in Puritan times, has since been lost sight of.

The usual tradition of a secret passage, said to lead to Jaynes Court, is current, and certainly there was a sub-terranean opening in the so-called Queen's garden, which was recently covered over by a former owner, and in the cellar of Jaynes Court there was the opening of a passage, since walled up.

The clothier family of Tayloe now become the most prominent of the people in Bisley in the seventeenth century. The first known of that name there is Simon Tailo, Prebendary or Rector of the first portion in Bisley Church, between 1316 and 1337. Another, Simon Tailo, was holding land of the Earl of March, one toft which Agnes Coppesgrave sometime held and another toft and acre of land in the field which Seth Tristram formerly held at 12d., on 25 October, 1369, and 12 May, 1393. In the Lay Subsidy rolls of 1523-4, Robert, John and Richard Tailo are mentioned, and at the Court of Thomas Wye, in 1558, William Tayloe does service for a Tuck and Gyggemill. He appears to be a brother of Thomas Tayloe (I), tenant of Overcourt, who died 13 September, 1600, when 26s. 8d. heriot was paid.

Thomas Tayloe (II) who purchased Overcourt, as we have seen, in 1621, was son of Thomas Tayloe (I.) and Alice Snowe, his wife (married at Bisley 11 August, 1589), and he was born in 1591, baptized at Bisley, 17 December, being barely eleven years old at the time of his father's death. Thomas Tayloe (II) assigned to Henry Twissell and Roger Scott, in trust, Overcourt, and all demesne lands belonging thereto in 1621, for sixty years, he receiving the profits, and the trustees to assign the said term to such persons as Tayloe should appoint. In 1633, Twissell and Scott, by appointment of Tayloe, assigned the residue of the term of sixty years as far

as it concerned eighteen acres in Over Lypiatt field or Stancombe field of the demesne lands of the manor of Bisley,
fifteen acres being then in the possession of John Stephens,
Esq., and three in the possession of Thomas Clissall, to John
Browne and Edward Stephens. This land formed four closes
of meadow, namely Cow lease, the Mowing Ground, The
Greater Lott, and the Lesser Lott mead, which were ultimately
bought by Thomas Stephens, Esq., in 1687.[1] Thomas
Tayloe (II.) married Joane Townsend, at Bisley, 13 October,
1638, their eldest son, Thomas, being baptized there, 30
August, 1639.

It must have been soon after this time, that the Tayloe
children left such charming memorials of themselves cut in
the stone splayed window jambs of their nursery and also
in the attic, where besides the quaint figures of men duelling
in the tall hats of the period, the inscription reveals the name
of Marrie Tayloe and W. T. besides certain only partially
legible letters.   (see plates 17 and 18)

The various changes which have passed over the Overcourt
estate make it impossible to picture quite what state it was
in during the seventeenth century, but the memory of the
park of early days is preserved in the two enclosures (504 and
505 on the Tithe map) bounded by the " Back Lane " and
still known as " the Park " and " Part of the Park."

Little is recorded of Thomas Tayloe (II) beyond the fact
that he was one of the Feoffees, and is spoken of as " yeoman "
in their deeds. As there was another Thomas Tayloe living
at Todsmore, and there is nothing in the Bisley registers to
distinguish between the two and their families, the will of
Thomas Tayloe (II), dated 18 April, 1661, is our only reliable
source of information. The preamble refers to his indenture
of 10 June, 1637, enfeoffing his land at Bisley to Thomas
Tayloe, his son. He wills to his wife, Joane, to augment
her jointure, all the part of the house he dwells in, namely, the
room called the hall, the buttery within the hall, the parlor,
the entry between the hall and the parlor, the three chambers
over the hall entry and parlor and also the chamber over

[1] Lypiatt MS book.

the outer Whitehouse, the outer garden adjoyning unto the Barns Close and the one half of the pigeon house and garden with free liberty unto the well to fetch water and to sett her wood in the Well Court with free ingress and Regress. She is to have two wayne loads, namely two cords of hard cleft wood and two loads of faggots, namely, one hundred of double faggots as in the country they are usually made between the first of March and the first of May. Also his little silver bowl and all his linen except the long table cloth for the Hall. She is to have the use of all tableboards, presses, cupboards and side tableboards in the room formerly and free liberty at all times to brew her beer in his furnace during her life.

To his three sons Robert, Samuel and Nathaniel Tayloe, measures of faggots.

" Item I give unto Samuell Tayloe my sone, All that my Meadow ground called Lordsmead with all the plott and parcell of meadow ground lying therein which I bought of Roger Fowler lying under Westerley wood and all the meadow ground adjoining to the said Lordsmead which he had in exchange of one John Twissell and adjoining to a meadow called Mill meadow the land of the said John Twissell and from thence divided with a quick-sett mound for rent of 4s. due to be paid out of the said scite and farm of Bisley. Item further my will is that my said wife Joane shall have the little garden ground that is over against the Hall one light window and the buttery and kitchen windows as now it is bounded out thereon and the wall next the lower farm Barne close for such use and uses as she shall imploy the same during her life."

He further bequeaths to his son, John, 20s. To his daughter, Jane, £100. To his daughter, Sara Hancox, £10. To his son, Thomas Tayloe, all the scite and farm called Overcourt, with all lands and rents belonging. He confirms the grants of land to his other three sons, as they held them. He wills all the tableboards, side tables, cupboards, presses, bedsteads, and his brass furnace to remain in the house as " Standills " for his heirs. To Samuel Tayloe, an annuity, and his best suit and cloak.

To Nathaniel Tayloe, an annuity, his lesser silver tankard, and the curtains lately bought of carpetting stuff, the tableboard in the middle chamber and the bedsteads in the Parlor. The brass and pewter is to be equally divided between his three sons. The will is witnessed by Francis Baker, Thomas Thacke, Richard Blake, Anna Walk (her mark) and John Wood.[1]

By a codicil dated 6 January, 1664, Thomas Tayloe directs Samuel Tayloe, who was to pay a yearly sum of £20 to his son, John, to pay the said £20 to his grandson Thomas Tayloe, son of John Tayloe. His executors are to take care for his breeding up and when of fit age to place him as Aprentize to some lawful callings. At 21, his grandson is to have £100 over and above the £20 and his breeding up and apprenticeship. Signed, Thomas Tayloe and witnessed by Thomas Thacke, Richard Blake, Anna Walk (mark) and John Wood.

Having survived the troubled times of the Civil War and Commonwealth, Thomas Tayloe witnessed the Restoration and did not die till 1666, being buried at Bisley on 23 October.

In 1659, Thomas Tayloe, senior, yeoman, had, by Indenture of Lease, granted to Nathaniel Tayloe, his son, the arable and pasture ground called the Ridings, of twelve acres, being parcel of the farm of the manor of Bisley. Nathaniel, by his will dated 24 June, 1667, bequeathed the same to John Ridler, of Standish, Glos., yeoman, the Ridings being then in the possession of Thomas Eckold. John Ridler sold the same land to Peter Clissold for £49.

Thomas Tayloe (III), clothier, succeeded his father at Overcourt. He made his will 1 August, 1685, bequeathing to his wife, Anne, the house he dwelt in and all the lands in the parish of Bisley which he inherited from his father, also all rents reserved on lands given to his brother. After settling certain loads of wood from Calfway wood yearly on her, he bequeathes to her all his household goods except such as came to him as heir of his father, which are to remain to his heirs who have the house. To his brother, Samuel

1 Overcourt Title deeds.

Tayloe, £20, his wearing apparel and books. He forgives his kinsman, Thomas Sparrow, the money he owes him. To his kinsman, Thomas Tayloe, his " Shares " and other tools for dressing of cloth and such teasels as he shall leave. To his cozen, Ann Corderoy, all that right he had in the house and land she and her husband live in, called Long Tunn. His sister-in-law, Sarah Hancox, her children and their father, to have certain monies divided amongst them. He wills Widow Townsend the land she has under his writing, and that Mrs. Ridler shall enjoy the privilege in and about his house she formerly had. He charges his lands in Bisley, with £300, whereof £100 to his cosen, Edward Tayloe, son of his brother, Robert Tayloe, £60 to Mary Trotman, £40 to Elizabeth Poole, also the same sum each to Jane Butt, Rebecca Tayloe, and Sarah Tayloe, all being daughters of his brother, Robert Tayloe.

Calfway wood is not charged with the above legacies, but all his part of the said wood is to go to his cosen, Thomas Tayloe, son of his brother, John Tayloe, after the decease of his wife.

A codicil directs that Thomas Tayloe, out of Calfway wood, is to pay £100 in money to Samuel Tayloe. His signature is witnessed by Simon Preist (vicar of Bisley), John Tayloe and Henry Smart. A further codicil directs his wife to cut £5 worth of wood in Calfway wood to give to his cosen, Thomas Sparrow, and he is to have half his wearing apparel. To his sister, Jane Fettiplace, his silver watch.[1]

Anne Tayloe continued to reside at Overcourt during her widowhood till her death in 1704, her burial being recorded in the parish registers as taking place on 3 March.

Thomas Tayloe (IV), nephew of her late husband, lived there with her, but the estate passed to Robert Tayloe, nephew and heir to Thomas Tayloe (III) who by Indenture of 5 June, 1695, sold the reversion of the same to his cousin. By this it was agreed that Robert Tayloe of the parish of

---

[1] Overcourt Title-deeds, the source also of information regarding the various legal documents quoted in this chapter, the use of which is owing to the kind permission of Hugh Coles, Esq., and of R. J. Dyson, Esq.

Bisley, clothyer, nephew and heir at law of Thomas Tayloe, sometime of Bisley, clothyer, deceased, and Thomas Trotman, of Bisley, clothier, of the one part, and Thomas Tayloe, of Bisley, gentleman, of the other part, for 5s. paid by the said Thomas Tayloe, the said Robert Tayloe and Thomas Trotman have bargained and sold to the said Thomas Tayloe " All that messuage or farmhouse in Bisley commonly called or known as Overcourt and all barnes, stables, cowhouses, gardens, courts, yards and outhouses belonging and all that little close neare adjoining to the said messuage or farmhouse called by the name of the barne close and sometymes called the Home close containing two acres and also those two enclosures or tyneings containing ten acres more or less adjoyning together save only a little Lane divides them called the back lane and all hedges, trees, wood, underwoods, the same being first enclosed the said premises being situate in Bisley aforesaid, now in the occupation of the said Thomas Tayloe and Anne Tayloe, widdow, and were sometime heretofore amongst other lands bought by Thomas Tayloe, the late grandather of the said Robert Tayloe of and from the late Duke of Buckingham and others, the reversion of which after the decease of the said Anne Tayloe, widow of the said Thomas Tayloe, uncle to Robert Tayloe, is descended and come to the said Robert as heyre at law to his said uncle together with all commons and feedings (not exceeding fifteen Rother beasts, four horse beasts, two hundred sheep and fifteen swyne) for one year."

The Release, dated 6 June, 1695, is between Robert Tayloe and Elizabeth, his wife, and Thomas Trotman, of Bisley, clothier, of the one part and Thomas Tayloe, of Bisley, gentleman, of the other part. After reciting all as in the previous lease, mention is made of the right of Anne Tayloe for life, and also the estate and interest which William Eldridge, claymeth to have of and in the tenement and premises now in his possession by virtue of a lease granted to him by the said Thomas Tayloe, deceased, together with all the writings and evidences of the said premisses after the decease of Anne Tayloe for the yearly rent of £1 17s. 6d. to be paid yearly to the right owners of the manour of Bisley. To be held of the chief Lord or Lords of the Fee for and under the rents and services therefore due and of right accustomed. Signed Robert Tayloe, Elizabeth Tayloe (mark), Thomas Trotman.

Not only does the mansion of Overcourt appear to have been divided into two dwellings at some period, but there was, and is, in the grounds, the Tudor house referred to as in the tenure of William Eldridge. This, I think, is to be identified with the tenement called " le Dowriee," the earliest mention of which occurs in the Bisley Court Rolls (P. R. O.) of 1601. " Richard Hopton surrendered the reversion of one messuage and one ferendal of land called le Dowriee then in the tenure of Henry Tailo. Came Richard Tailo, son of William Tailo and took from the Lady Queen the same reversion of the said messuage and ferendal of land to hold to the said Richard Tailo and Elizabeth Webbe, daughter of John Webbe, of Cowley, and Katherine Tailo, daughter of the said William Tailo for lives."

Richard Hopton was, at the same time, holding Mortimer's Farm, and probably both he and Elizabeth Webbe were connected with the Tailo family by marriage. The relationship with Thomas Trotman is established by the marriage of Mary, daughter of Robert Tailo, father of Robert, who was heir to his uncle, Thomas Tailo (IV), to Trotman, as stated in the will of Thomas Tailo (III).

The position of this building now known as Overcourt Cottage, would suggest its former use as a dower house, and though it has passed through many vicissitudes, it will be seen in the following pages that it has been inhabited at various times, though at present it is not used as a dwelling house.

Thomas Tayloe (IV) married Hester Cull, and made his will 14 January, 1716. In it he states that he was late of Bisley, but then living in Gloucester Lane without Lawford Gate, in the parish of St. Philip and Jacob, in the County of Gloucester. He is styled gentleman, and after bequeathing his soul to Almighty God, he commits to his kinsman, Samuel Tayloe, of Hide Hill, parish of Minchinhampton, clothier, all the houses, woods, lands and tenements which he has in the parish of Bisley and all reversions, he to pay all debts.   Also he is to pay to his well-beloved wife, Hester Tayloe, £15 per annum for life.   He is to pay also, to Anne Cull, daughter of his brother-in-law, John Cull, £10 after the decease of his wife, to whom he gives the best cow and £5, as also his two best beds and bedsteads and all belonging, with all the furniture in the Hall and parlour Chambers, for life, and after to Anne Cull.   To his well-beloved wife, the use of all such household goods as she shall have occasion for life.   Provision is made for a dwelling for his wife ; also for a suit of crape mourning for her and Anne Cull.   " Whereas I could never gett my brother-in-law Stephen Cull either by fair or hard words to any manner of account in all my life either of my wife's fortune or for several quantities of money I have formerly lent him nor for great quantitys of wood which he cutt and sold in the years 1696-97-98 in my wood Calfway Wood for all which my executors may give him a great deale of trouble, and whereas by reason I had given him noe discharge either for my wife's fortune or for the wood cut and sold as aforesaid, he made me give him a bond for £20 I had of him notwithstanding he knew much more was due to me from him, and whereas he has a bond in his keeping given by myself and my uncle Samuell Tayloe to Peter Clissold, of Bisley, blacksmith, for £30, and assigned by the said Peter Clissold, to my uncle Richard Townsend, and which my brother Cull knows I have over paid My will is that my said brother-in-law Stephen Cull doe deliver unto my executors the said bond cancelled and all other bonds and writings he shall have of mine."

But if he refuses to give them and a general release, his said wife is to be paid only £10 per annum and they shall not be obliged to pay £10 to Anne Cull.

To his kinsman Robert Tayloe, his best coate, wastcoat and breeches, his two best shirts, one best cravatt, one best pair of shoes and stockins and his best hatt.   To his well-beloved wife all the rest of his wearing linnen.   His executors are to give one suit of worst cloths to Thomas Short and his son Richard.   His kinsman, Samuell Tayloe, to be executor. He desires to be buried in the parish Church of Bisley near the pew where he used to sit and that a small monument be set up against a pillar for him.   W. Thomas Hodges, John Short. Proved 14 December, 1720.[1]

Whether the small monument on a pillar was ever erected cannot now be ascertained, but Thomas Tayloe (IV) is commemorated, with others of the family, on a marble monument now placed high up in the tower of the Church, which was put into the old building by Hester Tayloe, widow of William Tayloe, who died in 1749. " Thomas Tailo, Gent., of this town died Sept., 1720, aged about 58."   There is a shield of arms on this marble monument for Tayloe—(Vert), a sword in pale (erect or) between 2 Lions rampant addorsed (erm.).[2]

The unsatisfactory condition of the estate is apparent from Thomas Tayloe's will, and it was now heavily mortgaged. Though Overcourt appears to have been in the tenure and occupation of Hester Tayloe, his widow, and of Samuel Tayloe, yet on 26 and 27 June, 1721, by lease and release, the estate became the property of Daniel Watkins, of the city of London, who resided there till his death, in 1736. His widow, Sarah Watkins, returned to London, having let part of Overcourt to one, George, and part to Richard Champion, whilst the " messuage tenement or farmhouse adjoining to the said capital messuage (the Tudor house recently referred to and now known as " Overcourt Cottage ") with a malt house, stables, and other houses belonging, now or late in the occupation of Richard Driver, together with the several pieces or parcels of arable meadow and pasture land let therewith and containing together eleven and a half acres, and also that messuage or tenement with a barn and about fourteen acres of arable land lying at or near a place called Lugg's Frith, now or late in the occupation of Robert Arundell and also several coppices and woods, etc., known by the several names of Lug's frith, Litteridge Wood and Calfway Wood, containing about ninety one acres " charged with the annuity of £15 to Hester Tayloe and £10 to Anne Cull, together with the mansion of Overcourt, are specified in a deed of 8 and 9 September, 1766, and valued at £1900.   Daniel Watkins, had, by his will, devised the estate to his wife for

1 Glos. P. R.
2 *B. G. A. S.*, xxviii, 455.

life, and then to his son, Thomas, who having died before 1766,
his sister, Mary Watkins, purchased the estate during her
mother's lifetime.   It appears that this was in view of her
marriage with Henry Peckitt, of Compton Street in the parish
of St. Ann's, Soho, Mary Watkins at that time being described
as of Northumberland Street, Strand.   In an Indenture of
Nov. 1, 1770, it is stated that the messuage wherein Daniel
Watkins lately dwelt was then occupied by the Reverend
William Pitt, Clerk ; and Richard Driver was still in occupation of the farm and cottage, whilst Edmund Clutterbuck,
gentleman, occupied part of Overcourt.

Mary Peckitt died in 1793, and by her will, dated 26 March,
1767, left the Overcourt Estate to her husband, Henry
Peckitt, for life, and after his death, to Daniel Watkins,
youngest son of Thomas Watkins, " of Besley, Glos., gent.,
deceased."   She left bequests to the four children of her
cosen, Thomas Watkins of " Thurp " (Thropp), son of
Samuel Watkins, clothier, deceased, also to her cosen James
Bidmead, son of John Bidmead, late of Bisley, clothier,
deceased, James Bidmead, being of Chalford,   Some of these
are also mentioned in a codicil of 7 August, 1790. Administration was granted to Henry Peckitt, 8 April, 1793.

Mary Peckitt devised the estate, after her husband's life
interest, to Daniel Watkins, son of her deceased brother,
Thomas Watkins.   In a deed of 1772, the estate was then
described as consisting of three messuages, one malthouse,
three barns, five stables, twenty acres of land, ten acres of
meadow, ten acres of pasture, a hundred and twenty acres of
wood and £5 of rent, common of pasture for all cattle (not
exceeding fifteen rother beasts, four horse beasts, two hundred
sheep and fifteen swine)."

Daniel Watkins occupied Overcourt Cottage, and died in
January, 1838. By his will, dated 19 October, 1829, he
appointed Thomas Hall, of Througham, yeoman, and Samuel
Damsell, of Bisley, malster, as his trustees, providing for his
two sons, Thomas and John, and his daughter, Mary, out of
the estate.   Shortly before her father's death, Mary Watkins
had married John Bishop, of Bisley, mariner, and going out
to Australia, died there 26 May, 1839, after the birth of a

daughter, who only lived a few days. A marble tablet now in the tower of the Church records the death of Mary Bishop.

Mrs. Elizabeth Watkins (formerly Drew), continued to reside at Overcourt Cottage till her death, 10 January, 1847. Thomas Watkins, her son, bought out the interest of his brother, John, in the estate and on 10 March, 1852, sold Overcourt to William Gregory, of Bisley, builder, reserving the Cottage and malthouse, with the paddock known as the Park or Home Ground, for his own use. At this time, Overcourt being still divided into two messuages, had been in the occupation of Mrs. Lediard, and of the Rev. H. A. Jeffry, curate, as tenants. In 1852 Overcourt was inhabited by the Rev. Isaac Williams, curate, and it was there that he wrote much of his volume of poems, " Thoughts in Past Years."

From this time Overcourt frequently changed hands. William Gregory sold it on 5 July, 1854, to the Rev. Edward Pyddoke, then curate of Bisley. During his ownership he gave a portion of the small paddock, now garden, near to the well, for a site for the new school, which he mainly built, and on 21 December, 1862, he conveyed Overcourt, where he had for some time resided, to Philip Davies Rose, Esq., of Jaynes Court, the Rev. William Lowder, curate and architect, being tenant at that time.

Meanwhile Thomas Watkins, residing at Overcourt Cottage, died there 15 October, 1861, and on 6 April, 1866, his trustees, George Goddard, of Bisley, innkeeper, and William Teakle, of Abnash, farmer, conveyed the same with its malthouse, yard, garden and pasture land called the Park or Home Ground, to P. D. Rose, Esq., but excluding common rights and common lands then being enclosed, these being sold separately to Mr. Woodruffe Kearsey, of Stroud.

At this time certain small portions of the close called Middle Ground and the Farther Ground, abutting on the Back Lane, passed into various hands.

On the 25 March, 1875, P. D. Rose, Esq. (then of Norcliffe, Babbacombe, near Torquay), conveyed the whole estate of Overcourt, with the Cottage and paddock to John Gordon,

D

Colonel (and later General) in the Bengal Army, who resided there till his death 1 January, 1899.

Overcourt Cottage was occupied, from 1878 to 1894, by Mrs. Dean, widow of the Rev. Nelson Dean, vicar of Bussage.

On the death of General Gordon, the Overcourt estate passed to his widow, Mrs. Mary Madeleine Gordon, and after letting it to Mrs. George Abell for some years, on 29 August, 1913, she leased it to Mrs. Marie Kathleen Dawes (otherwise Capell) for twenty-one years, but dying on 25 October, 1914, she devised the estate to her daughter Sarah Madeleine Sempill Gordon.

The unrest and difficulties caused by the Great War are evidenced by the rapidity with which Overcourt has since changed hands. Mrs. Capell sub-let to Mrs. Violet Mary Cooper for one year, 1918, and wishing to surrender the remainder of her term of lease, Miss S. M. S. Gordon sold the property to the then tenant on 27 June, 1919.

On 21 July, 1924, Thomas Alfred Walker, Esq., acquired the property from Mrs. V. M. Cooper, and in 1930 disposed of it to Reginald J. Dyson, Esq., the present resident owner.

It would appear that the mansion of Overcourt was considerably larger at one time than it is at present, and that it had a wing running out towards the School, near where the well lies, and forming the Well Court mentioned in the Tayloe will of 1661. It is not known when this was removed, but the malthouse which lay between the Cottage and the front of the house, was pulled down in the middle of the nineteenth century, the stones being bought by Mr. Dorington and incorporated into Eastcombe Manor Farm, which was then in course of erection. Owing to the fact that a portion of the Saxon font was found amongst these stones, it is probable that many of them came from the original Saxon Church.

The summerhouse or gazebo of early eighteenth century date, with a dog-kennel beneath the steps, is a fine example of its kind, and the adjoining gateway, now restored to its contemporary appearance, must have witnessed many a procession of joy or sorrow passing down the ages from Overcourt to the Church and Churchyard.

The stone coffin which for many years has lain in the garden at Overcourt was found in the Churchyard when the foundation of the present school was dug. It must have originally been constructed for a very tall person, being 7 ft. 4½ ins. in length, 27½ ins. in breadth at the head, and with concave sides, tapering to 18 ins. at the foot, whilst it is 18½ ins. in depth. Though it might be of Roman date, it is more probably of mediaeval times. It is without a lid and none of the mediaeval coffin lids in the Church fit it.

When found, the coffin contained the bones of a young girl which gave rise to a fiction which was invented by Canon Keble and others purely for their own amusement, now known as the tradition of " the Bisley Boy." The story ran, that the Princess Elizabeth, on a visit to her manor of Bisley, died, and was buried in the stone coffin, and, that (out of the fear her attendants had of her father's wrath) a Bisley boy of similar age and appearance was substituted for her, for which reason Queen Elizabeth never married! There was, and is, in Bisley, a family which bears a remarkable resemblance to Queen Elizabeth, more especially noticed by those who remember certain members of the family in the ruff and jacket of the Blue coat boys, and probably this fact suggested the romance to their Vicar's mind. He had not reckoned, however, on the story being sufficiently attractive to be the cause of a book being written on the subject, which reaching the United States brought visitors thence to see the coffin of the Princess Elizabeth ; nor was it foreseen that this pure fiction would be credited in the parish as their most cherished tradition beside which true history pales.

CHAPTER IV

PART 2

JAYNES COURT

In Chapter III it is stated that Richard Clarke was farming the lands of the Nether Manor (otherwise Jaynes Court) between 1446 and 1462. Later this estate was known as Higgons Court, the name of one, Thomas Higons, appearing in the Lay Subsidy Rolls of 1523-4. In the Indenture of 1594, already quoted, it was stated that Walter Compton had held and occupied the parcel of Bisley Manor.[1] He may have sub-let to Henry Broughton of Bisley, yeoman, who in 1581 demised the remainder of his years of the lease of his farm of Higgins Court, to James, his son.[2]

Meanwhile, the Jayne family, from whom the Nether Court presently took its name, appears in the Bisley parish registers first in 1548. (2 November, William, son of John Jaynes, baptized).

The next mention of Higgons Court is in an Indenture of 29 October, 1633, when Robert Tomlins and Clutterbooke Deane demise the five acres of arable land pertaining to Higgons Court in Stancomb field, for sixty years, to John Browne and Edward Stephens.[3]

The first title-deeds of Jaynes Court are non-existent, the earliest preserved being an Indenture between Thomas Jayne, of Frampton Mansell, yeoman, and Thomas Tayler, of Tarlton Co., Glos., gent., of the first part and Henry Townsend of the parish of Painswick of the second part, but containing nothing to our purpose.

1 Overcourt Title deeds.
2 P. C. C. 13 D'arcy.
3 Lypiatt MS. Book.

In 1715, there is an Indenture of release between William Jayne, of Frampton Mansell, gent., heir of Thomas Jayne, deceased, and Thomas Jayne, of Brimpscomb, Glos., clothier, another son of Thomas Jayne (of the first part), and Richard Aldridge, of Stroud, mercer, of the second part.   No further documents disclose the events of years till 1752, when on 12 and 13 June lease and release passes between Thomas Jayne and Henry Jayne, of the first part, and Rowland Tomlinson, of Gray's Inn, London, of the second part, and also a release between the said Thomas Jayne, described as then of Brimpscomb and then of Bisley, gent., and Henry Jayne, as then of Staple Inn, London, gent., only surviving son of Thomas Jayne and Sarah, his then wife, deceased (1), and Rowland Tomlinson of Gray's Inn (2), and Thomas Tyndall, of Coats, Esq. (3).

There is a recovery later in the year between Thomas Jayne, Esq., demandant, Rowland Tomlinson, tenant, and Henry Jayne, Vouchee.   These proceedings are followed on 20 October, 1752, by an Indenture of release between Thomas Jayne, of Bisley, and Henry Jayne (1), William Tyndall, of Coats, Clerk and Frances Tyndall, daughter of the same spinster (2), Thomas Tyndall, of Coats, gentleman, son of the said William Tyndall and Edward Aldridge, junior, of Bisley, gentleman (3), and John Cox, of Lypiatt, Glos., and Samuel Shepherd, of Minchinhampton, Esq. (4).   This was in view of a marriage which took place between Henry Jayne and Frances, daughter of the Rev. William Tyndall, rector of Coates.

Henry Jayne, of Bisley, gentleman, made his will 18 March, 1764, being then sick and weak of body, confirming the deed of settlement on his marriage with Frances, his late wife and bequeathing all the premises therein comprised, to his son, Thomas Tyndall Jayne.   To his servant, Mary Vizard, in consideration of her faithful service, his dwelling-house with garden, situate at Oakridge, known as Kirbys, or the Pigeon Hole.

All his other messuages, etc., in the parish of Bisley or Sapperton, or elsewhere, to his said son, but he authorises his brother-in-law, Thomas Tyndale, Esq., to let the same

premises devised to his son, but to pay the rents to him for his
education, he to be his son's guardian till he is twenty-one.
Also his messuages and lands at Oakridge, called Trilleys,
let to William Royatt, at the rent of ten guineas, to his sister,
Mary, wife of Peter Clissold, of Bristol. All his interest in
the wood called Oaklands Grove, of seventeen acres, and his
interest in a piece of land called Herringate, of one acre, to
his sisters, Mary Clissold and Catherine Saunders, equally, as
tenants in common. To his said sisters, all his interest in
his messuages and lands at Frampton Mansell. All the rest
of his estate in Bisley, not particularly given, he devises to
his sister, Aldridge, wife of Edward Aldridge, of Bisley. His
goods, except plate and such furniture as his son reserves,
to be sold at his death. If his son die, than all his goods to
his sisters. W. William Burroughs, Richard Driver, Charles
Coxe. Proved 7 March, 1765.[1]

During the intervening years the parish registers of Bisley
give us no help regarding the Jayne family of Jaynes Court,
and perhaps, this it to be accounted for by the family's
connection with Frampton Mansell and Brimscombe, but in
the Bisley Court Baron, of John Stephens, Esq., of 23
October, 1736, Thomas Jayne, is enrolled as free tenant for
Higgins Court, Mortimers Farm, Baldwins and Otesland in
Aveness, Blackwells and Hancoxes.[2] We may assume that
this Thomas Jayne was descended in direct line from William
Jeyne, who, in 1585 (30 December), came to the Manor Court
and took (and in 1589 surrendered and re-took for his own
and his son, William's, lives), one cottage, with a close and two
acres of wood and subwood, called Otesland, after the death
of Elizabeth Clerke, widow.

At the Court of the Manor, held 24 March, 1599, William
Jeyne is presented by the jurors, who state that he forfeits
his customary tenement into the hands of the Lady Queen,
in that he has not repaired the house of his tenement after
four penalties imposed on him and because he has permitted
his grange house to fall and has sold the " miren " of his
barn, and because he has sold certain oaktrees growing on

1 Glos. P. R.
2 Bisley Court Rolls, Lypiatt.

his land, and because he has converted the " miren " into charcoal and spoiled and consumed the wood growing upon his tenement. He had been warned in the Court of 22 September, 1589, that his house was not properly repaired.[1] No doubt this refers to Jaynes Court.

The Thomas Jayne above mentioned, and his son of the same name, appear in the Feoffees' documents as feoffees from 1714 to 1751, under various designations,—clothier in 1734, yeoman, that same year, and gentleman in 1740.

In Bigland's Glostershire, of 1786, mention is made of the heraldic shields in Bisley Church, and amongst them those of Jayne, namely—A chief vaire, impaling—on a chevron between three eagles' heads erased three trefoils slipped, for Kite, dated 1730.

From an Indenture of 1 May, 1778, it is clear that Thomas Tyndall Jayne, only son and heir apparent of Henry Jayne, late of Bisley, by Frances, his wife, owned Jaynes Court at that time, but was living at North Cerney, Glos., and on 23 and 24 March, 1787, Indenture of lease and release conveyed the property from him to William Yarnton Mills, Esq., who may have resided there for a time, but on 27 and 28 September, 1811, he sold Jàyne Court to Captain John Hamstead, R.N.

Great changes were immediately effected in the Court and its surroundings, Captain Hamstead, as it appears from a lease in 1814, having partially rebuilt and enlarged the house, stables and out-buildings, formed " yards, lawns and pleasure gound out of a close of land called the Orchard of two acres, and out of another close, called the postern way of two acres, now all enclosed by walls and divided by the road on the south and west parts and contain together with the site of the buildings about four acres."

Further there is a lease of 29 May, 1818, of a tenement erected by Captain Hamstead and then in the occupation of Daniel Woodfield, together " with a close of pasture ground called the Innock of fifteen acres, now divided into three closes called the Plantations, the Hither Innacres and the

1 P. R. O. Bisley Court Rolls.

Far Innacres, which was, with other lands, not included in these presents, now converted into a lawn and garden of twenty acres."

This is the only record preserved of the extensive gardens and grounds laid out by Captain Hamstead ; the cottage has long since disappeared, a pump alone remaining to mark its site, and the Innacres themselves have returned to their former condition, almost the sole indication of the transient change left being the stone pillars and iron gate marking the entrance just opposite the lodge gate of Jaynes Court.

What tragedy overtook Captain Hamstead and his wife is now unknown, but their ownership ended in 1813, and a marble tablet, re-erected in the Church tower, alone remains to mark the close of their short residence at Bisley.

" In this chancel are deposited Captain John Hamstead, of the Royal Navy, and Mary, his widow. He died 14 May, 1813, aged 46. She died 26 June, 1813, aged 41."

Sir Paul Baghott, of Lypiatt Park, knt., immediately acquired the whole property, and on 27 December, 1813, sold, for £1800, the mansion house and outbuildings adjoining and all enclosed within the garden walls (except the new granary, the peachery and greenhouse, and brewing utensils, etc, to be removed by Sir Paul Baghott), to Joseph Grazebrook, of Farhill, parish of Painswick, Esq.[1] The object of this purchase was the marriage of his daughter, Hester, on whom the property was settled 22 January, 1814, immediately before her marriage to the Rev. Edward Mansfield, Vicar of Bisley, who finding the Vicarage " small and incommodious," had already taken up his abode at Jaynes Court, which then and for some time later was called the Grove.

Captain Hamstead had acquired possession of the cottage house and garden and pastureland adjoining on the north to Chantry Farm, called Brattons and covering five acres two roods and thirty perches, for which a chief rent of £3 5s. 8d. was due, and a Reeve rent of 15s. 1d., payable

---

[1] He was for some time owner of the Stroud Bank (see ' Fisher's Stroud ') and together with his father, Benjamin, and other members of the family, lies interred in a double vault on the N.E. of Bisley churchyard.

out of Brattons Piece. It is interesting to note, in the out-house, a pair of those thirteenth century windows of which several are still to be seen in the parish. Brattons was also sold to Joseph Grazebrook and settled on his daughter Hester.

It is noted in the Indenture of settlement that the sum of £1 10s. 0d. per annum is chargeable on the whole estate for ever for the poor.

The Rev. E. Mansfield having died in 1826, his widow, Mrs. Hester Mansfield, continued to reside at Jaynes Court for some years, and by Indenture of 19 August, 1839, she purchased the cottage and Innacres (or Innocks). This property had been mortgaged by Sir Paul Baghott to Charles Cripps, Esq., in 1818, together with its common land of five acres (called Seven Acres), in Stancombe Field in Cook's Hill, being altogether 20 acres ; and by the latter it was sold in 1831 to Handey Davis,[1] who becoming bankrupt, it was disposed of by his creditors to Mrs. Hester Mansfield.

At some time, Sir John Shelley was tenant of Jaynes Court, and one piece of the garden between the kitchen and flower gardens, has been since called Sir John Shelley's garden.

Philip Davies Rose, Esq. became tenant of Jaynes Court in 1857, and on 23 March, 1861, that estate, together with the Innacres and cottage, was conveyed to him by Mrs. Hester Mansfield. He resided at Jaynes Court till 1874, and on 25 March, 1875, he sold the whole estate to Colonel Gordon.

On 18 June, 1892, Francis Robert Miers, Esq., purchased Jaynes Court, and after residing there for many years, sold to to Hugh Coles, Esq., to whom I am greatly indebted for access to the Title Deeds of this estate.

Paul Woodruffe, Esq., the eminent stained glass artist, became the owner of Jaynes Court in 1934.

The present house of Jaynes Court, though on an ancient site, is not of great antiquity. In the Indenture of 1814 already referred to, it is stated that the house had been

[1] Handey Davis and his brother Jesse, were well-known clothiers at Chalford, and became bankrupt in 1838. They built the house called Spring-field at Chalford.,

recently re-built, but this statement is not borne out. The front part of the building is manifestly of the reign of William and Mary, with its fine staircase and powdering closet, and its Dutch curved roof, but the bay window on the south side dates from the early nineteenth century, whilst the back part of the house is probably seventeenth century.

The octagonal building beyond the stables (strangely enough omitted in surveys and maps), crowned by a pigeon-loft, is of the eighteenth century and contains a fine cock-pit. There are many anciently worked stones on the premises, and some foundations have been found, but no definite remains of a former mansion can be identified, and all traces of farm buildings have been obliterated.

We have seen, that, in an Indenture of 1594, it was stated that Walter Compton had held and occupied the parcel of Bisley Manor, otherwise Jaynes Court. There is a small stained glass window in the house, between a passage and the pantry, the origin of which is unknown, but on an octagonal portion of it, there is part of an inscription, evidently in memory of a Compton.

D. JOANN. . .

COMPT. . .

PASTOR. . .

SIE P . . .

The window is made up of pieces of foreign glass, one bearing the name of Bauldwin Ryckman 15 (9 or 2) 3, and there are two foreign coats of arms, also a part of a Last Supper, with an angel and other figures. It is possible that this window was bought at Sir Paul Baghott's sale at Lypiatt, in 1825, as he had a large collection of foreign stained glass.

It is an undoubted fact, that, from the cellar, a passage led underground, possibly to Overcourt, but though several attempts were made to investigate it during the time of Mr. Rose's occupation, the light always went out at a certain point, and it was considered wise to block up the entrance to it.[1]

---

[1] Communicated by Miss M. Rose.

MORTIMER'S FARM

The name and locality of this farm has completely passed out of all recollection at Bisley, though existing and known in 1827, when Mrs. Hester Mansfield was paying a rate for Mortimers.[1] The name is significant, connecting it with the former lordship of the Mortimers, and it would appear probable that the farm was located on, or near, the site of the present lodge to Jaynes Court.

The earliest mention of it is in Ministers' Accounts of 1448-9 (28 Henry VI), as follows :—" 12d. of rent of Elies Serche for one messuage and one virgate of land formerly Mortimers of the Superior Manor at 18d" (repeated in 1450-1), but it more frequently appears in connection with Jaynes' or Higgons Court. It is mentioned in the will of Thomas Smart of Througham of 3 July, 1561. " I will that Alys, my wife, shall one whole year after my decease have nothing of my sonne James, for my house at Bisley called Mortcmers, saving only for house rowm." In the Court Rolls of 6 April, 1601, it is recorded that the barn called Mortymer's barn in the tenure of Richard Hopton has a defective roof.

Five acres of land in Stancombe Field went with Mortimers as described in an Indenture of 29 October, 1633, whereby Robert Tomlins and Clutterbuck Deane demise to John Browne and Edward Stephens, for 60 years, five acres of land in that Field parcel of the Site of the Manor of Bisley called Higgons Court and five acres of arable in the same, parcell of Mortymers Farm.[2]

The list of free tenants at the Court Baron of J. Stephens, Esq., of 23 October, 1736, includes Thomas Jayne for Higgons Court, Mortimers Farm, etc., and in 1770 the heirs of Henry Jayne, gentleman, for the same.[3]

From these scanty references it may be assumed that Mortimers was the demesne farm for Jaynes Court.

---

[1] Lypiatt MSS.
[2] Lypiatt MS. Book.
[3] Bisley Court Rolls at Lypiatt.

CHAPTER IV

PART 3

THE MANSION

There is every reason to believe that the manor house of Stokesend, as stated in Chapter III, is represented by the building now known as the Mansion, but some years ago, as Paulmead Place. Evidences of great antiquity have been found on the premises, most of which have now been removed. The cellar, at one time, contained the stone bases and parts of columns, considered to be Transition Norman, and there was a pair of thirteenth century windows cut out in one stone, in the out-building, now the garage. These windows were removed by the contractor employed to adapt the building for its present use, and have since been lost sight of.[1]

Till recently, also, there was part of an octagon shaft near the front door, and two small round pillars on the lawn, about eight inches in diameter. All these were of the type common to domestic architecture, and there is no ground for suggesting that they ever came from the Church. On such an ancient site it would be remarkable if no such remains of former buildings had existed. One of the walls in the house, at one time an outside wall, is two yards thick less one inch. This alone betokens great antiquity.

The main part of the house dates from the time of Charles II or James II, the part adjoining the present road being of rather later date. The back part of the house is of earlier origin, and during recent repairs a large Stuart fireplace was opened up, which had formerly had a little window in it, now blocked up.

---

1 Letter from Mr. Wilfrid Randall.

Another large Stuart fireplace has also recently been restored to its original state in the later part of the house. A flight of stone steps leading down to the lower lawn was also unearthed, but covered up again. These were probably used when the road which now passes at the end of the house, followed the avenue past the lower side of the garden into Joiners' Lane. The new road divides the house from part of the grounds which stretch up the hill.

The ownership and descent of the Mansion in old times is unknown ; if any ancient title-deeds exist, access to them has not been granted. It is known that General Daubeny at one time owned the house, and on his death it was bought by Mr. Wilson, who sold it to the Rev. F. M. Raymond Barker, in 1854,[1] from whom it passed into the possession of his grandson, H. E. Raymond Barker, Esq.

---

1 From notes by the late Mrs. F. M. Raymond-Barker.

CHAPTER V

Independent Manors

Througham with Clyffisale and Greys, Sydenhams, Sturmye's Court, Tunley and Denway, Ferris Court.

Througham with Clyffisale

The lesser manors within the ancient parish of Bisley present rather a difficult problem, as in most cases very little is known about their early history, owing usually to complete destruction of all ancient deeds connected with them, or to the inaccessability of those that remain.

In the case of Througham (formerly Troham, " the homestead by the trough or hollow valley ")[1] certain historical documents afford information about it in mediaeval times. It is a site of great antiquity, as witness the pre-historic remains, situated at, or near, Througham (see Chapter I), and it is bounded on the east by Holy Brook, a name which, perhaps, implies a connection with Pagan worship. The whole district is romantic in its beauty and remoteness.

The earliest mention of Througham is in Domesday Book, where it is stated to have been held by Lewnod of King Edward the Confessor, and by Hugh, Earl of Chester of William I, there being then one tenant there with 120 acres, and four borders (or cottagers) with one plough tillage, and four acres of meadow worth 20s. Earl Hugh was said to hold half a hide in Troham worth 10s., which Roger de Laci claimed as belonging to Edgeworth. Probably Througham lay in both parishes. In 1234 the Earl of Chester still held three carucates in Troham.[2]

[1] Letter of F. T. S. Houghton, Esq.
[2] Testa de Nevill.

The records of the Curiae Regis preserve the next notice of Througham in the following extract :—

"1201. Glouc. Ricardus de Troham positus loco Hardwini de Troham petit versus Robertum Achrad quod teneat finem factum in Curia dominu regis Henrici patris Domine regis per cirographum, in quo continetur quod idem Ricardus (sic) quiet-clamavit rationabilam partem suam 1 hide terre et capitale mesagium in Troham inperpetuum et pro hac quieta clamantia idem Hardwinus quietam clamavit eidem Roberto eadem villa, quam Willelmus filius Fulchonis tenuit de eo unde idem Robertus et heredes ejus debeant adquietare ipsum Hardwinum et heredes suos de forinseco servicio quod pertinet ad illiam virgatam terre et unde ipse pro defectu ejus reddedit 111 marcas de reragiss illius servic. Robertus venit et cognoscit finem et defendit quod pro ejus defectu nichil perdidit et quod servicium fecit plenare quod ad feodus pertinet. Dies datus est eis a die Sancte Trinitatis in XV dies apud Westmonasterius ad audiendum judicium suum."[1]

From this, we gather that Robert Achrad was holding the hide of land and the capital messuage at Troham under Hardwinus de Troham, which formerly William, son of Fulk, held, the fine for foreign service attached to the fee having been neglected by him to the extent of 111 marks of arrears, which he acknowledges. In the margin, a note states that this matter was submitted to King John.

There is a fine of 11 Edward II., 1317-8, made between Henry de Clyveshale and Richard de Clyveshale, respecting two messuages and one virgate and three parts of one virgate of land[2] and two acres of meadow in Througham and Clyveshale, which Henry let to Richard for life. The latter was to present annually, for rent, one rose, at the feast of the Nativity of John the Baptist, rendering all services to the Chief Lord of the fee which pertained to the said tenement. After the death of Richard de Clyveshale, the tenement was

---

[1] P. R. O. Rolls and Records, Curiae Regis, Vol. ii, 448.

[2] A virgate or yardland was a quarter of a hide and varied from 12 to 40 acres.

to remain wholly to Emma, daughter of William de Bisleye, holding it from the aforesaid Henry and his heirs, for her life, on the same service, and after her decease it was to revert to the said Henry de Clyveshale. Probably this fine was made on the eve of a marriage between Richard de Clyveshale and Emma de Biseley.[1]

The name of Clyveshale, or Cliffisale, and later Clissold's glade, occurs frequently in mediaeval documents, but its locality has passed out of knowledge now. As it is always mentioned in close connection with Througham, there is every reason to think that it was the name for the valley lying between Througham Slad and Battlescombe, but further evidence will be noted presently.

Meanwhile, at some date unknown, Cirencester Abbey had the gift of certain lands at Througham from Reginald de Througham and his son, for in 1319, licence was granted to the Abbot to celebrate divine service and cause it to be done by others in the Chapel built within his manor of Througham, in the parish of Byseleye, the license to last for one year.[2] The Abbot acquired common of pasture for 60 sheep on all the lands of Richard of Througham, by an exchange made with John Hatheway and his daughters, and this was given to the chapel.[3] The manor remained with the Abbey till the Dissolution.

In 1448, Isabella, wife of John Dudbrigge, quit-claimed to John Gerveys, Thomas Chedworth and William Frost, in perpetuity, two tofts, one virgate of land and four acres of meadow in Clyffeshale and Thoroweham.[4]

On 17 May, 1477, at Westminster, pardon was granted to Thomas Clyssole, late of Byslegh, yeoman, alias "husbond-man, of his outlawrie in the said county for not appearing before the justices of the Bench to answer the King and Richard Beauchamp, knt., etc., for having forcibly entered into a messuage, 100 acres of land, 20 acres of meadow, 20

---

[1] P. R. O. Feet of Fines, Glouc. 180.

[2] Reg. Bp. Cobham, p. 16, fo 14.

[3] Fosbrooke.

[4] P. R. O. Feet of Fines, Glouc. 110. A toft was a place where a house formerly stood.

acres of pasture and six acres of wood of the said Richard, John Cussy, Esq., Robert Kynne, Thomas Kingescotte and John Bennet in Byslegh, Clyssale and Througham Co. Glos. and disseised them and afterwards made an enfeoffment of the same to defraud them contrary to the form of the statute in Parliament at Westminster, 8 Henry VI, and to satisfy Henry Clyssale of £26 which the latter recovered against him for a trespass committed at Byslegh, Clyssale and Througham, in the late reign and to answer him touching another trespass, he having surrendered to the Flete prison and paid 6s. 8d. to the King for fine and satisfied the said Henry as appears by the tenure of the records and processes of the outlawrie and the certificate of Thomas Bryan, chief justice."[1]

On the dissolution of the monastaries in 1539, the manor was retained in the King's hands, till on 18 July, 1544, request was made by Thomas Strowde, Walter Erle and James Pagett, gentlemen, that they might purchase the manor, particulars thereof being set out as follows[2]:—

" Manor of Througham, parcel of the possessions of the Monastary of Cirencester, valued thus—

" Rents of Assize of free tenants in Cliffissale in the said Manor, 19s. 11d.

" Rents of customary tenants at will in those townships and hamlets to the said manor belonging, viz., Througham, 18s. 4d. Westwode 31s., Tonley 5s., Abbenesse 4s., and Frampton 10s.—68s. 4d.

" Farm of the site of the manor with all houses, etc., demesne lands and a pasture, both several and in common, lying in Rudgehill and " le Chapell Pece " in " le Greenewey " (excepting manorial rights, woods and rents of all tenants there) was demised to Thomas and Margaret Smarte and William, their son (20 February, 3 Henry VIII, 1512), for their lives, and a rent of 100s. for the said farme, doing suit every year at the Abbot's Court of Bisseley and giving a heriot of their best animal or 10s. at the Abbot's choice, and

---

1 Cal. of Pat. Rolls.
2 P. R. O. Aug. Office. Particulars for grant 1073. (Hockaday).

F

every year, at Christmas, a couple of rabbits, 101s. 4d. Farm of a tenement and close of pasture called Trylles and a small close adjacent in Okeruge in the parish of Bysseley demised to William Frome and Isabel, his wife, and William and Thomas Cockes, sons of the said Isabel, 20 September, 30 Henry VIII, 13s. 4d. Farm of two acres and three virgates of land in Througham and Cliffisale demised to William and Margaret Turner, Thomas and Henry, their sons, for a terme of years, 17s.

Fines, etc., 29s. Total, £11 19s. 11d.

There be growing, about the said manor, 140 oaks and ashes, whereof 100, of 80 and 100 years' growth, are not valued, being reserved to the farmer for repairs, etc., the remaining 40, of 60 or 80 years' growth, are valued at 20s."

The purchase of the manor by the three named, appears to have been merely a speculation, as William Compton, of Chalford, acquired it probably the same year, for he died possessed of it in 1546, and it passed to his son, Walter Compton, who, on 14 February, received license to grant two messuages, 120 acres of land, 12 acres of meadow and 70 acres of pasture in Clissall, Bysseley, Westwood and Edgeworth, parcel of Througham manor, to Thomas Smart and Richard Smart (afterwards cancelled).[1]

In this grant, Walter Compton is stated to be of Avenyage, but in the next grant, of 1 June, 1552, it is allowed to Walter Compton of Aveninge, gentleman, to grant his house called " the mannour place " of Througham, Glouc., in the tenure of Thomas Smart and 250 acres of land, 15 acres of meadow, 40 acres of feeding and pasture and two acres of wood in Bysley, pertaining to the said manor or house and also the free rent of 18s. 9d. paid by the free tenants of the same, to William Stumpe, of Malmesbury, Esq., and his heirs and assigns. On 23 November, of the same year James Stumpe, Knt., son and heir of William Stumpe, had license to let this estate to Matthew Kynge, of Malmesbury, clothier.

The manor of Througham, was, apparently, ultimately sold by Sir J. Stumpe to Matthew King, for " All that manor

---

[1] P. R. O. Grants, 4 Ed. VI. Pt. 2.

called le Maner place alias le Fearme place de Througham with all its appurtenances within the parish hamlet or fields of Bysley (Glouc.) " was sold on 26 January, 4 Elizabeth (1562), by Matthew King de Malmesbury to Johannes Rycheman and William Rycheman, the latter of whom complains against the said Matthew for refusing to convey the said premises to him. (11 Elizabeth m. 88 d. 9.)[1]

It appears, from the Feet of Fines, that Robert and William Partridge, of Wishanger, parish of Miserden, had acquired both the manors of Bysley and Througham, and conveyed them, in 1591, to William Lambarde and William Blocker, Esqrs., for the sum of £1360.[2]

Hitherto the Sovereign had been Chief Lord from whom the Manor was held, but records now fail us as to the names of owners of the manor house and lands, though it is probable that the Smart family, who continued to reside at the Manor house through all the vicissitudes mentioned, finally bought the property, and manorial rights lapsed. In 1736, Thomas Smart, gentleman, attended the Court Baron of John Stephens, at Lypiatt, for the manor of Througham.

In 1841, William Turner, Esq., was the owner and occupier of the Manor house estate, as well as that of Lower Througham farm (occupied by George Young), whilst Charles Harvey, Esq., owned Upper Througham Farm (occupied by Thomas Hall), and Thomas Mills Goodlake, Esq. owned Througham Slad farm (occupied by Samuel Butcher). The manor house is now the property of Professor O. L. Richmond.

Amidst all the changes in ownership, the lands attached to each farm have varied in extent from time to time. The whole of Througham was bought by Sir John Dorington, but the heir to his estates sold it in 1919, and now each farm has passed into the hands of a separate owner. The title is now registered, and as is the case with all the estates acquired by the late Sir John Dorington, no ancient documents are to be found.

---

1 P. R. O. Alphabetical Cal. of enrolments of Exchequer of Pleas.
2 B. G. A. S. Trans. xvii. Pedes Finium in Co. Glos.

CLIFFISALE

Cliffisale having been frequently mentioned in the foregoing pages, appears to have been of considerable importance in mediaeval times. Richard de Cliveshale was bailiff of the liberty of Byseleigh in 1355.[1] John Clyvethale is mentioned in the Court Rolls of 1413 as making default and owing sac. Also John Taunton, who held one tenement called Clyffeshallys in Bisley, had died.[2]

There are two further references to residents at Cliffeshale, besides those already recorded. The first is in the will of William Torner (or Turner), husbandman, of the parish of Bisley, dated and proved in 1552. He desired to be buried in Bisley Churchyard and bequeathed to his godson, Robert Hunte and William Clarke, each a ewe with her lamb, as also to Elinore Trolope. To John Here his blewe cote. The remainder of his goods to Margytt, his wyffe, and Henry, his son, both his executors. Overseers. Henry Browghton and John Whytyng, of Bysley, W. Thomas Torner, his son, and John Fowler, vicar of Bysseley. Provided always, that his wife and son, Henry, shall occupy and enjoy his purchase or messuage called Smethesmeade lying in Clyssal Glade, as long as his said wife keeps her widowhood, but if she decease or marry, it is to remain during the rest of his lease to his son. Except, if his son, Thomas Torner, provides and helps the said Henry, his brother, to a part of a living in another town, according to the approval of Henry Browghton and John Whyting above-said and Robert Hancock, the messuages are to remain to the said Thomas.

The second and last mention of Cliffeshale found under that name, is in the will of Richard Clyssale, 1 February, 1576. He bequeathed to his brother-in-law, John Looker, for ten years, his " mansion house " with all edifices, buildings, barns, stables, bartons, courtes, together with all land, arable, lesowes, meadows, pastures, common feedings, costom woodes underwoods, rentes, suites, with all other profits, etc., liynge and being in Clissold's Glade and in all other feeldes within the parish of Bysly, known or reputed to appertain to the

---

[1] P. R. O. Coram Rege roll, 379. m. 69.
[2] P. R. O. Bisley Court roll. Port. 175.

said mansion or dwelling-house. Except and reserved to Alice, his wife, one convenient chamber in the sayd house to dwell in. The said John bringing at his own cost and charge yearly during the sayd ten years three lodes of customs woods and certain hedge woods, clopes of trees, to the use of the said Alice. Also he shall pay 13s 4d. yearly and that year twenty bushells of barley and yearly sixteen bushells of barley, four bushells of wheat and four bushells of oates. One cowe is to be kept for her use and six sheep during the ten years. She is to have the garden they now occupy, with two pigs, six hens and a cocke going in the said commons and bartons about the house if the said Alice live so long. She is also to have all his household stuff for life with all the settles in his house. After her death to his son John, or at the end of ten years, and in case of his death, all is to go amongst his sisters equally. All is to be delivered up by his overseers in good order as it is now. John Looker to be his executor. Overseers, Richard Snow, Richard Smart and Robert Hunt, W. Walter Perse, Edward Reem, William Downton, Thomas Pope, and John Lightfoot, Vicar of Byseley.[1]

Richard Clissold died in 1577 and was buried on 5 February, at Bisley. His widow, Alice, did not long survive him, as she was buried on 20 May of that same year. John Looker, likewise, did not live long to enjoy the mansion house. He made his will in 1579, being then sick in body, and after pious commendation of his soul, left all to Marjorie, his wife, his overseer being Robert Hunt and his witnesses Richard Smart, William Whytting and John Lightfoot, Vicar of Bisley (who appears to have written the will).[1]

The question is, where did all these inhabitants of Cliffisale live?

We have, in the house known as Througham Slad farm, which overlooks what I take to be Cliffisale or Clissold's Glade, one of the most ancient dwelling-houses in the parish. It possesses one pair and a single one of small Early English lancet windows, each cut in a single stone, and the pair in its

---

[1] Glos. P. R.

original position, the other moved to what was formerly the barn, but which is now kitchen quarters ; and at the recent restoration by Mr. Cadbury, the present owner, a fourteenth century window, in its original setting, with grooves for wooden shutters, was discovered. There were remains of two spiral staircases which were destroyed. A carved oak cupboard beside the old fireplace in the entrance hall, the date " J. C. 1689 " on the chimney of the kitchen wing, a Queen Anne fireplace with a keystone, discovered in the parlour, the date 1850 on the barn and " T. M. C., 1862 " on a stable, all point to a continuity of occupation of this house from mediaeval times. It may reasonably be assumed that this was the residence of Richard de Clyveshale and his ancestors, and that the cottage near by, with its pair of Early English lancets, is of an equal antiquity.

The description of Richard Clyssale's " mansion house " in Clissold's Glade, may, of course, refer to Througham Slad farm, but it appears to allude to something on a grander scale, and I would suggest that, perhaps, this mansion lay on the south side of the glade at the east end of the field called Tomlines, where distinct traces of foundations of a large building, with a terrace having round projections, can be seen. It is significant too, that a field adjoining Upper Laines to the north west is called " the Park."[1]   There is no tradition to guide us to a more definite conclusion as to Cliffisale.

THE MANOR HOUSE AND OTHER FARMS AT THROUGHAM.

The Manor House occupies the central position between the Upper and Lower Farms, and is the least imposing of the three. The south front had, until recently, a gabled addition of the late seventeenth century, which has now been removed ; the north side is of Tudor date with mullioned windows and leaded lights. There are extensive cellars beneath the house, two of which are now walled up. In the

[1] Tithe Map, 1017.

third, when heating arrangements were being installed, the workmen found that the east wall, built of the natural stones dug from the site, heavily embedded in mortar, was seven feet thick, and was thought to be a thousand years old. If this is the case, it would have formed part of the Saxon owner's house. Further evidence of antiquity is now to be seen in the small, rudely-cut, early thirteenth century window, which was found in the grounds and is now lighting the kitchen entrance.

The Upper Farm, also built of local stone, is of Tudor date, gabled back and front, and having a Stuart balustrade to the staircase. The farm buildings exhibit indications of early date and monastic origin, there being two stone buttresses of ecclesiastical type still remaining, one on an old building and the second on a barn. Here, doubtless, we see the site of the original manor farm buildings, and the abode of the farmer, though there is no trace of the chapel, which at one time the Abbot of Cirencester had here. Perhaps the field known as Churchway piece (No. 1070 T.M.), may have some connection with its site.

The Lower Farm, at Througham, formerly the home of the Turner family and now owned by Michael Sadleir, Esq., is a fine specimen of the Cotswold gabled architecture of the early seventeenth century. It has remarkable stone water shoots, and a unique stone gutter-pipe ; also a very large pigeon loft.

The ancient house known as the Greys, formerly stood on a knoll over-looking the Holy Brook, to the east of Througham Slad farm and cottage. The origin of its name is unknown, but it may possibly have connection with Lord Grey de Wilton, owner of Bidfield Manor. The house was a sixteenth or seventeenth century gabled mansion, the south approach to which is still marked by the remains of massive gateposts on either side of the former carriageway leading to Battles-combe Lane and Bisley. This house was the residence of the Smarts during the eighteenth century, after they had ceased to be at the manor house apparently, or perhaps, it was occupied by a younger son of that family. After the death of Richard Smart, of Greys, in 1776, the Througham

Smarts were extinct, and the property was purchased by Marmaduke Bardoe, M.D., whose widow possessed it in 1789 ; later one of his sisters married John Edwards, Esq., who sold it to Sir William Harvey, of Bristol, the proprietor in 1807.[1] Traditional accounts of this ancient house, relate that it was tenanted by farmers or farm labourers, and despoiled of its former treasures, handsome tapestries being used as carpets on the floor. It was finally bought by Sir John Dorington and pulled down by him about 1878, its staircase being saved and re-erected in the new building at Lypiatt Park.

A descendant of one of the families occupying the house in the nineteenth century, relates that, at the time of the Civil War, The Greys was used as a farmhouse, and that one morning, when the farmer was out at work and his wife busy making bread, a troop of Roundhead horsemen was seen coming down the Packway from Edgeworth, and presently, arriving at the door, a trooper entered. The farmer's wife, alarmed at his appearance, hurled the dough she was kneading in his face, made good her escape by the back-door, and joining her husband, went with him to safer quarters at Bisley. Possibly the troopers were connected with the siege of Lypiatt House which was garrisoned by Col. Massey for Parliament, and later, in 1642, taken by Sir Jacob Astley.[2]

THE FAMILIES OF SMART AND TURNER OF THROUGHAM

In the Lay Subsidy Rolls of 1523-4 we find the names of several of the inhabitants of Througham, as follows :—

Richard Clyssale was assessed at £16, Thomas Smart at £19, William Turner at £12, John Hunt at 100s., Richard Lowe at £4, William Dorowe at £4, Robert Hunt at 40s., Richard Joyce at 40s., William Smart at 49s., and Richard Clyssale, in wages, at 20s.[3]

---

[1] Fosbrooke.
[2] Letter of Mr. Fred. Kirby, also see *Stroud News*, Feb., 1930.
[3] P. R. O.

Of these inhabitants, the Smarts and the Turners were the principal, and of longest standing in Througham.

The Smart family first apears in Bisley records in 1512, when Thomas and Margaret Smart became tenants of the Manor under the Abbot of Cirencester, as already stated. Where they came from is not certainly known, but the parish registers, from 1549 onwards, indicate the existence of five families of that name in Bisley parish in the sixteenth century, though as a rule without any record of the locality in which they resided. The earliest will of the Smart family in Gloucester Probate Registry is that of William Smart, 1558, of which the first part is missing, so that, though in all probability he was the son of Thomas and Margaret, his identity cannot be proved. He died in December, and was buried on the 26th of that month, 1588, being survived by his wife (not named) and seven children, of whom Katherine was the eldest, and of age, and therefore was to have twenty sheep. His wife was to deliver twenty sheep to each of his children on their marriage or coming of age. His son, John, appears to be next in age, and is to have a cart and wayne and four oxen. To his son, Thomas, a colt, at Rydyngs, to be bred up by his wife up to four years. To each of his children one yearling or a bullock of three years of age. He mentions his brother, James Smart, and also his debt to Bysseley Church of twenty shillings, two shillings thereof to be allowed for timber. The poor people of Byssley were to have twenty shillings at his burial and the Church two bushells of mawlt, the vicar of Byseley 3s. 4d. The rest of his goods and his house of Byseley, and also at Dyryse to his wife, who is sole executrix. John Whytyng and Robert Smart, supervisors, to have 6s. 8d. for their pains. W. Thomas Tayler, vicar of Byseley, John Whytyng and Robert Smart.[1]

Owing to the number of children, of whom nothing certain is known, it is with some hesitation that one suggests the line which probably continued at Througham Manor house. However, it may reasonably be assumed that Thomas Smart of Througham, yeoman, whose will is dated 3 July, 1561, is a brother of the preceding William. He desired to be buried

[1] Glos. P. R.

in the Churchyard of Bisley, and left to the use of the Church 3s. 4d. To Alys, his wife, all his household stuff, four kine and four score sheape as they come out of the folde, all his swine and poultry being in and about his house and farm at Boninghame. To his son, James, forty sheep as they run out of the fold, two kine which he has now in his company. To Henry, his son, twenty sheep. To Richard, his son, twenty sheep and to both sons, half the crops at Boninghame. To his wife, Alys, other quarter of his crops there and to William his son. To his son, Richard, two kyne and a yerling calf. The same to his son, Henry, also a wain with all gere belonging. To his son, Richard, a wayne and gear. His oxen were to be divided between Richard and Henry, except those given for the harriott.

To Margaret, wife of James Smart, his son, six sheep. To James Barker, two sheep and a calf. The keeping of twenty sheep to be allowed to William, his son. To Chrycham Dowell, one sheep. To Elizabeth Hop, one cow and to every one of her four children, John Hop, her son 20s., and Richard Hop, 20s. To Courle Hop, 20s., and to Pendrill Hop, 20s., by equal portions, which £4, given by him, shall be out of the hands of James Tokknell, out of the sum of £10 which he owes. (Other gifts are torn away).

To his son, William, his whole house at Cawdwell with all appurtenances . . . between them. To his son, William, his reversion of Wilkyns House lying . . . of Bysley. To his sons, Henry and Richard, each a horse. To . . . of Bysley, for writing hereof 3s. 4d. Alys, his wife, to have her dowry of all his hole lands.

Overseers, Thomas Hayle, of Tofeley and Wm. Nicolon, of Badgeworth. (10s. apiece).

"Item. I will that Alys, my wife, shall one whole year after my decease have nothing of my sonne, James, for my house at Bisley called Mortemers saving only for rowm." W. James Smith, James Brown, Walter Peers, Richard Wall, William Shyllam and others.

The will was proved at Gloucester, 27 September, 1561.

Alice Smart, widow of Thomas Smart, made her will 2 April, 1578, being then sick of body. She committed her soul to the Holy Trinity. To her son, Richard Smart, her great brass pot, and after his death, to John, his son, also eighteen shepe which were in the keeping of the said Richard, a frame and borde and bedstead and a roff. To Jane, daughter of Richard Smart, a fether bed, a bolster and a boxbed.

To Thomas Smart, son of the said Richard, a broche and a payr of colbernes. To Alice Smart, daughter of the said Richard, a candlestyke, a platter and a basen. To Ane Smart, daughter of the said Richard, a platter and a pottenger. To Henry Smart, son of Henry Smart, her second brass pot. To Anthony, son of Henry Smart, a brass pot. The residue to Henry Smart, her son, who is executor. W. Thomas Pope, Thomas Jones, and John Lightfoot, clerk, vycar there.[1]

The will was proved at Gloucester, 9 January, 1578 (old style), but the burial is entered in the registers as on 3 March, 1578, so that there is some mistake in dates somewhere.

From these wills, one gathers that the interests of the family, whilst entirely agricultural, lay in several directions other than Througham, namely at Boningham, Cawdwell, (both unidentified) and Wilkyns House, lying somewhere near Bisley, as well as Mortimer's (whither Thomas Smart's widow Alice, apparently retired), and this accounts for the dispersal of the family and the confusion of the registers, where there is no indication of domicile.

James Smart, parson of Brimpsfield, at the end of the sixteenth century, had some connection with the Smarts of Bisley, as his son, James, was buried there 29 September, 1616.[2]

The accompanying tree is a suggestion of descent gathered from the registers and wills, but is not authoritative, and it is impossible to say from which of the Smarts here recorded the Througham line continued and was finally represented

[1] Glos. P. R.

[2] Extracts from Brimpsfield Parish Registers, Glos. Notes and Queries, vol. i, 403.

in the Smarts of Greys.   Edward Smart seems to have risen
in the social scale, and it may be that from him, Thomas
Smart of Greys was descended, through his son and grandson,
both of whom were named Richard.

We are on surer ground with Thomas Smart, of " Trow-
ham," gentleman, as the recorded inscriptions[1] in the Church
of Bisley give the date of his death 24 January, 1725, aged 78,
(b. 1647), his first wife, Ann, having died 24 February, 1710,
and his widow, Sara, died 25 July, 1736, aged 85 (b. 1651).

Thomas Smart of Greys, Througham, gentleman, is probably
the son of the preceding Thomas, and was born in 1684.
He was present at the Court Baron of John Stephens, at
Lypiatt for the manor of Througham, in 1736.   He died in
1746, his will being dated 12 January, 1738.   He bequeathed
to his eldest son, Thomas Smart, all his messuages, lands and
tenements, etc., lying in the parish of Duntisbourne Rouse,
which he held by lease from the president and scholars of
Corpus Christi College, in Oxford, together with the said
lease and all interest therein.   Also to his son, Thomas,
all his Leasehold Estates whatsoever, in the County of
Gloucester during their terms.   To his son, Richard, £10 for
mourning.   All the residue of his estate and all his goods
and chattels, plate, etc., to his eldest son, Thomas, who is
executor.   W. J. Stephens, Thomas Stephens, Peter Leversage,
Proved, 26 February, 1747.

Thomas Smart of Greys, Junior, died in 1752, without
having made his will.   Letters of Administration were granted
to his brother, Richard Smart.

The monument erected by Richard, now in the belfry of
the Church of Bisley, gives all the information to be gleaned
at Bisley of the Smarts of Greys.   Under the coat of arms of
the Smart family, namely :—Argent, a chevron between
three pheons, sa.—on a marble tablet, is the following
inscription :—

> " In the North Aisle of this Church lie the remains
> of much loved wife, father, and mother, and those of
> Thomas Smart of Greys, in this Parish, who, having

---

[1] Bigland's History of Glos.

with integrity and the most enduring good nature and cheerfulness filled all the offices of his life, exchanged it for immortality on the 26th of December in the year of our Lord, 1746. Here also lie the bodies of his sons, William and Thomas, the former died in his infancy, and the latter on 26 April, 1752, aged 44.

This monument, with the highest sense of affection, gratitude and duty, was erected to his memory by their surviving son and brother, Richard Smart, Esq.

The above Thomas Smart had issue, another son of the name of Richard, elder brother to the said William Thomas and Richard, who died very young and lies buried at Stonehouse."

Richard Smart, Esq., the only surviving son of Thomas Smart and the last of Greys, died in 1776, having made his will on 7 April, 1772. By it, he charges his freehold manor, messuages, farms, lands, woods and tenements in the parish of Bisley and all his leasehold estate for years in the parish of Lower Duntisbourne, with payment of all his debts, and chargeable with the several sums of £1000 and £800, and the several other legacies given to the benefit of his kinsman, John Parry, of Clifford's Chambers, in the said county of Gloucester, gentleman, and the Rev. John Chapman, rector of Daglingworth, and heirs, according to the nature of the said estates. The said sum of £1000 is to remain a charge on the said estates during the life of Sarah Bishop, now living with him as a servant, payable at quarter days at 4 per cent. After her death, the said principal sum is to go to her neice, Sarah Bidmead. The said £800 to Catherine Blackwell, daughter of the late Mr. John Blackwell, of Chalford, at 21 years of age, but the 4 per cent. interest thereof is to be paid to Sarah Bishop for life. To Mrs. Mary Jennings (late Miss Mary Tyndale), £100. To each of his servants, £50. All his household goods to the said Sarah Bidmead. John Parry and Joseph Chapman, junr., to be executors. W. Anthony Pye, David Rees, William Cummins, servant to Mr. Pye. Proved, 14 June, 1776.[1]

1 Glos. P. R.

THE TURNER FAMILY

The second most notable family in Througham is that of the Turners, who appear in Bisley registers from 1552 onwards, there being five families of the name in Bisley parish at that time. Possibly, they sprang from the Turners numerous in Bristol and neighbourhood, especially at Mangotsfield, and if so, they were connected with the Turners of Lincolnshire. (See Madison's Lincolnshire Pedigrees, p. 1016). The same difficulty of identification arises with them as with the Smarts.

We have already had the will of William Turner, of 1552, in connection with Cliffisale. He, and Margaret, his wife (who died in 1570 and was buried 20 January), with Thomas and Henry, their sons, were tenants, of the Manor of Througham, under the Abbey of Cirencester, renting a farm of two acres and three virgates of land in Througham and Cliffisale, for a term of years, at 17s.[1]

Henry Turner, the second son of William, married Grace Mason, in 1567, and had a son, William, born November, 1568, and two daughters, Margaret, married to . . . Greene, and Joane, married to . . . Hughes. His will, dated 7 August, 1599, describes him as of Througham, husbandman, and after pious commendation of his soul to Almighty God and Jesus Christ, he bequeaths to James Greene, his black heifer of one year and the vantage. To Alice Greene, his other black heifer, etc. To Mary Greene, his daughter's child, a sheep. To his daughter, Margaret Greene, the rome of the house which she dwelleth in during the terme of his lease for it, if she so long live, and after to James, her son, or else to her other children. To each of Edward Haynes' children, a sheep. To his daughter, Joane Hughes, his reade heyfer. The rest to his son, William Turner, who is sole executor. W. John Smart, Edward Haynes, and John Turner.[2]

The next will is that of John Turner, of Througham, yeoman, dated 15 April, 1609, and then being sick of body,

---

[1] P. R. O. Aug. Office. Particulars of Glos., 1073. Hockaday
[2] Glos. P. R.

he commends his soul to Almighty God, his only creator and Saviour and to Jesus Christ, his redeemer, by Whose death and passion he trusts to be saved. To his daughter, Elizabeth, £80 at nineteen years of age. To his other daughter, Elinor, £80 at nineteen and to each of them six silver spoons. If either of them dies, then £20 to go to the other sister and £60 to his sons, John and Edward Turner. To his son, John, all his lands lying in the parish of Stroud and Pakenhyll, that was purchased of William Borne for eighty years and one, yeilding and paying to his heir 5s. on St. Michael's day. To his son, Edward, all his lands in the parish of Harsfield that was Newtons, for eighty one years, paying to his heir twelve pence a year at St. Michael's day. Also to Edward, his son, all his lands at Longney, purchased of Thomas Smart, for 101 years, paying to his heir 3s. 4d. a year at St. Michael's day. Also to his son, Edward, for his maintenance and breeding up, the house that was Borrowes, with the close adjoining and seven acres of arable in one field and six in the other, with the Sheephouse close, now in the tenure of William Maysey, for eight year, paying to his heir 15s. a year at St. Michael's day. To his godson, John Smart, £6 when out of prenticeship. To each of his sisters a sheep. To Thomas, his son, and executor, all his goods and cattels, but Alice, his wife, is to have the use of them during eight years to breed up her children, and the profit of the house and land during that time, paying yearly in consideration of Roger Turner's chamber and maintenance as appears in a pair of Indentures made by him, John Turner, of the one part and Thomas Poole and Elinor, his wife and George, their son of the other part. If his wife, Alice, happens to marry, he gives her one bed furnished. To the poor, 40s. To everyone of the poor of Througham a peck of barley, and to Edward Haynes, a bushell. Overseers, John Smart, Thomas Poole and Edward Smart (10s. each).

Memorandum. " My will is that Alice, my wife, shall have all that is above sayd for and concerning the eight year, excepting the Kinge's part which I mean in no wise to defraud touching Capit in land. Item my will is to give to John and Edward, my sons, £40 each, to be payed at twenty-one years." To Alice Buck, his sister, £6, to be paid in one year after his decease.   W. Thomas Knight, cleric, Richard Smart, William Snow, Edward Haynes.   Proved, 15 July, 1609, by Alice, his relict.[1]

It appears, from the registers, that John Turner married Alice Smart 2 October, 1592, their children being Thomas (b. 1598), Edward (b. 1605), Elizabeth and Elinor (b. 1606). The will makes it evident that interests in landed property were not confined to Througham.   Though the Smarts and Turners lived in such close proximity for two centuries or more, there are only two marriages recorded between the families, that of John Turner and Alice Smart, just mentioned, and that of John Smart with Elizabeth Turner, on 29 November, 1591.

Relations between the two families must have been considerably strained at that time, as a son had been born to this last couple out of wedlock in the preceding May, baptized the 12th of that month.

Roger Turner, mentioned in the foregoing will, was son of Thomas Turner, who was probably the brother of John Turner. Roger was born in 1576 and died in 1612.   The registers are incomplete during the disturbances of the Civil War, but we have the will of Henry Turner of Througham, husbandman, dated 20 February, 1663, and proved 29 March, of that year. He appears to have had no son, but left his daughter, Elizabeth Shewell, 10s.   To her children as follows :—To his cozen, Thomas Shewell, 40s.   To his cozen, Elizabeth Shewell, 40s. To his cozen, Jane Shewell, 40s. at eighteen years of age. All the rest to Joane, his wife, and Robert Burrow, his son-in-law, who are executors.   W. Edward Turner, Gyles Bennett, John Turner, Junior, and John Turner.[2]

John Turner, of Througham, husbandman, whose will is dated 12 August, 1681, is obviously one of the same family, but cannot be definitely placed.   He bequeathed to his well-beloved wife, the house he now dwells in, in Througham, with nine akers of yearable land, three akers thereof lying in a tineing on the East side of Througham butting upon the

1 P. C. C. 70 Dorset.
2 Glos. P. R.

orchard of Edward Turber's one aker in the Commonfield of
Througham shuting upon the Lippiat Lodge, one and a
half aker shuting upon the Church way in the same field,
and half an aker moore which heads the three half akers,
one aker shuting upon Sowmead helds, and one aker at
Lilbarn, one aker in the Lower feild. Item, he gives also. to
his wife, a house called Parkers, with four akers of yearable
land called Parkers Leaze, and to enjoy the house he now
dwells in in Througham with the nine akers of yearable land
during her widowhood, otherwise his son, John, is to have it.
To his wife, all his household goods. To his son, John, four
horses with plow, carts, sadles, etc., and ten ewes. To his
daughter, Elizabeth, £5. To his daughter, Mary, £10. His
wife to be sole executrix. W. Thomas Gegge, Robert Barrow,
Samuel Turner.

(NOTE.—Samuel Turner, son of Edward Turner, was born
in 1645. He married and had two sons, Thomas, b. 1683, and
Henry, b. 1684).

Edward, the third son of John and Alice Turner, is commemorated on a small brass tablet now in the church tower
as follows :—

" Edward Turner, of Througham, yeoman, died 24
September, 1691, aged 86." He married Elizabeth (who
died 1681), and is probably the father of Edward Turner, of
Througham, yeoman, also of William Turner and John
Turner, of Pillhouse, Painswick.

Edward Turner, by his will dated 24 February, 1726, after
pious commendation of his soul, bequeathed to his nephew,
John Turner, son of his brother, William Turner, deceased,
his two tenements in Througham, one in the occupation of
Thomas Brown, and the other of Thomas Denman, with the
gardens belonging, adjoining, also an enclosed garden below
his orchard, called the " tinning," for life. To his niece,
Elizabeth Turner, who then lives with him, £10 for mourning,
also £100. The residue to his brother, John Turner, of
Pillhouse, in the parish of Painswick, chargeable with payments aforesaid and his debts, and he to be sole executor.
W. Thomas Cook, Elizabeth Bennett, and Thomas Smart[1].

---

[1] Glos. P. R.

G

Memorandum. £5 per annum to his nephew charged on his Througham estate. Also to his niece Susannah White-head £50. Proved, 21 April, 1727.

John Turner, of Througham, was present at the Court Baron of John Stephens, 23 October, 1736, and William Turner, gentleman, was present at Bisley Court, 20 December, 1744, to be admitted tenant for land then held of Bisley manor.

One other memorial to the Turners is recorded by Bigland, as being in the Churchyard, to—

William Turner, died 7 February, 1714, aged 79.

Elizabeth, his daughter, 31 March, 1703.

Sarah, wife of William Turner, died 14 May, 1721, aged 21.

In these two modest memorials that remain of the Turner family, there is no indication of any coat-of-arms, as is the case with the Smarts and Tayloes, but if the Througham Turners were connected with those of Mangotsfield, their arms were :—Erm. on a cross quarter pierced argent four millrinds sa.[1]

SYDENHAMS

Of the lesser manors of Bisley, Sydenhams is one of the most ancient, and its manor-house, now in excellent preserva-tion, retains a single thirteenth century window and a pair of fourteenth century windows, and an entrance of the fourteenth century, besides much work of somewhat later date, showing a continuous occupation for many centuries. And yet it is the case, as with so many other lesser manors, that nothing is known of its history, there being an entire absence of any ancient deeds. Its name, spelt in varying forms as Sidenham, Syddenham, Sidnams or Sydnams, appears first in two documents, one, the charter of William de la Pere, about 1302, in which the path to Sydenham is mentioned[2] and the other in 1304, when William of Syddenham was one

---

[1] *B. G. A. S. Trans*, xxviii., 469.

[2] See Chapter III.

of the jurors at the Inquisition P. M. of Edmund Mortimer. But the origin of this name is unknown, and whether it, or Piedmont, which latter name still continues for the wood below Sydenhams, should be the name of the manor, is uncertain. Piedmont is found spelt "Pidemount" in a late eighteenth century paper amongst the Lypiatt deeds.

If, however, the name originated with the Sydenham family, that family was, in Queen Elizabeth's reign, renewing its connection with Bisley, when John Sydenham, Esq., who married Mary, the widow of Francis Codrington, (who was a descendant of John Clifford of Daneway, and, as such, held land in Bismore for which she rendered service before 1592), is mentioned in a note to the Bisley Court rolls of that year.

In 1620, James Burrowe or Burrows, who had been living at Sydenhams, made his will,[1] leaving his house at Sidnams, to his wife, for life, and the remainder of the term of years for which he held it, to his sons, Roger, James and Thomas, successively. James Burrow's brother, Robert, was son-in-law to Henry Turner, of Througham.[2] The Burrows seem to have left Sidnams and entered the wool trade, for in 1717, the will of John Burrows, of Bisley, clothier, records that he was of kin to William and Richard Tayloe, of the eminent clothier family.[3]

Their successors, at Sydenhams, were the Sevills, or Savills, who lived there for over a century. They appear to have come to Bisley from Stroud, their first connection being in 1545, when the Royal Licence was granted to John Pope to alienate to Richard Fowler a moiety of his manor of Nether Lypiat, and also to alienate to William Savell, clothier, of Strode, the other moiety of the said manor and messuage in tenure of Thomas Sewell, John Shereman, John Bulkeley, and Thomas Freme.

The name of Sevill is found in the will of William Fream, of the parish of Bisley, dyer, of 15 August, 1651, wherein it appears that his daughter, Sarah, had married a Sevill, and

---

[1] Glos. P. R.
[2] Will of Henry Turner, Glos. P. R.
[3] Glos. P. R.

to her he left his mead, called by the name of Ayshmeade, after his wife's decease, and his two houses in Framton parish. After the decease of his said daughter, his " two housen which be in the parish of Minchinhampton " to William Sevill, his daughter's son. Also, he gave to Sarah Sevill, his daughter's child, his meadow ground called Ashmeds, lying in the parish of Bisley. His wife, Susan, was to have the rent of the " two housen " in Minchinhampton for life. To William Sevill, £5, at 21. To Sarah, Mary, and Mathew Sevill, each, £5. Overseers and witnesses, Samuel Sevell and William Rutter. Proved, 5 June, 1654.[1]

William Sevill, the elder, of Sidnams, presumably the son of Samuel Sevill and Sarah Fream, his wife, made his will 16 January, 1713, and died between January and March of that year. His wife, Hannah, and son, William, to be executors. He had another son, Samuel, and five daughters.

Samuel Sevill was present at the Court Baron of John Stephens, as tenant of Sydenhams, 23 October, 1736. He was one of the Feoffees of Bisley in the early part of the eighteenth century, and was described as yeoman and clothier, and William Sevill, clothier, was a feoffee at the same time. William Sevill, the elder, gentleman, is named in Bisley Court roll of 1770, as tenant of Sydenham ; he had married Ann, daughter of Richard Butt, of Chalford,[2] dyer, and had a son, William Sevill, the younger, and three daughters. William Sevill, senior, was still living in 1781, and owned a wood adjoining the ground called Rideings.[3] He had exchanged lands near Calfway with Robert Shewell in 1742.[4]

The pursuit of the cloth industry was probably the cause of the Sevill family leaving Sydenhams and settling in Chalford Bottom. A tablet in Bisley Church (recorded by Bigland), perpetuated the memory of Mr. William Sevill's wife, Scholastice, who died 175-, aged thirty years, and three of their sons, who died in 1752 and 1759. A coat of arms was depicted, namely—on a bend, three owls.

---

[1] P. C. C. Alchin, 82.
[2] Will of Richard Butt, Glos. P. R.
[3] Feoffees' Papers.
[4] Lypiatt MSS.

Sydenhams ultimately passed into the hands of the Driver family, and was lately owned by Lionel Clarke, Esq., who thoroughly repaired it. The house still retains its ancient stone spiral staircase, and an Elizabethan bedstead, (said to have once been occupied by Queen Elizabeth on her mythical journey to Bisley). There is a remarkable series of mediaeval gateposts, of stone, erected on the wall in front of the house. They were made for gates, which, at that period, were constructed with their bars projecting beyond the cross battens, and fitted into a recess in the stone.

Sydenhams is now the property of Captain Stokes.

Sturmye's Court

The small manor of Sturmye's Court, lying in Aveness, has been completely lost sight of in recent years, having passed into the possession of the Bisley Feoffees at some remote period. At what time it was first held by the Sturmy or Stormy family, is unknown, but John Stormy was one of the witnesses at the Inquisition P. M. of Edmund Mortimer, in 1304.[1] The family is found elsewhere in Gloucestershire, and in Wiltshire, and two coats of arms are assigned to them, viz. :—Argent, three demi-lions rampant, and couped gu. for Sturmey or Esturmye, and Sa., a lion salient ar. for Sturmye.[2]

Though the owners of Sturmye's Court either gave or sold that estate to the Feoffees, with its manorial rights, descendants of the family are found to have continued at Bisley for a long period.

In 1547, the tithing men presented that John Sturmy was a good miller. On 13 August, 1599, Henry Sturmye, the elder, of Hasill House (now known as Hazel House, near Camp), in the parish of Bisley, husbandman, made his will, and his widow, Alice, did so also in 1602, dying in February, 1603,

---

[1] P. R. O. Chancery Inq. P. M.
[2] Burke's Gen. Armoury.

and leaving three sons, Edmund, Thomas, and George. Edmund Sturmy, who married Jane Currier, 6 September, 1602, is mentioned in an Indenture of 18 March, 1620, between the Marquis of Buckingham and Thomas Ward, of Edgworth, clerk, when one close of one acre called Calves Close, one close of pasture called Blackwell grove of two acres, one close abutting upon Hieghmead of one acre, five acres of arable land in Battlescombe field lately belonging to a messuage now or late in the tenure of Edmund Sturmy, passed to Thomas Ward.[1]

This is again mentioned in similar manner as having been in the tenure of the said Edmund Sturmy, in a mortgage of 1671, between Walter Shewell and his son, Walter, and Henry Elshawe and his wife, of Minchinhampton, this land having come into the possession of Walter Shewell.

The estate of Sturmye's Court is described in Chapter VIII.

Tunley or Denway

It has been thought that in Denway and Tunley we had two separate manors, whereas they are interchangeable names for the same manor. This is made clear in the Feet of Fines of 1 James I (1603), when an agreement was made between Peter or Robert Hancox, and Edward Bromwich, gentleman, and Margaret, his wife (a descendant of the Cliffords), regarding the Manor of " Tunley alias Denway," with appurtenances and two messuages, etc., in Bisley and Tunley.

The name of Tunley (the woodland clearing, leah, marked by an enclosure)[2] appears as Tunleya, in 1220 (Fees), as Thonleya and Tonley (Pleas), in 1248, and as Tunlee, in 1287 (Pl. Cor.). William of Tonlye, was a witness of Maria de Bohun's Inspeximus, respecting Frithland or wood[3] and also at the Inquisition P. M. of Edmund Mortimer, in 1304.

1 Lypiatt Deeds.
2 F. T. S. Houghton, Esq.
3 *B. G. A. S. Trans*, li, 212.

But by 1338-9 a member of the Clifford family from Frampton-on-Severn appears as owner of property in Tunley, Denway, Over Lypiatt and Frampton.

In the Feet of Fines of 12 Edward III (1338-9), an Agreement is recorded in the Court of the King, at York, on Easter day, and afterwards confirmed there on the octave of the day of the Holy Trinity, between Henry de Clifford and Matilda, his wife, and William de Longe, chaplain, regarding three messuages of three carucates of land, ten acres of meadow, ten acres of wood and 30s. rent in Tunleye, Overlepeyate and Frompton.[1]   Henry and Matilda de Clifford had taken up their residence at Denway, for in 1339 the Bishop of Worcester granted to his beloved children, Henry de Clyfford and Matilda, his wife, the right to have an oratory in their manor of Deneweye, in the parish of Byleslegh, for celebrating, etc.[2]

This, perhaps, was granted owing to the perils of the way through the forest to the parish Church at Bisley at that time. William de Longe was probably their appointed chaplain, of whom no further mention has been found in Bisley records.

In 1347, Hugh de Biseleye quit-claimed to Henry de Clifford and his heirs, the holding and rent of 2s. and 6d. of silver, together with all services in Perelonde and Peweslonde, which he had of the gift of Walter and Richard, his brothers. This is sealed by Hugh de Biseley, at Byseleye, in the presence of Robert Cronste, Thomas Roberd, Henry de Geneworthe, Robert de Stonehenge, Thomas Mody and others, on Wednesday next after the feast of St. James, April, 1347.[3]

In 1349, Hugh de Bysleye quit-claimed to Henry de Clifford and Macilla or Matilda, his wife, and to Henry, their son, and heirs, all his rights in the half virgate[4] of land in Overlepeyat, called Stertelond (otherwise the remarkable promontory of land known as the Sterts, below Middle Lypiatt Farm), together with all rent hitherto paid. This deed was

---

[1] P. R. O. Ft. of Fines, Glouc., 159.
[2] Reg. Bp. Braunsford, Fo. 33b.
[3] Lypiatt MS. Book.
[4] A virgate varied from twelve to forty acres.

executed and sealed at Bisley on the vigil of the Annunciation of Blessed Mary, 1349, and witnessed by John de Monmouth, John atte Feld de Pagunhull, Andrew Clavyle, Robert de Eggesworth, Richard de Clyveshale, Thomas Mody, Hugh Galon, William de Wyks and others.[1]

In 1355, on 1 August, came Henry Clifford, to pay homage for Ferreys at Bisley Court, he being, probably, the son mentioned above. The transactions suggest that a marriage had taken place with the de Bisley family or the Maunsell family, or possibly with both.

This same year John de Clifford bore witness at Westminster to a charter granted by King John to John de Alspach of a quarter of the Manor of Bisley (Stokesend) then in dispute between Roger de Mortimer, Earl of March and Edmund de Alspach. Whether he was son of the elder or younger Henry de Clifford is not apparent, but he was residing at Denway, and in 1367 he, together with Thomas Mauncel of Over Lypiatt, shared the patronage of the newly built chantry chapel there, presenting Master Adam to the perpetual chantry thereof.[2] This shows that John de Clifford had had some share in the building of the Chapel and points to the closer relationship suggested.

The Lypiatt MS Book quotes from a Bundle of Eschaets of 1372-3 wherein the jury stated that John Clifford of Denneway, held one knight's fee in Lypiat worth 100s., and he appeared at Bisley Court on 13 April of that year, but he died on All Souls' day, 1397-8. His Inquisition was taken at Painswick, Nicholas Mauncell being one of the jurors. They said that John Clifford held his demesne as of fee on the day he died, from the king in chief by knight service, a messuage with £3 rents in Frampton-on-Severn, worth 14 marks clear. Long before his death he had demised those premises to Henry Champneys and Margaret, his wife (one of the daughters of the said John Clifford), to hold for 21 years from the feast of St. Aldelm, 20 Richard II, paying the first year, a red rose at Midsummer, and each year after, 14 marks.

[1] P. R. O. Coram Rege Rolls.
[2] Reg. Bp. Wittlesey fo. 27.

He held, also, a messuage and virgate of land in Lupeyate from the Duke of Hereford, by the service of 4s. yearly worth two marks clear, also a messuage and one carucate[1] of land in Dennewaye from Robert Hille by service of a $\frac{1}{2}$d. yearly, worth two marks clear ; also 15s. rent from a tenement in Coweley held of the Duke of Hereford by service of 1 lb. of cummin yearly. His daughter, Margaret Champneys, had died the previous 22 September, and his heirs were his two other daughters, Elizabeth and Alice, aged respectively, sixteen and twelve.[2] Elizabeth died s. p., and Alice, being sole heiress married, William Teste. About this time enquiry was made as to the tenure of John Clifford of Denway, whether he held it from Robert Hille, or of Hugh Bysleye, by knight service.[3]

The descent of the heirs of John de Clifford will be noted when treating of Ferris Court, but though it seems to be the case that Denway was bought by the Hancox family in 1397, yet Clifford's descendants appear to have retained an overlordship of the manor, according to a note in the Lypiatt MS Book, which, however, does not seem quite accurate as to dates. There, quoting from an extract of Lypiatt Court rolls, it is stated that Ferris Court and Denway were held by Lawrence Teste in 1447-8 and by Giles Teste in 1477-8. The Hancox family is not mentioned in the Lay subsidy rolls of Bisley of 14-15 Henry VIII, or of 3 Edward VI, or of 36 Elizabeth, but John Hancox is mentioned in those of 2 Charles II.

There is also in the Feet of Fines of 1 James I, the record of a transaction between Peter (later called Robert) Hancox and Edward Bromwich and Margaret, his wife, descendants of John Clifford, when for £80 the manor of Tunley alias Denway with appurtenances and two messuages in Bisley and Tunley, passed to the possession of Robert Hancox.[4]

---

[1] A ploughland of possibly 100 acres or less.
[2] Inq. P. M., *B. G. A. S. Trans.*, iii, 205.
[3] P. R. O. Coram Rege Roll, 560 m. 17d.
[4] *B. G. A. S. Trans.* xvii, 205.

THE HANCOX FAMILY OF DENWAY

The name of Hancox is found in various parts of Gloucester-shire and is sometimes spelt Handcocks, or Handcock. The first mention in the parish registers at Bisley is of the baptism of William, son of Robert Hancox, 31 March, 1549. A possible relation of the Denway family may have been a monk of that name at Winchcombe, otherwise John Augustine, prior, and after the Dissolution, perhaps rector of Shipton Oliffe from 1554. He was drawing his pension of £8 in 1552, and died in 1562.[1] Beyond the county, William Hancox was Mayor of Coventry in 1608, and Thomas Hancox was a bell-founder of Walsall, whose work has been traced at Stanway and Swindon, 1622-40.[2] A monumental effigy at Twynning Church, of William Hancock and two sons, of 1676, is adorned with a coat-of-arms, Gu. a dexter hand couped at wrist argent, on a chief of the second three fighting cocks of the first.[3] This coat-of-arms occurs also in three places in Tewkesbury Abbey,[4] and once at Malmesbury Abbey.[5] The Denway Hancoxes appear to have borne a chevron between three fighting cocks, and possibly this coat-of-arms was granted at the Herald's visitation of 1682-3, to which William Hancox of Denway, was summoned. The family has preserved its pedigree, but the following notes are of local interest.

The first Hancox will to be found in the Gloucester Probate Registry, is that of John Hancock, of Denway, yeoman, 27 November, 1619. He bequeathed his soul to Almighty God and his body to be buried in Bisley Church or Churchyard, and he left his lands at Litteridge, called North Ekins, to his son, Walter Hancox, after his wife's decease or widowhood. His part in Hill House, half he gives to his son, William, who is to pay to his daughter, Jane Hancock, £40, after the decease or re-marriage of his wife, when his son enters into it. To his daughter, Jane, £100. To his daughter, Anne Hancock, £60.

---

[1] *B. G. A. S. Trans.*, xlix, 86.
[2] *B. G. A. S. Trans.*, xli, 170.
[3] *B. G. A. S. Trans.*, xxvi, 168.
[4] *B. G. A. S. Trans.*, xxviii, 277.
[5] *B. G. A. S. Trans.*, xxvi, 14.

To his son, William Hancock, two oxen, two horses and certain tableboards in the hall, a press and bedstead, etc. To his son, Henry Hancock, one ox, one cow, one horse, after the decease of his wife. To his son, Walter, one bedstead, etc. To his daughter, Catherine Jeane (or Jayne) two sheep. To his daughter, Margery Bridges, two sheep. To his servant, Robert Netell, one sheep. He gives the lease of his living called Denway Farm, to his son, William Hancock, after the decease of his wife and he is to have £3 a year for his maintenance. The rest to his wife, Alice, who is sole executrix. Overseers, William Hancock and William Jeane, to whom 5s. each. W. William Martin, George Bridges. Proved, 25 March, 1620.

John Hancock had married Alice Twissell on 20 January, 1585, and their daughter, Margerie, was baptized at Bisley, 27 August, 1598. She was married to George Bridges on All Saints day, 1619.

Their daughter, Ann, or Annis, married John Magee, and her inscription, formerly in the Church, stated that she was the youngest daughter of John Hancox " of the Manor of Tunley, also Denway," and that she was born the first Friday in Lent, 1597, and died 7 April, 1649.

Alice Hancox survived her husband till 1625, making her will 11 July of that year. After bequeathing her soul to Almighty God, etc., she left to her son, Walter, six sheep, the best caldron save one, three pieces of pewter, eight bushells of barley, one black coulte and half of the best pan, the ten acres of corne of barley and oates that she rents of Mr. Freeme, he paying the rent for the land and £3 in money.

To her daughter, Margery Bridges one heifer of one year, 20s., her wedding ring and best brass pan.

To her son-in-law, George Brydges, one piece of gold of 22s. and two sheep. To her daughter, Jane, £10, three pieces of pewter, lynnen, one piece of medlye cloth and various household effects and eight sheep. To her daughter, Annis, half the lynnen and six pieces of pewter and a coffer which stood at the stayr head, etc. To her daughter, Catherine Jayne, one heifer, one pair of large hooks, one sylver piece

and one gold piece of 5s.   To her son-in-law, William Jayne,
22s. in gold and to him and his child, William Jayne, one
heifer, two sheep and to his son, Harry Jayne, two sheep
and one calf.   To her son, Harry Hancox's two children
each a heifer and two sheep, and each a silver spoon.   To
her son, William, one cubborde in the haule and half of the
best pan, the best pot and the lennye coffer and best caldron.
To her son, Henry Hancox, one cow and various household
furnishings.   To her sister, Margrett Haukins, a noble
yearely during her life towards her maintenance.   To her goddaughter, Joan Harbert, one Aperne, one earoseife and a
perleit.   Her two sons, William and Henry Hancox, to be
executors.   Overseers, her sons-in-law George Bridges and
William Jayne.   W. John Harbert, George Brydges (his
mark).   Proved, Gloucester, 16 October, 1625.[1]

John Hancox had leased Hill House, Tunley, in 1572-3,
from the Lord of Lypiatt Manor, the property then consisting
of 66 acres of arable land in two of Tunley fields, one meadow
near Denway Bridge, of one and a half acres, one meadow
called le Branches in Tunley of half-an-acre, a small close
of half-an-acre, and one close of one-and-a-half acres under
Sackritch.[2]   The Court roll of Robert Wye of 1316-7, states
that Thomas Brown then held of the Lord one third part of
a messuage called Hill House for 4s. 8d. rent and one sixth
part of a knight's fee.[2]

Concerning this same property there is an account of the
purchases of Mr. Throckmorton copied by John Stephens of
Lypiatt Manor in form of a Court of Survey.   Mr. Walter
Hancox showed a deed of 27 October, 1609, whereby John
and Julian Throckmorton sold the reversion of Hill House,
Tunley, then or late in the tenure of Walter Hancox, and
Robert and John Hancox, with Hill House Grove in the
occupation of Walter Masters, except a parcel of ground
lately enclosed within a wall called Pinbury Park.[2]

It would seem that John Hancox had procured Hill House
for the use of his relations, as Walter Hancox, probably his

[1] Glos. P. R.
[2] Lypiatt MS. Book.

brother, attended at the Court of the Hundred, 3 October, 1584, and was at the Court of John Throckmorton, Esq., and Julian, his wife, 6 November, 1589. He had married Marjorie, daughter of William Shewell, of Ferris Court, who was mentioned in her father's will of 4 January, 1583, of which Walter Hancox was an executor.

Henry Hancox, of Oakridge, yeoman, was a brother of John Hancox, his will being dated 4 April, 1625. He appears to have had two daughters, Ann and Joan, to each of whom he bequeathed £10. To his wife, Edith, his lands. His overseers where his brother, John Hancox and his wife's brother, John Munden, of Rodmarton, yeoman, both of whom witnessed his will together with another John Hancox.[1]

The registers note the death of Martha, daughter of John Hancox, of Hill House, 19 August, 1638.

Meanwhile William Hancox, son of John and Alice Hancox, was in possession of Denway. He is said to have been a Captain serving under Oliver Cromwell, and was with that traitor when he expelled the Rump Parliament in 1633. A letter from him describing this scene was in the possession of a descendant, Henry Hancox, but was unfortunately destroyed in 1874. He was also High Constable of the Hundred of Bisley. His wife, Susanna. died 16 September, 1633, and there is a brass plate to her memory in the belfry of Bisley Church, and another one to him recording his death on 27 December, 1670, and the fact of his having served under Cromwell.

The death of Walter Hancox is notified in the Bisley Court rolls of 31 March, 1681, his land called Ekins being mentioned. By his will which is dated 26 September, 1670, he left to his nephew, Thomas Jayne, of Frampton Mansell, all his farm in Bisley, called Higgins Court and Mortimers' Farm. Also Ockfolds Mead near to the same. To Walter Jayne, his lands at Avenis then in the tenure of Thomas Witts.

To William Hancox, son of Henry Hancox, his lands in the parish of Bisley purchased of John and Thomas Baldwyn.

[1] Glos. Pro. Reg.

To John Hancox, his brother, £5 per annum. To Henry Hancox, the son of Henry Hancox, his land at Litteridge.

To his brother, William Hancox, £10. To his nephew William, son of William Hancox £50. To Nathaniel Hancox, the son of Henry Hancox £20. To his sister, Jane Hancox, £200. To Ann Jayne, £100. To John Taylor, of Torlton, £300. To Ann Aveland, £20. To his cousin, Thomas Jayne, land in the parish of Miserden.

Executors, Thomas Jayne and John Taylor.

William Hancox appears to have been succeeded at Denway by his son or grandson, William Hancox, yeoman, who was summoned to the Herald's Visitation in 1682-3, and who died in November, 1707-8, having made his will in August, 1701. He bequeathed to his kinsman, Nathaniel Hancox, of the parish of Bisley, son of Nathaniel Hancox, deceased, his messuage and manor house with the buildings, barn, stables, court, garden, orchards, etc., situated in Denway and all arable lands, meadows, commons, etc., belonging to his other lands in Bisley, and pasture ground lying in the parish of Edgeworth. To Anne Trustem, daughter of Thomas Trustem, of the parish of Duntisbourne, £200. To his kins-woman, Susannah Hancox, sister of Nathaniel Hancox, £5. To his cozen, Henry Hancox, 1s., and the same to his kinsman, Walter Hancox, son of the said Henry. To his kinsman, Thomas Jayne 1s., with other small legacies. The residue to his kinsman, Nathaniel Hancox, who is sole executor. W. Henry Witts, William Hall, Thomas Trustram.[1]

Nathaniel Hancox, yeoman, succeeded his kinsman, William, at Denway, making his will there 20 January, 1728. He bequeathed to his cousin, William Hancox, son of his brother, William Hancox, the close in the parish of Bisley, which he lately bought of Charles Payton, called the rough leaze with the grove of wood belonging and £100. To his cousin, Anne Fowler, wife of John Fowler, £30. To his brother, Walter Hancox, his capital messuage wherein he then dwelt known as Denway, with the closes, groves of wood, arable lands, etc., for life, and after his decease to his

---

[1] Glos. Pro. Reg.

cousin, Thomas Hancox, son of his brother William Hancox, and his heirs. To his said brother, Walter Hancox, all his estate at or near Tunley, called King's estate, with all closes, tenements, etc., and a grove of wood called Countermead Grove, and after his decease to his cousin, Thomas Hancox. To his brother, Walter, his two closes of pasture ground in the parish of Duntisbourne Abbotts and a close in the parish of Edgeworth called Newman's close, and after his decease to Thomas Hancox. The residue of his goods, to his brother, Walter Hancox, who is sole executor. W. Richard Mason, Robert Boulton, John Panting. Proved, 9 April, 1729.[1]

There is a brass to the memory of Nathaniel Hancox, now in the belfry of Bisley Church, stating that he was born 14 January, 1670, and died 24 January, 1729, aged 59.

Walter Hancox enjoyed his brother's estate till his death in 1743. By his will, dated 21 March, 1742, he bequeathed to his nephew, Thomas Hancox, the estate known as Tunley Farm as well as all other of his freehold lands. To his brother, William Hancox an annuity of £5. To his nephew, William, an annuity of £4, which sums his nephew, Thomas, was to pay half yearly as a charge on lands bequeathed to him. To Mary and Ann, the daughters of his nephew, William, £10 each at 21. To Ann, daughter of John Fowler, £5 at 21. All his goods and chattels and leasehold lands and personal estate to his nephew, Thomas Hancox, who is sole executor. W. John Fowler, Robert Boulton, John Clappen, E. Aldridge. Proved, 8 June, 1743.[1]

The brass to his memory in the belfry of Bisley Church records that Walter Hancox, of Denway, died 22 March, 1742-3, aged 64.

Thomas Hancox, who inherited the estates mentioned in the fore-going wills, died in 1792, aged 82. He was present at the opening of the Thames and Severn Canal by King George III and Queen Charlotte, in 1788, part of this famous construction running through his lands.

Thomas Hancox was a big and powerful man, weighing twenty stone, and it was with ease that on one occasion he

[1] Glos. Pro. Reg.

picked up an offensive individual and dropped him over Denway Bridge into the lock.   He had no son, so his only daughter, who married Mr. Bidmead, of Beacon Tump Farm, Sapperton, inherited the Denway estate.   After her death it was sold to Mr. Dangerfield, who cut down the timber and then sold the estate to Mr. Chapman, a silk merchant of Chalford.   He re-sold it to Mr. Smith, builder and timber merchant of Chalford, who again sold it to Earl Bathurst, in whose possession it remains.

One member of the family, Henry William Hancox, son of John Hancox, was a sufferer in a tragedy of 1832, when he was living in the farmhouse at Tunley.   In those days, before the enclosure of the Common, violence was rife, and one night, hearing two men approach and guessing they had come to rob him of the proceeds of a sale of a bull, which he had that day made, he armed himself with a gun, but before he could recover from a fall as he climbed a fence, one of the men discharged a pistol in his face, which destroyed the sight of both eyes and inflicted other injuries, he being then 23 years of age, and suffering till his death at 67.   Both the men were apprehended and tried, one named Hunt, who had been employed on the farm, being sentenced to penal servitude for life, and the other, named Berryman, was hung at Gloucester.   So barbarous was village society at that time, that the wife of the latter, then living at Brownshill, is said to have allowed visitors to view the corpse of her husband at 1s. a head.

DENWAY HOUSE

Denway House is a delightful example of one of the lesser manor houses, lying in a remote and beautiful vale at the head of the Stroud Valley, and adjoining the parish of Sapperton.   The oldest portion of the house, that on the north side, is of the fourteenth century, and may rightly be regarded as the building of John de Clifford.   The south front or wing, and the tower-like block at the east, date from Queen Elizabeth's reign.   These two portions are separated by a small court, which has a screening wall on the south, entered by a round-headed doorway, with rusticated arch-stones, of Jacobean date.

On entering through the south main doorway which is sheltered by a square dripstone, a pointed fourteenth century arch faces one, leading to the more recent additions, where a Tudor doorway is seen. To the left of " the Entry " is a fourteenth century foliated and shouldered doorway, leading to an older part of the house, now the kitchen. A fine gothic wooden ceiling covers the living room on the right, from whence stairs ascend to a room on the first floor of the adjoining south block, the entrance being covered by an interior wooden porch of Jacobean date.

The plaster ceiling of this room is of Elizabethan date, and may be attributed to John Hancox. It is adorned with ribbing and panels containing bold but rather coarsely worked wreaths and rosettes. Quadrants of sprigs in the smaller panels, and single sprigs or fleur de lys in the corners of the panels, with a running vine pattern for cornice, or honeysuckle, form the scheme of decoration. Above one door the cornice device is broken by the figures of five horses. The mantel-piece has a large trout in the centre with fleur de lys on each side. Two little figures between the fireplace and the door, may represent Adam and Eve, with the Tree of Knowledge.[1]

When Denway became the property of Lord Bathurst, about 1899, the building was carefully repaired, but happily retains its air of antiquity.

HILL HOUSE

Mention has already been made of Hill House as having been owned by the Hancox family from 1572 onwards, but there is evidence of a greater antiquity of this estate, which when John Clifford died in 1397-8, appears to have been the residence of Robert Hille, who claimed an over-lordship

---

[1] See the well-illustrated article in " *Country Life*," for 6 March, 1909.

H

of Denway, or of part of it, for which 1s. 2d. a year was paid by John Clifford, (as described in his I. P. M.) It seems as if Hill House estate, which probably received its name from the Hill family, was of greater antiquity then the Denway estate, and it is now impossible to state how this claim to a certain over-lordship of Denway arose, seeing that Hill House was subject to Over Lypiatt and the Duke of Hereford, and Denway to the Lord of Bisley manor.

The present house, the back part of which appears to be early seventeenth century, must have been built, together with the very fine farm buildings, by one of the Hancoxes, in whose family it remained for many years. It is now the property of Miss Bruce.

Other land in Tunley, not identified, was purchased by Sir William Nottingham from Robert de Cotes in 1466.[1] At his Inquisition P. M. it was stated that he possessed 7s. rent of assize from one messuage and one virgate of land in Tunley, held of the service of Cecily Duchess of York, as of her manor of Bisley.[2] His name is still attached to certain other lands he held in Bisley namely, Nottingham Scrubbs.

Sir Henry Poole bought from George Raleigh, unnamed messuages and rents in Bisley and Tunley in 1601.[3] His son, Sir William Raleigh, having been a Royalist, was mulcted as a delinquent and mortgaged his manor and lands, including those at Tunley, and the Hundred of Bisley, to Becke and Walker.

These lands were bought by Sir Robert Atkyns in 1676-7.[4]

---

[1] B. G. A. S. Trans., 1, 190.

[2] B. G. A. S. Trans., 192.

[3] B. G. A. S. Trans., 220.

[4] The Raleigh family, whose name appears in Bisley Court rolls, owned land in Edgeworth which they inherited from the Helyoms, who were heirs of Thomas and Geoffry de Eggeworth, temp. Ed. III. (See Fosbrooke's Hist. of Glos, I, 359).

FERRIS COURT.

It has been mentioned that the Cliffords, about the time of appearing at Denway, also owned Ferris Court, which was a lesser manor, held under homage to the Lord of Lypiatt. Henry de Clifford paid homage for Ferreys Court in 1355. John de Clifford holding it up to the date of his death in 1397-8, Alice, his ultimately sole surviving heiress, carried it to the Teste family, she having married William Teste. Laurence Teste, their son, citizen and clothier, of London, married Joan . . . and died in 1507-8, having two sons, John, d. s. p., 1507-8, and Giles Teste, clerk, also d. s. p., in 1542-3. There were three daughters, of whom Mary, the eldest married William Codrington of Frampton, and carried to him all the Clifford property which she inherited. Their son, Francis Codrington, married Margaret, daughter and heiress of William Shefin, of Bristol. Their son, Giles Codrington of Frampton and Pucklechurch married Isabel, daughter of Arthur Porter, and attended Bisley Hundred Court in 1584. Of their two sons, Richard Codrington held Bismore in 1598, according to the Bisley Court rolls of that year, but ignored the service and alienated the same to Nicholas Throgmorton, Esq., and Francis Codrington married Mary, daughter of Sir Nicholas Poyntz, of Iron Acton. She married, secondly, John Sydenham, of Nymphsfield (his will being dated 4 February, 1590). Their daughter, Margaret (or Mary in the Court rolls of 1592), married first, Edward Bromwich, and secondly John Sydenham.[1] From that time the connection with the Clifford family ceases to be represented.

Giles Codrington was at the Court of Thomas Wye, Esq., 16 March, 1558, as " free tenant for his manor called Ferres Court and Denway." The Jurors presented that Francis Codrington, his father, who held the manor of Ferres Court and one virgate of land from the Lord by military service and four pence per annum, had died since last Court, and that Giles was his son and heir and nineteen years of age. They

[1] Fosbrooke's History of Gloucestershire. It has been necessary to trace this descent at some length, as the above names appear frequently in ancient Bisley deeds.

also said that a certain spring lying between land called Little Ferres and Ferris Court, was the common spring for all the tenants within the manor, but it was stopped and in defect of the tenant, John Arundell, who was ordered to amend it.

Ferris Court, occupied as it was by John Shewell (who died in 1515) and his family, early in the sixteenth century, continued to be owned by the Codringtons, who appear at the Courts of the Lords of Lypiatt up to 1581, at which date John Shewell paid homage for it. Apparently, after the death of John Shewell, of Ferris Court, the property was broken up into three parts, 20 July, 1647, and sold to John and William Nash.

John Nash reserved to himself a house on the third part of Ferris Court which comprised the lower part of the barton and lower barn, half the dovecot, one orchard and garden lying within the said messuage and five closes of pasture, then in the parish of Bisley, but later in that of Stroud. As described in the Lypiatt MS. Book, there were the following lands. :—

" A close of pasture or arable, three acres, having Ferris Court Lane on the south and the ground late of John Nash, but now of John Stephens on the north, and shooteth down upon the wood of the said John Stephens and is called the Wood leaze.

A close of arable called the upper Cow Leaze, four acres.

A meadow called Lower Cow Leaze, four acres.

A meadow called Cowleaze Patch, two acres.

These lands extend from the Barnfield down to the wood of John Stephens, being bounded by Ferris Court Lane on the south and Honyhills on the north."

Looking at the meagre remnant of the former Ferris Court, which now stands on the site, it is difficult to picture the manor house as it was originally, but after study of the Court rolls the conclusion may be reached that the old house was built on both sides of the lane, and perhaps was joined by a gateway across it. The lane itself, below Ferris Court, was held (in the Court of Robert Wye, Esq., 24 April, 1516), to belong solely to the Lord of the Manor of Lypiatt, and it was only by his licence that the tenants could use it.

The house continued to be occupied by three families for many years. At the Court Baron of Mrs. Anne Stephens, 13 October, 1724, the death of Thomas Pettit, who held part of Ferris Court, was announced, the messuage descending to his three sisters ; also it was stated that James Brown held part in right of his wife, and the third part was held by the Lady of the Manor.

John Nash had sold his land at Ferris Court to John Stephens, Esq., reserving only his house, etc., and paying 6d. for it a year. After John Nash's death in 1737, his nephew, Nathaniel Nash, of Bristol, to whom the house at Ferris Court was devised, sold it to Mr. Stephens, of the Inner Temple, London, Peter Leversage acting as his attorney to deliver it to Mr. Stephens. The house was probably reduced to its present condition about that time.

The Nash family appear in Ministers' Accounts of 1452-3, as paying rent for a cottage called Stonyend in the manor of Bisley. From this same family probably descended John Nash, of Brownshill, parish of Bisley, clothier, who died 30 November, 1716. (*See* Chapter X, Part 4.)

The Pettet family lived in the manor of Lypiatt for several generations. The will of Richard Pettet, son of John Pettet, husbandman, of Over Lypiatt, 1574, is extant (Glos. P. R.) as well as that of Mary Pettet, 1701, but they belonged to Stroud parish.

Ferris Court passed into the possession of the Leversage family, from whom it was bought by Sir John Dorington.

THE SEWELL FAMILY.

The Sewell or Shewell family are the best known of the residents at Ferris Court. The oldest brass in Bisley Church which commemorates Katherine, wife of Thomas Sewell, who died in 1515, records the fact that they had seven sons

and five daughters,   (see plate 22)   so it is not surprising to find that there are many confusing registers of
their descendants, some of whom drifted to Bisley, Nether
Lypiatt and Stroud.   Indeed, Thomas Sewell himself, after
his second marriage, moved to Stroud, and was engaged in
the cloth trade.   The following is an abstract of his will,
dated 1 October, 1540, in which he is described as of the
Lymitacion of Stroud.   He desired to be buried at Bisley,
by Kateryn, his wife.   He bequeathed to Alice, his wife,
£100, 200 sheep and £12 in plate.   Also a medowe grounde
called Muggemore, in Mynchen Hampton, to remain to his
sonne, Thomas, during the date of the indenture, which he
held on one, William Chamber, late heire of the said meadowe.
To the said Thomas, £100, and the remnant of his shepe
reserving oon to everyone of his godchildre, and halfe his
grayne growing in the parishes of Mynchen Hampton.   To
Richard Sewell his part of the parsonage of Byssley, which he
held of the College of Stoke Clare.   To his son John, £10.
To his sonne Thomas, his dwelling-house, fullyng mylles,
and Dyenge house which he held of John Whittington of
Pauntley, esquire, with all the Burne landes that he held
of William Freme, gentleman, by indenture, also all his vattes
and furneys, with sheares and other shoppe stuffe, at the age
of twenty one.   His household goods to be divided among
his wife and sons, William and Thomas.   He makes his wife
and son, Thomas, his executors.[9]

W. Thomas Powell, clerk, parson of Mynchen Hampton, Sir
Richard Gravener, chauntry priest there, William Martyn,
Thomas Cooke.   Proved 14 July, 1543.

Possibly the son of Thomas Sewell is to be identified with
that Thomas Sewell, who with John Shereman, John Bulkeley,
and Thomas Freame, was tenant in 1545 of a moiety of the
manor of Nether Lypiatt, purchased that year by Thomas
Pope after the suppression of the Knights Hospitallers, its
former owners.   Licence was obtained to alienate this
property to William Savell, of Stroud, clothier.[1]   At the
Bisley Court of 8 October, 1547, the Lower Lypiatt tithing
presents that Thomas and Richard Sewell are good millers.

---

[1] Hockaday.

Richard and William Shewell were at the Court of the Hundred, 3 October, 1584 ; and at the View of Frankpledge, 13 May, 1586, Thomas Sewell and Richard Tocwell were common millers at Lower Lypiatt. Thomas Sewell is mentioned in Bisley Court rolls of 1598, as surrendering one cottage called Wyesland in Byssridge (Bussage) in his own tenure. This was taken by John Dyer for lives of himself and William Shewell, son of Thomas and Elizabeth Sewell.[1] The will of William Shewell, of Ferris Court, yeoman, 4 January, 1583, is, to be buried in Bisley Church, bequeathing all his goods in Herefordshire to Jone Shewell, his wife. To his son, Richard, a mare and all his wearing apparel and two sheep. To each of his daughters, Marjorie Hancox, Kathrin Bradly, Mary Winchcombe,[2] and Elizabeth Whitt, a cow. Walter Hancox, to be executor. Overseers, Thomas Kynge, William Griffin, 6s. 8d. each. W. John Lightfoot, Vicar, Thomas Phillip, Robert Brad, Thomas Wylle, and William Verrender. The " Fuerin mead " is mentioned as let on lease.

William Sewell, had, for some years, been a " farmer " of the rectory of Bisley with Henry Compton, Esq., Both of these lay rectors were censured in the Gloucester Consistory Court of 1569 for allowing the chancel of the Church to become ruinous. Henry Compton, Esq., of Bisley, in his will of 1593, refers to William Sewell's (" gentleman ") share in the rectory.

[1] P. R. O. Port., 175.

[2] Mary Winchcombe's will is dated 30 March, 1587. (Glos. P. R.) She left two sons, Henry and William, and a daughter, Alice. The will of Alice Winchcombe alias Whiting, dated 6 April, 1591, is, perhaps to be identified with this Alice Winchcombe ; it contains an interesting list of household furnishings. To John Winchcombe, one fetherbed and flock bed, two pair of blanketts, ten tablecloths, four coverletts, two of the best and two other, three pair of sheets, the second brass pot, the tallowe cawthren, the scalding cawthren, the formes, five platters, one pottinger, five sawcers, two candlestickes, two salt-selleres and two brass pans, the grater and the least. To John Cooke, three charakers, a tablecloth, a pair of sheets, four pewter disches, the fourth brasspan, her best frocke and petticote. To Anne Wimbery, the brass pan, which is peart and two white towels. To Margaret Gotheridge one towell with blewe wurke, one fine sheet, two pair of pillow bears, the middle brandierne, one cawtherne, one bed and coverled. To William Winchcombe a Calfe, candlestick and salt-seller. . . . The rest to Walter and Henry Winchcombe, her sons. W. Richard Mason and William Snowe, " whritor."

Walter Sewell, who made his will 14 May, 1593 and was, the 31st of that month, of the parish of Bisley, commits his soul to the hands of Almighty God, our gracious hevenly father and of Jesus Christ our only Redeemer by whose mercie only he has trust that he shall be saved, his body to be buried in Bisley Church amongst his ancestors. To his daughter, Elizabeth, £13 6s. 8d., unless she wilfully marry against his wife's agreement, in which case half that sum. To his son, Walter, £6 13s. 0d. To his son, John, one sheep. To his son, William, a quarter of barley. To his daughter, Annes, landes of the fee so many as shall make the debt of £5 which he owes. To his son-in-law, William Birt, £3 6s. 8d. that is behind of the marriage portion of his wife, and twelve bushells of barley due. The residue to his wife, Agnes, who is executrix, including the rent of the house that Thomas Web, of the parish of Miserden, brodeweaver, dwells in, 39s. per annum. She to have the house and ground for life where his son, John, now dwells, so much as was at any time his, whensoever she shall come to dwell in the house which he do now possess and inhabit, as agreed. W. Christopher Windle (vicar) and William Broughton.[1]

Richard Sewell appears to have succeeded his father at Ferris Court and to have died in 1607. Of him nothing is known, but his son, Richard, is entered in the registers as " gentleman " and his Inquisition P. M. of 24 July, 1683, taken at Painswick, reveals him as possessed of a messuage, two fulling mills, one gigg mill and one water grain mill called Huckwills Cort. He died at Nether Lypiatt, 30 December, 1635. Besides the mills mentioned, Richard Shewell possessed two orchards and one close of meadow called Flagghey meadow lying in Nether Lypiatte ; one way which leads to the Borne ; all that meadow called Foxhall meade : one meadow of two acres, late parcel of the lands of Henry Sherman called Sadwells ; one parcel of pasture called the Hale, containing one acre of land ; four acres of meadow called Stubby Close ; and two acres of pasture in Nether Lypiatt in the parish of Bisley, which said premises are held of Thomas Freame, Esq., as of his manor of Lippeate in

1 Glos. P. R.

free and common soccage, by fealty, suit at court and yearly
rent of 4d. and are worth per annum a clear 10s. His son,
Giles Shewell, was his next heir, aged 21 years and more.[1]

Whilst Huckwills Cort may have been identical with
Huckvale Place, which formerly was the centre of an estate
running from Nelson Street, Stroud, down to the River
Froom in the valley, part of which estate is now called " the
Field," the mill of the same name would have been situated on
the river. Richard Sewell died at Nether Lypiatt, the manor
house of which was then occupied by the Freames, and the
description of the land at Nether Lypiatt suggests the
probability that Flagghey meadow may have been the
meadow still full of flags in the spring which lies just above
Todsmore Mill, and in which traces of a more recent grist
mill may be seen.

The will of John Sewell, yeoman, of Over Lypiatt, dated
8 June, 1624, may have been connected with Ferris Court.
As it gives a picture of the simplicity of the yeoman's life
at that period, it is here given in detail. After a pious preamble, he bequeaths his body to the parish Church of Bisley,
and to the poor there 30s., to those of Stroud 10s. To his
son Richard Sewell, all his wearing apparel, save his best
cloak, which is for Walter, his son. To his son William
Sewell, 40s., on condition that he does not at any time trouble
his brother Thomas, with any suit at law for the house wherein
the said Thomas dwells, otherwise he is to lose the 40s. To
his son Thomas, £5. To his daughter Jane, one sheep.
To his daughter Margery, one cowe, two heifers, one yalow,
one red, and four sheep, and her mother's cheste. To her
three children each a sheep. To his daughter Anne, five
sheep. To his godsone John Heaven, one sheep. To his
son Walter, senior, his redd marre and a bed with its
appurtenances and one best candlesticks, two platters and
two potengers. To his godson John Sewell, one sheep.
To his son John Sewell, the residue, and he to be executor.
Overseers. Thomas Clissold of Over Lypiat in the parish of
Bisley, yeoman, and kinsman, and Walter Sewell, of Bisley.

---

[1] Glos. Inq. P. M. *B. G. A. S. Trans.*, 1625-42, p. 5.

W. Robert King, Thomas King, John Davis, William
Stephens.   Proved, 19 November, 1625.[1]

John Sewell had married Anne Pearce, 10 April, 1600.
She pre-deceased him, being buried at Bisley, 27 December,
1619.

Amongst the five sons and three daughters of John Sewell,
it is impossible to identify the descent of the family from the
registers, but the burial of John Sewell of " Pherris Court "
is recorded on 14 July, 1646.   He may be the son of the
preceding John Sewell.   The Sewells were drifting to Stroud
and the district, being drawn away from agricultural pursuits
to the clothing industry, as we find in so many of the old
Bisley families.   There is a will of Walter Sewell of Over
Lypiatt, yeoman, 16 October, 1635, who leaves a wife, Anne,
probably a Webb, as he speaks of his brothers, Richard
Webb and William Kynne, and there were three sons, Walter,
John and William, and four daughters.   There is no indication
as to Ferris Court in this will.

Amongst the deeds preserved at Lypiatt Park there are
many concerning the exchange or acquisition of land, mostly
in the common fields, by the Sewells.   For instance, in 1647,
Walter Sewell of Stroud, dyer, buys a messuage and lands in
Bisley, called Redes (late the residence of Thomas Hunt)
from Samuel Allen, of Daventry, Northants.   In 1656,
Richard Pope of Bisley, clothier and Walter Sewell, of the
parish of Stroud, yeoman, exchange lands in Battlescombe
fields.   In 1657, Walter Sewell of the Bourne, perhaps the
same as the foregoing, disposes of his meadow in Bisley,
called Hardings, to George Smart.   It has the lands of
Walter Hancox, called Ekins, on the West, and a ground in
the parish of Edgeworth called Ohell, on the East, and a
ground belonging to the rectory or parsonage of Bisley,
called Parsons Meade, on the south, and the land of Richard
Taylor, on the north, of one acre pertaining to the tenement
of Walter Sewells lying near a wood called Calfway Wood,
heretofore the land of Thomas Ward, clerk.

[1] Glos. P. R. Original.

Thomas Ward, clerk, of Edgeworth, had acquired a messuage and lands in Bisley in 1620, from the Marquis of Buckingham, who at that time had received them by grant from James I, together with part of the Manor of Bisley. The lands consisted of one messuage and one yardland called Redes, of 61 acres, a close of one acre called Hardinges, 15 acres in Stancombe field and 15 in Battlescombe field, one acre called Calves Close, a close of two acres called Blackwell Grove, and one close of ten acres abutting upon Hieghmead. These lands were all bestowed by the Rev. Thomas Ward upon his nephew, Francis Raleigh, then of Bycester, Oxon, by deed of 1632, to take effect after the death of Thomas Ward and Ann, his wife. By June, 1639, Francis Raleigh, then of Cullworth, Northants, being in debt to Samuel Allen, of Daventry, Northants, maltster, conveyed all these lands to him.

In 1658, John Sewell, of Stroud, tailor, son of Walter Sewell, released his rights in a messuage and lands in Bisley, which his father had conferred on him in view of a marriage between John Sewell and Mary Millard. The next year, Walter Sewell having acquired most of the lands of the Rev. Thomas Ward above mentioned, placed them in trust with William Gryme and Charles Wood for the use of himself, his wife Elizabeth, and his younger sons, Robert and Henry Sewell.

The will of Walter Sewell, senior, of the parish of Bisley, yeoman, dated 16 May, 1653, gives to his wife Alice, all the " monney " he has in the parish of Bisley (excepting one cottage with two orchards adjoining it), no wood to be felled except what is used on the premises. To his son Walter, £5. To his son John, £5, and to his son Thomas, £5. To his daughter Anne, £15. To his son Edward, the cottage and two orchards aforesaid for 14 years after the expiration of a lease granted to William Bradley, paying 12s. a year rent. If he minds to sell the said cottages, his brother William is to have the first refusal. To his grandchild William Sewell, the dovecote, garden and backside, which Thomas Pinchin, Henry Pinchin, and Joan Greer do hold for the term of their lives, for eighty years, paying 5s. 6d., after their decease.

To his daughter Burdocke, 5s., and her daughter Alice, 5s.
To his son William, the table boards, round bord, formes,
benches, joyne stools, chairs, cubbard, and presse in the
parlour, the tableboard in the hall, the form and benches and
the best pot and biggest kettle, but his wife is to have the
use of his goods for life. . . . Bedding also and the great
chest in the Chamber. To his son William, all his land
lying in Miserden parish (except the lease before excepted).
To his son Walter, his great Bible. The residue to Alice his
wife, who is sole executrix. Overseers, his well-beloved
friend, Samuel Sevill, and his son-in-law, Richard Denton,
2s. 6d. each. W. Richard Denton, Richard Blade, and
William Sevill. Proved, 6 April, 1665.[1]

In the will of Henry Turner of Througham, husbandman,
of 1663, his daughter Elizabeth Sewell, is mentioned and his
cozens, Thomas, Elizabeth and Jane Sewell. The marriage
of Elizabeth Turner and Thomas Sewell is entered in the
Painswick register on 19 February, 1655, for during the
Commonwealth period many of the marriages were registered
there by the civil magistrates.

Robert Shewell sold Holbrooke to Edward Turner, in 1684,
and his death was presented at the Court of 25 March, 1686.[2]

There was a settlement of land between Robert Shewell of
Bisley, baker, and Elizabeth, his mother, and William Ridler,
of Kimsfield, yeoman, on occasion of the marriage between
Robert Shewell and Francis Ridler, in 1698. This land had
been in the tenure of Richard Denton, son-in-law of Walter
Sewell, who died in 1665. Throughout the eighteenth century
there was constant exchange of lands in the common fields
by the Sewell family. Robert Sewell was still at Redes or
Calfway Farm, for which he is acknowledged as free tenant,
at the Court Baron of John Stephens, 23 October, 1736, but
some of the Sewells were living at Timbercombe, a remote
combe lying below Nottingham Scrubs.

There is the will of William Sewell, of Timbercombe,
yeoman, dated 25 March, 1708, by which he left to his son

---

[1] Glos. P. R. Original.
[2] Bisley Court rolls at Lypiatt.

William Sewell, his two pieces of arable and pasture ground, called the two Gratton Grounds, lying below the house called Stonedge House, in the parish of Bisley, for the term of his natural life only (he being provided for by a former settlement made upon marriage with his mother). After his decease, the said grounds to go to the first son of the said William, lawfully begotten, whom failing, to his second son, etc. Failing such issue, to testator's second son, Walter. The said grounds are mortgaged for £40, which must be paid off by the devisee. To his son William, 10s. in lieu of a chest, formerly intended for him, and a further 2s. 6d. To his son Edward Sewell, all the dwelling house, garden and orchard, in the parish of Bisley, where his brother Edward, now dwells, and has an estate for life. Sundry household bequests including the tableboard that stood in the Hall, and one pair of fire-dogs, follow. To his daughter Judith Trapp, 2s. 6d., as a taken of his love, and to her four children, 10s. equally divided. To his daughter Alice Sewell, two pewter dishes and one bed. And whereas he had £15 given to his said daughter by her Grandmother Hall, and as she is at present unable to provide for herself, she is to have maintenance out of his personal estate. His son Walter, to be sole executor. W. William Keene, Edward Pleydell, junr., John Drinkwater. Proved, 25 March, 1708.[1]

Amongst the deeds at Lypiatt Park there is a Terrier of "Mr. Shewell's land in Bisley," which, though not dated, appears to have been of about the end of the seventeenth century. It shows forth the highly inconvenient method of cultivation of land in separate acres in the Common fields, and though too long to give here in full, there are several interesting allusions of value in historical research, such as—

One acre shooting over Sidnams Way leading to Bisley.

Two acres lying between Calfway Wood and the Whitten Tree adjoyninge to land of Mr. Shepperd's.

Three acres lying in Stancombe threate.

One acre lying at Sterwell in the threate.

[1] Glos. P. R.

One acre lying at the upper end shooteing upon Sterwell well.[1]

One acre adjoyning to the highway that leads from the Butts to the end of the hay hedge.[2]

One acre shooting from the butts by the way that leads from Etheridge Wood.

One acre called a Legg acre shooting over Litteridge Way.

Three acres in a peete in the same furlong.

One meadow plot (in Battlescombe) the brooke running through it.

One half acre lying in Herringale.

John Shewell, of Bisley, cloth-worker, who died in 1684, left a will in which he bequeathed to his sons, Walter, John, and Henry, and his six daughters, the furnishings of his house, which are enumerated in detail.

The family at Ferris Court left only one other memorial of itself beside that of the brass of 1515 in the Church, in the Churchyard, opposite the south porch, where the following inscription is to be seen :—

" John Sewell, of Ferris Court, in the Parish of Stroud, yeoman, who departed this life, January 5, 1780, aged 45 years.

John, the son of John Sewell, departed this life, 105 December, 1781, aged 23 years.

Mary, the wife of John Sewell, senr., departed this life December, 1785, aged 57 years.

Keep death and judgment in your Eye,
Nones fit to live that is not fit to dye,
Tis Dreadful to behold the setting sun,
And Night's approach before our work is done."

[1] This well is marked Starveall Well on the Ordnance Survey Map, to the south of Limekiln Lane, and in direct line south of the copse on the east side of which was the so-called Roman well, or dip-well, which was obliterated in the last century. (No. 916 on Tithe map, and Starwell no. 911).

[2] The road from Bisley to Battlescombe is called Hayhedge Lane.

This would seem to be the last of the Sewells, of Ferris Court, but it does not appear how it came about that, in spite of the recorded sale of the estate and its division into three parts, as we have seen, there were Sewells living there so long after this arrangement. Possibly they returned to the old home after having left it many years before.

CHAPTER VI

PART 1

ECCLESIASTICAL HISTORY

RECTORS, RECTORIAL TITHE AND RECTORY HOUSE.

The Ecclesiastical History of Bisley begins with the
statement in Domesday Book that there were two priests in
the manor of Bisley, a circumstance which is unique in the
annals of the county. That there had been a church here in
Saxon times is evidenced by a few scanty remains of that
period which have been found. For instance, two roof ridge
tiles[1] were dug up in that part of the Churchyard known as
the ' New Ground ' near which it is thought the Saxon Church
stood. They are marked with finger and thumb indentations.
A pair of small Saxon windows cut out in one stone is now
fixed in the wall of a garden which lies opposite the vicarage
garden, whilst a precious portion of the Saxon font is preserved
in the south porch of the Church. The latter exhibits a
very usual form of Saxon ornamentation, bearing figures of
saints under round arcading, and this relic had been, as
already stated, built into the wall of the malthouse at Overcourt, removed thence by Sir John Dorington with the other
stones, to Eastcombe Manor Farm, recognized there as Saxon
by the late Mr. W. F. Randall and restored to the Church.
There are also the remains of a Saxon Cross shaft in the south
porch. (see plate 4)

Further spiritual provision for this large parish in Saxon
times appears to be indicated by the remains of a chapel
at Brownshill, an account of which is to be found in
Transactions, B. G. A. S., xlvii, 259.

[1] Now at the Vicarage.

The existence of two priests in Bisley parish indicates the origin of the two rectors who continued to hold the title down to the Reformation. The destruction of all early records[1] of the diocese of Worcester, in which Bisley lay, leaves us with no Episcopal Registers earlier than that of Bishop Giffard, 1268-1302. There is nothing to show that any regional jurisdiction was assigned to the two rectors, and they were probably both resident during the early years after the conquest, and even after non-residence became the rule, their stalls would be kept for them at the North and South of the entrance to the chancel. The Christian name of one rector of the time of King John survives in the charter of Roger Mortimer to Cecily of Rodborough, to which Master William ' persona de Biselee ' is a witness. We must then place him as the earliest rector known to us, the next name, that of Osbert, before 1274, being that of the first vicar, reputed to have founded Our Lady's Chantry. Meanwhile, a Norman Church had been erected on the site of the present building, and of this there are a few remains,—a Romanesque capital which was sent up to the British Museum, with the two Roman altars, found built into the wall near the tower, (see Plate 1, fig. 2), another capital with some fragments of carved work now in the South porch, but above all the font bowl of late Norman work, which will be described later on. Some stones in the South aisle are said to be Norman and to bear the marks of fire.

The Church has always been known as that of ALL SAINTS.

The patronage of the benefices of Bisley parish will be noted with each presentation, the variations arising from the change of ownership of that part of the manor to which the patronage was attached, or as it would appear, from certain portions of the manor having alternate rights to the advowson.

The right of presentation to the vicarage and to the Chantry benefices normally belonged to the First Portioner, or Rector.

---

[1] The registers of Bishops Giffard, Gainsborough, Reynolds and Sede Vacante are now in print.

I

RECTORS OF THE FIRST PORTION OR PREBEND.

WILLIAM, temp. King John.

Before 1257. HUGH MORTIMER. On 2 September, 1257, Pope Alexander IV, granted an indult to Master Hugh Mortimer (Mortui Mare), rector of Biselie diocese of Worcester, to hold also the Church of Old Radnor, in the diocese of Hereford,[1] this being the parish in which Wigmore Castle, the home of the Mortimers, is situated. Hugh Mortimer had, doubtless been presented by Roger Mortimer, and he held both the first and second portions, as stated in Bishop Giffard's register in the record of the institution of Richard de Lynthon as chaplain to the Chantry of the Blessed Mary of Bisley in 1285, on the presentation of Hugh Mortimer " Rector of two portions in the Church of Bisley."

On 28 November, 1270, the royal licence, at the instance of Roger Mortimer, was granted for life to Hugh Mortimer, parson of the Church of Biseleye, to hunt with his own dogs, the fox, the hare, the badger and the cat, through the forests in the Counties of Oxford, Gloucester and Worcester.

In 1280, a dispensation was granted by Bishop Giffard to Hugh Mortimer, rector of the Church of Bisleyea, that from Easter in the 12th year of the Bishop's pontificate he may lawfully dwell with the Lady Matilda de Mortui Mari in Ireland, and in the meantime let to farm his Church. That he had already had a dispensation to let his rectory to farm (though record thereof is lost) is apparent from the fact that THOMAS, to whom the care of the possessions assigned for the maintenance of divine service, etc., in the chapel of the Chantry of Blessed Mary, in 1274, is addressed by Bishop Giffard as rector of the Church of Bysseleya. Hugh Mortimer ceased to be rector of Bisley in 1290, whether owing to resignation or death is not known.

1290. HUGH MORTIMER (II) was presented as rector of the first portion by Sir Edmund Mortimer, but not being in Holy Orders, Bishop Giffard, on August 10, 1290, committed the custody of the first portion to Walter Bordon until the presentee should be in Holy Orders. Hugh Mortimer, clerk,

[1] Cal. Papal Reg., i, p. 350.

was inducted to the Church of Bisleya, in 1290, but was not instituted because he was absent. In 1291, on "Saturday on which is sung 'Scientes'" at Bredon Church, Hugh Mortimer was ordained sub-deacon, He is mentioned in the charter of William de la Pere quoted in Chapter III, as holding land in Bisley, 'Persona de Bysseleye,' but his appointment seems to have been wholly unsatisfactory, for in 1294, Bishop Giffard issued a mandate to the deans of Stonehouse and Cirencester to cite Hugh de Mortimer holding the Church of Biseley, who obtained the same since the Council of Lyons (1274), to answer for not being ordained in priest's orders and for plurality, both of which abuses the Council had forbidden. Hugh Mortimer (II) must have been deprived of his rectory, for the following day the Bishop issued a Commission to John of Evreux, archdeacon of Gloucester, and to Thomas Stokes, his official, giving the Church of Biseleye into their charge.

1295. HENRY HERVEY, clerk, was instituted in the kalends of August, by the Bishop, to the first portion, on the presentation of Edmund Mortimer. He is known also as Avery or Uphaveon. It was in his time and with his consent, namely in 1304, that a deed of endowment was made for Stroud Chapel, which will be considered when enumerating the vicars.

1316. JOHN HAKELUT, acolite, was admitted by Bishop Maydeston, to the first portion on the Kalend of October at Hampton Episcopi, on the presentation of Roger Mortimer, Lord of Wigmore. He presented himself at the office of the Archdeacon of Gloucester, made canonical obedience and obtained letters dimissory to all Holy Orders, and license to study for a year. His leave of absence for study in England was confirmed and increased to two years by Bishop Cobham on 26 December, 1317, in London.[1]

Before 1337, RICHARD DE CLAVILL was rector of the first portion, but there is no record of his appointment.

1351. PETER DE LACY received permission on 30 November from Bishop Thoresby, on vacating his rectory of Hildeber-

---

[1] Maydestone fo., 483. Cobham fo., 1.

werth, in the diocese of Norwich, to exchange with Richard de Clavill, who had resigned the first portion.[1]   On 23 May, 1353, King Edward III ratified the estate of his Clerk, Peter de Lacy, as prebendary or portioner in the Church of Byseley.[2] De Lacy's family had been previously connected with Bisley, as Walter de Lacy in Edward I's reign had held part of the Hundred, and Theobald be Verdun's father, John, had married the grand-daughter and co-heiress of Walter de Lacy, all the family being closely connected with Ireland.[3]

1351, Bishop Thoresby appointed the Prior of Llanthony, Master Henry de Neubole, vicar general, Mr. John Wyndesore, Rector of Clynce, and Mr. Henry Fenton, as a Commission to reply to the enquiry of Peter de Lacy regarding the cure of souls, of which he desired to be relieved as Rector of the first portion in Bisley.   The Commission sat in St. Nicholas Church, Gloucester, on a day after the feast of St. Valentine, with others named to assist including the perpetual Vicar of Bisley (Edmund de Elcombe).   The Bishop pronounced the finding of the Commission in his London house, 20 March, 1351, to be that all his predecessors in the first portion had, from time immemorial, held the same free from residence or cure of souls and that the latter rested entirely in the possession of the perpetual vicar, who gives a part of the rents and tithes to the said portioner.[4]

The abuse of non-residence and alienation of tithes originally given for the sustenance of the priests of the parish, had reached its climax, and Edward III looked upon such sinecures as fitting and economical rewards for his Clerks.

Peter de Lacy resigned in 1366, and at some time he became Prebendary of Swerde in Dublin Cathedral, and rector of Northfleet, Kent, where he died and was buried, a fine brass (which is mentioned in most books on Monumental Brasses) marking the reputed place of his interment, on the chancel floor.   The height of the effigy of Peter de Lacy is 4 ft. 6 ins., and he is depicted in full Mass vestments, alb, maniple,

[1] Thoresby fo., 29B.
[2] Cal. Pat. Rolls.
[3] *B. G. A. S. Trans.*, xi, 133, 143.
[4] Thoresby fo., 34.

amice, stole and chasuble, with his hands in the attitude of prayer. He has long hair and a tonsure, and originally lay under a canopy, now gone. The inscription (which may have been altered in restoration) runs as follows :—

" Hic jacet Dominus Petrus de Lacy, quonda rector istius ecclesiae prebendarius p'bende de Swerde Cathedral Dublin qui obiit XVIII die Octobr Anno XXXX millimo CCCLXXII. Via vite mors." The last three words are probably a substitution for the usual commendation of soul, and the word after Anno is not distinctly legible. A note in Suffling's " English Church Brasses " states that " About 1780 the body of Peter de Lacy was exhumed in Northfleet Church when it was, after 400 years found to be in an excellent state of preservation, being entirely enclosed in a leather covering."[1]

1366. JOHN BACOUN, on the resignation of Peter de Lacey, and on the presentation of King Edward IV, in whose custody were the lands and hereditaments of Roger Mortimer,[2] Earl of March, deceased, was admitted to the first portion on 8 November, at Hartlebury, by Bishop Witlesey. He resigned in 1383.

1383. RICHARD DE MEDFORD, king's clerk, by patronage of Richard II, custos for the heirs of the Earl of March, deceased, was appointed on 15 January, 1383, in the person of Thomas Barton, his procurator. He resigned in 1386.[3]

1386. WALTER HAKBORN was appointed the year that the " venerable Dominus Richard Medeford " resigned, on 8 August, but a fresh grant was made 13 June, 1389, his institution taking place at Wythynden, 20 September of that year. Nothing is known of Walter Hakborn, but he appears to have ceased to be rector about 1402.

1402. WALTER MEDEFORD, clerk, succeeded as both first and second portioner, and began to present to the vicarage of Bisley in 1404, he at that time being Chancellor of Salisbury Cathedral (1402-4). He became Archdeacon of Salisbury in

---

[1] I am indebted to the Rev. Montague Cox, Vicar of All Saints, Swanscombe, for the details of the Northfleet brass.

[2] Cal. Pat. Rolls.

[3] Wakefield fo., 37.

1404, but resigned the same year for the Archdeaconry of Berkshire, which post he held till 1423. His last recorded presentation at Bisley was in 1416, to the Chantry.

1423. THOMAS DONECAN, M.A., succeeded as first and second portioner, his institution to the latter being registered as taking place on 27 July, 1423, on the presentation of Edmund, Earl of March.[1] A possible defect in the registers accounts for the omission of Thomas Donecan's appointment as first portioner, but he was presenting to the Chantry as such in 1428.

1441. RICHARD SHIRBURN also second portioner.

1461. ROGER MALMESBURY, clerk to Edward IV, was presented by the King on 26 June to the first portion, vacant by the death of Thomas Donecan.[2]

.... RICHARD HIDDE (of whose institution no record was found) died as first portioner in 1465.

1465. THOMAS GAWDE, Professor of Sacred Theology (in the person of his proxy Adam Gawde), was instituted to the first portion 13 April, at Fladbury, by Mr. William Vauce, Commissary to Bishop Carpenter. The presentation was made by the Dean and Chapter of the College of St. John Baptist, Stoke Clare, but it would appear that he died before 8 November that same year, judging from an entry in the register of that date relating to a presentation to the vicarage.

There is some confusion, perhaps owing to the Wars of the Roses, respecting the date of the concession of the patronage of the first and second portions to Stoke Clare College, for this presentation of 1465 is the first recorded in the Bishop's register. On 8 March, 1480, Bishop Carpenter held an enquiry into the matter in Worcester Cathedral, regarding the appropriation of two portions or prebends in the Church of Byssley to the College of St. John Baptist, Stoke Clare. The College pleaded that it was greatly impoverished and in difficulties, and humbly begged these two portions, the first being worth £20 and the second £10. It was stated that Letters Patent of Edward IV showed that

[1] Morgan II fo., 23.
[2] Cal. Pat. Rolls.

Richard, Duke of York, Lord of Wigmore and de Clare, his father, and others, gave to Stoke Clare the patronage, etc., of Dunmow, in 1427-8, also the first and second portions in Bisley.[1] This house had been founded as an alien priory in 1248 by Richard de Clare, Earl of Gloucester, from whom descended the Mortimers, Earl of March and the Royal House of York. In 1395-6 Richard II made the priory native, and gave it as a cell to St. Peter's, Westminster, but at the request of Edmund, Earl of March, Pope John XXIII transformed the house from a priory of monks to a College of a Dean and secular canons (1419-20), to whom Edmund Mortimer confirmed all the lands and privileges of the previous priory.[2]

It was unfortunate for Bisley that this transfer of patronage to a religious community was made, less than a hundred years before the Dissolution of the Religious Orders, for it enabled Henry VIII to lay his avaricious hands on the endowments of the prebends.

JOHN THORP, appointed in 1480, after Bishop Carpenter's enquiry, by the Dean and Chapter of Stoke Clare, receives no mention in the register, neither is there any record of his successor to be found, though the College continued to appoint to the Chantry up to 1534. Possibly this is to be accounted for by the loss of many pages in the register of Bishop Merton.

RECTORS OF THE SECOND PORTION OR PREBEND.

Before 1285. HUGH MORTIMER (I) held the second Prebend in conjunction with the first which see.

1290. RICHARD LE BAUDE " rector of the Church of Byseleye was ordained Priest at Bredon in 1291, on the same occasion that Hugh Mortimer (II) was ordained sub-deacon, as Rector of the Church of Biseleya."[3] Though it appears

---

[1] Carpenter fo., 69. In fo. 232 b., the Confirmation of this Act by Richard III in 1484, is recorded.

[2] Dugdale's Monasticon.

[3] Giffard.

probable that Richard de Baude's appointment was to Bisley, there is just a possibility that Billesley or Bushley, Worcestershire might be intended, both of which are liable to be mispelt in the episcopal registers.

1304 or earlier. ROBERT LE EYRE, of the de Bisley family, is recorded in the Endowment of Stroud, as being rector of the second portion and in 1310 " Robert Rector of the second, portion in the Church of Biseleye, priest," received license from Bishop Walter Reynolds to let his portion to farm in order that he might study.[1]

1313. March 1. BARTHOLOMEW DE ELMHAM was granted letters dimissory for admission to all minor orders not yet received and to all holy orders. On 28 March he did obedience for his appointment as second portioner, after his ordination as deacon.[2]

By 2 December, 1313, letters dimissory were granted to him to be promoted to priest's orders by any bishop of the Apostolic See, the Bishopric of Worcester being vacant after the appointment of Bishop Reynolds to the see of Canterbury.[3]

On 19 June, 1314, Bishop Maydeston granted licence to Bartholomew de Elmham to be absent for study, in compliance with the request of the King, Edward (II) to whom probably his appointment was due.[4]

Walter by Divine permission Bishop of Worcester to the beloved son Bartholomew de Elinam Rector of the second portion of the Church of Byseleye in our diocese, greeting etc. " Tue devocionis previbus inclinati ut pro annum a tempe cosceccionis presencm continue inimmandum ab Ecclesia tua predicta In obsequis domini nostri Regis Angliae illustris morari valeas Ita per ad proaleni residenciam per dictum tempus minime tenearis ac et porcione Ecclesie tue predicte durante dicto tempore cum fructibus et pro muntibus eidem ad firmam alicui persone edifiastice prouidea honeste

---

[1] Reynolds, fo. 20.
[2] Reynolds, fo. 78d.
[3] Sede Vacante.
[4] Maydeston fo. 7.

dimetter seu fructus eosdem cui pro tua veclitate videris expedire vendere possis liberam etiam tenore presente concedimus facultatem permyo per porcio ecclesie tue pro oerute inter non debitis non fran detur obsequus et aiaz cura fue ad ultatene negligatur In cuis rei testimonium sigillum nostrum presentitibus appensim.

Datur London XIII kal Junii Anno Dm. MCCCmo XIIIJ Et consecrationis nre primo."

Before September, 1316, HENRY DE UPHAVENE (Upavon near Marlborough), otherwise Harvey, who by September is spoken of as rector of two portions in the Church of Biseleye, when he presented Robert de Cherleton to the perpetual Chantry of the Blessed Mary of Bisseleye. Henry de Uphavene probably died that year, as in October John Haklut was presented to the first portion by Roger Mortimer. There is no record of any presentation to the second portion till 1331.

1331. 11 October. RICHARD CLAVILLE presented by Edward III to the two portions,[1] the prebends being in the King's gift by reason of the lands of the rebel Roger Mortimer being in his hands. Richard Claville resigned the first portion in 1351 but must have resigned the second portion by 1344.

1344. JOHN HOYLOUN, clerk, was presented by Humphry de Bohun, Earl of Hereford. He was instituted at Hartlebury on 25 May, and died in 1361.[2]

1361. 23 September. STEPHEN ATTE ROCHE was admitted, in the person of Richard Jobelif, his procurator, by Bishop Reginald Bryan, at Pershore, on the death of John Hoyloun, being presented by Humphry de Bohun, to whom the patronage fell owing to the minority of Hugh, son and heir of John de Bisleye. On 1 October, 1370, he exchanged with Mr. Roger de Wodenorton, Rector of Fenny Ditton, diocese of Ely.[3] There seems to have been some difficulty about this exchange, as it was held that the presentation lay with

---

[1] Cal. Pat. Rolls, 5 Ed. III.
[2] Braunsford fo. 37b.
[3] Lynne fo. 11.

the Pope, who, however, issued a mandate of confirmation of Stephen atte Roche's appointment 20 May, 1372.[1]

1370. 1 October. ROGER DE WODENORTON, Rector of Fenny Ditton by exchange with Stephen atte Roche, on presentation by Humphry de Bohun. He remained second Portioner until 1377, when desiring to exchange with Dom. John Waldyn, Rector of Chelusfeld, diocese of Rochester, his cause was on 20 December, preferred to the Bishop at Hartlebury by Hugh de Byseleye.[2]

1377. JOHN WALDYN, or Waldene, from Chelusfeld, by exchange. He died 26 March, 1388.[3]

1388. 10 April. RICHARD DE WHITHAM, chancellor of the diocese of Worcester. An enquiry had been held by the Archdeacon of Gloucester at Estynton (Eastington) by desire of Henry, Earl of Derby and Richard de Whitham, chancellor, on the vacancy caused by the death of John Waldene. Richard de Whitham was nominated to the second portion by his procurator, John Galby, and presented by the Earl of Derby.[4]

1402. WALTER MEDFORD, also first Portioner, which see.[5]

1423. 27 July. THOMAS DONECAN, also first Portioner, which see.[6]

1441. 25 October. RICHARD SHIRBURN, who was also first Portioner. His appointment was ratified by the King, his presentation probably being due to Richard, Duke of York, who had acquired the advowson of the second Portion from John Stonehouse, who had exchanged his fourth part of the manor of Bisley (namely Stokesend) and the advowson of the second Portion in 1434, for the manor of Over Sodington.[7]

1480. 8 March. RICHARD SHIRBURN, according to the report of Bishop Carpenter's enquiry was to be the first

---

[1] Cal. Papal Reg. Hockaday.
[2] Lynne fo. 11.
[3] Wakefield fo. 18.
[4] Wakefield fo. 51.
[5] Clifford fo. 77.
[6] Morgan II, fo. 23.
[7] Cal. Pat. Rolls.

appointment of a second Portioner by the College of Stoke Clare. Whether the College was only confirming the Portioner of that name appointed in 1441, or whether there was a second person of that name is not indicated. At any rate, he is the last of the second portioners recorded in the Episcopal registers.[1]

After the middle of the fourteenth century there appear to have been no duties attached to the office of second Portioner. Before that time there are indications of residence being required, unless license was granted by the Bishop for absence to study and the necessity of proceeding from minor orders to Holy Orders.

The Great Tithe of the Rectory of Bisley.

The Great Tithe of Bisley, allotted from time immemorial to the maintenance of the clergy of the parish and consequently to the two priests mentioned in Domesday Book, and to their successors (whether with or without the cure of souls), was in the Valor of Pope Nicholas, of 1291, reckoned at £25 13s. 4d. for the first prebend, and £14 6s. 8d. for the second. At the time of the appropriation of the two prebends to Stoke Clare College the first is stated to be £20 and the second £10.

The Great Tithe passed into Henry VIII's hands in 1536-9, and ever since then there has been a " Lay Rector." Shortly after the Reformation, the impropriation was granted to Walter Compton and William Shewell, a rent of £10 being required to be paid by them to the chaplain of Stroud.[2]

In 1569, the Gloucester Consistory Court censured these two farmers of the Rectory for allowing the chancel of Bisley Church to become ruinous, and in 1572, it is recorded that the chancel still required repairs, glazing and mossing.[3] Walter Compton had however rebuilt the Rectory house, as will appear from the will of Henry Compton, his grandson.

[1] Carpenter fo. 69.
[2] Fosbrooke.
[3] Hockaday Eccles. File.

" In the name of God " the 9 February, 35 Elizabeth (1593). Henry Compton of Bisley, gentleman, weak after long sickness, but of perfect memory. He commits his soul to his Lord and Saviour Jesus Christ trusting by the merits of his death and passion to be saved, and his body to the earth, his funeral to be done decently as shall please his wife Johane.

To his wife and her assigns, he gives his rights in the farm at Aveninge then in the tenure of Henry Bridges, esquire, and Alice, his wife. To his wife for life one yearly " schiffe " rent or rent service of 8s. issuing and going out of certain lands in Colcombe in the parish of Minchinhampton now in the tenure of one — Cox.

He owns that by his deed of 20 June, 34 Elizabeth, he had let to Sir Henry Poole, knight, to Henry Bridges, Esq., his father-in-law and to Richard Byrd, gentleman, the moitie of the Rectory or prebend of Bysley otherwise called the first and second portion or prebend of Bysley and the moiety of all houses, edificies, buildings, glebe lands, tythes, meadowes, feedings, pastures, rents, services, perquisites of Courts and laetes, hereditaments and of all other things demised in and by certain letters patent of lease dated 31 October in the 28 Elizabeth made unto one William Lingard and to one William Heynes for term of 21 years excepted, to have and to hold by the said Henry Poole, Henry Brydges and Richard Byrde and to their assigns to their use and all his claim and right term of years, reversion, etc., to the capital messuage of the rectory parsonage or prebend of Bysley aforesaid and the close whereon the said messuage is situate, and the garden thereunto adjoining and all the edifices and buildings belonging of late newly erected and built by Walter Compton, Esq., deceased together with the said letters patent of lease and certain Indenture of assignment.

He signifies that the said deed was made to avoid any benefit of survivorship which William Shewell, gentleman, may should or ought to have in the rectory parsonage or other premisses specified or intended to be demised by the said letters patent of lease, if the said William Shewell outlived him and that the said Poole, Brydges and Byrd should hold these premises on trust for his wife during the 21 years, therewith to pay such moneys as shall be borrowed for and towards the purchase thereof and to dispose thereof at her will.

Whereas his grandfather Walter Compton, by his last will gave to him and his wife, Johane, the longest liver of them, the moitie of the parsonage of Bysley and being possessed thereof by a deed in writing of his said grandfather, he gives to his said wife the said parsonage moiety and all his estate and interest of the same rectory or parsonage for the term of 21 years specified. He gives to her all his indentures and writings, etc., concerning the said farm of Avening and parsonage of Bysley, and the deeds of the said sheife rents of 8s. he gives only for her life.

He gives the education breadings up and preferring in marriage of his two daughters to his wife, she to be sole executrix. (No witnesses mentioned). Proved at Cirencester, 9 November, 1593.[1]

Johane Compton enjoyed the rectorial tithe, and presumably resided at the new-built rectory, till her death in 1606-7. Her burial took place at Bisley on 7 March of that year.

James I granted the Great Tithe to Lawrence Baskerville and William Blake, scrivener, by Letters Patent of 17 July, 1606, reserving, however, out of the rectory of Bisley and other premises belonging thereto a fee farm rent of £33 10s. 0d. The grantees undertook " from time to time for ever at their own proper cost and expenses to find and provide a sufficient curate or minister at Stroudwater in the County of Gloucester, and two deans, namely one at Stroudwater, aforesaid, and the other at Bisleighe in the said County of Gloucester, for the celebrating there of divine service and whatsoever belonged to divine worship there to be done."[2]

The Lay Rectors have ever since paid the sum of £10 to the incumbent of Stroud, and the patronage of that parish lay with them, but apparently the exercise of it lapsed, and about 1750 was claimed by the Bishop of Gloucester, with whom it remains.

[1] Glos. Pro. Reg.
[2] Fisher's Stroud, pp. 232 and 364.

After passing to one, Willis, the lay rectorship was sold by him to Lord Coventry, the Lord Keeper of the great seal (1625), who died in 1639-40, with whose descendants it remained until 1808, when the Hon. Thomas Coventry Bulkeley sold the impropriation to William Yarnton Mills, an agent, who himself lived in the Rectory house. His grandson, Thomas Mills Goodlake, whose mother was daughter of William Yarnton Mills, inherited the same and bequeathed it to his daughter who married the Marquis de Lastyrie. The Marquise realized her responsibility as Lay Rector, and gave generously to the Church schools and other parochial charities. After her death, her nephew became Lay Rector, but within recent years sold his rights to the Rev. William Francis Buttle, Rector of Alwalton with Chesterton and Haddon (diocese of Ely), the present owner of the Great Tithe, the tithe rent charge Impropriation being £1300 in 1933.[1]

The lands scattered about in various parts of Bisley, Stroud and Paganhill, known as Coventry Lands and consisting of 301 acres (see Bisley Tithe Terrier), represent the glebe land formerly belonging to the Rectors of Bisley. These all came into the possession of Thomas Mills Goodlake, and after his death were sold. The lands consisted for the most part of arable, houses, and gardens, with the Rectory farm, and Hawkley wood.

The Rectory House.

The Rectory House formerly stood near the Vicarage in the upper part of the present Vicarage garden. We have seen that it was rebuilt by Walter Compton, and nothing more is heard of it till the Rev. Stephen Philips (Vicar from 1715 to 1740, or his son of the same name, 1740 to 1782) wrote to Lady Coventry complaining of the annoyance caused by the tenants : not only did they withhold the portion of tithe which was due to him, but his garden was rendered unpleasant by the odour of the tenant's pigs.[2]

---

[1] Crockford.
[2] Bisley Parish Magazine, August, 1898.

The Rectory House was a ruin when the Rev. Thomas Keble came to Bisley as Vicar in 1827 ; consequently he pulled it down, and exchanging another piece of land for that on which it stood, he included the site in the present Vicarage garden.

THE RECTORY FARM.

The Rectory Farm lies rather strangely placed as regards the farmhouse, which is situated on the High Street, remarkable for its Georgian front, and its back of earlier date. Between it and the farmyard an old house, formerly the Red Lion, intervenes, and on crossing the upper road the yard with the stately tithe barn of the eighteenth century is seen abutting on the old road to London. Within the barn the tithes in kind (which will be more fully dealt with when the vicarial tithe is considered) were collected in olden days.

CHAPTER VI

PART 2

VICARS OF BISLEY

Owing to the abuses current in the Church of the later Norman period, resident vicars responsible for the cure of souls were appointed by non-resident or negligent rectors to carry out their priestly duties for them, but at what time the first vicar of Bisley was appointed is not known.

The following list of vicars has been compiled from every known available source, and mainly from the episcopal registers at Worcester.

Before 1274. OSBERT, founder of the Chantry.[1]

1282. ROBERT DE BISELEYE, presented by Richard de Bisleye, and instituted when still sub-deacon, 22 February, to the third portion of the Church of Bisleye.[2]

1302. WILLIAM CALF of Campden, was inducted on 5 September, and instituted to the Church of Bysseley and swore canonical obedience and residence.[2]

It was shortly after William Calf's appointment that an important change was made in the parish through the separation of Stroud from the mother church and the provision of a chapel there. This led to a deed of Endowment or Composition agreed to in 1304, enrolled in the Bishop's registers, copies of the translation of which are in the first volume of Bisley registers, and also in Fisher's " Stroud."

" Be it known to all men, that whereas, between Masters Henry Avery and Robert, called le Eyre, Rectors of the first and second portion of the church of Bysseleye, and William, Vicar of the same place, of the one part,— and Thomas of

---

[1] Chantry Certificates, P. R. O., No. 22, 47.
[2] Giffard.

Rodeborowe, William Proute, Henry of Monemuwe, Nicholas le Seymour, Henry le Fremer, and the other inhabitants of the chapel of Strode, appearing by William Benet and Richard son of Richard, jointly and severally, according to law appointed their proctors, and afterward appearing personaly ratifying the deed of the proctors themselves, of the other part :—Concerning the restoration and repair of the chancel of the chapel of Strode and certain other matters, subjects of strife and disagreement had arisen ; which at length, in the presence of us W. Burdon, Archdeacon of Gloucester, hath been set at rest after this manner, that is to say : That whereas there is no manner of doubt, that between the chapel itself of Strode, and its mother church of Bysselye, so great and so dangerous a distance exists that, in the baptizing of young children, and the administration of the other sacraments of the church, it is not unlikely that grievous peril of souls may happen ; and inasmuch as the Rectors and Vicar aforesaid are bound of their own free will to remedy this evil as far as in them lies,—They will and consent that in the Chapel of Strode itself, at the expense of the inhabitants of the same, henceforth shall be made a place for baptizing, and in it shall be administered the Sacrament of Baptism ; the minister of the chapel also, by the aforesaid rectors equally chosen and admitted, in order that he may administer day by day the sacraments of the church, in the chapel itself, shall for the future be continually resident ; with this understanding, however,—that the open piece of ground or tenement in la Strode, which piece of ground or tenement, John of Pridie hath hitherto held of the aforesaid rectors at a certain rent, may be appointed by them for the residence of the same priest, but shall have a competent building erected on it by the above-mentioned inhabitants of la Strode themselves, since it is for their own benefit that this piece of ground is so assigned. And as often as, or whensoever this building shall need repair or improvement of any sort, the whole shall be done at the expense of the same inhabitants. The same inhabitants shall also pay there yearly, for it, eighteen pence to the Rectors themselves, as they have hitherto been accustomed to do. But toward the stipend of the aforesaid Minister of the chapel, the inhabitants them-

K

selves shall contribute yearly fifteen shillings at three periods
of the year, to wit, at the feast of Saint Michael, the Birthday
of our Lord, and on the Feast of the Purification of the Blessed
Virgin. If, however, wilfully, and to the detriment of the
Minister of the chapel, they shall cease to give satisfaction in
the same, which Heaven forbid ! the aforesaid parties will
and consent that the before ordained Chantry as it was
formerly accustomed to be held, shall entirely cease, although
had and obtained there. Also the aforesaid tenement shall
revert to the same Rectors freely, and without any hindrance
whatsoever. Also the same Minister of the Chapel shall
administer all and singular the Sacraments in the villages of
both Lepeyates, Strode and of Pagunhull, together with the
whole vill of Bourne from the house or tenement which
formerly was commonly called Serded house (Seredhous)
unto the afore-mentioned Chapel of Strode. But the clerk
who is continually to wait on the minister of the Chapel
(himself admitted at the good pleasure of the rectors and
to be removed by them whenever they think fit), shall receive
for the future for his stipend what he has been accustomed to,
together with that which the beneficed Clerk in the Chapel of
Pagunhull for their burial used to have from the inhabitants
themselves for their services. With regard, however, to
the repairing and restoring of the Chancel of the Chapel of
Strode, the parties have unanimously agreed in this manner,
that is to say : That the rectors themselves shall repair the
front of the chancel now in a ruinous condition (if necessary
building it up from the very foundations), and shall make in a
competent manner in the same, the window which has been
ordered at their own proper charge, for this one time only :
but, for the future, the before-mentioned inhabitants shall
repair and make good all and singular the other defects of
the aforesaid place, taking upon themselves and their
successors for ever, the burden of repairing, rebuilding, and
roofing in, as well the front and the window, as the whole of
the aforesaid chancel as often as need shall require.

" In all oblations, however, obventions, tithes, and payments, collected as well for the maintaining of the bells, as
of the body of the church, or in all other contributions and

rights of what sort soever they may be, in what way soever from of old due and accustomed, the before-mentioned chapel of Strode and its inhabitants for ever, as hitherto they have been, shall remain obedient and subject to the aforesaid Church of Bysseleye, as to their mother. For the observance of all these things and each of them the above-named parties have mutually bound themselves, having taken their corporal oath upon the holy Gospels of God. In witness and assurance whereof, we, W. Burdon, Archdeacon aforesaid, to this present writing made after the manner of a Chirograph between the two said parties at their procurement and instance, have thought fit to have our seal affixed. Written at Gloucester, on the fourth day before the Calends of August, in the year of our Lord One Thousand three hundred and four.''

It was this same year that the death of Edmund Mortimer took place and his Inquisition Post Mortem was held at Minchinhampton on the 10th December. At that time William of Reom (Freame), Thomas of Eggesworth, Nicholas of Seymor, Henry the Farmer, William the Pronte, William of Bysrugg (Bussage), John Sturmy, Thomas Acchard, Reginald Jurdan, William of Syddenham, William of Tunley, and Robert Selwynne, declared on oath that the said Edmund was seised of the advowson of two parts of the Church of Byseleye which were worth fifty marks per annum.[1]

In this inquisition and in the preceding deed we have the names of the principal men of the neighbourhood at that time. William Calf died in 1305.

1305. JOHN OF WYVELESFORD, sub-deacon, was granted the custody of the vicarage of Bisseley vacant by the death of William Calf, by Bishop Guisborough, until the next ordination, on condition that he then was ordained deacon. His institution by the Bishop of Worcester after his ordination as deacon (on the presentation of Henry of Uphaven or Avery, rector of the first portion) took place 14 March, 1305, at Hylyngdon, and on 12 June he was ordained priest.[2] It was during his vicarship that the chancel was rebuilt.

---

[1] P. R. O. Chanc. Inq. P. M. Ed. I.
[2] Guisborough.

1317. HENRY LE EYR, clerk, was admitted 8 December, by Bishop Cobham, at London, to the office of parson of the third portion of the Church of Bisleye, then vacant, on the presentation of Hugh le Eyr de Biseleye, son of Richard of the same. He was admitted and inducted by Mr. John Bradewas,[1] but not being yet in Holy Orders he received letters dimissory to orders of acolyte and subdeacon the same day, and having been admitted to these orders, 18 February, 1318, he also received license for absence to study in England for one year.[2] He was admitted to the priesthood at the Trinity ordinations of 1319. Thus for the second time the comfortable arrangement of squire and parson being of one family arose, he being son to Hugh de Bisley, then lord of the manor of Overcourt.

1325-6. WILLIAM DE LEGHE, chaplain, on presentation of John Haklut first rector, the benefice being vacant by resignation, and he having effected an exchange from Cowley. He was instituted in March at Hartlebury and inducted by the rector of Minchinhampton, William of Prestbury. The vicarage was taxed at this date at ten marks of silver.[3]

1328. WALTER DE YANEWORTH, presbyter, exhibited letters patent of John Haklut, first rector, upon presentation, in London 19 February, when he was inducted. He died in 1337.[4] His name continued to be attached to certain land he held in Bisley and known as Yaneworthy's land in 1462.[5]

1337. HUGH DE CALDECOTE, priest, was admitted 25 July, by the Vicar General of the Bishop of Worcester to the vicarage vacant by the death of Walter Yaneworth, on the presentation of Richard de Clavil, first rector.[6]

—. ROGER, of whose appointment no record was found, but it appears from the institution of his successor that he died in 1348, the year when the Black Death was raging in England. There is no record or indication that it affected Bisley.

---

[1] Cobham fo., 1b.
[2] Cobham (printed), p. 265.
[3] Cobham fo. 109b.
[4] Horleton fo. 18b.
[5] *B. G. A. S. Trans*, li, 215.
[6] Hemenhale fo. 9.

1348. EDMUND DE ELCOMB, priest, presented by Dom. Richard Clavyll, first rector, to " Byslee perpetual vicarage " and instituted 17 Mareh, on the death of Dom. Roger, last vicar.[1] From his name, his birthplace was Elcombe in Bisley parish, a small and remote hamlet, of which mention is made in the Bisley Court roll of 5 October, 1357, being the court of Roger Mortimer, at which William Boskenals exhibited a charter of the same lord, by which he gave to William Sered one grange called Elcombe to be held of him and his heirs for 4s. per annum with four lands, etc., as Anis Stanton had held. Edmund of Elcombe may have belonged to the Sered family.[2]

In 1349 during the vacancy of the See, a visitation of clergy and people of the deanery of Stonehouse was held at Bisley Church on Tuesday after the feast of St. Denis, by the Commissioners of the Prior of Worcester, keeper of the spiritualities during the vacancy.[3] Edmund de Elcombe resigned in 1355.

1355. ROBERT CAPEROUN, priest, presented 17 May by Bishop Reginald Bryan to whom the appointment had fallen on the resignation of Edmund de Elcombe.[4] He died in 1356.

—. SIMON TAILO.

1356. ROBERT BURGEYS, priest, was instituted 12 July at Nubberlye, being presented by Peter de Lacy first Rector, on the death of the last vicar.[5]

The question of the vicarial tithes appears to have been a matter of long contention between the vicar and the first rector, so in 1360 Bishop Bryan issued the " Ordinance of the Vicarage of the Church of Bysseleye,"[6] which gives us a wonderful picture of the Church life at that time. A copy of the translation is to be found in the Bisley registers, vol. I. in the handwriting of the Rev. Stephen Philips.

[1] Braunsford, vol. ii., fo. 24.
[2] Hockaday.
[3] P. R. O. Portfolio, 175, 7.
[4] Bryan fo. 13b.
[5] Bryan fo. 18b.
[6] Bryan fos. 99b and 100.

" To all the children of the Holy mother the Church to whom these presents shall come—Reginald, by Divine permission Bishop of Worcester, sendeth greeting. Amongst other desirable things of our heart, we have earnestly wished to take away all hurtful doubts of law, and contention, between our subjects, and establish peace among them ; especially long since between our beloved sons in Christ, Peter Lacie, portionary of the first portion of the Church of Bisley, on the one part ; and Robert Burgess, perpetual Vicar of the said portion in the Church of Bisley, on the other part. A question being raised concerning the sufficiency of the allowance of the Vicar himself and his Vicarage, and of the profits and revenue allowed to the Vicar who shall be there for the time being, We, well weighing and, as belonging to our inspection, considering,—and the parties aforesaid sufficiently appearing before us,—after deliberation, and by the counsel of the learned, and also with the express consent of the aforesaid parties, both portionary and the vicar and vicarage aforesaid, we have judged and ordained in form following, that is to say : We will and ordain that the Vicar of the aforesaid portion, who is now or hereafter shall be for the time being, shall have and receive for his portion, and the portion of the vicarage of the aforesaid Church, these plain things under written, viz. : the Mansion house which the said Robert Burgess, the vicar, doth now dwell in, together with three curtilages adjoining, which were late in the tenure and occupation of Simon Tailo, portionary of the said portion ; also the oblations to be made in the said Church and parish ; all obventions and duties at the altar, or otherwise within the limits of the parish aforesaid ; and also whatsoever heriots which pertained to the aforesaid portionary or his predecessors till this time, and ought to appertain. Also the tithes of flax, milk, hemp, butter, cheese, calves, cocks, hens, swans, geese, ducks, pigs, eggs, wax, honey, apples, pears, gardens, grist mills, fulling mills, or soever like, dovehouses, fish-ponds, fowling, rabbits, hunting, merchandizing, herbage, firewood, and the small tithes of the whole parish ; and also the entire tithes of all hay of lands and meadows, in the tenure of the said portionary, commonly called Worlands, and the herbage of the churchyard of the said church ;

also the entire tithes of wool and lambs, sheep, pigs, pigeons, geese, ducks, eggs, apples, pears, and all fruit tithable of the portionary of the aforesaid portion, as well in his demesne lands called Worlands, as which is in his own possession. Also all the tithes of hay, wool and lambs, as well of the tenants of the said portionary, besides Worlands, as also of the whole parish aforesaid. And the same vicar and his successors may receive all tithes and re-decimations, as is allowed and granted to him and his vicarage, in the mansion of the said portionary of the church aforesaid. Also that the said Vicar who shall be for the time being, shall claim of the portionary of the portion aforesaid for the solid or entire portion of his vicarage nothing besides the premises aforesaid,—but shall hold himself contented with those fruits, tenths, oblations, and obventions, which exceed the clear value of ten marks of silver ; unless the said portionary of the portion aforesaid shall of his special favour provide more plentifully for the said Vicar. But the said Vicar and his successors shall bear these burdens under written :—that is to say, that he and whosoever is Vicar shall, either by himself or some other sufficient Chaplain, perform Divine Service as is fitting in the said Church, and undertake the cure of souls, bind the books, wash the surplices when it shall be necessary, and as the said portionary is obliged. And that all the wax to be burned in the chancels of Bysseleye and Strode, on what account soever it shall happen, the same Vicar and his successors shall provide for the same. And also whosoever shall be Vicar for the time being in the first portion of the said Church, shall pay the synodals and procurations to the Archdeacon, and provide wine for the people to communicate, at his own charge all other burdens being excluded. Always reserving to ourself and our successors, Bishops of Worcester, the Special Power of adding to or withdrawing from the aforesaid premises, and changing the same, and also declaring, interpreting, correcting, and supplying, if any thing in the same shall be obscure or doubtful. In witness whereof we have caused our seal to be set to these presents. Dated at Alvechurch, the eighth day of July, in the year of our Lord 1360, and of our translation the eighth."

Robert Burgeys died in 1365. There is no record of the appointment of Simon Tailo, mentioned above, as vicar.

1365. JOHN HULLE, chaplain, was admitted to the vicarage on 15 May, on the presentation of Peter de Lacey, first rector.[1] In 1367 an important event took place at Lypiatt, namely the building of a Chantry chapel there, and the appointment of a chaplain, which must have made some difference to the ecclesiastical life of Bisley. John Hulle died in 1368.

1368. JOHN PROUT, priest, was presented by John Bacoun, first rector, to the " perpetual vicarage," the date being destroyed.[2]

—. ROBERT MERIET, the date of whose appointment is missing owing to the loss of records for two years in Bishop Lynne's register. He exchanged with John Edward to the less strenuous office of Chantry priest in 1383, the exchange being ratified at Hembury on 28 April.[3] He resigned from the Chantry in 1386.[4]

1383. JOHN EDWARD, Chaplain, presented 28 April by John Bacoun, first rector.[3]

—. JOHN WOLRUGGE, whose appointment was not found recorded but whose resignation in 1402 is mentioned.[5]

1402. JOHN GRAUNGER, priest, instituted 13 July at Alvechurch on presentation by the first rector, and resignation of the last vicar.[5] He stayed only two years at Bisley, and then exchanged with John Smalrugge to the Rectory of Hywyssh in Sarum diocese.[6]

1404. JOHN SMALRUGGE, rector of Hywyssh, exchanged to Bisley and was appointed 20 July, on the presentation of Walter Medeford, first rector.[6] He died before 13 September of that year.

---

[1] Wittlesey 1364-8.
[2] Lynne fo. 1.
[3] Wakefield fo. 36.
[4] Wakefield fo. 44b.
[5] Clifford fo. 61.
[6] Clifford fo. 77.

1404. ROBERT OPPI or ORPY was instituted 13 September, on presentation by Walter Medeford. He, however, resigned in 1406.[1]

1406. JOHN POLE was admitted vicar at Hillyngdon, on 5 January, on presentation by Walter Medeford.[2]

——. JOHN WANSFORD, of whose appointment there is no record. He was vicar in 1424-5 being mentioned as such in a deed of John Frampton conceding lands in Chalford and Colcombe to him and John Solars in that year, to hold in trust.[3] He is also mentioned as vicar in the Court roll of Bisley held 10 April, 1427.[4] He exchanged with Richard Totty, vicar of Hundlavyngton (now Hullavington), Wilts.

1430. RICHARD TOTTY, presented 22 April, by Thomas Donecan, first rector.[5]

——. ROGER CARPENTER, whose appointment is not recorded. He died 1439.

1439. WILLIAM BYAN, chaplain, instituted by the Bishop at Alvechurch, 16 April, on the death of Roger Carpenter, and on the presentation of Thomas Donecan "second portioner."[6] He resigned in 1445.

1445. THOMAS OLYVVER, chaplain, instituted by the Bishop in his manor of Alvechurch.[7]

——. THOMAS SKYNNER, the record of whose appointment did not appear, but whose death as vicar is noted in the appointment of his successor in 1465.

1465. JOHN ROGERS, admitted 8 November at Alvechurch, by Mr. William Vause, the right of presentation falling to the Bishop, owing to the death of Thomas Cannye or Gawde, first rector. During the incumbency of John Rogers the churchyard of Bisley was desecrated, in 1468-9, owing to an

[1] Clifford fo. 79.
[2] Clifford fo. 95.
[3] B. G. A. S. Trans., li, 213, 216.
[4] P. R. O. Port., 175, 10.
[5] Pulton fo. 82.
[6] Boughcher fo. 59.
[7] Carpenter.

attack made by one David Jones, on Thomas Dolman[1] within the sacred precincts, which ended in the effusion of blood, about which inquisition was made during the Christmas festival of that year by Mr. William Vause, Commissary of the Bishop, at Chipping Sodbury.

Mr. Vause declared the Churchyard to be polluted and under an interdict, so that no burial could be made there till it was reconciled.

From the tradition at Bibury, where a portion of the Churchyard is known as the " Bisley piece," it would appear that any burials during the time of an interdict on Bisley Churchyard, took place at Bibury, eighteen miles away, as being the nearest place beyond the bounds of the Worcester diocese, and according to Abel Wantner, the road thither passed over Perrot's Brook, formerly Barrod's Bridge, alias Bearwoods, alias Biersway or Burialsway Bridge.

A possible earlier interdict of the thirteenth century will be considered in the next chapter, but on this occasion in 1469, the interdict did not last long, as on 26 February, by Commission from the Cardinal, the Bishop of Down and Connor, acting as Suffragan, came to Bisley to reconcile and re-consecrate the Churchyard. The heavy expense of this must have taught the parishioners a lesson, 250 marks being the fee paid, Mr. John Botiller, who was probably the Chief Registrar of the Diocese having interceded and obtained remission of the remaining 33s. 4d. demanded. Fifty marks went to the Bishop for his trouble, which must have been considerable in reaching such a remote spot at that time of the year, and his chaplain and Marshall, Chancellor and Registrar all received their due fees.[2]

After this nothing is heard of Bisley's vicar until 1491, when Thomas Whytington of Over Lypiatt, Esq., bequeathed to " John Rogers, Vicar of Bysseley his best gown of scarlet with the hood," whether for his personal use, or for adaptation as a vestment for the Church, does nor appear. It is

---

[1] Laurence Dolman held lands in Over and Nether Lypiatt in 1367. P. R. O Feet of Fines, Glouc., 466. Also William Dolman is mentioned in Bisley Court Rolls of 25 September, 1599, as over-loading the commons of the manor.

[2] Carpenter, fo. 299b.

interesting as an early mention of that scarlet cloth for which Stroud valley has been so famous.[1]

In 1493, the Churchwardens and more important people of the parish came before the Bishop of Worcester at Gloucester to exemplify their copy of the Composition of 1304. A copy of the deed of Exemplification is in Bisley register, Vol. I. as follows, the original deed of Composition having vanished.

" To all sons of Our Holy Mother the Church to whom these presents shall come, John Thour, Doctor of Laws, Chancellor and Commissary General, of the Rev. Father and Lord in Christ, the Lord Robert, by divine permission, Bishop of Worcester, sends greeting. We made known, that in the year of our Lord 1493, in the eleventh Indiction, in the first year of the Pontificate of Our Most Holy Father and Lord in Christ, the Lord Alexander the Sixth, on the eighteenth day of the month of July, in the Great Cloister of the Monastary of the Blessed Peter at Gloucester, in the diocese of Worcester, before us sitting in the place of Judgment, appeared, as well the Wardens as the greater and the more discreet part of the parishioners of Bysseleye, and produced the real and original Composition between the former rectors and the vicar of Byssleye of the one part, and the inhabitants of the Chapel of Strode of the other part,—not decayed, not cancelled, not erased, nor in any part altered,—though in some degree impaired by age and obscurity of the writing, as it appeared to us ; and humbly prayed that, whereas the said wardens as well as the parishioners, present and to come, might have need to use the said Composition—which they have not in duplicate, nor among writings of modern date—in different parts of the country far distant from each other, and that they might be able to exhibit it for establishing their rights ; and that, because this Composition might probably be lost by the risks of travelling, or by other mishaps, —We would take care that it should be copied, exemplified, signed, and brought by the undersigned Public Notary, (taken to be our scribe, for this purpose), into a public form, so that, to the copy so made, credit may attach equally with the original Composition ; of which the true tenor follows in

[1] P. C. C. Milles 45.

these words : ' *Universis pateat*,' etc. (Here the original Composition is inscribed).

" Wherefore we, John Thour, Chancellor, etc., having examined the said original Composition, and found it not erased, nor decayed, not cancelled, nor in any part of it open to suspicion ; that the means of proof may not hereafter be taken away from the aforesaid Wardens and the other parishioners, present and to come, owing to the age, decay, or faintness of the writing ; therefore, sitting in our place of Judgment, we have published by our authority and decree the Composition, and have caused the same to be copied by the undersigned public notary, and reduced into public form, and to be signed with his accustomed signature, and to be exemplified. To which copy, so brought into public form, we decree by these presents full credit shall hereafter be attached, as to the said real and original Composition. In witness and assurance of all and singular the above, to this present instrument or copy we have considered that the seal of the aforesaid Bishop of Worcester, which we have at hand, should be affixed. These things were given and done as above written and recited, in the year of our Lord, Indiction, Pontificate, month, day and place in the beginning of this instrument or copy described. Then follows the attestation of James Botiller, clerk of the Diocese of Dublin, Public Notary and Chief Registrar of the Reverend Father and Lord in Christ, Robert, Bishop of Worcester, that, at the time and place aforesaid, and at the command of the aforesaid Chancellor, he had copied and exemplified the said Composition, and published the copy, and reduced it into public form ; and with his accustomed signature and name, together with the appendage of the seal of the aforesaid Reverend Bishop as aforesaid, he had signed,—in assurance and witness of all and singular the premises."[1]

John Rogers' long term of office closed with his death in 1504.

1504. HENRY WYRESDELL, chaplain, was admitted to the perpetual vicarage on the last day of January, on the

---

[1] See also Fisher's Stroud.

presentation of the Dean and Chapter of Stoke Clare, who had acquired the right to present, with the rectorship which lay with them.[1]   He died in 1509.

1509.   JAMES LOWE, chaplain, was admitted 21 December, having been priest of the Chantry from 1503 till his resignation in 1509.[2]   He was one of the overseers of the estate of John Grymes (whose will was dated 19 January, 1509-10, and proved on 14 February), who left to the Church of Byseley 3s., and to the torches there 12 pence, and to the service of St. Mary of Bysseleye 20 pence.[3]

At the Visitation of Bishop Bell in 1532, Sir James Lowe was mulcted to the amount of 26s. 8d., his curate Sir Ralph Hauchell of 7s. 1d., Sir Robert (or Roger) Jones, Chantry chaplain, of 7s. 8d., the "Praemunire penalty" imposed in 1531 by Henry VIII, who had placed all the clergy in outlawry in that year, and extorted this iniquitous charge in five yearly portions, payable at Michaelmas.

James Lowe died in 1534.

1534.   RICHARD BLYSSE, M.A., was admitted by Mr. Hazard pr. 8 July, on presentation by the Dean and Chapter of Stoke Clare.[4]   He took his degree of B.A. in November, 1527, at Oxford.[5]

Richard Blysse probably belonged to the local family of that name, who were parishioners in the sixteenth and seventeenth centuries, and who have left their name to the Blisse Mill.

In 1541, during Richard Blysse's incumbency, Roger Fowler, of Bisley, left 6s. 8d. for tythes forgotten to the "highe Awlter" of Bisley, and in 1542, Joan Freme, widow (of Nether Lypiatt) buried in the Churchyard of All Saynttes in Bisley, had arranged by her will of 1541 for her month's mind to be kept the whole year, one of her witnesses being

---

[1] De Giglis fo. 40.
[2] De Giglis fo. 62.
[3] Hockaday.
[4] Ghinucci fo. 68.
[5] Boase Reg. Univ. Ox. i, 149.

Sir John Trevyllyan her " gostely father,"[1] who was curate at that time, and for some years later.

1543. JOHN FOWLER, M.A., Clerk, record of whose appointment was not found, but he compounded for first fruits 29 June of that year, at £19 10s. 5d., payments to commence at Michaelmas, 1544. As one of his sureties was Richard Fowler, of Stonehouse, clothier, he was doubtless a member of this local family.[2]

John Fowler took his B.A. degree at Oxford in October, 1540, and became M.A. in May, 1543, having been made fellow of Corpus Christi in May, 1541.[3]

In 1544 began the despoiling of the estates held by the Abbey of Cirencester at Througham and elsewhere in the parish, whilst in 1545 the property of the Knights Hospitallers of Quenington[4] Priory, at Nether Lypiatt, was also alienated to secular hands, and in 1546 our Lady's Chantry was abolished. Yet still in 1545 devotion to the " hight Auter of Bysely " is shown in the will of John Egerly of Byssely, who bequeathed a bushel of barley to it,[5] whilst in 1546 John Fre . . bequeathed 12 pence to our Lady Image and to the mayntynans of the Church lyghte and the belles, a boschell of whete.[5] In 1548, Richard Peryn, of Byssley, left to the high Aulter of Byssly, 2s. To our Lady servys 20 pence. To the coffer 20 pence.[5] The number of houselling people in the parish in this year was 628.[6] So that Church life had continued much as formerly throughout the terribly unhappy years of Henry VIII's reign, and that of his son. John Fowler must have used the first prayer book of Edward VI issued in 1549, but probably that of 1552 did not reach him as he died in 1553, and was buried at Bisley 18 February.

1553. DAVID CONDON, clerk, presented 2 March, by King Edward's Chancellor, and instituted 14 March.[7] He was deprived by Queen Mary.

[1] Glos. P. R.
[2] Hockaday.
[3] Boase Reg. Univ. Ox. ii.
[4] Hockaday. .
[5] Glos. P. R.
[6] Chantry Cert. No. 22, 47.
[7] Hockaday.

1558. THOMAS TAYLOR, presented by Queen Mary, 18 March and instituted 1 August.[1] The Queen died 17 November of that year. Thomas Taylor appears to have been active amongst his parishioners : he witnessed the will of John Dower, 25 August, 1558, also that of William Smart (who left two bushells of malt to the Church and 3s. 4d. to the vicar) the same year, and that of Henry Pers on 15 September, 1559, in which he bequeathed 3s. 4d. to the " hyght Aultar of Byseley and to the Church two bushells of malt,"[2] For how much longer Thomas Taylor remained vicar is not known.

Meanwhile the county of Gloucester had been separated from the diocese of Worcester and the new diocese of Gloucester formed in 1539, the first Bishop being John Wakeman, late Abbot of Tewkesbury. The confusion apparent as regards the Vicars of Bisley is to be noted also in the history of the Bishops, and the great religious changes effected in the sixteenth century are reflected in the decay of the Church life and neglect of the Church which are recorded during the next three centuries.

1563. RICHARD RAWLYNS, who may have been appointed a few years earlier. He took his B.A. degree at Oxford in 1532, M.A., 1534,[3] and was presented to Bisley by Queen Elizabeth. Complaint was made in 1563 by Thomas Eccles and Thomas Wakeman, Churchwardens, and three parishioners at the Archdeacon's Court that Sir Richard Rawlyns served two churches, Bisley and Rodborough. The church itself was neglected and needed glazing, and the vicarage was not repaired with timber, wattle and thatch. In 1566, on 2 May, Thomas Powell, D.L., Chancellor, by permission of Richard Cheyney, Bishop of Gloucester, furthered the imprisonment of Richard Rawlyns, who remained excommunicated forty days and more, after being denounced as so in his parish church. Sentence of Greater Excommunication was also pronounced in respect of his contumacy in not having paid her Majesty's subsidies at a

[1] Hockaday.
[2] Glos. P. R.
[3] Boase, Reg. Univ. Ox. i.

certain day as ordered.[1]   He was free and in his parish again
in 1564 for on 6 August of that year he was writing Elizabeth
Bowton's will.[2]

1568. ROBERT ARMONDE, clerk, presented 20 February,
by the Lord Keeper, on the vicarage becoming vacant, either
by the death or resignation of Richard Rawlyns.[3]   On 5
May of that year Robert Armonde entered into a bond of
£100 to Richard Bishop of Gloucester, on his institution.

He assumed the duties of his office to find the chancel of
his church ruinous through the neglect of Messrs. Compton
and Shewell, farmers of the rectory, the lay substitutes for the
former ecclesiastical rectors.   The Consistory Court took up
the matter in 1569, and found also that the Church had
suffered through the dishonesty of several persons.   Thomas
Eales, who owed the Church £6 6s. 2d., was excommunicated
on 2 December, for his contumacy in not appearing before
the Court, and was only restored on 7 January, 1570, in the
house of Master Chancellor.   At the same time Thomas
Workman owed the Church £10, Edward Kene, 20s. (he was
excommunicated), William Ireland, 53s. 4d., and Henry
Stevens, 40s.   To judge from these large sums, dishonesty
must have prevailed for some years during the ecclesiastical
confusion, which had told disastrously on the morals of the
people.   In 1569 and 1570 several cases of immorality were
dealt with by the Court, one couple being sentenced to do
penance on 19 April, 1570, in the market-place at Stroud, to
confess their sin before the people, and also on the next
Sunday in the parish Church of Bisley.[3]

Robert Armonde resigned in 1572.

1572. JOHN LIGHTFOOT, clerk, was instituted 11 June.
Probably his family was connected with Bisley of old time,
for in the Ministers' Accounts (P. R. O.) of 1448-9, one, John
Lightfoot held land here, and again in 1452 William Lightfoot,
the same.

---

[1] Hockaday.

[2] Glos. P. R.

[3] Hockaday.

He entered on his office with the chancel and Church still out of repair and in need of glazing and mossing. He is the first priest of Bisley whom the records show to have been married. His first son, Thomas, was born at Bisley, and baptized there, 25 July, 1573, his daughter, Joane, 12 November, 1574, and another daughter, 29 June, 1578.[1]

In 1579 some unrecorded epidemic must have devastated Bisley homes for there were 52 burials that year, and amongst them the vicarage was heavily visited. John Lightfoot lost two sons, Richard, buried 25 April, and John, buried 27 April, while his wife followed them and was buried 4 May.

On the 21st May in the following year, John Lightfoot married Margaret Gatley, at Bisley. A daughter, Anne, was born to them and baptized 21 January, 1583.

John Lightfoot must have been greatly beloved by his parishioners and entirely in their confidence, for it is remarkable in the wills of that time that he was often the writer of them and very frequently a witness. Those wills that he wrote out invariably begin with a pious commendation of the soul to Almighty God, or to the Holy Trinity, a custom which was gradually weakening since the Reformation, the mention of the " Holy company of Heaven " having become quite obsolete. John Lightfoot resigned in 1588, and some time about 29 March, died at Brainford (Bramford), and was there buried.

It is strange that having assisted so many others to make their wills, he himself should die intestate, but so it was, and administration of his estate was granted to his widow, Margaret, 3 April, 1599.[2]

1588. CHRISTOPHER WYNDLE, clerk, presented by Queen Elizabeth and instituted 17 April. He took his B.A. degree at Oxford in 1579-80, and on 28 July, 1588, he married Mary Townsend, at Bisley. They had a large family— Thomas baptized 10 June, 1589, Sarah baptized 19 December, 1590, Phoebe, 9 February, 1595, Christopher, 27 March, 1597.

---

[1] For all dates of births, marriages and deaths see Bisley Registers. Glos. P. R.

L

This year was marked by a grievous epidemic, during which no marriages are registered, but there were 145 burials, amongst them his son, Thomas, on 20 July, his servant, Alice Cowles, being buried 5 December. Thomas John, his son, was baptized 18 March, 1599, but died 20 March, Mary, baptized 4 September, 1600, Elizabeth 11 March, 1604. In 1605, on 12 May, Israel, his son, was buried on Sunday evening, and his daughter Phoebe was buried on 18 May in the Chancel, under the altar. His son, Matthias, was baptized 25 May, 1606, and Juliana, his daughter, 2 November, 1608. Death again visited the vicarage, his daughter, Elizabeth, being buried 27 January, 1618, and his son, Matthias, on 25 April, 1624. Christopher Wyndle had a dispensation in 1592 to hold Syde rectory in plurality.[1]

Having become very old and infirm, Wyndle agreed to resign in 1625, on receiving an allowance and with the permission of the Bishop of Gloucester and the Bishop of Lincoln, then Lord Keeper. He died in October of that year, and was buried at Bisley on the 18th.

Christopher Wyndle appears to have made his will the day of his death, namely 17 October, 1625, and he desired that the money due to him by bond from Thomas Taylo, Henry Twisle, Richard Rogers and Nathaniel Yates, all of Bysley, and all other his debts due to him, should be bestowed upon land or some annuity by Christopher Windle, his son, either during the lives of Mary his wife and of Julian his daughter, or else by the term of 21 years, and that Sara, his daughter and her children, should have £4 per annum paid to her quarterly during the lifetime of Mary his wife only, but his will was that Francis Ludlow, husband of the said Sara should not have anything to do with her estate, Sara to have the disposing of the £4 for herself, for her own and her children's benefit. All the rest of his estate was to be equally divided between his wife and daughter, Julian, and after the decease of his wife all was to be divided between Jaspar Windle and Christopher Windle, his grandsons, sons of Christopher, his son. His wife to be sole executrix and Robert Tomlyns, of

[1] Hockaday.

Bysley, overseer. W. Katherine Townsend, Agnis Allen, Joane Doule.[1]

Mary Wyndle survived her husband till 1639, and was buried at Bisley, 24 April.

1625. JOHN SEDGWICK, clerk, M.A., instituted. He was a native of Wiltshire and matriculated at Queen's College, Oxford, 18 June, 1619, took his B.A. degree at Magdalen Hall in 1622, M.A. 1625, and was admitted B.D. in 1633.

No marriages were recorded in 1627, and no registers at all in 1628, 1629, 1630, or 1631, but in 1632 the only register of the year is that of the burial of Katherine, wife of John Sedgwick, on 14 January. He must have married again very quickly, for on 30 May, 1633, his son, John, was baptized, on 4 January, 1635, his daughter Abigial, and on 1 October, his son Obadiah. John Sedgwick was deprived of the living in 1638 on a charge of simony, brought against him in the Court of High Commission by Daniel Lawford, who obtained his own institution to the living, many of the parishioners being put to great expense on the same charge, and having to pay £30 to Sir John Lambe, besides costs, before they could clear themselves.[2]

1638. DANIEL LAWFORD, clerk, M.A., instituted to the vicarage on the 17 July. He entered Oriel College, Oxford, in 1619, from Warwickshire, and took his B.A. degree in 1622, M.A. 1628. He was licensed to preach 18 November, 1637, and was admitted B.D. 10 October, 1638, after his appointment as vicar.

In 1640-1, a petition was brought from John Sedgwick, clerk, and the parishioners of Bisley before the House of Lords, praying for the restoration of John Sedgwick, their former vicar. In this petition, having stated as above, they declare that Lawford is superstitious in observance of ceremonies, but lax in performance of duties, being frequently drunk and at that time lying a prisoner for debt in the King's Bench. A list of witnesses sworn is given and the deposition

---

[1] Glos. P. R. Robert Tomlyns, M.A., was a doctor at Bisley, where he died and was buried 24 February, 1635. (Reg.)

[2] Report on Hist. MSS, Ho. of Lords Calendar, p. 49.

of Anthony Coxe and others that Mr. Lawford is a drunkard
and bows to the Communion Table, etc. There is a further
petition of John Stephens and others, parishioners of Bisley,
to the House of Lords in 1642, that Mr. Britton may have
liberty to officiate in the Church there and that some of the
profits of the vicarage may be allotted for his payment, the
present vicar Daniel Lawford, having led a scandalous life,
and still being in the King's Bench prison for debt. On 7
October this permission was granted, with Lawford's
consent.[1]

1641. RICHARD BRITTON, clerk, M.A., was instituted 8
October, and began his ministry with the troubled period of
the Civil War and Commonwealth, but lived to rejoice in the
Restoration. One gathers that he had been curate before
becoming vicar. Little is known of how the war affected
Bisley and its vicars, but he was one of those who subscribed
to "The Gloucestershire Ministers' Testimony to the Truth
of Jesus Christ, and to the Solemn League and Covenant as
against the Errours, Heresies, and Blasphemies of these
times," in 1648.[2] This acquiescence in the prevailing
religious movement seems to have carried Britton unmolested
over the Commonwealth period, throughout which he
continued to marry, baptize, and bury his parishioners as
before. He was reported in the Parliamentary Survey of
1650 to be a constant preacher and the living to be worth
about £50 per annum.

Britton's wife died in 1671, being buried in the Chancel,
and the tablet he erected to her memory is now in the belfry.
"Here resteth the body of Sarah, the wife of Mr. Richard
Britton, Pastor of this Church, who deceased August 14, 1671,
Etatis sue 54.

> The glory of her sex loe here doth lie,
> The perfect modell of true pietie,
> Cover'd with dust thus oftentimes are found
> The richest treasure in most barren ground.
> Her Soul's but to its center gone to shine
> In Heav'n to which here it did incline."

---

[1] Report on Hist. MSS., Ho. of Lords Calendar, p. 54.
[2] Rare tract in the British Museum. See Glos. Notes and Queries, i., 329.

In 1655, Richard Brittaine sued Lord Coventry, the Lay Rector of the Parish, before the Bishop of Worcester's Court, for detention of certain of the Tithes which were his due, and judgment was given in his favour, as appears from the following extracts, quoted in the Parish Magazine for 1898.

" Richard Brittaine, Clerke, did in the year 1655 exhibit an English bill into this Court against Lord Coventry, Hereby showing that he is Vicar of the Church of Bisley in the County of Gloucestershire, and that the Parsonage of the said Church is a Rectory impropriate, held and enjoyed by Lord Coventry, and that in the said Parish there is an ancient Vicarage, endowed with an ancient house (here follows the list of Tithes in kind, due to the Vicar), and that the Complainant and his successors should have and receive all the tithes before mentioned, for which the said complainant and his successors are to officiate in the said Church. Further showeth that the Parish of Bisley is a great Parish, and hath within it diverse Chappells of Ease, and consisteth of a great number of Communicants, and the gift of the Vicarage hath always been in the Crown of England, and is now in his Highness the Protector, and that the Complainant was about 20 years ago lawfully presented to the Vicarage, and continued there ever since, and doth officiate the Cure there, and is accountable for the First fruits and Tenths, and yet Lord Coventry doth endeavour to deprive him of the small Tithes. Lord Coventry receiveth the whole benefit thereof. The Complainant is obliged to pay his Tenths and First fruits, and the Vicarage is not worth £20 per annum besides the Tenths so detained."

Judgment was given as follows :—" It is this day ordered by the Court that the Defendant, Lord Coventry, shall forthwith satisfy and pay to the complainant the Tithe arising within the Parsonage of Bisley, and detained from the Complainant, from the time of his Institution, the 18th of October, 1641, until the 18th of October, 1656."

In 1662, the year after the Restoration, Richard Blake, former teacher at Cirencester school, was licensed to teach in the parish of Bisley, and on 24 May, 1673, William Clutterbuck, B.A., of Magdalen Hall, Oxford, was ordained deacon and appointed curate of Bisley, being admitted to priests' orders the following year.[1] These two circumstances point to a revival in Church life at Bisley.

Richard Britton died 13 November, 1679, being buried in the Chancel on 16 November with his wife. A tablet to his memory is now in the belfry :—

"Richardi Britton Qui hoc institutendo Ecclesiam per septem et triginta annorum seriem Pastoris munere quam vigilantissime perfunctus est. Obijt 13° Die 9bris A.D. 1679, Aetat suae 65." (A latin verse follows.)

Richard Britton made his will 6 August, 1678, "In the name of God" and being through the mercy of God in some measures of health of body and perfect memory. He commends his soul into the hands of the Lord Jesus, his dear Saviour and Redeemer, whom he has to his power faithfully served in the Gospel. His body to decent Christian burial in the Chancel of the Church of Bisley, by Sarah, his beloved wife, there to rest together till the Resurrection.

And for that small portion of wordly goods which the Lord of His goodness hath lent him he gives and bequeaths as follows. To his brother, Cananuel Britton, £10. To his sister, Abigail Duck £10. If any die before receiving their legacy then it is to go to their children. To his nephew, Mr. William Clotterbuck, all his study of books and as much of his goods and chattels as with his study of books shall amount to one moiety thereof, the other moiety he gives to his sister Jane Ferneley, in consideration of her paines in keeping his house since the death of his dear wife, and he wills that she shall dwell in his house called Patts for her life if the lease hold so long, and if his executors be not forced to sell it. Mr. William Clotterbock to be his sole executor, he to hold all the money in the house or owing, his lease at Patts, his lease at Copsgrove, his Barn and stable, and all things therein, his cattell that he shall possess, his household goods and plate, all to be divided between him and his sister Ferneley. His executors are to give rings to his cousin, Thomas and Cousin John Pope, of Cam, with their wives, his cozen,

---

[1] Hockaday. Wm. Clutterbuck was Britton's nephew.

Richard Pope and his wife, at London, and his funerall ring which he wears for his wife, to be given to his sister Abigail. W. Richard Blake, John Hede, Sarah Hide.

" An explanation of one branch of my will, my study of books cost me above sixstow pounds, and it is my will they should be valued to my Executor at £40 to equall which I give to my sister, Ferneley, £40 out of my goods and chattels, and for the remainder of my estate let my executor and sister divide it equally between them." Proved 10 September, 1680, by Wm. Clutterbock.[1]

1680. JOSEPH LODGE, M.A., priest, was instituted 18 March, having been presented by the King, but he did not remain vicar more than a few months.

1681. SIMON PRIEST, M.A., was instituted 12 August. Beyond the various changes in his curates and school teachers nothing is recorded of his ministry. He preached an excellent sermon on 23 July, 1710, in Bisley Church entitled " The Danger of Bad Company with respect to our Obedience to God : or the Impossibility of their keeping God's Commandments that keep Bad Company." The text was Psalm CXIX. 115. " Depart from me ye Evildoers, for I will keep the commandments of my God." In 1686, Simon Priest's sister Martha, of Great Shelford, Cambridge, died at Bisley, where she was buried 16 January, leaving him her sole executor and the residue of her goods. In 1682, on 15 September, Isaac, son of Simon and Elizabeth Priest, was baptized, and on 4 January, 1684, their daughter, Mary. Isaac died in 1685, and was buried 11 June, and on 14 January, 1689 their son John was baptized, his other children being baptized, Francis on 25 June, 1692, and Secundus Isaac on 27 December, 1694. His daughter, Elizabeth, died in 1712 and was buried 29 April, and his daughter, Mary, on 3 October, 1714. Simon Priest himself died in 1715 and was buried on 19 July.

---

1 Glos. P. R. Patts or Patts Place continued to be known by this name well into the eighteenth century. At the Bisley Court of Oswald Charlton and the Countess of March in 1401, permission was sought by William and Matilda Enpare to rebuild at their own cost a larger house upon the cottage and half ferendell of land called Pattesplace. P. R. O. Bisley Court rolls.

Simon Priest, the elder, of Bisley, Clerke, made his will 14 November, 1711, commending his soul to Almighty God, hopeing through the merits and satisfaction of his Blessed Lord and Saviour Jesus Christ to have full and free pardon, etc. To his three sons Simon, John, and Secundus Isaac all books and £3 to be divided equally. Any remaining money to be divided between his wife and daughter equally. The residue of personal estate and goods and chattels to Elizabeth his loveing and beloved wife for life, after her death to be divided between his four daughters, Elizabeth, Martha, Mary, and Frances. To his wife Elizabeth, the close or enclosed parcell of ground lying in the parish of Bisley called Hay Hedge, of three acres which he formerly purchased of one George White, then of Browns Hill in the said parish, gentleman. Also to his said wife all that other close in the parish of Bisley, called the wall'd Tyning, of four acres and one farundell, together with the tenement or dwelling-house thereon and the garden and orchard adjoining formerly purchased of John Mill, senr., of Bisley, yeoman. Both properties are to be to his wife's sole use for life and after her death to his daughters and their heirs. His wife to be sole executrix. W. Gyles Watkins, Hester Tayloe, John Wall, als. Caudell. Inventory. £39 10s. 0d. Proved 12 October, 1715.

From this will it appears that Simon Priest had purchased a dwelling-house and grounds at Bisley, to be identified with the house known still as Priests ; and the family continued to live there and elsewhere in Bisley for some years.[1]

---

[1] Isaac Priest, of Bisley, clerk, son of Simon Priest, made his will 2 February, 1751, and mentions his brother, Simon. To his niece, Anne Priest, daughter of Simon, all the messuage wherein he dwelt at Bisley with garden and court. she to be sole executrix. W. Thomas Rowles and Mary Mason. Proved 1 September, 1765. Frances Priest, daughter of Simon Priest, vicar, died in 1768, and bequeathed the house she lived in mentioned in her father's will and her Tyning at Hay Hedge, to her niece, Ann Priest, daughter of her late brother, Simon, and to his son, Simon, and his daughters Frances and Elizabeth, she left £10 each charged on the land given to her neice, Anne Priest, who is sole executrix. W. Sarah Aldridge, Jane Collings, E. Aldridge. Proved 20 October, 1768. Elizabeth Priest died in 1770, Ann Priest in 1776 (being buried 26 September), aged 63, and Simon Priest in 1780, buried 30 March, aged 65. He seems to have been the last of the Priest family at Bisley.

All the wills quoted are in the Gloucester Probate Registry.

1715. STEPHEN PHILLIPS, instituted 25 August. It is due to his care that the register book has copies of the Compositions and much other information, and that the deeds belonging to the Feoffees were put in order. During his incumbency the Workhouse for the poor was started, also the Blue Coat school, and the years 1726, 1727, 1731 and 1738, were marked by epidemics of small pox and fever.[1] Stephen Phillips lost a son, Henry, who was buried at Bisley, 24 March, 1725.

1740. STEPHEN PHILLIPS, junior, M.A., son of the preceding, was instituted 30 June. He was ordained Deacon 23 September, 1733, and Priest, 9 June, 1734, by the Bishop of Rochester. During his long incumbency of 42 years the chief thing that appears in the records is the registration in the Bishop's Court of the intention of various parishioners to hold non-conformist prayer-meetings at their houses, this registration being required by the Act of I. William and Mary.[2] Though this shows there was a great desire for religion, it also shows the state of neglect into which the parish had been allowed to sink. A son of Stephen Phillips, Charles, was baptised 30 January, 1744.

On 11 August, 1743, Stephen Phillips effected an exchange of land with Robert Shewell, of Nympsfield, Baker, to whom he granted one acre in Stancomb field near a place called the " Whittentree Quars," bounded on W. by land of Thomas Jayne, S. by land of Robert Shewell, and headed by a road leading to Sidenhams, lately in possession of Mr. Richard Buttler, but then of the said Stephen Phillips. In exchange for one acre which Robert Shewell confirmed to Stephen Phillips and his successors as Vicars of Bisley, in Battlescomb field, headed by half an acre of John Shewell's, N., by the highway leading from Bisley to Cirencester on E., and the lands of Mr. John Iles on S. and W.[3] Stephen Phillips also exchanged various other pieces of the glebe lands for more conveniently situated fields, as will be noted when the Vicar's tithe is considered.

[1] Feoffees' MSS.
[2] Hockaday.
[3] Lypiatt MSS.

Stephen Phillips, junior, died in 1782.

1782. EDWARD HAWKINS, M.A., instituted 16 July, and presented to Bisley by his father's friend,, Lord Thurlow, then Lord Chancellor. In 1798 he obtained a dispensation to hold the living of Kelston, Somerset, in plurality, and he appears to have lived there, leaving a curate to look after Bisley. He died in 1806 and there is a monument in Kelston Church to his memory, with the following inscription :—

" In the family vault in the adjoining churchyard are deposited the remains of the Rev. Edward Hawkins, M.A., Vicar of Bisley in Glostershire and Rector of this parish. He was the youngest son of Sir Caesar Hawkins, Bart., and died 5 January, 1806, aged 53. ' Leave thy fatherless children, I will preserve them alive ; and let thy widows trust in me." Jer. XLIX, ver. 11."[1]

1806. EDWARD MANSFIELD, B.A., instituted 3 March. He was the second son of Sir James Mansfield, Knight., Chief Justice of the Common pleas, being born 21 August, 1779. He was educated at Westminster school, and afterwards was fellow of St. Peter's College, Cambridge. He married in 1813, Hester, daughter of Joseph Grazebrook, banker, of Farhill, Stroud, and resided at Jaynes Court, then called " the Grove," until his death, 20 July, 1826, the vicarage being too small and inconvenient. A carriage accident in George Street " whilst proceeding on an errand of benevolence." as his inscription records, brought his life to a close after a few days' illness. A monument to him (and to his second daughter, Hester, who died 20 July, 1834), was erected on the north wall of the chancel, giving much of the above information, together with a long and laudatory summary of his character in the fashion of that period. There is a coped recumbent stone to the memory of Mrs. Hester Mansfield, in the N.E. part of the churchyard adjoining a railed in double vault of the Grazebrook family.

1827. THOMAS KEBLE, senior, B.A., instituted on presentation by the Lord Chancellor. He was the second son of the Rev. John Keble, scholar and Fellow of Corpus Christi

[1] Glos. Notes and Queries II, 193-4.

College, Oxford, Vicar of Coln St. Aldwyns, and of Sarah
Maule, his wife, daughter of the vicar of Ringwood, Hants.,
having been born at Fairford, in 1793, one year after the birth
of his brother, John Keble, afterwards vicar of Hursley, and
the great Tractarian leader.

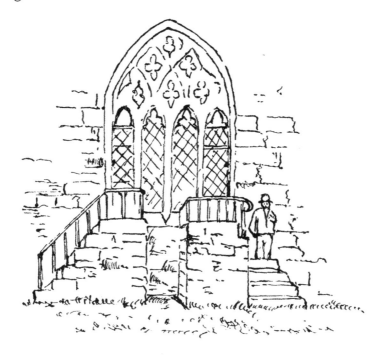

Fig. 1.—WINDOW ENTRANCES TO PRIVATE GALLERIES, BEFORE
RESTORATION.

(From a sketch by Mrs. Raymond-Barker).

Thomas Keble, senr., matriculated at Corpus Christi
College, Oxford, 1 April, 1808, aged 14, was scholar from 1809-
20, B.A. 1811, M.A. 1815, fellow 1820, Junior Dean 1822,
B.D. 1824. About 1825 he married at Cirencester Parish
Church, Elizabeth Jane, daughter of the Rev. George Clarke,
Rector of Maisey Hampton, Glos., whose sister Charlotte,
married his brother John. On entering on his duties at
Bisley, Thomas Keble found a Church sinking into a ruinous

state, the roof of the nave propped up with a fir-tree, disfigured with galleries and pews and private entrances through the windows, (See Fig. 1.), which made it more like a theatre than the House of God ; the vicarage was small and inconvenient, and the enormous parish without any other Church than the parish Church with the exception of Chalford Chapel, and dissenting meetings consequently abounding. He secured a succession of curates, many of them later much distinguished in the Church (see section on Chaplains and Curates of Bisley), and with their ready assistance he brought about such a revival of Church life, as the parish had not known since the Reformation.   The first restoration was in 1829, when the top of the spire was repaired : the vicarage was pulled down and a new house built in 1832 ; the chapel of ease at Oakridge was built in 1837, with schools in 1860 ; Christ Church, Chalford, was consecrated and formed into a separate parish and schools built in 1842 ; Bussage parish was formed and Church and schools built in 1846, and France Lynch Church and schools were built in 1857.

Having thus provided for the spiritual needs of the remoter portions of his parish, Thomas Keble took in hand the restoration of Bisley Church, which he carried through in the face of great opposition from many of his parishioners.   Though one can understand their resentment at seeing the body of the Church pulled down and an apparently new building erected, and though one regrets that so much of ancient work was abolished, yet Thomas Keble has left a very fine Church, fittingly furnished for Divine worship, and containing far more of the old building than is at first realized.

Throughout all his activities Thomas Keble was entirely in sympathy with the Tractarian Movement, and was in touch with all its leaders, of whom his brother John was chief.   They frequently resorted to him for advice, and few of them passed Bisley by when on their way from Oxford southwards or westwards.   It was here that the Tractarians saw their views and the doctrines of the Church worked out in practice in the pastoral life of the active parish priest.

Thomas Keble resigned the living of Bisley in 1873, and died 5 September, 1875, being buried at Bisley.

1873. THOMAS KEBLE, junior, was instituted, being the only son of the preceding Thomas Keble, senior, born at Southrop near Fairford, on 24 March, 1826. When he was only a year old his father came to Bisley, and it was there that he spent his boyhood under his father's tutorship, until he became a Demy at Magdalen College, Oxford, 1842-6. He took his B.A. degree in 1846, M.A. in 1849, and was fellow of his College from 1849-65, being ordained deacon in 1849, and priest in 1850, in the diocese of Exeter and parish of St. Marychurch. In 1851 or 1852 he became curate of Bussage and chaplain to the House of Mercy there until 1858. From there he went to Sidmouth for a year and then returned to Bisley for three years to help his father and to take up his work again at Bussage till 1862. After serving various curacies in other places, he came back again to be near his father, and was once more chaplain at the House of Mercy. Finally, after his father's resignation, the Lord Chancellor presented him to the living of Bisley, where he remained for the rest of his life. He became Rural Dean in 1881 and an Honorary Canon of Gloucester in 1893.

Thomas Keble, junior, married firstly in 1851, Cornelia Sarah, daughter of the Rev. Charles Cornish, Rector of Landkey, Devon, and secondly, in 1862, Mary Caroline, daughter of the Rev. Charles Turner, Incumbent of St. Luke's, Norwood, Surrey. Canon Keble's four sons all entered Holy Orders.

During the thirty years of his incumbency Canon Keble carried out his priestly duties most exactly and reverently, imbued as he was with the teaching of the Tractarian school. His pastoral work was incessant, and no part of his large parish was left unvisited, neither were the daily services omitted. His father had seen to the formation of three new parishes, which lessened the size of the ancient parish of Bisley, but left it still large in area.

The call to rest came suddenly to Canon Keble on 1 January, 1903, and he was interred at Bisley on 7 January. A tablet to the memory of both the Keble vicars has been erected in the Sanctuary of the Church, but Bisley, with its daughter parishes is not likely to forget what it owes to the labours and generosity of the Keble family.

1903. WILLIAM JAMES CLAY, B.A., of University College, Durham, was ordained deacon in 1887, and priest in 1889 at Chichester. He was curate of Hailsham from 1887 to 1900, and of Broadwell with Aldestrop from 1901 to 1903, in which latter year he was appointed Vicar of Bisley, on the presentation of the Lord Chancellor. He resigned in 1935, and died 9 January, 1937, being buried at Edenbridge, Kent.

1935. GEORGE ADSLEY PIPER, B.A., Queen's College, Cambridge. Formerly curate of St. Paul's, Bunhill Row, E.C., 1899-1901. Curate of Holy Trinity, Bishops' Stortford 1901-1903, of St. Johns, Coleford, 1904-1909, Curate-in-charge of Tuffley, Gloucester, 1909-1917, Hon. Chaplain to the Forces 1914-1916, Vicar of Lower Cam 1917-1922, of Nailsworth 1922-1935.

THE VICARIAL TITHES

The Valor of Pope Nicholas of 1292, states that the vicarage portion of tithe was £6 13s. 4d., which by the time of Henry VIII's Valor equalled £19 10s. 5d. The detailed Endowment of the Vicarage of 1360 already given was confirmed by the Barons of the Exchequer, Nicholas Parker and Hill, on 9 November, 1657, upon the complaint of Richard Brittain, then Vicar, and their pronouncement was as follows :—

" The Plaintiff shall ever hereafter have all ye Tithes of wool Lamb, ye Easter book and all and singul ye minute tithes of and with, in ye sd Psh of Bisly, and ye Tithable places thereof and all and singular other ye Tithes, retithings and profits wtsoevr mentioned and expresst in ye same Composition ordination or Endowmt, according to ye purport and true intent and meaning of ye sd Composition, ordination or Endowment and to ye end ye Pft may hereafter for ye time to come hold and enjoy all such tithes as are or shall be due to him of ye corn and hay growing wthin ye sd Psh of Bisly and ye Tithable places therof in kind, ye Defts Parishioners are hereby orderd to set forth their Tithes and ye sd Lord Coventry and Tenents and Farmers are to retithe and set apart ye Tenth of ye Tithes so set out, to ye intent ye sd. Plf may duly take and carry away ye same ; which tithings and retithings Rd. Brittain took in kind one year 1657, after which an agreement was made between ye sd Ld. Coventry and Rd. Brittain at 45 lb. pr ann in lieu of ye said tenth of ye tithes, wool and lamb, but we cannot find yt his successors ye vicars of Bisly recd more than 42 lb. p. ann wh was paid quarterly to ye sd Vicars without any diductions of Land-tax poor cess, or any other payments whatsoever. By two Terriers one in 1680 ye other 1704, it is asserted yt ye vicr of Bisley is entitled to 10s. for every Mortuary, 2d. for every Comunict, 6d. for every servant, 6d. for evy saddle horse, 3d. for evy milch cow, 4d. for evy Thro cow, 6d. for evy Mill wheele, 1d. for evy cock or hen, 1d. for evy Garden, 6d. for evy Christening. " Besides the vicarage house " it had 16 acres and an half of Glebe dispersed in several parts of ye comon feilds, wch lands or some of ym ye psent Vicar Stephen Philips hath exchanged by ye consent and approbation of ye Rt. Revd. Fathr in God, Martin, by Divine permission ye prsent Ld. Bp. of Glou' for 18 acres and half and are contained in three Inclosures.

1st. Three acres and half near Peer Yate in ye Westfield adjoining to ye Road leading from Bisley to Hampton, north west, and ye grounds of Mr. Rd. Champion on all other sides.

2nd. Eight acres and half in Battlescomfeild near ye Thornrows bounded by ye road leading from Bisley to Avenis or Lillyhorn West, lands of Jon. Cook and Wm. Sevil S. East, of Thos. Keen and a Road to ye Lime Kill N. East.

3rd. Six acres and half in Stancombfeild bounded by an Inclosure of Mr. Rd. Butlers N. East, by a Road from Stroud to Cheltenham N. West, by another Bisley to Sidenhams S. West, by grounds of Edmd Alldridge S. East."[1]

The tithes were commuted in 1841, when the lay rectors' rent charge was assessed at £1200, and the Vicar's at £750, with seventeen acres of glebe. In the apportionment, it is stated that all the tithes, both great and small, of the lands

---

[1] Bisley Registers, vol. i.

called Coventry lands belonged to the vicar. At the same time all the vicar's tithe arising from land in Lypiatt and Stroud was given to Stroud parish.[1]

THE VICARAGE HOUSE

The present vicarage house built in 1832, occupies nearly the same site as the old house, which was inconvenient and small, and was built in two parts at right angles to each other, with no communication between them.

The earliest mention of the vicarage house occurs in the presentment of the parishioners against Sir Richard Rawlyns, vicar, in 1563, when they complained that their vicarage was not repaired with timber, wattle and thatche.[2]   This building was replaced by one of stone, the front part, according to a note in the Registers, being attributed to John Sedgwick, Vicar from 1625 to 1635. A terrier of the vicarage of 1744 states that "the vicarage house is in very good repair, containing nine bays of building, part of which has been lately rebuilt, with a courtyard next the churchyard, a garden behind ye house, a stable and barn of eight bays lately rebuilt, with a carthouse and small tenement.[3]   Time had wrought considerable changes during the eighteenth century. The present garden, at its upper end covers the site of the former Rectory and its garden, which Mr. Keble acquired in exchange for a portion of five and a half acres of glebe land at Stancombe Ash.

---

[1] Bisley Tithe Terrier.
[2] Hockaday.
[3] Bisley Registers, vol. i.

CHAPTER VI

PART 3

THE CHAPLAINS OR CURATES OF BISLEY.

It is worth placing on record the names of the numerous clergy connected with the parish of Bisley, though little is known about most of them. With such an extensive parish to serve, several chaplains were needed, and it may well have been that some of them were promoted to the Vicarage, for frequently it is to be noticed in the records of the Vicars, that they are spoken of as " chaplain " when presented.

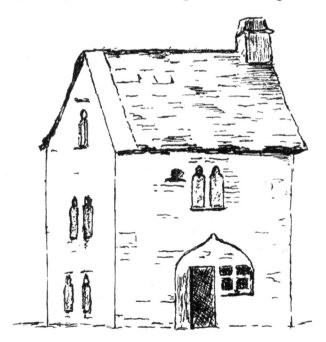

Fig. 2.—CHAPLAINS' HOUSE, BEFORE ALTERATIONS.
(From a sketch by Miss Grace Keble).

M

The house in which the chaplains resided in old times, formerly part of the " Coventry Lands," still stands at the S.E. corner of the churchyard, and though much altered at the end of the last century, it yet retains two of its fourteenth century windows. From having been the property of Mr. Yarnton Mills, and then of Mr. Goodlake and his daughter, the Marquise de Lastyrie, it has finally passed into the ownership of Mr. Gardiner who, whilst adding a wing to it, also altered the East front considerably, taking out the window and large arched doorway of the fourteenth century, and placing sashed windows in their stead. The large stone fireplaces were also removed, and a carved oak beam which was in the living room, was cut up and used as lintels for the new windows. The stonework was broken up and buried in the walls of the new wing. (See Fig. 2).

There have been several old coins dug up in the garden, now lost to Bisley, and human bones, but in the adjoining garden, when excavations for a new tank were being carried out, a whole skeleton was found. As it was lying facing west the inference is that the gardens were the burial ground of pre-Christian inhabitants.

It is not known when this house ceased to be the residence of the chaplains or curates.

———

List of Clergy and those in minor orders connected with Bisley, other than the beneficed clergy.

Before 1174, Gerard, chaplain of Biselye, witness to a grant by Jordan de Sanford and his wife, of land in Chelworth, to the monks of Gloucester. (Early deeds of St. Peter's Abbey. *B. G. A. S. Trans* xxxv., 225).

1314. Ember Saturday, first week in Lent, Ordination by Gilbert, Bishop of Armaghdown. Ralph de Biseleye on presentation of the Prior of Llanthony.[1] (Maydestone).

---

[1] The pre-Reformation ordinations are found in Worcester Episcopal registers.

1314. Rades de Biselye ordained on Trinity eve to title of religious house, Llanthony, Gloucester, at Worcester. (Maydestone).

1317. 5 February. William de Bisseleye, Canon of Llanthony, letters dimissory to all orders. (Cobham fo. 4).

1318. 3 June. Richard de Byssele, letters dimissory for orders of acolyte and sub-deacon. (Cobham fo. 8b.)

1320. John de la Rok de Bisseleye ordained deacon, "ad tit. patrimonii." Priest, 1320. This, perhaps, is Bushley, Worcs. (Cobham, p. 52).

1326. 19 April. John Mauncel de Lepeyate, Acolyte, at Cirencester. (Horleton fo. 1b.)

1331. Ember saturday in Whitsun week, Henry Rogers of Pagenhull, Acolyte, at Campden. (Horleton) fo. 1b.

1349. William, of Bysseley, clerk, M.A., to a benefice in the gift of the Bishop of Worcester in the Collegiate Church of Westbury. (Calendar of Papal Briefs.)

1349. Walter de Martelye, Chaplain did homage at the Court of Hugh de Byselye for one messuage and twenty four acres of land. (Bisley Court Rolls. P. R. O.)

1349. Brother Henry de Biseleye, monk of Little Malvern, received letters dimissory for priest's orders.

1354. 15 September. Nicholas, John and Thomas Lupyete, Acolytes, at the ordination at Henbury. (Bryan fo. 44b.)

1358. 23 October. Thomas de Bisseleye and John de Bisseleye, Acolytes, at the ordination at Tewkesbury Abbey. (Possibly of Bushley, Bryan fo. 73).

1367. 5 January. Adam Robyn instituted to the perpetual Chantry of the Chapel at Lupeyatt. (Wittlesay fo. 27).

1374. 17 March. William Stonehenge of the parish of Bysele, ordained sub-deacon to the title of the hospital of St. John of Jerusalem, to all holy orders, of which he gave particulars.   (Sede Vacante, p. 333).

1374. Richard, Priour of Chalforde, by letters dimissory of the Bishop of Lincoln to all holy orders to the title of the prior and convent of Coldnorton, of which he gave particulars. (Sede Vacante, p. 333).

1392. 21 December. John Bysely, ordained Secular Acolyte. (Wakefield fo. 165).

1400 and 1401. John Burgess, chaplain of the parish of Strode had hunted with others in the Lord's warren without licence. (Bisley Court Rolls, P. R. O.)

1407. 17 December. John Byseley ordained at Cirencester as secular acolyte and deacon on the title of the Monastery of St. Augustine, Bristol, and on 9 June, 1408, he was ordained secular priest at Lechlade. On 28 September, 1413, Dom John Bysley, chaplain, was instituted to the parish Church of Whytyngton, vacant by the death of Nicholas Hodges, last Rector, on the presentation of John Beauchamp, Lord of Bergaveney, John Greynde, knight, and Thomas Walweyn, Esq., patrons. (Peverill fos. 82, 85b. and 68b).

1420. 16 December. Dispensation to Robert Bysseley, clerk, upon defective birth. (Morgan fo. 226).

1444. 20 February. Philip Lepeyate ordained secular Acolyte at the Convent Church of Blessed Mary, Cirencester. (Carpenter).

1486-97. Deanery of Stonehouse. Dom Oliver Vale, chaplain of Stroud for taxation 6s. 8d. (Morton).

circa 1513. Dom Henry Ball, curate of Bisley, for subsidy to the King, 6s. 8d. Dom. William How chaplain of Stroude 6s. 8d. (De Giglis fo. 95).

1531. Sir John Trevylyon, curate of Bisley,[1] witnessed many wills of parishioners. Joan Freame, of Lower Lypiatt speaks of him in her will, dated 1541, as " my gostely father."

1531. Sir John Shaw, curate.[1]

1532. Sir Ralph Hauchell, curate.

1544. John Edwardes, priest at Over Lippiat, mentioned in the will of Robert Wye, to have meat and drink in his house

[1] Bishop Bells' Visitation.

at Lypiat and his chamber during his lifetime, and four marks yearly, for his wages, and to continue to serve the chapel there.

1546. Richard Gravener, clerk, witness to William Compton's (of Chalford) will.

1558. John Harttelond witness to the will of Thomas Nicholls " my goostlye fathyr and curate of Strowde."

1562. Sir Richard Rawlyns, curate of Bisley. Also Sir Richard Hunt, curate of Stroud, the same year.[1]

1568. George Harrison, curate of Bisley, mentioned in the will of Sybil Field, of Chalford.

1593. John Knight, clerk, ordered to pull down his building on the common before the next court (Bisley Court rolls, P. R. O.) He had dug stones on the common (20d. fine), and also had encroached on the common with pigs.

1595. The same John Knight had cut down twenty-eight oak saplings on lands he held, price 12d., and also opened a close called Quarley before Whitsun, for which he was fined 20s.

1638. 23 May. William Lord, clerk, married to Elizabeth Watts at Bisley. (Bisley Registers).

1641. 14 May. John Watkins, clerk, buried. (Bisley Registers).

1673. 24 May. William Clutterbuck, B.A., Magdalen Hall, Oxford, then to be admitted deacon, curate of Bisley. He was ordained priest at Gloucester in 1674.[2]

1692. 11 October. Richard Horston, licensed to be curate of Bisley.

1698. 15 October. John Taylor, B.A., of Bisley, to be admitted deacon, and on 21 September, 1700, ordained priest.[2]

1790. John Jones licensed to the curacy of the free chapel of Chalford.[2]

1804. John Green, clerk, M.A., curate of Bisley.[2]

---

[1] From a small MSS book in the *B. G. A. S.* Library, Gloucester.
[2] Hockaday.

1819. Thomas Housman, B.A., curate.[1]

1820. John Gathorne, M.A., curate.[1]

1825. Arthur Roberts, B.A., curate.[1]

1828. George Prevost, baronet M.A., licensed as curate of Bisley. He was born in 1804, and married 18 March, 1828, Jane, the only daughter of Isaac Lloyd Williams, of Cwm-eyn-felin, Co. Cardigan, sister of the Rev. Isaac Williams. He was Archdeacon of Gloucester, from 1865 to 1880, and vicar of Stinchcombe, Glos. His second son, Charles, succeeded him as third baronet, and married in 1856, Sarah Margaret, daughter of the late Rev. Thomas Keble, B.D., vicar of Bisley. He died in 1893.[2]

1835. Henry Anthony Jeffry, M.A., licensed as curate at Bisley.[1]

1840. Erroll Hill, M.A., curate.[1]

1841. Richard Champernowne, B.A., curate (for Oakridge).

1843. 15 April. Isaac Williams, curate of Bisley. He was the son of Isaac Lloyd Williams, and was born in 1802, at Cwm-eyn-felin, near Aberystwyth. He matriculated at Trinity College, Oxford, 1822, in which year he first met John Keble and fell under his influence, ultimately becoming one of the leaders of the Oxford Movement, and also an accomplished poet. He was ordained deacon in 1829, and was curate of Windrush. On becoming fellow of his college in 1831, he took priest's orders remaining there as tutor, till in 1843 he came to Bisley as curate to the Rev. Thomas Keble, residing for part of his time at Overcourt. He is also said to have occupied Paulmead Cottage at one time. He married Catherine Champernowne, sister of the Rev. Richard Champernowne, both of Dartington Hall, Devon. Isaac Williams left Bisley for Stinchcombe in 1848, and there devoted himself largely to writing. He died in 1865. His writings include a Devotional Commentary on the Gospels and Revelation, that about the Resurrection being dated from Bisley, at which place also he wrote much of the volume

---

[1] Hockaday.
[2] Lodge's Peerage, etc.

of poems entitled "Thoughts in Past Years." He was the author of several well-known hymns, and his longest poetical works were the "Cathedral" and the "Baptistery." The proceeds of his "Plain Sermons" he devoted to the restoration of Bisley chancel, and the present altar was his gift.

1843. 22 December. Robert Gregory, B.A., licensed as curate, "to reside at Brownshill, two miles distant." Robert Gregory took his B.A. degree at Corpus Christi College, Oxford, in 1843, M.A. in 1846, and was ordained deacon in 1843, and priest in 1844. In 1890 he became Dean of St. Paul's Cathedral, London, having been a Canon from 1868.

1847. Edward Whateley Piddoke, M.A. (See France Lynch, Chapter X, Part 4.)

1860-1864. William Henry Lowder, B.A., St. Edmund Hall, Oxford, 1860, M.A. 1861. He was ordained deacon in 1860, and priest in 1861 in this diocese, but had previously been an architect. He supervised the restoration of the Church, and later became Vicar of Southminster, near Malden, Essex, where he died.

CHAPTER VII

PART 1

THE PARISH CHURCH OF ALL SAINTS, BISLEY.

The dedication to All Saints of Bisley Church is ancient, being mentioned in Hugh de Bisley's will of 1415 under that title.

There is a tradition about the site of the Church on its commanding plateau,—that originally the builders began to erect it on what is known as the Church Piece at Lillyhorn, the site of the Roman villa mentioned in Chapter I, but that nightly the stones were removed by Satanic agency and deposited near to where the Church now stands. This tradition may have originated from the fact that when the nave walls were pulled down in 1862, the Roman altars mentioned as being now in the British Museum were found embedded in the wall of the tower. There are also Roman or Saxon stones built into the exterior of the east end of the chancel, so probably the ruined villa had been used as a quarry, either for the Saxon church or later.

Of the church of the thirteenth century there are two remarkable external remains, the well-cover in the S.W. part of the Churchyard, and the canopy attached to the south chancel wall, now covering the effigy of a mailed figure, where till the last restoration the priest's door opened. (see plate 6)

About the former, which has been called the Bone House and the Churchyard Cross, there is considerable mystery, but there is no reason to doubt that the beautiful Early English structure with its double rank of arcading covers a disused well. (see plate 7)

Abel Wantner, in his MS. history of Gloucestershire,[1] writing in 1714 gives the following account of a local tradition :—

" I shall conclude my discourse of Bisley with a Gloucestershire proverb, viz. : " There is one, says Pearse, when he fell into the well," which saying was thus occasioned. The Church of Bisley was out of repair, and the officers of the parish set some men to mend what was amiss ; amongst those labourers there was one whose name was Pearse, who, with the rest at dinner-time, came into the churchyard, where was a winch-well, and where they usually sate round whilst they did eat their victuals. Now it fortuned, that as they were just waiting for the striking of the clock to go to work, that as the clock struck, Pearse replyed, " There's one," which word was no sooner spoken, but he fell backwards into the well and was drowned. Whereupon the churchyard was excommunicated, and the parish did bury their dead at Bibury, which is eighteen miles a sunder, and the burial way thereunto, was over Biers-way (or Burials way) Bridge, the same that is now called Bearwoods (or Barrods) Bridge, which was no more than a foote path before, though now it be become the maine Roade way from Gloucester to London."

This tradition hardly supplies a reliable reason for the existence of a well cover of the thirteenth century, as it seems unlikely that at that date a remote church should have a clock, neither does it appear to afford a sufficient cause for laying the churchyard under an interdict.

A more likely tradition relates that, on one dark night the priest was summoned to take the Blessed Sacrament to a dying parishioner whom he never reached, but later his body was found down the well, into which he had fallen in the dark, and that thereafter the well was built over so that it should never be used again. Unfortunately, the episcopal archives at Worcester before 1274 were lost, so no record of an interdict early in that century is to be found there. It is possible that there may be a record preserved amongst the Papal archives.

[1] Bodleian Library.

At the restoration of 1862, the Norman font already mentioned was found fixed upside down on the top of the well cover, and was then restored to its rightful position in Church, a modern cross being set in its place.

As regards the canopy referred to, it will be seen in Chapter VII, Part 2, that there is reason to think it originally covered a memorial to the founder of the Chantry. At what date it was placed in its present position is unknown, and though it is depicted in an early nineteenth century view, it does not appear in a print of the Church in Bigland's History of Gloucestershire ; but drawings of that period can not be relied on for accuracy.

The effigy now reposing under this canopy formerly lay on an altar tomb, represented in Mr. Lowder's sketch as divided in its length into six panels, adorned with foliated arcading and a shallow moulding under the slab, but with no indication of further enrichment, which if it ever existed would have been in the form of painting. Atkyns says that this tomb was formerly in the South aisle of the Church, and the tomb being removed at the restoration of 1862, the effigy was then placed in its present position.

This life-sized figure, six feet in length, has been habitually spoken of as that of a knight, or Knight Templar, a crusader, and more particularly as one of the Mortimers.

There is more ground for thinking it to be one of the de Bisley family, for the plain armour strikes one as more suited for an esquire than for a knight : there is no special indication of a knight or Knight Templar, and it is most unlikely to be a Mortimer, seeing that none of the family are known to have resided at Bisley and that as a rule they were all buried at Wigmore.

Mr. Lowder deemed the effigy to be of the early part of the thirteenth century. Miss Ida Roper dates it as possibly 1302, and describes it very fully as follows :—

" The knight is enveloped in a suit of chain mail. The hauberk, reaching to the middle of the thighs where it is slightly cut up, has long sleeves covering the hands and divided at the fingers, beneath is seen the quilted gambeson. The hood of mail over the head and shoulders is further protected by a ridged chapelle de fer ; chausses of mail cover the legs and feet with wide straps buckled on the instep and passing under the foot to hold pryck spurs, and at the knees tight poleyns, probably of cuir bouilli. Over all is a long flowing surcoat so full about the waist that the cingulum is hidden. Buckled across the hips is a wide drooping belt passed around the scabbard of a long sword ; and borne upright on the left arm a plain heater shield fastened by a broad guige passing high up over the right shoulder. Small rectangular ailettes add a further protection to the shoulders and are an unusual adjunct on effigies. The hands are raised in prayer. The head rests on a rectangular pillow. The feet are on a hound lying down and facing the knight."[1]

Miss Roper is further of opinion that the rings of mail were originally of gesso, now worn off. The finger tips and spurs are missing and the ailettes partly broken off ; there is no inscription and no arms are depicted on the shield. The meaning of the crossed legs which used to be held to indicate a crusader being now considered as unknown, the question of identity cannot be solved.

Beyond the scanty remains of the Norman and Early English periods mentioned, the Church of that time seems to have been swept away and replaced in the reigns of the Edwards much in the form we now have it, namely, with chancel, nave with north and south aisles, south porch, tower and spire. The chancel and north aisle are of the reign of Edward II, and probably the lower stage of the tower ; and additions in late Decorated of Edward III's time were to be traced before the restoration in 1862, especially in widows then removed of which Mr. Lowder preserved sketches. A great deal was done in Richard II's reign (1377-99), the rest of the tower and the broach spire being built and the aisle and nave roofs being taken down, the floor removed and old coffin lids broken up to be used for building material. The aisle wall was raised and the clerestory

---

[1] " Effigies of Gloucestershire." I. M. Roper.

of rude work was concealed by the aisles which were provided with richly carved flat oak roofs, covered with lead.[1]   Several perpendicular windows were introduced at that time, but the masonry was bad and the windows placed at all levels.

The chancel can be dated with accuracy, as Bishop Walter Maydestone is stated to have come to Bisley in September or October of 1315, when he was on a tour consecrating churches and altars, amongst others, those at Miserden and Cherington, and the great altars of Sapperton, Bisley, and Minchinhampton.[2]

One consecration cross remains on the south-east angle buttress of the chancel, together with a small I.H.S. in a roundel beside it.   One window on the south side of the chancel was unfortunately removed in 1862, leaving the chancel very dark.

The nave and porch as we see them now are rebuilt, but the tower is original.   There are faint traces of a consecration cross on its S. W. buttress.

On the exterior of the north aisle are four ancient carvings which formerly were placed on the parapet ; the Holy Name, curiously repeated, is now over the north door, and shields which have borne the arms of De Clare and the Duke of York, now much weather-worn, are as near their old position as possible.   There is also a figure on a stone at the west end of this aisle which may be a dragon, and is of such rude appearance that it might be Saxon work.

The vestry on the north side is modern.   The Church exteriorly was roughcast and whitewashed.   Before the restoration the north aisle and west end were sunk in earth which was removed, and a stone paving, mainly composed of the old floor of the Church, six foot wide, was laid all round the building.

There were many entrances to the Church, several being through the window lights, into private pews in the galleries which surrounded the Church, access being gained by flights

[1] *B. G. A. S. Trans*, v., 38.   Rev. W. H. Lowder's account.   There is a tradition that the flat roofs were brought from Hayles Abbey.
[2] Thomas' Survey, Glos. Notes and Queries II, 13-4.

of steps up to the windows. There was even a gallery across the chancel arch. (Fig. 1.)

The interior of the Church had been choked with pews, and the roof of the nave was in such a precarious state as to require the support of a firpole. On entering the nave now, we stand in a fine and lofty building, re-erected exactly on the old foundation, the roof having been raised to its original height, as indicated by the ancient weather-moulding, and supported by arcades of three bays, the style adopted for nave and aisles being of the Decorated and Perpendicular periods. The new pillars of the nave were found to be unequal to the weight of the heavy roof so that the arches had to be shored up and stronger pillars of grey sandstone inserted. These pillars stand on the ancient foundations.

Mr. Lowder's specification for the restoration of the Church provided for the retention of much more of its ancient features than was found to be feasible, for as soon as the walls were touched they were seen to be in such a bad state that it was necessary to pull them down entirely. It is to be regretted though that the Church was deprived unnecessarily of many of its ancient treasures, now frequently met with in houses in the parish. For instance, the flat Perpendicular roof of the old church was condemned as unsound, only a few of the carved beams being retained and used in the vestry, and for the support of the belfry floor, but Sir John Dorington procured ten quite sound beams and placed them in his gamekeeper's cottage, then being built at Bismore. Three interesting beams are preserved in the vestry roof, supported by oak figures, and having carved bosses with the York rose, the Stafford knot, and a sunflower enclosing a man's face. The figures, with the exception of one hidden by the organ, which is a man in puffed sleeves with a dagger, appear to be deacons in tunicles, holding a book, or similarly vested figures, only having a band round the head and a cross above the forehead, one of which holds a shield and the other, above the organ, a scroll.

There are two loose oak figures of the same age, now resting on the sill of the west window in the north aisle, one representing a man playing a bagpipe, and the other a pipe.

THE CHANCEL.

The Chancel, of the Decorated period, retains the original height of its roof.   The east window, the old tracery of which was removed and replaced by similar tracery and mullions, preserves its exterior hood moulding as it was, and the interior hood, carefully restored, terminates in corbels with portrait heads of Edward II and Queen Isabella.
(see plate 20)

The double piscina is masked by tracery like a little decorated window of two trefoil-headed lights, with a five lobed opening above, enclosed under a hood moulding terminating in small corbels. that on the east side having a man's face enclosed in foliage, and that on the west being foliage only.

The sill under the south window was lowered so as to form a sedilia and the hood moulding of this window has interesting heads of a bishop and priest, which presumably are portraits of the consecrating Bishop, Maydenstone, and of the then parish priest, John Wyvelesford.

The corbels supporting the main roof timbers are ten in number.   Beginning on the north side, the most westerly :—

1.   A queen's head under foliage.

2.   A mocking face under the branch of a tree.

3.   The figure of a man in a tunic, under a tree.

4.   A half length figure holding two boughs of a tree.

5.   At the north east corner of the sanctuary, strawberry leaves.

6.   At the south-east corner, a man's head with a moustache, under foliage.

7.   A figure gathering grapes.

8.   A mocking face, under maple leaves.

9.   A dragon, out of whose mouth foliage grows.

10.   South-east corner.   Foliage.

Interesting relics, now in a glazed recess in the north wall of the sanctuary, are a small pewter chalice and paten, which were dug up outside the south porch, and had evidently been buried with a priest, after the custom of mediaeval times.

The old chancel arch was removed and the present one took its place with a wall above it raised to the requirements of the new elevation of the nave roof, and to the west of the chancel arch (which still retains the temporary decoration designed by Mr. Lowder) are to be seen two piers, pierced with arches originally connected with the rood screen.

One uncommon feature is the double piscina set in the sill of the lower arch on the north side, which, if it is in its original position, as it appears to be, indicates the existence of an altar at the east end of the north aisle. It is, however, remarkable in a church of this size that there is no trace of such an altar and no mention in the numerous wills examined of any altar other than the High Altar and that of our Lady's Chantry, to both of which bequests are frequently made.

Adjoining this north pier and in front of the modern screen the only really ancient brass the Church contains is set in a slab in the floor. The inscription is as follows :—

" Pray for the soule of Kateryn Sewell, late the wyf of Thomas Sewell whiche Kateryn deceised the VIII day of January, the yere of our Lord MVCXV, on whose soule Jhu have mercy Ame."

A small figure of Katherine Sewell is accompanied by those of seven sons and five daughters (see plate 22).

At the restoration the floor was raised seven inches above the level of the old stone paving, and underneath it were packed many portions of the old marble monuments which cumbered the walls, some of which fragments have been unearthed during excavations for the heating system.

The nave walls were somewhat lowered to receive the high pitched roof, and a doorway in the east face of the belfry looking into the Church was uncovered. Its purpose may have been to enable the ringer to observe the right moment for ringing the sacring bell.

In the apex of the nave roof is a series of wooden niches, the most easterly three of which contain ancient carved wooden figures, of which no record has been preserved. Being but dimly seen, it is only possible to suggest that they may represent Our Lord, our Lady, and St. Peter.

The present clerestory took the place of the old one which however stood at a slightly higher level.

On stripping the north wall of the nave a large fresco was discovered under the whitewash : it was impossible to preserve it, but Mr. Lowder made a sketch of it before it was destroyed. This fresco had been uncovered in 1771 when the Church was repewed, but it was immediately defaced. It was ten feet square. The subject was St. Michael weighing souls. His figure was very crudely executed, but whilst holding the scales in the right hand he points to our Lady with the left, and she has a chain from her right hand fastened to the scale containing a small naked figure, whilst a demon is trying to force up the balance. Our Lady, who has long flowing hair under a low cap, and who is clad in a short tight-fitting coat partly of pink material heavily trimmed with ermine, and a red skirt with a deep ermine flounce, all in the fashion of Henry VI's reign, is sheltering the souls of the blessed beneath an ample pink cloak, which was edged with ermine and had a cape of the same fur, kept in place by straps crossed on the breast and jewelled. (see plate 8)

This representation of the sheltering of souls is commemorated in the right hand light of the east window, where a figure of our Lord in a large cloak, is depicted in similar action.

THE FONT.

Much has been written in the Transactions of the Bristol and Gloucester Archaeological Society and elsewhere regarding the font and expressing the most conflicting ideas about its age. It has already been stated that the bowl of the font, of late Norman work, was found (in 1850), inverted on the top of the well cover, and restored to its proper place in 1862.[1] It is of very rough workmanship, being carved in

---

[1] A new font had been put in the church in 1771, made by Mr. Bryan, costing £2 7s. 0d. (Churchwardens' Account).

hard rag-stone, and it has a basketwork moulding round the rim and a cable moulding round its base, between which is a nine inch depth of carved work. It is remarkable for its attempts at an early form of fleur de lis, which is developed into a double florescence. In the somewhat random arrangement next to the fleur de lis a cable moulding separates them from a squared space occupied by two interlaced vesica piscis, next to which is a roundel containing a four-lobed flower ; another square is filled with basket-work. Within the bowl there is a unique feature, namely, two fish carved lying at the bottom, which Mr. St. Clair Baddeley thinks may represent a seal and a salmon.

Of the pedestal of the font it is imperative to state that it is absolutely modern, and it was carved by the Rev. T. Meyrick of Corpus Christi College, Oxford, in imitation of old work. As he was an amateur in sculpture, given a piece of similar stone he undertook to produce something that would not clash with the original work, and he chose the subjects of the Good Shepherd and the Disciples drawing the net with fishes. His imitation of ancient work has been so successful as to deceive many experts.[1]

The base on which the pedestal stands is modern. (see plate 9)

THE NORTH AISLE.

The walls of the North aisle had to be rebuilt and lowered so as to receive the new lean-to roof. Three new windows were inserted in this aisle, though two of the old hood mouldings and jambs of the former windows were re-used : that in the West wall is new. If any of the tracery was preserved and used again according to the specification, it is hardly possible to distinguish it after being re-tooled by modern workmen.

All the carved corbels in this aisle are ancient. One near the organ depicts an angel playing a musical instrument, and

---

[1] This was attested by Canon Keble and his daughter in the Parish Magazine in 1897. The stonemason who prepared the stone for Mr. Meyrick, is still living in Bisley (1933).

N

on the South side of the aisle six other corbels support the principal roof timbers.

1 and 2.   A grotesque man.
3.   An angel with an escutcheon (plain).
4.   A man with his hands under his chin.
5.   An angel with an escutcheon (plain).
6.   A bishop with his hands hanging down.

The most remarkable of the corbels, though, is that at the West end of the North side of this aisle, which represents a Saxon King, with the characteristic forked beard and low crown of that period, holding a sceptre or spear in his left hand, and something that has been broken off in his right hand.   Seen in a good evening light this corbel appears extraordinarily life-like, and is obviously a portrait, the right side of the face showing a sunk cheek where the original lacked teeth.   It has the appearance of Saxon work, and may very possibly be a relic of the Saxon church.   (Fig. 3).

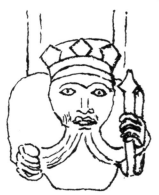

Fig. 3.—CORBEL OF THE SAXON KING.

The north door occupies the same position as formerly. Fixed along the wall of this aisle is a series of twelve stone coffin lids, some being whole and some only portions. These had been found in the roof of the aisle, cut up, reversed, and utilized for gutters in the rebuilding of Edward II's time. Numbering this series from the East end, and having obtained the opinion of Miss I. M. Roper on the subject, the following dates may be suggested.   (Fig. 4).

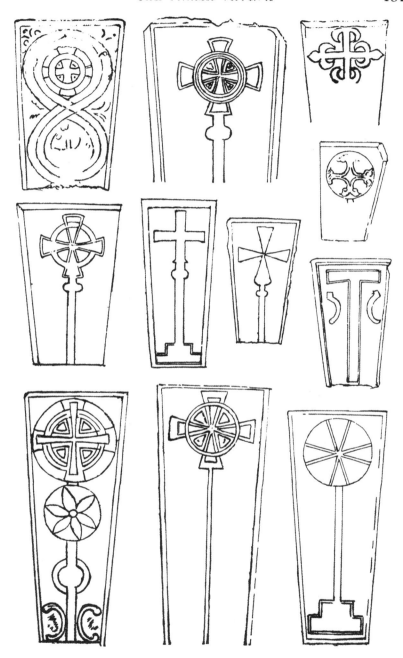

Fig. 4.—INCISED COFFIN LIDS.

No. 1, is considered to be like Irish examples of the eleventh century, and this may have been possible through the intercourse with Ireland maintained by the Mortimers and De Verdons.

No. 2, which is very rough in workmanship, the stone being of the same kind as that of the font bowl might possibly be Saxon, " as the ornamentation is not unlike that found on a fibulae unearthed from a Saxon burying ground at Banbury, Oxon." But as Saxon slabs are very rare, this suggestion is only tentative.

Nos. 3 and 4 are probably eleventh century, because the six-rayed star or flower is common in Norman work.

Nos. 5 to 12 may be assigned to the twelfth century.

No. 9, would appear to have covered the coffin of a person of great stature, being seven foot six inches in length, but the extraordinary narrowness of one foot eleven inches at the head, tapering to one foot three and a half inches at the foot, raises the question as to whether it could possibly have been for the tomb of a man, or was it for an abnormally tall woman ?

THE SOUTH AISLE.

This aisle was found to be in such a ruinous state in 1862 that its walls had to be taken down to the ground level, being rebuilt on the old foundations and of the same thickness, and with preservation of part of the plinth.

This aisle had been disfigured with an outside stone staircase leading up over the roof of the porch to an entrance to a pew in a gallery. At the east end of the aisle the later Chantry chapel had been formed, entered under a much decayed arch, on the east side of which the Early English scalloped corbels (now in the south porch) appear to have supported short columns and brackets, from which it is thought a groined roof sprang. Portions of the reredos and groin stones discovered and preserved in the arch leading to the rood-loft, enabled Mr. Lowder to reproduce in a sketch some idea of what the chapel had been. That there was a statue of our Lady in the chapel we learn from the will of John Free, who in 1546 bequeathed " To our Lady's Image 12d. To the maintenance of the Church lights and the bells a bushell of wheat."[1]

The east window of the chapel was of the early perpendicular period. It has been replaced with a new window, but with the trefoil headed internal hood, with a round moulding and carefully restored corbels, which formerly covered a window in the south wall.

The piscina which is placed in the south wall near the porch in a position usually occupied by a holy water stoup, was probably removed from the Chantry chapel at the restoration.

THE TOWER.

The tower, entered from the nave through a lofty arch of the time of Edward II, and now enclosed by a screen erected in memory of parishioners who fell in the Great War, was filled with a gallery for singers and organ. At the restoration a new approach was made to the upper floor by external steps, the west window was repaired and the west door renewed. A new floor resting on the old corbels was provided for the belfry, its joists being formed of some carved beams from the old Perpendicular roof, having several figures laid along them, holding shields, whilst on the bosses the Stafford knot, foliage, and a large M embracing a C and I and enclosed by feathers can be seen. The stone louvres were removed from the belfry, and replaced by glazed windows, but the stone louvres of the windows above the belfry were preserved and repaired.

The spire which is such a notable landmark in the neighbourhood (the Church standing on a plateau 784 feet above sea level), has required frequent repairs, in 1795, 1829, 1896, and again in 1933.

[1] Gloucester Probate Registry.

THE BELLS.

The Church formerly had only six bells, which were recast in 1747 by Abraham Rudhall, of Gloucester. His bill, paid in 1748 amounted to £64 12s. 4d. John Baker charged £24 15s. 0d. for hanging them, the carriage backwards and forwards and candles costing £4 15s. 6d. " To Matthias Welch for Lime and for carriage of the little Bell to and from Gloucester, and for John Panting's journey to Gloucester to weigh the new bells, 14s."

During the incumbency of Stephen Phillips, junr. much was done to the Church. In 1770 Richard Baker, junr., made a new Ringing loft and singing gallery, £10 8s. 9d. In 1788, there were expenses about " dialls ", each time being 5s., the second time being for ropes for the clock, and letters, etc. " Stephen Dangerfield for halling Dialls to Gloucester and back again, 12s. 6d. To Mr. William Hardwicke, Gloucester, new painting the dialls, £5 5s. 1d. To Joseph Baker for taking down and putting up the Dialls £1 11s. 6d. Repairing them 16s. 6d." In 1794, Mr. Brown provided new Dialls for £3 3s. 0d., and the clock was cleaned. The bell wheels required repair again in 1800 at a cost of £2 12s. 9d., and all the iron work of the bells, 4s.[1]

The following are the inscriptions on the bells, which were increased in number to eight in 1864, one only (no. 3) of those of Abraham Rudhall's casting being recast at that time.

No. 1. Holiness to the Lord. Cast by John Warner and Sons, London. 1864.

No. 2. Angels music heard beyond the Stars. Cast by John Warner & Sons. 1864.

No. 3. Peace and good neighbourhood. 1864.

No. 4. Prosperity to this parish. A. R. 1748.

No. 5. William Taylor, Esq., and Thomas Rogers, Church Wardens. A. R. 1748.

No. 6. William Seval and Thomas Hancock, Church Wardens. A. R. 1747.

No. 7. Stephen Phillips, Vicar. A. R. 1748.

---

1 Churchwardens' Accounts.

No. 8. I to the Church the living call and to the grave
do summon all. A. R. 1748.

There are two special occasions recorded in the tower
when the beauty of the Bisley bells rang over the countryside
for some hours, namely, on 22 May, 1899, when the Society
of Bisley change ringers rang Holt's Tenpart peal of Grand-
sire's Triples 5940 changes in three hours seven minutes, and
on 16 March, 1912, when the Ancient Society of Painswick
youths and the G. and B. Association of change ringers rang
Mr. J. Parker's one part peal of Grandsires Triplets 5040
changes in two hours fifty-nine minutes.

In the tower the many monuments of the old Church were
collected at the restoration and affixed to the walls, largely
deprived of their florid marble embellishments (which were
broken up and placed under the new floor of the Church).
In some cases the monuments are placed so high up that it is
impossible to read their inscriptions.[1]

The Royal arms, recently rehung on the tower wall in the
nave are of the time of George III.

The stained glass windows are all modern. If there was
any ancient stained glass in the old Church, it was removed
by the contractors, but enquiries on the subject have met
with no success. Some of the Bisley glass found its way to a
Gloucester dealer, but whether stained or not is not now
ascertainable. In the Chancel the east and south windows
bear no inscription but the north window was dedicated by
John Edward and Susan Dorington to the memory of a son
in 1863.

In the north aisle the easternmost window commemorates
the marriages of the Rev. John Keble (of Hursley) and
Charlotte Clarke (sister in law of the Rev. Thomas Keble,
senr.), and of the Rev. Richard Champernowne and Elizabeth
Keble (daughter of the above Thomas Keble). The west
window of that aisle is the gift of the Freemasons.

---

[1] Bigland's History of Gloucestershire (1786), gives a list of all then existing
monuments inside and outside the Church.

The east window of the south aisle is in memory of John Edward Dorington, died 16 June, 1874, aged 88, and Susan, his wife, died 4 October, 1866, aged 72.

There is one small stained glass window in the clerestory.

THE CHURCH PLATE.

All the Church plate of Bisley is modern, the two large chalices which were in use before the restoration having been disposed of. The Chalice, Paten and Flagon of parcel gilt have the Birmingham hall mark of 1862, and the maker's mark S & Co. The Chalice stands on a six-lobed base and the knob is set with six crystals. The Paten, six inches in diameter is engraved with an Agnus Dei. The Flagon is ewer-shaped and stands twelve inches high.

There are two pewter almsplates. One is stamped with the name of Richard Going, an Agnus, and a cross crowned. The other has the stamp of Hard, with crown and rose and lion's head erased. The inscription is " Thomas Smart, Thomas Iles, Church Ward. 1696."

Another plate of pewter is marked with double crosses and inscribed MMJMM, possibly Churchwardens. The maker's mark is nearly obliterated, but may be that of George Bacon.

Nothing is known of the Pre-reformation vestments and furnishings or ornaments of the Church.

THE PARISH REGISTERS.

The registers of the Church begin in 1547 and up to 1700 are contained in one volume in excellent preservation. As far as one can tell they are complete down to the present time with the following exceptions as recorded in the registers.

" 1589. Here are many Christenings through negligence omitted." About 1598 " order was given throughout the Diocese of Gloucr for the providing of a Register Booke in parchment according to the late Canon."

No marriages are recorded in 1627, no registers at all in 1628-29-30 and 31, and only one in 1632, namely the burial of the Vicar's wife, Katherine Sedgwick.

In 1635 only two marriages are recorded.

1644. " The Christenings of the month of May was lost by reason of the troubles of the times."

1663. " By a mischance there were many names lost of this year, of baptisms. Many of the weddings were lost of this year."

1673. " Many Christenings lost this year, I know not how."

With very few exceptions no indication is given in the registers of the place of residence of those mentioned. In such a large parish with its several villages, this is a great drawback and detracts from the interest and use of the record. Also there are no notes added by the Vicars such as one finds in many registers, enhancing their historical value.

Amongst the curious Christian names of women may be noted Tibolta, Tybulla, Tiballa, Isoda. Moda, Tacita, Abisag, Annage, Culpersandy.

It has been computed from the registers that in 1548 the population of the undivided parish of Bisley was about 920, and in 1828 about 5500. In 1897 the population of the ecclesiastical parish of Bisley was about 2000.

THE CHURCHWARDENS' ACCOUNTS.

The accounts kept by the Churchwardens (Parish Book B.) afford some interesting glimpses of parochial activities from 1740 to 1827. After the renewing of the bells in 1748, Thomas Hunt was paid £2 3s. 0d. for " Doing Alter piece " in 1767. In 1771 Edward Keen was paid £30 for alterations in the Church and £15 for a new pulpit. He also made a new desk at a cost of £16 11s. 3d. and a new Vicar's seat was provided in 1772 for £3. In 1774 a curtain of 4 yards of Calaminco with binding cost 7s. 6d., and a new surplice £2 9s. 6d.

In 1777, there was a great outlay on a new cushion for the pulpit, Mr. Dawson providing the gold fringe and two gold tassels for £4 1s. 6d. Mr. Wood of Gloucester, two yards and two nails of best Ginway velvet at £1 8s. 0d. a yard, and ticking and silk for its inside case, £3 2s. 4d., with 8 lbs. 4 ozs. of feathers at 1s. 4d., 11s. 8d., and the making of the cushion by Anthony Owen, 7s. 6d. ; to Mr. Drake for ticking for the cushion, 2s. 4d., and to Mr. Harmer for glaze Holland for the outside case of the cushion 2s. 11d. :—in all, the sum of £8 8s. 3d. was expended on this one cushion.

In 1785, three shillings' worth of beer was consumed when the Church was whitewashed, and that same year new pewing cost £7 10s. 0d. In 1786, William Lidiat received £6 2s. 0d. for whitewashing the Church, and in 1787, John Baker repaired the " Alter piece, etc., £4," and Mr. Hardwick received towards " lettering the Alter peice £8." From this it may be concluded that the " Alter peice " consisted of the table of the Commandments, Creed and Lord's Prayer. Mr. Lowder mentions the removal of " battlements " of the old reredos in 1862.

Two " joynt stools " were bought for 2s. this same year, and also Joseph Baker built a gallery for the use of the Minister costing £12 6s. 0d., and Giles Franklin was paid £11 0s. 4d. for " Stone and halling for steps to the Gallery," etc.

In 1788, a new prayer book was bought from Mr. Stephen, of Cirencester, and another in 1792. In 1788, Mr. Sevill's Gallery required 22 foot of guttering 11s., and a new curtain 15s. 6d.

" Matts and green Bay Cloth " cost £1 17s. 6d. in 1790, and in 1794 the North Aisle was releaded for £9 19s. 9d. besides new timber being required.

In 1796 William Lediard rough cast the Church and white-washed it several times with other repairs amounting to £46 16s. 10d.

In 1797, the Church was again whitewashed as well as the tower both inside and out, £8 1s. 6d. In 1804 a Pitch pipe for the singers was bought, 2s. 6d., and green baize to cover the Sacrament cushions 10s. This is a significant difference from the outlay on the pulpit cushion.

The iron chest for the Church costing eight guineas was bought in 1813, and a new surplice made, also the Chancel was then newly paved, and a new " Tabel Cloth and a Napkin for the Sacrament table " were procured. In 1814, Joel Chew provided a new Bassoon costing 6 guineas.

Throughout the accounts there are frequent payments for the destruction of vermin ; in 1746 for 39 foxes, 49 hedge-hogs, and one polecat £3 1s. 6d. was paid. In 1749, 42 hedgehogs 7s., and two badgers 1s., but that same year Mr. Clissold earned 17s. for killing hedgehogs. In 1807, Robert Phelps' boys received 2s. 4d. for waging war on eight dozen sparrows and a hedgehog, and so late as 1812 Capt. Hanstead's man had fourpence for killing two hedgehogs.

The office of dog whipper was one of importance judging from the entries concerning it. John Chew had £1 as salary in that capacity in 1767 and in 1797 Isaac Stephens succeeded him. In 1800 the following entry shows that a uniform was worn :—

" March 28. Thomas Keen, dog whiper, £1 0s. 0d.

Makeing and Trimming the dog whiper

Sute of Close and Hat £2 7s. 6d."

The last entry for the payment of a Dog whipper is in 1812.

CHAPTER VII

PART 2

THE CHANTRY OF THE BLESSED MARY

The Chantry of our Lady " within the churchyard " of Bisley Church was founded by Osbert,[1] sometime vicar of Bisley, before 1274, in which year a letter is recorded in Bishop Giffard's register addressed to Thomas, rector of the " Church of Byseleya " committing to him the possessions assigned for the maintenance of divine service and the organs (organa) of praise in the chapel of the Blessed Mary of the Church of Byseleya, with the consent of Richard called the Heir, patron. Dated at Cirencester the Nones of December.

From this letter we gather that the Chantry was already built and furnished by 1274 and was placed in the custody of the Rector of the first Portion, who himself was presented by Richard de Bisley (or the Heir), then Lord of the Manor. The mention of " organs " might possibly mean part-singers, as suggested in the note to the printed register, but whether part-singers or a musical instrument, " a pair of organs " (as they were then called), it indicates a building of some importance which, in the Early English period, had been erected by its founder, and endowed in order to find a priest to celebrate in the same chapel for the founder's soul and for those of all Christian people for ever. (see plate 21)

An interesting point is, where was the original chapel? " Within the churchyard " does not necessarily mean a building separate from the church. Indeed at the last restoration of the church, the architect states that the chantry chapel was at the east end of the south aisle, but in such a bad condition, the aisle having been rebuilt in the reign of

[1] Chantry Certificate P. R. O. No. 22, 47, 1548.

Richard II, that it was impossible to preserve it.[1] Some remains of the reredos were found in an arched way in the South arcade leading to the rood loft and are still there (with possible further portions now in the Vicarage shrubbery near the gate leading into the churchyard). All this work is of much later date than the original chapel, and the east end of an aisle could hardly be the site of an important foundation, such as the Chantry. The original chapel may indeed have lain east of the aisle end, but externally, and almost as a separate building. The late E. E. canopy over what was originally the priest's door of the chancel, appears not to have been exposed to the outer air so long as the surrounding masonry, nor is it usual to have so ornate a decoration to such a doorway. Its shape irresistibly suggests that its original purpose was to enrich a tomb, though not of course, that of the figure now reposing under it.

I would suggest that the original chapel stood somewhere within the angle of the chancel and S. aisle, and that the E.E. canopy formed part of the tomb of the founder Osbert. The windows of the chancel on that side (one having been filled in at the last restoration) were of Edward II's reign, by which time the chantry chapel may have become ruinous, and therefore was reconstructed within the S. aisle.

It is not till after 1430 that the chapel is spoken of in the episcopal registers as being " within the Church."

The sketch of the chantry chapel made by the Rev. W. Lowder before it was actually demolished, but in a ruinous state, depicts the arch that separated it from the south aisle, looking through it from the east. On either side of the arch is to be seen a corbel of a much earlier date than its surroundings, which probably came from the E.E. building. Both corbels are of a rough shell pattern and are preserved in the south porch. (Fig. 5.)

The names of several of the Chantry priests have come down to us. The first known is RICHARD DE LYNTHON, who was instituted in 1285 by Bishop Giffard, on the presentation of Hugh de Mortuomari, rector of two portions of the Church of Bisley.

[1] *B. G. A. S. Trans* **v, 38.**

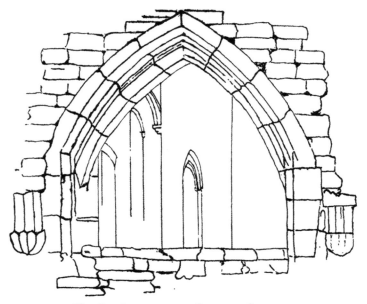

Fig. 5.—ARCH OF THE CHANTRY CHAPEL.
(From a sketch by the Rev. Wm. Lowder).

In 1316, the Chantry was vacant, and ROBERT DE CHARLTON, clerk, was admitted as chaplain, in the person of his proxy Stephen de Scottheye, at Bredon, on the presentation of Henry de Uphaven, rector of two portions of Bisley, and on the understanding that he should be admitted to all holy orders within the year.[1]

In 1376, the Chantry being vacant, THOMES PYPER was collated thereto by Bishop Wakefield on 6 July, in his chapel in London, the right of appointment having devolved on the Bishop.[2]

In 1378, JOHN EDWARD, chaplain, was presented by John Bacoun,[3] first portioner, and instituted by the Bishop, 19 March. In 1383, John Edward exchanged with the Vicar of Bisley, Robert Meriet.[4]

---

[1] Maydeston's Reg. fo. 46b.
[2] Wakefield. fo. 6b.
[3] Wakefield, fo. 30.
[4] Wakefield fo. 36.

In 1383, ROBERT MERIET was instituted by the Bishop at Hembury, 28 April. He resigned in 1385.

On 7 November, 1386, HENRY TYMBERHULLE, priest, was admitted to the Chantry in London, on the presentation of Richard Medeford, first portioner.[1]

The Chantry was again vacant in 1405, and the appointment devolving on the Bishop, he instituted JOHN GRANGER, priest, on 18 March, at his Hospice in London.[2] John Granger (or Graunger) had become vicar of Bisley in 1402,[3] had then exchanged with John Smalrugge,[4] Rector of Hywyssh, and returned to Bisley as chaplain in 1405. He died in 1409, and was succeeded by RICHARD MORE, chaplain, who on 4 December, of that year was admitted at Blockley, on the presentation of Walter Medeford, first portioner.[5]

The Chantry being vacant in 1413, JOHN TUMBRELL was instituted on 10 December, at Hyllyngden, presented by Walter Medeford,[6] but in 1416 JOHN SPEDOUR, chaplain, was instituted on 3 March " on the free resignation of RICHARD MORE, last chaplain,"[7] also on the presentation of Walter Medeford. There is no record of More's appointment, except that given above, so one does not understand how John Tumbrell intervened.

John Spedour died and on 1 April, 1428, THOMAS CULHAM, priest, was instituted, being presented by Thomas Donecan, first portioner.[8] Owing to the death of Thomas Culham in 1430, Thomas Donecan presented NICHOLAS CLYST, clerk, who was admitted 14 July, at Alvechurch.[9]

On 13 December, 1446, Bishop Carpenter issued letters of Commission to his commissary William Vauce, B. Litt. to enquire into the vacancy of the Chantry, which for the first

---

[1] Wakefield fo. 44b.
[2] Clifford fo. 88b.
[3] Clifford fo. 61.
[4] Clifford fo. 77.
[5] Peverill fo. 14.
[6] Peverill fo. 70.
[7] Peverill fo. 75b.
[8] Pulton fo. 40b.
[9] Pulton fo. 84b.

time is described as " within the Church of Bysseley," and whether the Bishop had the right to confer the same on MR. WILLIAM AMENER, chaplain, for his sustenance, who continued chaplain till his death in 1486.

Mention is, however, made in the Minister's Accounts of 27 Henry VI of one, Robert Hipkyne, Clerk of the Chantry, who, in that year, 1447-8, and the following year, paid one pound of cummin as rent for a croft called Calstoo.[1] He may have been assistant chaplain to William Amener, whose appointment " for his sustenance," suggests old age.[2]

The College of St. John Baptist, Stoke Clare, having become Rectors of the first and second Portions of Bisley, the patronage of the Chantry also fell to them, and they presented MAURICE UNWIN, chaplain, he being admitted at the Palace, Worcester, 31 August, 1486.[3] He died in 1503, and the Dean and Chapter of Stoke Clare presented JAMES LOWE, priest, on 25 October,[4] who in 1509, 21 December, became Vicar of Bisley,[5] and was succeeded at the Chantry by Roger Jonys, chaplain, who was admitted 25 January, following.[6]

At this time devotion to the " service of St. Mary of Bysseley " occasionally shows itself in bequests in wills. In that of John Grymes of 19 January, 1509-10 he bequeaths twenty pence to her service, and even so late as 1546 John Freme left twelve pence and in 1548 Richard Perryn left twenty pence for the same object.

Sir Roger Jonys was the last Chantry priest of Bisley. The Commissioners who suppressed the Chantry in 1548 state in their certificate that Roger Jonys was aged 80 years, and had no other source of income than the Chantry, valued at seventy shillings a year. The Churchwardens and parishioners had presented that the " mansion place of the Chantry

---

[1] The Sede Vacante Register p. 415 speaks of Robert Hopkyns, clerk, who was presented to Laschevington as having a chapel in the Churchyard of Bisley worth 40s.

[2] Carpenter fo. 95b.

[3] Carpenter II, fo. 260b.

[4] Silvester fo. 27b.

[5] Silvester fo. 62.

[6] Silvester fo. 62b.

priest of Bisley is in decay in the default of Sir Roger Jones." The lands and tenements belonging to the chantry are stated by the Commissioners to be worth £4, goods belonging thereto £6 0s. 8d., " catell " to the same at 41s., and plate and jewels none.[1]

THE CHANTRY HOUSE AND LAND.

The present house known as the Chantry is to be identified with the " mansion " of the original chantry priests. The oldest portion of the house, that to the right of the porch, is of great antiquity, the walls being over four feet thick. The southern aspect of the house was completely altered by Sir John Dorington, through the addition of gabled front rooms. During the alterations of that part of the house a mutilated portion of a stone crucifix showing undoubted Early English carving, was found built into the wall, and is now placed in the Church porch.

In a small sunk panel over the front door there had been a device carved and defaced beyond ordinary recognition at some time subsequent to the suppression. A bright reflected light one sunny day revealed that the device had been an Agnus Dei, facing to the sinister side, and no doubt placed there when the Chantry was granted to the College of St. John Baptist, Stoke Clare, the Agnus Dei being the symbol of that Saint.

In the grounds the ancient spring flowing into a large stone tank, the sundial across the corner of the west end of the house and three coped headstones of gateposts testify to the antiquity of the place.

Rudder states that the Chantry house and lands had belonged to the College of St. Mary, Westbury, but there is no confirmation of this statement in the Worcester Episcopal registers. On the contrary it is there stated (Carpenter Register, Vol. II) in Letters Patent of Edward IV that Richard, Duke of York, the King's father, and others, had

[1] P. R. O. Chantry Cert., No. 22, 247.

o

granted the first and second portions of Bisley Church to the College of Stoke Clare before 1428, the first portion carrying with it the patronage of the Chantry. At the suppression, the revenue of the chantry was granted to Walter Compton in 1548, according to Rudder, but the house and lands were granted to Francis Maurice and Francis Philips in trust for Anthony Cope and others in 1612-3. It appears from the will of Thomas Bowton, 10 August, 1563, that he was residing at the Chantry, the remainder of his lease being bequeathed to his widow Elizabeth, to enjoy with his son Roger. As she died in 1564, presumably Roger Bowton continued to live there alone. John Butler, of Rookwoods, in his will, dated 12 October, 1716, mentions having bought the Chantry of one, John Webb, and that it is to remain as settled on the marriage of his son Richard with his present wife. Margery, elder daughter, of William Compton, had married Edmund Webb who, in all probability was ancestor of the John Webb, owner of the Chantry. In the rates list among the Feoffees papers, Mr. Butler is at the Chantry in 1722, and in 1752, Mr. Richard Butler paid £4 5s. 6d. rates, and in the Bisley Court Roll for 1770 he is again mentioned as free tenant of the Chantry.

In the absence of ancient documents it is impossible to gather more precise information regarding the passing of the Chantry to recent times. When Mr. William Lewis was in possession of Lypiatt, from 1825-42, he appears to have owned the Chantry, which in 1841 was in the tenure of Maurice Faulkes, and it was then a farmhouse. In 1842, it passed into the possession of Samuel Baker, Esq., who, in 1847, sold it to Sir John Dorington. On the break-up of the latter's estate in 1919, it became the property of Major Drummond.

At the time of the survey of the parish of Bisley, in 1841, the Chantry farm included the following lands :—

Gascoign piece, 4-2-4, arable.

Windmill Tyning, 18-0-0.

Chestergate piece, 6-0-0.

Rough ground, 13-0-0, pasture.

Meadow, 6-0-0, pasture.

Orchard, 1–2–0, arable.

Little grounds, 2–2–0, arable.

Chantry Coppice, 4–0–0, wood.

With the suppression of the chantry and the secularisation of its revenues a most beneficent foundation came to an end after an existence of three hundred years. It was an important feature in the life of the place, and the chantry priest, who usually assisted the vicar and attended to the education of the young, must have been greatly missed by all classes.

Among the tenants, after the restoration of the Chantry House were William Miller, Esq., the Rev. J. Maude, curate of Bisley, and Miss Keyl.

CHAPTER VIII

BISLEY FEOFFEES, CHARITIES, AND SCHOOLS.

The origin of the body entitled the " Bisley Feoffees " is now unknown, owing to its great antiquity. They have held certain properties for charitable purposes from time immemorial, but the original documents connected with these estates have long since disappeared. The Rev. Stephen Phillips, in 1715, endeavoured to recover certain old deeds of the Feoffees which had been carried off by George Smart, senr., who had been one of that body, into Wiltshire, in 1692. Such deeds as Mr. Phillips, was able to recover he placed in the chest in numbered bundles, the earliest being dated 1647. He notes that Sturmye's Court, the chief property held by the feoffees (now known as Ponting's farm) was bought of one Washbourne, the first feoffments dated 2 July, 1558, and 22 April, 1566, and the next in 1615.

There is mention in the Bisley Court Rolls of courts of the Feoffees held yearly from 1413 to 1417, but, there is no special information conveyed about the properties.[1]

The full number of feoffees was originally sixteen, but the Charity Commissioners of 1853 found only five left, namely :— Edward Aldridge, Charles Ballinger, Nathaniel Hancox, Thomas Packer Butt, and Archer Blackwell.

The charitable estates were held for ever to pay a schoolmaster, the clerk, and the repairs of the Church, or to be applied to other Godly use as the feoffees might think proper, the yearly amount being then £49 10s. 5d.[2] This last clause was not allowed by the Commissioners to cover any contribution to the cost of the new organ in the Church, which amounted to £450.

[1] P. R. O. Port. 175, no. 7.

[2] I am indebted to the Rev. W. J. Clay for free access to the Feoffee's and all other parish documents.

The following list of the estates held by the Feoffees is taken from one dated 17 June, 1732. They were let on leases of three lives, until the Court of Chancery altered this to yearly tenancies.

1. An estate called Sturmye's Court, where all their tenants are obliged to meet, to pay suit and service to the said Feoffees whenever they think fit to hold a Court.

2. An estate called Stone-hing or Stonehouse at Brownshill.

3. Four acres of Wood called Church Grove or Stonage, Brownshill.

4. Church Grove near Sturmye's Court.

5. Another six acres of Church Grove with a cottage.

6. Two Hilly Grounds in the Bottom called Bidcombe.

7. One acre of Grass ground, near Sturmye's Court.

8. One acre of Pasture and two tenements.

9. A ground called Timbercombe in Fee of the Manor of Sturmye's Court.

10. A ground called Ashlands, adjoing to Bidcombe and in the Fee of the manor of Sturmye's Court.

From this list two estates emerge, namely that of Sturmey's Court, with the grounds noted from 4 to 10, and that of Stonehing at Brownshill, with its four acres of wood (No. 3.)

————

STURMYE'S COURT.

Sturmye's Court, now represented by Ponting's farm, has long since lost its manorial rights. The particulars of the estate are as follows :—

House, Barn, Stable and outhouses, Home Mead (one acre) another adjoining to the barn one acre. The Upper ground having the Common to the E. five acres. The Layings two acres. Pennymead three acres, the Hill three acres, Wood ground five acres, Lower ground five acres,—total 25 acres.

The earliest deed preserved concerning this estate of 4 November, 1647, relates that by an Indenture of lease of 1626, Sturmye's Court situated in Aveniss was devised to William Restell to hold to him, his wife and son. Their rights were apparently foregone, for on 4 November, 1647, this estate, "lying in Abenesse" with the wood called the Church Hill, before granted to William Stephens, and another part granted to William Blisse, and anciently belonging to the manor of Sturmye's Court, were granted to Samuel Shepherd of the parish of Bisley, gentleman. It is probable that he lived at Sturmye's Court, which in 1711 is described as a "mansion or dwelling-house, with a great courtyard," a little outhouse situate eastwards, and the little courtyard and orchard lying on the South side. Foundations of some large buildings can be traced behind the site of Ponting's farm, which probably belonged to the old house.

After Samuel Shepherd's decease, Philip Shepherd, of Minchinhampton, Esq., his son, in 1684, assigned the remainder of the lease to Thomas Hurdon (or Harndon), broadweaver, whose daughter, Sarah, married James Ponting. Thomas Hurdon died in 1704,[1] and after passing through several hands, Sturmye's Court was let to Nathaniel Damsell in 1714 : the latter sold his rights to James Ponting (or Panting), in 1733. This was confirmed by the Feoffees who already in 1732 had let to John Panting broadweaver, a pasture land at Dimallsdale, on condition that on some part of the premises he should erect before 25 March, 1734, a messuage 24 ft. by 14 ft. by 14 ft. high, (the Feoffees allowing the materials of the old house), and this he had done by 1736. In 1784 this cottage was let to Thomas Matthews.

The name of Ponting or Panting[2] first occurs in the registers on the occasion of the marriage of William Ponting to Alice Sheete, 17 August, 1622, and throughout the seventeenth and eighteenth centuries the name is repeatedly found. The family appears to have prospered, for William Ponting, who died in 1688, is described as gentleman in one document.

---

[1] Will, Glos. P. R., also tomb in the churchyard.

[2] In Gloucestershire dialect o is usually pronounced a, hence variations in spelling.

John Panting, who died in 1729 (weaver), left to John Panting, his son, his messuage in Aveniss, known as Barns, with all the closes and groves of wood belonging, paying to his son, Thomas Panting, £3 10s. 0d. per annum for life.   To his son, Thomas Panting, the house wherein he now dwells when twenty-one, or failing that £40.   It was the son John, who rented the land in Dimallsdale.[1]

James Panting, baker, died 29 November, 1765, aged 79, his wife, Sarah, dying 25 February, 1769.[2]   In 1767, after the death of James Ponting, Sarah, his widow, held Sturmye's Court, part of the premises containing four acres lately woodland, but now grubbed up and converted into arable land, and together with the acre in Dimallsdale this estate was confirmed to her during the lives of William Hall and John Hall, sons of William Hall, of Hankerton Wilts., yeoman, and Thomas Shuring, son of Mark Shuring, of Hankerton, carpenter.

In 1747, the Feoffees had leased Bidcombe's to James Panting for 99 years. In 1771, Bidcombes, lately held by John Panting, deceased, was let to William Davis, of France Lynch, yeoman, during the lives of himself, Mary, his wife, and William, his son.   Part of Bidcombe's had been purchased by the Feoffees from Edmund Clutterbuck about 1771, and in 1783 it was leased to John Innell for seven years.

In 1719, the Feoffees let the western moiety of their Common wood ground known as Church Hill, lately occupied by John Sevill and also one cottage sometime since built on the said Common wood, lately occupied by Peter Clissold, to Thomas Westmacott of Chalford, whose widow, Ann, devised these premisses to Gabriel Clissold, in 1729, and in 1732 Joseph Clissold had a lease of the same for his own life, that of his wife Ann, and of William Tayloe, junr.

The eastern moiety of the Common wood, or Church Hill, formerly in the possession of Philip Shepherd, with the cottage, was leased to Rebecca Kerby in 1731 for 99 years, but it was again with the Feoffees who assigned it to Mr. John

---

[1] Glos P. R.

[2] A brass to their memory is in the Church tower, Bisley.

Haines, of Duntisborn Rous, gentleman, in 1773. Finally in 1797 it was assigned to Mr. John Walker. With this date the available documents end. The name of the Church Hill or Church Grove in Aveniss may indicate, as in the case of Stonehing at Brownshill, the existence of a Church or Chapel in old days in that locality, or it may simply have received the name as being Church property. There is no tradition to guide one to a solution of the origin of the name.

THE ESTATE OF STONEHING OR STONEHOUSE AT BROWNSHILL.

This estate appears to have been in the possession of the Feoffees from very early times and there are evidences of great antiquity to be found in or near the present farm buildings. The name of Stonehinge or Stonehouse has ceased to be known, but it is so named in the terrier of 1732 and in an Indenture of 1740. There was a family known as de Stonehenge residing here at the end of the thirteenth century and throughout the fourteenth when their names occur as witnesses to many of the deeds connected with the Corpus Christi property at Chalford. Robert de Stonhenge is the earliest, in 1291.[1] John de Stonheng appears in the Court rolls of 1354, and William de Stonehenge of the parish of Bysele was ordained in 1374.

It appears probable, from the name of Church Hill attached to the old lane leading up from the valley, as also that of Church Grove to the former wood, that a church or chapel existed here from Saxon times, on a site lying east and west within the grounds of Tanglewood (now Templewood) where there are indications of a building having an apse and south aisle. Many stones of ancient working have been dug up in the grounds or may be seen built into the Feoffees' farm buildings and walls near by, the greatest proof of an ecclesiastical building being a portion of an Early English

---

[1] *B. G. A. S. Trans.*, li, 213, 223-4.

holy water stoup, with a cross carved on it, which was here found. A pair of possibly Saxon windows are now in the south end of the barn, and the masses of stone lying about, and utilized in neighbouring walls indicate the destruction of some large building.

Before Tanglewood was built, there was an ancient house on that site with very thick walls, besides a length of very solid foundations, and an ancient well with steps, now covered over. If there was indeed a chapel of Saxon or even later foundation the adjoining estate of the Feoffees is accounted for as glebe land attached to it.

The terrier of 1732 describes the estate in detail as follows. " An estate called Stonehing or Stonehouse at Brownshill now in possession of Mr. Thomas Keble wch he holds by Lease of 99 years or three Lives, viz. himself, his wife, and Anne, his daughter bearing date . . . at ye yearly rent of £12 . . . upon wch there is a house, barn, stable, malthouse, etc. An orchard ½ acre, The Paddock, 1 acre Broad Lease 4 acre. The uppr ground Arable near Mrs. Parker W. 4 acre. A piece bounded by ye Road W. ye wood S. 3 acre. The Hill 7 acre. Sharley, Mr. Waltr Ridlers W. Highway N., Brook Thomas E. 4 acre. Two half Acres in Westfeild near ye Tump (bounded by) Blisse's and Aldridge W. (by ye path and hedge N.) Road N. and Mr. Mills E. 1 acre.

24½ acres.

He likewise holds 4 acres of wood called Church Grove or Stonage by a Lease of 99 years or 3 Lives, viz., Thomas Beale Dead, James, son of Mat. Beale and Wm., son of Geor. Beale at 20s. pr. an.

All Oak Ash and Elmm reserved to ye parish, bounded by ye highway N.W. and S. and by Jos. Mayors East which Lease is dated February 2d., 1714."

A second account adds that Mr. White leased Stonehing before Thomas Keble and that Samuel Web succeeded him, both the former being dead by 1740.

Thomas Keble came from Southropp, perhaps on his marriage with Mary, daughter of William Tayloe, of Chalford, and his daughter, Anne, was baptised at Bisley 11 August, 1704, his son, Thorway, 30 July, 1707, his daughter, Mary, 25 August, 1708, and his son, William, 27 September, 1709, after which there is no further mention of the name in the eighteenth century.

In 1708, the Feoffees had let to John Coxe, of North Cerney, clerk, and Charles Coxe, Esq., of Lincoln's Inn, (later of Lower Lypiatt), Stonehing with the two and a half acres of arable lying in the Westfield of Bisley (the Common holding attached to this property). The Church Grove of six acres having been let separately to Thomas Beale, clothier, in 1714, the whole estate by 1740 was surrendered to the Feoffees who confirmed it to Samuel Webb, whose widow was in possession in 1744 according to the terrier of that date. The terrier of 1750 makes the Church Grove to be seven acres and twenty perches, and the Little Grove one acre and thirty two perches, and it is now impossible to identify the exact site of the wood, but the rick barton mentioned in this terrier appears to have been that on the East side of the bridle path leading up from Brimscombe, and probably the Church Grove covered the site of the supposed chapel and beyond it eastwards. The Sharley at this date has the note " part of this now in the New river " or canal.[1]

On 12 May, 1748, Edward Gregory had an Indenture of lease from the Feoffees, renewed to his son Thomas on 29 September, 1761.[2] The Gregorys gave their name to the hilly ground below the bridle path leading down to Brimscombe, which was for long known as Gregory's Hill. Edward Gregory was a baker and maltster, and died 19 June, 1750 ; his son, Thomas, following the same occupations, was Reeve in 1770. The latter died in February, 1787, his will being dated 27 January, of that year. To his wife, Eleanor Gregory, he leaves all the household furniture standing in the room over the Hall. To Sarah Coopey, servant, £3. To Edward, son of Edward Gregory, his brother, All that piece or parcel

---

[1] The remainder of the Sharley or Charlea was let to the Parish Council in 1922 for allotments. It lies below the G.W.R. station at Brimscombe.

[2] The name of Gregory appears at Colcombe (Cowcombe) in the Corpus Christi College deeds of 1304. *B. G. A. S. Trans.*, li, 220, 224.

of land called or known by the name of the Park with appurtenances thereto belonging or used situate lying and being on Bisley Common . . . All the rest of his goods, chattels, cloath, stock in trade, securities for money and personal estate to his brother, Edward Gregory, whom he appoints sole executor. W. Martha Randell, Richard Drew, Daniel Witts.[1]

All the children of both Thomas and Edward Gregory (II) died in infancy and with the death of the latter in 1814, aged 71, the name seems to have died out at Bisley.[2]

The available documents of the Feoffees cease with the Indenture of 1787, but the title deeds of Firwood, Brownshill, number amongst them a lease dated 5 April, 1794, from Joseph Cullurne, Surgeon and apothecary, who then owned Firwood (otherwise Paggonshill) and had acquired the lease of Stonehing after the Gregorys. He let Stonehing to William Bryan, yeoman, who remained as tenant to the Feoffees till 1809, Cullerne having become bankrupt in 1794.

In 1816, the " Old House " and farm were repaired, and in 1823 William Tayloe became tenant.

In 1845, the house of Stonehing was known as the Barley Mow, a Public house kept by Mr. Crook. Since then it has been a private residence and is now known as the Vines.

A new house built on their property by the Feoffees was rented by William Winn, clothier, in 1813. He died in 1816.

THE CHARITIES OF BISLEY.

Next in age to the two ancient estates administered for charitable purposes by the Feoffees is the gift by Mr. Thomas Butler, clothier, in 1688, of 10s. for a sermon, and £1 for a distribution of bread to the poor annually on Easter Monday.

[1] Glos. P. R.

[2] Tombstone in Bisley Churchyard. Thomas Gregory's sister Mary married Ralph Randle. (Title deeds of Thanet Ho., Chalford).

It appears from the will of John Butler, senior, of Rook-woods, (father of Thomas Butler), dated 1716, that his son, Thomas, in his last sickness had desired him to establish this charity, and this he had done and confirmed in his will, leaving to his son, Richard, " all his Upper Coppice wood with ground there lying in Calfway wood subject to the payment of 30s. yearly during soe long time as the Church of England as now Established by Law shall remain and continue."

In 1697, Walter Ridler, clothier, gave by will dated 10 May, £300, to the poor of Bisley.

In 1715, Mrs. Joan Ridler, sister of Walter Ridler, also left £300 to the poor.

In 1715, Mrs. Mary Ridler ordered Thomas Ridler, Esq., her executor to give the interest of £100 to " our parish if we would agree to apply ye interest of ye two last legacyes to ye teaching of poor children in ye said parish. It was, therefore agreed by ye Parishioners with ye consent and approbation of ye Family of ye Ridlers on Easter Munday, 2 April, 1716, yt ye Intrst of ye sd monyes should for ye future be applyed to ye instructing of Children and buying Bibles and other good books for them."

In 1734, Mr. Samuel Allen gave a house and orchard in King's Stanley and land near Calfway, now let at £6 2s. 0d., the Calfway land being two acres let at three guineas per annum—for clothing for poor widows yearly.

Mrs. Mary Barksdale gave £80 to which the parish added £20 and purchased therewith lands near the Holloways now let at £5. This charity is annually distributed in linen cloth, as is also the charity given by Mr. William Wise, namely £60 to purchase ground near Avenis Green, called Ridings, and let at £3. The parish also possesses a piece of arable land of five acres which was let to several tenants at £11 15s. 0d., to which was added 7s. per annum by the turnpike Road Commissioners.

Charles Ballinger of Chalford, by will dated 24 June, 1798, gave his two shares in Stroud Navigation in trust to be divided between Bisley and Chedworth and the minister of France meeting, Bisley (not being Baptist or Methodist), who, if he held no services for one month, lost the benefaction, and then it was all to go to the Churchwardens. The object of this charity was to purchase coarse woollen cloth to be made into garments for the poor of Bisley and Chedworth.

Theyer Townsend, of Steanbridge, Esq., by his will of 1 July, 1801, gave £100 to Bisley, the interest of 40s. to be spent on bread to be distributed yearly on St. Thomas' day by the minister and churchwardens.

The Charity Commissioners also found that the parish had £663 in 3 per cent. Consols, not explained.[1]

THE SCHOOLS.

The first mention of a school at Bisley is in 1662, when Richard Blake, who was formerly licensed to teach at Cirencester, was licensed to teach in the parish of Bisley. In 1686, John Tayler, literate, was licensed to teach children in the free school of Bisley. He was succeeded by James Owen in 1702 and John Wall in 1703.

By his will dated 19 January, 1732, John Taylor, of the parish of Stroud devised to William Jayne of Frampton, William Townsend of Steanbridge, James Winchcombe of Stroud, and Duncombe Colchester, in trust, all his lands and tenements in Upton St. Leonards, after the death of his mother Mary Taylor, for the teaching of ten poor boys in the parish of Bisley, to read English and write, and also to clothe them yearly for ever ; if the funds allowed of a surplus, this was to be used to teach and clothe a greater number of poor boys. This was the origin of the Bisley Blue school.

In 1817, the Upton St. Leonards property was surveyed and found to consist of some houses, a farm house and about 32 pieces of land of a total area of 32 acres 3 roods and 14 perches, let then, with a cottage at £55 10s. 0d. In 1820 it was found the rent was five years in arrears and trust duties

---

[1] Charity Commissioners' Report. See also the Church Tables now in the Vestry.

had been neglected. In 1863, the whole estate was sold by auction and realized £2641 19s. 1d. After various re-adjustments new investments brought in an income of £152 (in 1928).

In 1821, it is recorded that the Free school had a spacious and commodious schoolroom and that the master, who was appointed by the Blue School trustees, received £12 12s. 0d. per annum for teaching ten Blue school boys. In 1824 £18 6s. 6d. was spent on their clothing. The blue cloth of which the suits were made cost 8s. 6d. a yard, a pair of boots 8s., making the suits 9s. each,[1] and the distinctive caps and stockings. 3s. 6d.

The rules provided that no scholar should be admitted to the school unless he brought a certificate of his baptism ; that regular daily attendance was required and whoever absented himself without leave, forfeited his clothes and was dismissed from the school, his continuance at school depending on good behaviour.

In 1821, the master taught boys to read and write, and the Church Catechism and brought them to Church on Sunday.

By 1833, the income of the charity had increased so much that eighteen boys were clothed and educated, and the master was paid £15.

In 1902, the Education Act altered everything, elementary education being made compulsory and free, so no further salary was paid to the school master, but clothing was given to ten boys by the trustees.

Further interference by the Board of Education took place in 1915, and Bisley lost one of its most picturesque features with the abolition of the distinctive Blue School uniform. The income was then assigned to six scholarships of £20 a year, to boys from Elementary Schools of the Ancient parish of Bisley and who were examined by the Head Master of Marling School, which the successful competitors attend till they are sixteen. After paying the school fees, the balance, about £6, is given to the parents for clothing and travelling expenses of the boys. There is a further £20 yearly laid out

---

[1] Churchwardens' Accounts.

in boots for boys elected by the managers of the various day schools of the parish. The trustees now consist of nine persons.

There is a letter extant amongst the Lypiatt deeds from Nathaneal Rogers to Mr. Henry Pecket, Drugist, of Great Compton Street, London, of 21 May 1781, referring to the ruinous state of Bisley school roof, which was thought to belong to Mrs. Pecket, and the lower part to the parish, but whether this was so does not appear.

The Rev. Thomas Keble, senr., carried out the re-building and enlargement of the School, part of which now stands on ground given out of the Overcourt estate by the Rev. E. Pyddoke, who was largely instrumental in providing funds for the building also.

There were said to be several schools in 1717, erected for children between five and six years of age, at which schools above 160 children attended and nearly 450 bibles had been distributed besides expositions of the Catechism and other good books.

In 1804, there was in existence the Sunday Institution, and the boys who attended Church and behaved well, received a cloth jacket. There is an entry in the Churchwardens' Accounts at that date :—" Thomas Jones, for 100 yards cloth for Boys attending Church and their good behaviour, £30 0s. 0d. Paid for the making and trimming of 100 jackets from the above cloth for the Boys £17 10s. 0d." In " 1805, 20 September, James Mayo, for makeing the boys' Cloath, £11 8s. 0d. 24 December, Mr. Charles Innell, for the Cloth which made 80 coats for the Boys of the Sunday Institution as Rewards for good Behaviour, 81 yards at 6s. 6d., £26 6s. 6d."

In 1806. " Payment to S. Jenner, for Books, etc., for the use of Bisley Sunday Institution which though patronized by the Magistrats and principals of the parish is now no more. £16 6s. 8d." Although this well-intentioned effort failed for the time being, the Sunday Institution was revived in a better form as the Sunday School which was such a strong feature of the religious revival during the incumbencies of the two Kebles.

BISLEY WORKHOUSE.

On the 24 March, 1725, a meeting of the vestry was called to secure a building suitable for a workhouse at Bisley, subscriptions amounting to £300 having been already raised for that purpose. An agreement with Mr. John Mills, the owner of a house called Joiners, was made 24 May, 1725, as follows :—

" We whose names are herewith subscribed being met at a vestry legally called to raise money to erect a workhouse to imploy ye poor, or hire a house to ye same purpose, do agree with Mr. John Mills to pay him £14 pr. an. for ye building called Joiners and the ground thereunto adjoining with ye consent of Mrs. Deborah Mills for her life, the fee simple of ye same to be wholy in ye parish of Bisley after her death."[1]

This was signed by John Mills, and by John Stephens, Stephen Philips, Edw. Turner, Thos. Smart, Wm. Tayloe, Thos. Jayne, Nathl. Hancox, John Snow, Peter Clissold, John Cooke, Willm. Mayzee, Henry Stephens, Thomas Randell, John Panting, Samll. Damsell and John Moss.

Joiners, which is still remembered in " Joiners Lane " which leads from the Chantry to the present high road and the old Holloway, lay on the upper side of that lane, adjoining the grounds of the Mansion. It is mentioned in the Court roll of 5 September, 1601, when James Keene, who held Joyners of the Lady Queen, came to the Court and surrendered the reversion into her hands. It was at that time in the tenure of Robert Sollers. Though secured by the vestry in 1725-6, at the Court Baron of 1736 Richard Champion is named as free tenant for Joyners (amongst other properties), and in 1770 Edmund Clutterbuck, gentleman, is so named for Palls (otherwise Paulmead or the Mansion) and for Joiners, but the house continued to be used as the workhouse till the formation of the Stroud Union in 1837, when Joiners was pulled down. Its situation was unhealthy, standing as it did in a deep depression, with the stream that flows from the wells close beside it.

---

[1] Deborah Mills died in 1754, her monument being in the Churchyard.

The Workhouse was opened on 12 April, 1726, with ten inmates, and on the 19th many parishioners met there to arrange about the " butting and boundings " of the ground and to make rules regarding the inmates, one being that if verminous they " shall be stript of their Nauseous rags and new clothed."

In 1738, the vestry ordained that the Governor of the workhouse was to provide some meat for " our poor," such as they shall think convenient, three times every week, on Sundays, Tuesdays, and Thursdays, for their dinner. On Mondays, Wednesdays, and Fridays, the broth yt was made with the meat the day before was to be thickened with some oatmeal or Flowr for their dinners, and on Saturdays they were to have some milk victuals for their dinners in the summertime, and in winter some Onyon Pottage, or some pease, and some small beer with their victualls every day. The sick were to have such things as were convenient. Bread and small beer were to be provided every day for breakfast and supper, but there was to be no supper for those who swear or curse, or behave disorderly, or break open a gate. The workhouse in 1731 had an average of thirty inmates, the cost per head being 1s. 3½d. per week, without work, or about 11¼d. when the work is deducted.

On the whole the treatment of the inmates appears to have been more humane than in many workhouses; they at least had beds to lie on, which some houses had not. But the records of the house are pathetic reading. Frequent outbreaks of smallpox and fever occurred, especially in 1726 and 1727, 1731 and 1738, and it was not till 1779, that a separate house for the treatment of these cases was provided, namely the Pest House at Oakridge. The walls of Joiners housed a sad mass of human misery and disease, from which death offered the sole means of escape. Nature does her best each returning spring to clothe their nameless graves in the Church yard above with a beautiful covering of snowdrops, type of that purity and innocence which was so sadly lacking in the lives of many. Requiescant in pace.

P

CHAPTER IX

PART 1

THE MANOR OF OVER LYPIATT.

The Manor of Over Lypiatt is first indicated in the charter of Hugh, Earl of Chester, in the reign of King John, bestowing upon Humphrey de Bohun that part of his manor of Bisley which is covered by Lypiatt, Bussage, Chalford, Thrupp, Stroud and Paganhill (see Chapter II.) In the reign of Henry III, the Earl of Chester is stated to hold of the King in 1234 within the Hundred of Bisley :—

> " In Lip'pegat Rici IIIJ caruc '
> In Lopegat Henr' IIJ caruc ' "[1]

Unfortunately there is no information as to who these tenants then holding Lypiatt might be, but towards the end of the thirteenth century Alexander de Duntisbourne granted the manor for life to William Maunsell, as stated in the ensuing Inquisition P.M. of the latter in 1324.[2]

" Inquisition taken at Lupeyate before John de Hampton the King's eschaetor in Co. Glos. Wednesday the feast of St. James the . . April, 1324 (18 Ed. II.) by oath of John de Averynge, Richard Bynng, Nicholas de Seymer, Richard the Clerk of Paganhill, Henry de Stretford, Henry le Fermer, John Nugaz, Nicholas de Chircheye, Henry Allrich, Richard Perisson, John de Frompton and Henry Bateckok. They said :—

" William Maunsell on the day he died did not hold any lands and tenements in the said county in his demesne as of fee, but he held the manor of Lupeyate of the grant of Alexander de Dontesburne for the term of his life by fine

---

[1] Testa de Nevill, Glos., 19 Henry II, p. 79.
[2] Inq. P. M., *B. G. A. S. Trans.*, ii, 189.

levied between them in the court of the lord the King in which said fine it is contained that the said Manor of Lupeyate shall remain to William, son of the said William Maunsell and to the heirs of his body begotten after the death of the said William Maunsell, to be held of the chief lords of that fee by the services which belong to the said manor.

There is a certain court with houses and gardens which is worth p. a. 5s. 4d., One dovecote which is worth p. a. 40d., and underwood which is worth p. a. 10s. There are 192 acres of arable land which are worth p. a. 32s., price per acre 2d., also 6 acres of meadow which are worth p. a. 9s., price of acre 18d. Also 6 acres of several pasture, which are worth p. a. 5s. price per acre 6d. The pleas and perquisites of the court are worth p. a. 40d. sum 66s.

There are there 36 free tenants, who pay p. a. £12 12s. 0d. ; also four natives who pay p. a. 60s. for all services. Sum £15 12s. 6d. Sum of the whole value of the said manor £18 18s. 6d.

The said manor of Lupeyate is held of the Earl of Hereford by the service of one knight's fee by homage and fealty and suit at the court of the said Earl at Gloucester from month to month.

The said William Maunsell held in Byseleye of Joan de Bohun one vivary, six acres of land and three acres of wood, by service of 30s. p. a., and they are worth nothing per annum besides the said rent.

William, son of the said William Maunsell, is his next heir and is aged 30 years."

The vivary here mentioned is that known as the Fishpond at Todsmore, with its wood in Deptcombe, which has always gone with the Lypiatt estate until that estate was broken up in 1919. It has not been generally known that the Fishpond is of such ancient origin.

It is apparent from the entries in the Lypiatt MS. book in which are recorded abstracts of the ancient deeds which have long since disappeared, that the boundary between the manors of Bisley and Lypiatt is marked by the very ancient stone standing beside the high-road near Stancombe Ash.

This stone was for centuries known as the " Lord's Stone " being so mentioned in the Lypiatt MS. book under the date 1654, and it is again referred to by that name in the seventeenth century. At the Court Baron of Mrs. Anne Stephens, of 13 October, 1724, the homage presented " the Stone near Stancombe Ash to be the out-bounds of the manor of Over Lypiatt towards Bisley, and doe order the Lady of the Manor to fix a Mere Stone by it." There is no reason to doubt that it has always stood as the boundary mark between the two manors, and it was significant that its most richly carved front faced towards Bisley, evident even as it stood tilted in its late neglected condition. The zeal and care of those interested in its preservation have again set the stone upright and surrounded it with a railing, but unfortunately it is now facing the road, so that its ancient significance has been obscured.   (see plate 11)

Much has been written about this stone by Mr. St. Clair Baddeley[1] and there have been various conjectures as to its age and origin. On the front, (in spite of its weather-worn condition) the figure of a saint with uplifted arms standing beneath a round arch, is traceable. Conjecture as to the six holes on this side has been rife, but they were probably the plug holes for an iron plate as the stone appeared to have been used as a milestone in later times, and as an indication of the limits of Bisley parish in that direction, being marked with a comparatively modern " B.P."

The south side of the stone also has the figure of a saint, probably the Blessed Virgin Mary, under a round arch.

Careful study leads to the opinion that it never was an actual cross, and that it is not to be confused with the Cross which stood at the corner of the Cross field, near Fennells' Cottages, beside the ancient road from Painswick which led into the old approach to Lypiatt house, still marked by the gateway in the Park wall. The charter of Humphry de Bohun which is about to be recorded mentions that cross as "the cross of Mary," which was destroyed in the early nineteenth century. It is possible that the base of its

---

[1] *B. G. A. S. Trans*, li, 103-7.

thirteenth century shaft is that stone which is still to be seen beside the north-east approach to Lypiatt house, within the Park, though tradition asserts that it marks the site of a fatal fall from a horse. It may well be that the old base was used for that later purpose.

If the Lord's Stone has always been so called we probably have in it the original indication of the division of the Manor of Bisley in Norman times. At the same time it must be stated that experts have suggested the possibility of its being of Saxon or even of Roman origin.

The ensuing " Grant of Humfry de Boun, Earl of Hereford, of Wardship and Lands in Lupiatt," is recorded in the Lypiatt MS. book, and is of such local interest that it is given unabridged. " Sciant presentes et futuri quod Ego Humfridus de Boun Comes Hereford concessi et hac Carta mea confirmari Bartholomeo Labano omnes terras cum pertinentijs Suis quam Henricus de Lupegeat ei dedit de feudo meo in Lupegeate et omnia Servicia que ipse ei ibidem concessit Scilt Robertu Filiu Helye et terram qam tenet cum oibz pertinentitiijs suis Et Willm filium Reginaldi et terram quam tenet cum oibz pertinentiijs suis Hugonem Teper et terram tenet cum oibz pertinentibijs suis Et terram quam Eustachius tenuit cum omnibus pertinentiijs suis Et terram quam Helias filius Eustathij tenuit cum oibz pertinentijs suis Et terram quam Godricus tenuit cum omnibus pertinentijs suis Et Robertu de Hethermora et terram super quam sedet cum oibz pertinentijs suis Et Matillidam de Cumba et terram quam tenet cum omnibus pertinentijs suis Et omnia nemora (groves) forinseca cum oibz pertinentijs suis excepto parto ipsius Henrici cum Mora et prato suo de Brumescumba et salvo nemore quod pertinet ad dotem Dno Scilt Hegga versus Rugebrugge Concessi etiam dicto Bartholomeo terras Subscriptas quas predictus Henricus dedit ei de Dominico suo Scilt in Sethcumba in Sturta inferiori Subtus aulam Henrici versus orientalem partem novem acras terre In Sturta superiori unum gardinum tres acras et dimid In campo qui vocatur Uverfeld viginti Septem acras terre videlt in Stretfurlonga propinquiore curie et quator acras et dimidium in eadem cultura versus crucem Marie In Stipfurlonga in eodem

Campo decem acras et dimid que extendunt versus Strodam In furlonga de Borha in eodem campa tres acras In furlonga de Heffedlond in eodem campo Sex acras terre in Campo occidentali qui vocatur Netherfeld Scilt in Smithfurlonga Septem acras et dimid In cultura de Withittimore in eodem campo novem acras et dimid et unu quarteriu in curta cultura apud Spineam purnam in eodem campo una acram et dimid In cultura de Rueburga in eodem campo novem acras et dimidium et unu quarterium In lata cultura in eodem campo octo acras In Cattherudinge in eodem campo tres acras et dimid et unu quarteriu apud Inheperingate In eodem campo duas acras et unu quarteriu Apud Stanhurstham In eodem campo unam acram et dimid Apud Aldesmittham duas acras et unu quarteriu In cultura de Lesseburge in eodem campo quatuor acras et dimid In cultura apud Fripgrove in eodem campo quatuor acras et dimid et clausum de Aldelethtana et unam acram deintius ad domos suas edificandas Et Servitium Herdwini Pigar et Johis Spilemon et Emme amite Henrici Scilt annuatim tres libras cumini et medietatem Servicij quod faber debet facere in eadem villa Istas predictas terras concessi et confirmavi prefato Bartholomeo Labano tenendas et habendas de prefato Henrico et heredibus suis jure hereditario sibi et heredibus suis vel si de eo sive herede humanitus contigerit cuiscumq assignare voluerit libere et quiete In parte et honorifice In omnibus locis et in omnibus liberis consuetudinibus ad predictas terras pertinentibus Reddendo inde annuatim predicto Henrico et heredibus suis dictus Bartholomeus et heredes sui vel ejus attornati unam libras cumini ad festum Sci Michaelis pro omni Servicio et Sclari exactione Salvo forinseco Servicio quantum pertinet ad dictas terras Scilt quartum partem Servicij unius Militis Concessi etiam eidem Bartholomeo et heredibus suis vel ejus assignatis et hac present Carta confirmavi quod licet Wills de Ruem vel heredes sui quocunque casu vel quacunque de causa terras suas vel tenementa sua alicubi impignoraverint vel religioni Seu altero aliquo modo contulerint teneat dictus Bartholomeus et teneant ejus heredes vel ejus Atturnati predictas terras suas cum omnibus pertinentijs. Ita scilt indempnes per predictu Serviciu ut dictur Barthomeus vel ejus heredes aut atturnati inde aliquod dampnu vel aliquod aliud grevamen non int-rant nec inde namient quo alio alique Sclari modo vexentur a predco Willo vel a Matilo uxore sua vel ab heredibus suis qo ab aliquibus qui ab eis venire poterunt Pro hac autem concessione et confirmatione dedit mihi predictus Bartholomeus duas Marcas argenti Hijs testibus Luca de Grug Rob de Sipertune Johe de Berneres Petro de Eggeworthe Henr le Femmeng Willo le Femming avunclo ejus Henr le Femmung fre ejs Tristram de Ribbeford Walto decano de Biseleg Rogero de Langeburge Radulph de Tuneleg Willo de Budefield Henr de le Strode Willo de Tuneleg Willo de Rodeburg Rico de Eggewerth Thoma de Rodeburg er multis alia."

Henricus de Lupegeat of this charter is probably Henry de Clifford.

The last Humphry de Bohun who was Earl of Hereford only died in 1183, when his son Henry de Bohun succeeded him (born 1176), he having married Maud, only daughter of Geoffry Fitz Piers, Earl of Essex and heir to her brother William de Mandeville, last Earl of Essex. Their son Humphry de Bohun was created Earl of Essex in 1199, as well as inheriting the Earldom of Hereford from his father. The charter therefore must be attributed to the earlier Humphry de Bohun, Earl of Hereford, before 1183. The Sturta superior and Sturta inferior are identical with the Stertes which lie below Middle Lypiatt, and the Stretfurlong would be the land allotted to that property in the common field.

Nothing further is known of William Mansell (I) except that his wife's name was Margaret, so named in the De Banco pleas of 1327-8, when there was a dispute between her and Nicholas atte Chircheheye and Alice his wife, regarding land in Stroud.[1] It may have been a son, John Maunsel de Lupe-yate, who was admitted acolyte at the parish Church, Cirencester, 19 April, 1326, by Bishop Horleton. Also he had a daughter named Nicholla who married Walter le Bret, son of Richard le Bret of Pitchcombe, Knight of the Shire for Hereford.[2]

[1] P. R. O. Index of Placita de Banco, 1327-8, p. 171.
[2] *B. G. A. S. Trans.*, xiv, 144.

The Mansells bore for arms,—Gu. a fess arg. a label of the second.

William Mansell (II) succeeded his father at Lypiatt and at the time of the levying of the aid on the occasion of the knighting of Edward the Black Prince in 1349, he was assessed for one knight's fee in Lupogate superior and Tonlye, 40s.

He also paid 10s. for a quarter of a knight's fee in Frampton, which his father had held. Perhaps this is the vineyard, six acres of land and three of wood held of John de Bohun by service and 39s. per annum.

Thomas Mauncel was Lord of the Manor of Over Lupeyatt in 1367, when he, together with John Clifford, having presented Adam Robyn, clerk, to the perpetual chantry in the chapel of Lupeyate, then vacant, the latter was instituted by Bishop Wittlesey, 5 January at Hembury.[1]

This most interesting entry in the Bishop's register gives the approximate date of the building of the chapel at Lypiatt, and the double patronage indicates the close link which existed between the Mansells and Cliffords. As there is no other mention of this chapel in the Worcester registers, it is probable that the appointment of Adam Robyn was the first after the building of the chapel, to which both families contributed. That it was a chantry chapel also solves the problem of the burial vault below the sanctuary to which access is gained by a flight of steps before the altar. It may be that a sealed vault lies westward of this entry, or that any coffins that might have been lying in the vault were removed during the general desecration of the chapel, but no doubt it was meant to be the burial place of the Cliffords and Mansells.

Philip Mauncell, Esq., succeeded to the manor of Over Lypiatt and died in 1395, having incurred a debt of £500 to Richard Whityngton, citizen and mercer of London, on 23 February, 1394. This he ought to have repaid on the first of April following, but he failed to do so. Orders were sent for a valuation of lands and goods in the liberty of Bisley. This was made and presented before Hugh de Byseley, bailiff

---

[1] Reg. Wittlesey, fo. 27.

of that liberty, on St. Luke's day, 19 Ric. II, 1395, at Pains-wick, by oath of John Clifford, Thomas Freame and others, who said that Philip Mauncell had at Over Lypiatt, the manor of Over Lypiatt worth yearly ten marks six shillings and eightpence clear, five oxen worth five marks, one cow worth eight shillings, thirty quarters of dragett[1] lying in a heap, and so estimated worth sixty shillings. An endorsement states that the aforesaid lands were delivered on 18 November ensuing, to the said Richard Whityngton to hold, etc.[2] Thus Over Lypiatt passed away from the Mansells into the possession of the celebrated Richard Whityngton, Lord Mayor of London, who was of the family of Whityngton of Pauntley, Glos. In 1424, the year after Richard Whityngton's death, Robert Whityngton and Guy, his son, of Pauntley laid claim to Over Lypiatt as legatees of Richard Whityngton.[3]

It appears that Thomas Roos and others were feoffees of the manor to the use of Richard Whityngton, and that all the feoffees had died, Thomas Roos having, by his will, enfeoffed Robert Whityngton of Pauntley and Guy his son, of the said manor of Over Lypiatt. Robert Whityngton died in 1424, and Guy in 1440-1, but the Whityngtons had made good their claim to Over Lypiatt and Thomas son of Guy Whityngton was Lord of the manor on 11 October, 1457, which is the date of the earliest of the Court rolls of Over Lypiatt of which record is preserved in the Lypiatt MS. book. It appears from it that one John Smyth was farmer at Over Lypiatt and it was presented that he had neglected to repair a certain house called le Nursery and a room called le Geston Chamber, and also the barn and cattle shed were in need of lathing and tiling. He also had neglected the enclosure in the wall, called le Chappell Hey; also he was in defect in the bridge called le Sclak near le Pyked Inhoke, and in certain repairs in the Park.

It appeared as if John Smith lived in part of the Manor house which was larger then than it is now.

---

[1] A cloth of flax and wool.

[2] Glos. Inq. P. M., 1359-1414, p. 197.

[3] E. Chan. Pro. Bundle 69, 19. See Notes and Queries, May, 1926. Paper by St. Clair Baddeley, Esq.

Thomas Whityngton was a J.P. for Co. Glos. in 1485-6 as appears in Manor Court rolls of Corpus Christi College, Oxford.[1] In the Ministers' Accounts of 1448-9 there is recorded the fact that Thomas Mody (who rented Chalford Mill) was to pay 4d. of new rent for a parcell of the water-course called Burnewater, namely from the upper end of the field called the Stubbyng to the mill of William Whityngton, to him and his wife Matilda and their son Thomas.[2] What relation William Whityngton was to Thomas of Over Lypiatt is not manifest, but he may have been an uncle.

Thomas Whityngton died in 1491, his will being dated 12 April of that year. In it he desired that his body should be buried in his chapel of Strode. To the Mother Church of Worcester 12d. To the procter of the Church of Byseley 20s. To the procter of the Church of Rodmarton to erect a belfry there 40s. To the parishioners of Strode to make a new chapel there on the South side of the Church in honour of the Assumption of the Blessed Virgin Mary St. John the Evangelist and St. John the Baptist £40. To the chapel of St. Gregory of Pauntley to amortise lands and tenements to the value of 12 marks yearly. To the two chantries in the Church of Tetbury all his lands and tenements in that town and after the decease of himself and Margaret his wife in order that the priests of the said chantries may every year celebrate masses and exequies for their souls and for the soul of William Everard.

To each house of the three orders of friars in Gloucester 40d.

To the Abbot of Flaxley 100s. to buy lands to the yearly value of 6s. 8d., to have mass and exequies publicly there on one day of the year for the souls of himself and his wife, and of John Edwards and his wife. To Richard Whytyngton a messuage in Hawerugge called Morellys, etc. for term of his life with remainder to the prior of Little Malvern to pray for their souls and for John Edwards and his wife.

His wife is to enjoy all his manors and lands in the Counties of Gloucester and Worcester (excepting those of Corse and

---

[1] *B. G. A. S. Trans.*, li, 218.
[2] P. R. O. Ministers' Accounts, 850/28.

Langdon) for life, and if remaining unmarried. If she re-married, the profits of lands till the full age of Robert Wye are to go to priests and clerks, marriage of poor maidens, etc. Immediately Robert Wye inherits he is to find a priest to celebrate for nine years for the souls aforesaid. The Abbot of Kingswoode is to have a silver basin if he does likewise. A trental of masses for forty days after his decease, the priest to receive 10s. One thousand Masses to be celebrated at Gloucester and in other places in the County at the time of his death as quickly as may be. A thousand poor folk are to have a certain sum every fifth . . ., 1d. The poor of St. John Cirencester and St. Bartholomew's, Gloucester, 6s. 8d. each. (Other bequests follow) William Freame to have the tene-ment in Mynchynhampton called Gilles for life on condition that he holds certain courts of his in the county of Gloster.

After his death the said tenement shall remain to the new chapel of Strode for ever.

To John Whytington a cloak of scarlet and £10, etc.

To John Rogers, vicar of Bysseley his best gown of scarlet with a hood, etc.

All his tenements in Bisseley and Mynchinhampton, except Gillis and all lands in Chaulton, co. Wilts., to remain after his wife's decease to the new chapel of Strode to which he bequeaths two large spears with the cobardis to the same belonging. Thomas Petyl is to have his right, to wit, in a chief rent out of a mill called Veysie's Mill.

All the rest of his goods to his wife Margaret and she, Master John Whytyngton and Master Thomas Holford, clerks, William Greville and William Wye, gentlemen, his executors, and Robert Moreton, Bishop of Worcester, to be overseer.

The will was proved 25 June, 1491.[1]

Thomas Whityngton's interest lay in Stroud Church rather than in Bisley, and it was there he built the south aisle. He left an only daughter his heiress, and she by her marriage with William Wye conveyed Over Lypiatt to that family.

[1] P. C. C. Milles 45. Abstract from Hockaday's Eccl. File.

Sir Robert Atkyns states that there was a handsome monument in the south aisle of Stroud Church for the Whittingtons which had since been taken down. They bore Gules, a fess componee or and argent ; in the dexter chief an annulet of the second. With the omission of the annulet and the substitution of two crescents, one in chief and the other in base (the latter probably an error of the sculptor), these arms were sculptured on the left side of the porch entrance of the former church.[1]

Robert Wye, son of William Wye and grandson of Thomas Whittington, succeeded to Over Lypiatt and married Jane Baynham, probably about 1514, the trustees of his marriage settlement being James Clifford, William Throckmorton, Richard Tracy, Richard Coton, and Richard Davys.[2]

Besides his eldest son Thomas, other sons named in his will are Robert, William, Giles, Richard and Francis, and a daughter Elizabeth. He died 26 November, 1545, his son Thomas being thirty or more at the time. He was a very large landed proprietor, his property lying in the Manors of Rodmarton, Over Lypiat and Corse, held of the King, and 76 messuages, 1264 acres of land, 212 of meadow and 148 acres of pasture, 160 acres of wood in the above mentioned place and in Corse, Hanrigg, Frampton, Westerley, Bentham, Tewkesbury, Southwick, Tredington, and Walton Cardiff, and the advowson of the Rectory of Rodmarton. The manor of Over Lypiatt was held of the King as of his honour of Hereford by fealty and rent of 40s. per annum being worth £32 per annum.[3]

Robert Wye of Over Lypyate, Esq., made his will 23 November, 1544, bequeathing his soul to his most merciful Lord and Saviour Jhu Christ trusting now most faythfully to be saved through the merits of his bitter passion, and his body to be buried there where it is appointed. Touching his lands and goods tendering the zele and love that his wife Jane has had towards him he willingly therefore gives to her his manor of Over Lypyate with the demesnes thereto

[1] Fishers' Stroud.
[2] Lypiatt MS Book.
[3] Inq. P. M. Lypiatt MS. Book.

belonging, with all other manner of grounds arrable or unarrable that he occupied in his own hands and to his own use at the time of this will making, to enjoy the same with special favour during her lifetime, with all his whole goods thereupon, moveable and immoveable, praying her lykewise in God's behalf to be good and loving to all his children. He gives her his lands in Corsse and Longdon with two of his chiefest houses in Tewkysbury according as it is expressed in her jointure, confirmed with his seal before this time. He gives to his wife his lease of Losemore, Co. Glos., which he took of the monastery of Syon, late dissolved, with all his own goods and chattels thereon. Provided that his daughter Elizabeth, shall have the rent and charges deducted, the which £100 he gives to his daughter at marriage. After his said wife he gives the reversion of his properties in Losemore stored with all such number of cattell as be pastured upon the same at this present time, reserved always the £100 to be levied upon the profits of the said farm of Losemore. Reserved also to his sister Elizabeth a beast's pasture there both summer and winter. Reserved also to his brother, parson of Rodmarton, and to his tenants there the pasturage of their usual beasts in summer time, paying therefor as they did in his time and so to continue in the conditions in his wife's lifetime. Also he gives his daughter Elizabeth, all his lands both of Pyerhyncumbe and also of Gloucester to enjoy immediately after his time until she have her £100 which he gives also to her marriage. After she has been paid the said lands are to remain to his right heirs. To his son, Robert, the rent of his farm of Bentham during his life. To his sons William, Giles, and Richard, their leases and farms that they occupy in their own hands. To his son John, the lease of Duryste, Co. Glos. To his son Francis, his lease and farm of Hampton. To his sister Elizabeth, his tenements of Rodmarton next adjoining the Church house with the whole property belonging thereto upon his own domain in Rodmarten and four acres yearly out of the same for her tillage, also he gives her four loads of wood yearly out of Westerley. He gives her Specke's land and wills her to have his great Chamber that goeth up the stairs of the right hand of the hall to occupy it and all other legacies before-mentioned during her life peaceably quietly each without interruption. To his preste John Edwardes meat and drink in his house at Lypiate and his chamber during his lyftyme and four marcs for his wages to be paid him yearly out of his lordship of Frampton by his baily or other deputed there at the two usual terms, viz., the feast of the Anunciation of our Lady and St. Michael the Archangel by equal portions, to serve his chapel there and to pray for him and his friends. And if he be behind unpaid of his wages in part or wholly for one month, then he gives him full power to distrain thereupon any part of the said Lordship and the dysties to withhold until he be fully paid and contented.

He desires his wife to be good to his old servants. To his daughter, Margaret, his lease of Icombe during her life time and after to remain to James Wybury and Richard Wybury, jointly, paying the rent and performing the covenants thereof according as it is expressed in the said lease. He wills that every of his tenants at Rodmarten enjoy their houses and tenements during their lifetime according to the custom of the manor, paying no further fine therefor. The residue he leaves to his wife, Jane, whom he makes executrix, with Master Latymer, parson of Soubury.

Witnesses. Master William Wye, parson of Rodmarton, John Trevynon and John Edwardes, clerk, with others. Proved in London, 6 December, 1544.[1]

Johanna, the widow of Robert Wye attended the Bisley Court on 4 May, 1546, and rendered service for two messuages, one being Dowers and the other Coppisgrove, both to the use of Thomas Wye, gentleman.

Thomas Wye succeeded his father and was sheriff of the County in 1575.[2] He died in 1581, at Bradwell, Glos., and was the last of the Wyes of Lypiatt. He was buried in the chapel of Stroud amongst his ancestors and though no names, were recorded, a monument that bore the arms of the Wyes, namely,—sable, three griffins segreant or, with the crest, a

---

[1] P. C. C. 19 Pynnyng.
[2] Fisher's Stroud, p. 192.

wivern sieant in a plume of ostrich feathers,—stood at the end of the south aisle. Thomas Wye had made an Indenture, dated 12 October, 1576, whereby he settled his property for life on Juliana, his wife, and their children. This included the manors of Over Lypiatt and Frampton Maunsell, with fifty messuages, twenty tofts, ten mills, 1000 acres of land, 500 acres of meadow, 1000 acres of heath, 500 acres of marsh ground, £12 of rent in Over Lypiatt, Frampton Maunsell, Sapperton, Stroud, Bisley, Winston, Syde, Tredington, Walton Cardiff, Tarleton, Hollyroode Hamney, Somerford Keynes, Michell Hampton, Campden, Cheltenham, Charlton Kings, Tewkesbury and Southwick. Also manors and lands of Bentham and Pichincombe and lands with the moiety of Dowe manor.[1]

Thomas Wye's will is dated 23 February, 1580. He was of Bradwell, Glos., but wills his body to be buried in the chapel at Stroud by his ancestors there. To the poor people in and about Stowtholde (Stow-in-the-Wold) and Stroud, twenty marks within one month of his decease. To his nephew, Charles Morgan, £30. To his niece, Ann Morgan, £40. To William Wye, son of his brother, Gyles, £10. To Nicholas Wye, £10. To his daughter, Julian Wye, forty marks and double apparel, to be got against her marriage. To his servants, Alice Clopton and Robert Dower, £3 each. To his servants, Robert Hopkins, Henry Pearce, William Williams and Henry Deuth, 40s. a piece. To Albridges, Knight's, Windowes', Teales' and Doggers' sons, his god-children, 10s.

Failing lawful heirs, after the decease of him and his wife, his lands, etc., are to go to John, natural son of his brother, Giles Wye and his lawful heirs, failing which to the above-mentioned William and his lawful heirs, failing which to Thomas Wye, son of his brother William Wye, of Kemble, deceased, failing heirs to Robert Wye, son of Giles, failing whose lawful heirs to Thomas Wye, the natural son of John Giles Wye aforesaid, failing which then to the right heirs of Thomas Wye, of Bradwell.

[1] Lypiatt MS. Book.

To John Wye, his first heir, £4 per annum. If not paid regularly he may enter into and upon his manor of Frampton Mansell to distrain for the same and the distresses so taken to lead and carry away and detain, etc.

His wife, Julian, is executrix. Overseers,—his well beloved Sir William Cordell, knight, his brother, William Clopton, and his nephew, George Whitnty and William Whitnty, to each 40s.

Witnesses. Thomas Wye, Sir James Whitntye, knight, George Whitney, Richard Hiett, gentlemen, also Roger Bracegirdle, William Whiting, Harry Dewer, John Tydmarshe, the curate of Bradwell and writer hereof, Thomas Knight and Robert Dower. Proved in London 27 May, 1581.[1]

In 1583, Juliana, the widow of Thomas Wye, married again, her second husband being John Throckmorton, and in 1588 they bought out the interest of John Wye, Esq., of London, and in 1595, for £2100 that of Elizabeth Wye, of Coln St. Aldwyns, Glos., cousin and widow, and heir of Thomas Wye, deceased, namely,—daughter and heir of William Wye, son and heir of William Wye, who was brother and heir of Thomas Wye.

Besides the places already named the interests of the Wyes had extended to Morton Henmarshe, Cherington, Aston, Avening, one close called Burdens in Tartleton, one messuage and tenement called Langleys also in Tarleton, and the parsonage and tithes of Kemble, Co., Wilts., excepted. John Throckmorton paid for this £2860.[2]

John Throckmorton who was a Roman Catholic, is stated by Sir Robert Atkyns to have been concerned in the Popish Gunpowder plot, and he certainly was related to some of the chief conspirators, Catesby, Tresham and Winter. The name of Fawkes was and is common in the parish, and the panelled room at Lypiatt Park is said to have been the place where the conspirators met. It is unlikely that John Throckmorton

---

[1] P. C. C. 19 Darcy.
[2] Indentures, Lypiatt MS. Book.

would have escaped all punishment, as was the case, had he indeed been guilty. A letter, not dated, from Lord Mounteagle, to Robert Catesbye, then at Lippiatt, together with one from Thomas Winter to Catesbye, was discovered in a volume of the Cotton MSS in the British Museum. The former letter was thought to have been written in October, 1605, and is as follows :—

" To my loving kinsman, Robert Catesbye, Esquier, geve theise Lipyeat.

" If all creatures borne under the mone's spheare can not endure without the ellimentes of aier and fyre, in what languishment have wee lede owre lyfe, since wee departed from the deare Robin, whose conversation gave us such warmeth as wee neded no other heate to maintayne owre healthes. Since, therefore, yt is proper to all, to desire a reamedy for their disease, I doe by theise, bynde the by the lawes of Charitye to make thy present aparence here at the Bath : and let no watery Nimpes diurt you, you can better lyve with the aier, and better forbeare the fyre of your spirite and vigoure than wee, who accumptes thy persin the only Sone that ripene our harvest. And thus I rest

ever fast tyed to your friendshipp,

W. MOWNTEAGLE."

A copy of this letter is framed and hangs in the panelled room already mentioned. Whether its obscure diction, in the euphuistic style of those days veiled a secret message regarding the plot or not, it is now impossible to determine.

In 1610, John Throgmorton sold the manor of Over Lypiatt for £4550 to Thomas Stephens, Esq., of the Middle Temple, and Attorney General to Prince Charles. The demesne lands included The Great Meadow, Honeyhills, Picked Innock, Well Park, Michell Meade, Highmead, Lower Easton's Croft, Axton Meadow, the Middle and further Park, Kingsland, Conygarth, Upper Easton's Croft, Little Honeyhills, Axtons Layes, Broad Innock, the Lower Frith, Bartholomew furlong, Stroud and the Pingle, the Seventeen

Q

acres, the Barnefield and all arable land parcel of the demesne lying in or near Bysley field and containing 50 acres ; and a parcell of land called Prowles Grove and Avenas Grove, a messuage and 46 acres of land in the tenure of Thomas Freame ; the manor of Pitchcombe and all houses in Over Lypiatt, Bisley, Stroud and Frampton Mansell were included in the purchase.

Thomas Stephens who was the third son of Edward Stephens of Eastington, married Elizabeth, daughter and co-heiress of John Stone of London., By her he had five children :—

1. Edward, born in the parish of St. Michael, Cornhill, 22 April, 1596.

2. Mary, born in the same place 9 February, 1597.

3. John Stephens born at Watford, Herts., 26 September, 1603.

4. Elizabeth, born in the parish of St. Bride, London, 12 September, 1605.

5. Nathaniel Stephens born at Lypiatt, 29 July, 1611.

The eldest son, Edward, lived at Sodbury and became the ancestor of the Stephens of that place, as was Nathaniel, the youngest son, of those of Cherington.

Thomas Stephens (I.) died on 26 April, 1613, his sons all being under age at the time. He left a very long will.

This was dated 8 March, 1612, and by it he left Elizabeth his wife, and his brothers-in-law, Thomas Paramour and Edward Manwaring, and his cousins, William Hill, Esq., and Robert Ball, minister, his executors. He desired that his body should be buried at Stroud in the parish church. His wife to have for her life his demesnes and manor of Lyppiatt with his leases of Colliers and Copesgrove, the Peare and other grounds held by lease, and the Warren called the Tedbury Warren, held also by lease. Also all lands recently belonging to her father, John Stone, situated in St. Martins, Ludgate Hill, and the third part of the manor of Rushborne, Co. Kent, with various other houses in London held of the Dean and Chapter of St. Paul's. After his wife's decease, the manor and lands of Over-Lippiatt are to go to his eldest

son (if of 24 years of age).   His funeral he wishes to be without
any pompous costly ostentation.   If any monument shall be,
it is in no ways to be any tomb to incumber the Church wall,
but rather in brass or marble or alabaster in the Church
wall " Of this my loveing friend, Mr. Arnold Oldisworth
may be consulted withal if need require."   He leaves £50 to
the poor of St. Bride's parish, £10 to Stroud, and £10 to
Bisley poor.   He gives to his eldest son, Edward, his large
silver basin and ewer which his Honble. good Lady the
Countess of Warwick, gave him.   To his son, John, his
silver and gilt bason and ewer which his Honble. good Lord,
the Viscount Lisle gave him.   To his son, Nathaniel, one
other of his deep silver Basons and an ewer to it.   To his
daughter, Mary, one of his best silver gilt standing cuppes
with a cover, to be chosen for her by her mother.   Also to
his daughter, Elizabeth, another of the same.   He desires
that not much of his furniture or goods should be sold, but
kept in his houses at Lippiatt and in London, and repaired
and delivered to his children who shall enjoy his houses.
All is entrusted to the good discretion of his wife, " for my
heart doth trust her," and so Lippeatt was to be left stocked
for the use of his son as he left it.

He mentions amongst his legacies £10 to his Kinsman and
servant, Henry Mayo.   His kinswoman and servant, Elizabeth
Ball, 40s.   To his cosen, Thomas Clissold, 40s., praying him
to be helpful to his loveing wife and children as he had been
kind and loving to himself.[1]

Thomas Stephens was buried as he desired in Stroud
Church, where his monument is still on the east wall of the
south aisle.   Within an arched recess a stone effigy of Thomas
Stephens clad in a doctor of law's gown, kneels before a
desk, on which is an open book, the hands being folded in
prayer.   Beneath is a tablet with the following inscription :—

" Thomas Stephens Armiger, legum municipalium Regni
Angliae peritissimus, Henrico et Carolo, principibus Walliae
Attornatus generalis, obiit 26 Aprilis, An. Dom. 1613.
Aetatis suae 55.

[1] Lypiatt MS. Book.

Lege perit Stephanus ?   Vae nobis lege perimus,
Omnes peccanti lex datur una mori :
Non periit Stephanus ; Fertur lex altera Christi,
Quae Stephanon Stephano hat prohibetque mori."

Mr. P. H. Fisher, in his Notes on Stroud, gives the following translation of this verse :—

Died Stephens by the law ? The law alas ! kills all,—
That law which doomed our sinful race to die.
But Stephens lives : another law, Christ's law withal
Gives him a crown and immortality.[1]

It is interesting to note that Lypiatt Chapel was used for sacred purposes in Thomas Stephens' time, for the Bisley registers record the marriage there of Samuel Gurner and Frances Turner, 25 June, 1610.

In 1615, Mrs. Elizabeth Stephens married Mr. Sherley. In 1620, Edward Stephens bought from the Duke of Buckingham Colliers and Copsgrove, parcell of the manor of Bisley and adjoining the manor of Over Lypiatt. He also acquired another parcell of the manor of Bisley from John Davis, two closes called Davis Copsgrove, as well as the Peare, then owned by Anthony Field. These properties lay within view of Lypiatt Park, on the opposite ridge of Stancombe Valley.   Of the several houses then standing, only Copsgrove remains, though the sites of former human habitations can be traced, and their names remain in field or plantation, such as Colliers, Pontings Hill, and Blanche's Bank.

Edward Stephens who inherited Lypiatt Park from his father, sold his interest therein to his brother John Stephens, in 1624.   (see plate 12)

NOTE ON THE PEAR.

Reference has already been made to the field called the Pear in Chapter III, when the charter of William de la Pere is quoted, and the site of the Pear is indicated.   William " in Campo de la Peir " whose charter of lands in Bisley, Througham, Frampton and Westerhale is amongst the muniments of Corpus Christi College, Oxford, evidently

---

[1] Fisher's Stroud, p. 305.

owned it and probably resided there. The Pear had passed from the family of Pere in 1500 to Thomas Field, from whom his son Giles Field inherited the property in 1510. This latter, with his son, Edward Field, in 1557, leased the Pear to William Butt and Alice, his wife, for 61 years, following on a previous lease for 40 years, but the latter in her widowhood in 1571, assigned the remainder of this lease to Richard Hale, William Butt having died in October, 1570. In December, 1572, Richard Hale and Walter, his son, assigned the lease to Richard Arundell, who held it till 1608, when he assigned it to John Throckmorton, Esq. It again was assigned by John Throckmorton and Thomas Clissold. Having returned to its original owners after the lease had expired, Anthony Field with his wife, Katherine, and son, Richard, sold the Pear to John Stephens, 11 April, 1634.

The arable lands of nineteen and a half acres belonging to the Pear in the common fields are described in the Lypiatt MS book in an Indenture of 1632 of John Stephens to Thomas Clissold.—Seven acres lay in Stancombe field in a place called Pearhorne, near to Dagnish wood, one acre at the Downe rake, shooting upon one acre of the Chauntrie land, one acre near Hansteades (Ansteads farm) shooting upon an acre of the Vicarage land, one half acre near the acre of the parsonage land, etc., rent per annum 4d.

There is no record of when the house of the Pear ceased to exist.

NOTE ON COLLIERS.

Colliers had been granted on 5 August, 1619, by James I to the Duke of Buckingham. The messuage had attached to it eight acres of arable land, four being in Over Lypiatt Field and the other four in Stancombe Field. It later increased to twenty acres, the situations of which are described in the Lypiatt MS book. These properties, with Copsgrove, have continued ever since to form part of the Over Lypiatt estate.

John Stephens, of Lypiatt, is known to have married three times. His first wife was Elizabeth Ramme, whom he married in 1626, and who died about 1630, s.p. The second wife was Grace, daughter of John Browne, Esq., whom he married in 1631, and who died before 1636.

John Stephens married thirdly Anne, daughter of Sir Thomas Moulson, of Hargrave, Chester, the marriage settlements being dated 27 May, 1636. Their son, Thomas, was born in 1639, his baptism being entered in both Stroud and Bisley Registers as having taken place on 14 August of that year. For some years subsequent to this period the parish registers of Stroud are very defective, and there is no record of any other children of John Stephens and Anne Moulson, but probably Anne Stephens, who on 11 January, 1663, married John Delabere, Esq., at Bisley Church, was their daughter. Portraits of John Stephens and of Annie Delabere exist at Southam Delabere, and also in the possession of Mrs. Delabere of Prestbury (see plate 13)

Fisher, in his " Notes and Recollections of Stroud " states that John Stephens had four wives. Of this no confirmation has been found, unless the entry of the death of Elizabeth, wife of John Stephens, 23 May, 1679, in the Stroud registers, is to be taken as such.

During the troublous time of the Civil War, John Stephens' sympathies were with the Parliament, Lypiatt being garrisoned by Col. Massey. It is said that the families of Stephens, Cromwell and Ireton were related, but evidence of this is lacking until after the Restoration. Hester Stephens, of Lypiatt married a first cousin once removed of the Protector. John Stephens' cousin, Nathaniel Stephens, of Eastington, is said to have consented to measures against the King, though with reluctance, under the influence of Ireton, with whom he went up to London, against the advice and wish of his sister.[1] He was seized with a lingering illness the following May and died in the year of the Restoration, 1660.

Lypiatt, not being a fortified dwelling, was, in the absence of the Captain who commanded there, taken by Sir Jacob Astley who came from Cirencester, in 1642, a lieutenant and fifty soldiers being captured.

---

[1] *B. G. A. S. Trans.*, **xxii**, 130-1.

John Stephens was returned as Knight of the Shire to the Commonwealth Parliament of 1658-9.   There is an interesting account of his dealings with certain Quakers in 1665, contained in an old pamphlet quoted by Fisher in his Notes on Stroud (pp. 194-6.)   His treatment of them as Chairman of the Quarter Sessions at Gloucester, when they were bound over for " standing in the Steeple-house with their hatts on " during worship in Cirencester Church, was violent and not strictly just.   When their friend, John Roberts, protested, John Stephens threatened him with imprisonment, and even hurled a ball of wax at him in his rage.   John Roberts was freed the next day, but was moved to go and see John Stephens at Lippiatt.   In contrast to his violent behaviour at the Quarter Sessions, John Stephens was now in a subdued mood and had the grace to confess he had been in the wrong and to ask forgiveness.[1]

In spite of the disturbances of the times, John Stephens increased his estate by several purchases of lands.   In January 1632, he acquired fifteen acres of land, formerly parcel of Bisley Manor, of Thomas Tayloe, and three acres more adjoining from Thomas Clissall, with ten of Robert Tomlins, all of which together with two acres of his own called the New Tyning, were enclosed in a thirty acre field thenceforth called the old Warren.

In April, 1648, he bought Dagnesh Wood of eight acres from Samuel Webb.

In November, 1653, John Stephens purchased a meadow of two and a half acres and an acre of land in Bisley near Copsgrove from Robert Snow.   In June, 1667, a meadow was purchased from Jane Adey, called Bismore.   In May, he further increased his estate by purchasing Highmeads and Colliers of Henry Shewell, and three grounds called Stancombe of Thomas Pope.

John Stephens died in August, 1679, being buried at Stroud, on the twelfth of that month.   No monument exists to his memory.

---

[1] See " Some Memoirs of the Life of John Roberts, written by his son, Daniel Roberts," 12 mo., pp. 59, London.

Thomas Stephens (II) succeeded his father at Over Lypiatt, having married Ann, daughter of Sir William Child, of Northwick, Co. Worcs. By her he had two sons, Thomas, baptized at Stroud, 5 February, 1671, and Edward, baptized also at Stroud, 20 March, 1676. There is a letter extant from Thomas Stephens to Mr. Thomas Edwards, dated Sodbury, 27 April, 1696, in which he relates how his son is wasting his estate, had ploughed up lands and cut down timber with the approval of his sister. Also he had shut him (his father) and mother from table and told his mother he would provide for them no longer than to Mid-summer, and then have them away and their bedding. He threatens to dig up the side of the hill by the house. The deed of trust of 1675 made his son tenant for life. Particulars of his debts follow and provision for paying them, £3000 having been given by the grandfather Neale. His son denies them the use of the coach, though he still had horses coach and chariot at leisure.

This letter reveals considerable financial difficulty, and strangely unfilial conduct on the part of the son, Thomas (III). Apparently Thomas Stephens (II) continued to reside at Over Lypiatt, his wife having died by 1704. His will is dated 5 April, 1704, and he is described as of Over Lypyate, Esq., and then infirm. He commends his soul to Almighty God, etc., and his body to be buried in such decent and Christian but private manner in the parish Church of Stroud, near his loving wife. Whereas his son, Thomas, is engaged with him in several suits and bonds for payment of money for him he gives to his said son, Thomas, all his household goods, plate, furniture, etc., and as his son, Thomas' Marriage Settlements of 7 July, 1696, grants to trustees the manor of Over Lypyate for raising of £2000 for his younger son, Edward, when twenty one and £60 per annum till he is that age, his meaning is that Thomas shall not have to pay £60 per annum. His son, Thomas, is to be sole executor. W. Kinard De la Bere, Joan Field, Rachell Stephens, Thomas Stephens.

Thomas Stephens (II) died in 1708, and was buried at Stroud on 6 May, no monument existing for him. His will was proved 1 June, 1708.

The registers at Stroud record the marriage of Anne Mary Stephens, daughter of Thomas Stephens, Esq., of Lippiatt, to Edward Fust, Esq., son of Sir John Fust, of Hill Co., Glos., Baronet, on 5 June, 1688, in the Chapel at Over Lypiatt. Though there is no record of her baptism at Stroud, this must be the daughter referred to in the letter of 1696. Their daughter, Elizabeth Fust, married Thomas Warner, of Stroud.

Edward Stephens, younger son of Thomas Stephens (II), and mentioned in his will, is not the Edward baptized at Stroud in 1676, who appears to have died the following year, but an unrecorded son similarly named (after the usual custom), for he was under age in 1704. He died in 1711, his will being dated 6 July, 1711, and proved 17 November of the same year. He was sick and weak of body, but of perfect memory, and after commending his soul to God the Father, hoping through the merits of his dear son Jesus Christ his onely Saviour and Redeemer to receive a full and free pardon of all his Sinns and everlasting hapiness in the world to come, he leaves his body to be buried at the discretion of his executors, and after debts paid, to his Aunt Frances Diston £10, To his niece Warner, £10, to the children of his brother, Thomas Stephens, John, Thomas, Anne, Hester, Elizabeth and Katherine, £10 a piece. To his brother Thomas' said son, Thomas, his silver plate, namely a Salver, six spoons, two little cupps, and one large cupp. To his brother John's two daughters, Sarah and Anne £10 apiece. To John Jones, his servant all the furniture in his house and £50, and all his other goods and estates he gives to his loving brother, Thomas Stephens, of Lippiatt, Esq., who is appointed executor. W. Thomas Warner, Junr., Elizabeth and John Gold. Edward Stephens was residing at Painswick at the time of his death, and was buried at Stroud 3 October, 1711. His brother John, mentioned in his will was baptized at Stroud, 13 July, 1674, and married there Rebecca Davis, 19 August, 1697. He lived at Bourne, his second daughter, Anne being baptized at Stroud, 13 June, 1701. He died in 1704, being buried at Stroud, 22 November, his widow also dying the following year, was buried at Stroud, 12 March. Thus having pre-deceased his father he is not mentioned in the latter's will.

Thomas Stephens (III) who had been established at Lypiatt in his father's lifetime, became also Lord of the Manor of Bisley in 1709, his first court being held on 7 April, of that year. In 1696 he had married Anne daughter of John Neale, Esq., of Deane, Beds. Their Marriage Settlement is extant amongst the Lypiatt deeds, the Indenture Tripartite being between Thomas Stephens of Over Lypiatt, Esq. and Thomas Stephens, junr., his heir apparent (1), John Neale of Aldborough Hatch, parish of Barking, Co. Essex, Esq., and Anne Neale one of his daughters (2), Edward Fust, Esq., son and heir apparent of Sir John Fust of Hill Co. Glos., Kinard Delabere, of Southam, Co. Glos., Esq., Henry Neale, of Allesley Co. Warwick, Esq., and Edward Stephens, of Legrove, in Old Sodbury, Co. Glos., Esq. (3). John Neale, settled £2000 and the Manors of Over and Nether Deane with other lands in Co. Beds. and Hunts, and John Stephens and Thomas Stephens, senior and junior, settled the manors of Lypiatt and Pitchcombe, Glos., and Weelock and other lands in Cheshire and Staffs., on the trustees, Thomas Stephens, senr. retaining the use of the manor of Over Lypiatt for his life, and after his decease to the trustees for sixty-one years.

Thomas Stephens (III)[1] and his wife, Anne, are said to have had eight children, though only six are mentioned in his brother Edward's will.

John, the eldest son was baptized at Stroud, 25 March, 1697, Thomas on 21 December, 1699 ; his daughters Anne on 5 February, 1702, Esther on 18 April, 1704, Elizabeth on 4 September, 1706, whilst Katherine must have been born and baptized elsewhere.

Thomas Stephens appears to have worshipped at Bisley Church as a faculty for a pew at the West end of the Church was granted to him 16 August, 1716.[2]   He was High Sheriff of the County in 1693, and was Knight of the Shire in 1713. He died in 1719 being buried at Stroud on 3 March.

[1] There is some confusion in Fisher's Stroud between this Thomas Stephens and his father.
[2] Hockaday's Ecclesiastical Files.

Thomas Stephens (IV), the younger son, barrister-at-law, of the Inner Temple, died unmarried in 1745, and was buried in Bisley Church, where a monument (now in the belfry) tells all that is known about him.

The marble tablet has the following inscription beneath the Stephens coat of arms,—Per chevron Azure and argent, two falcons rising.—

" Underneath this Monument are deposited the remains of Thomas Stephens, Esq., Barrister at Law, Steward of the Sheriff's Court, Deputy Town Clerk of the City of Bristol, younger son of Thomas Stephens of Over Luppiat. Esq., who in several parliaments served as Knight of the Shire for the County and was Lord of the Manor.

His great candour and benevolence justly entitled him to the esteem of all who knew him and he was not only an ornament to his profession but also to the world and Ancient family from whence he descended.

He died greatly lamented the 7th day of December in the year 1745, aged 46."

Of Thomas Stephens' (III) daughters, Hester married William Baghot Delabere, whose grandmother was Anne Stephens. Elizabeth who was born in 1706, died in 1711.

Mrs. Anne Stephens, widow of Thomas Stephens (III) was Lady of the Manor of Bisley, and held her Court Baron in 1724. The next Court of which record survives was held by John Stephens, Esq., on 29 October, 1737. He had inherited Lypiatt on his father's death in 1719. On 21 January, 1724, John Stephens and Thomas, his brother, executed a deed to lead uses of a fine " sur Cognizance de droit," etc., to be levied by them to William Baghott of the Parish of Prestbury, gentleman, and Edward Stephens of the City of Gloucester, gentleman, for the destroying of all estates tail and remainders of the estates of Over Lypiatt, and its appurtenances in Stroud and Bisley, and the manor of Pitchcombe, appertaining to the said John Stephens and his mother Anne Stephens for her life.[1]

---

[1] Lypiatt MS.

In 1725, John Stephens married Elizabeth, daughter and heiress of Henry Phill, Esq., of London. They had several children, of whom Farrington was the eldest son.

Mrs. Anne Stephens appears to have lived with her daughter at Over Lypiatt during her widowhood, for she died there in 1722, being buried at Stroud, 16 March, as recorded in the registers.

John Stephens' affairs seem to have been embarassed in 1740, for he then arranged with his brother Thomas, for the sale of all the furniture mentioned in the inventory at Lypiatt, and to reimburse himself for expenses, and to pay off John Stephens' debts, mention being made of arrears of rent due to Lady Coventry for tithes of Lypiatt and to pay £43 to Peter Liversage, his "servant" at Over Lypiatt. If there was any surplus then the poor rate for all his Bisley estates was to be paid and wages to his servants at Over Lypiatt, and also towards paying the principal of £1200 and interest which he owes to his brother Thomas for the securing of which he had mortgaged Over Lypiatt.

The Bisley Courts of 1741-2 were held by William Baghott De la Bere, Esq., and William Neal, gentleman ; from 1744-8 by Samuel Hawker and William Tayloe, Esq., Lords of the Manor, who were trustees of the estates ; in 1749 and 1752-3 by Samuel Hawker as sole Lord, but in 1756 John Stephens again held Court as Lord, till 1777, so presumably his affairs were less involved.

In 1755, John Stephens lost his eldest son, Farrington, whose burial took place in the family vault at Stroud Church on 11 February. Laid to rest there with loving care, a century had not elapsed when ignorant workmen employed in repairing the floor over the vault, on removing a paving stone discovered a coffin, originally covered with crimson cloth, and with brass fittings, broke it open, cutting through the oaken shell and lead coffin, and with ghoulish curiosity unfolding the winding sheet, revealing the body which being well preserved in antiseptic fluid, exhibited the features of a handsome young man of twenty years of age. The corpse was clothed in a shroud of fine linen plaited on the breast, with a crimson neck-cloth and a " death crown " cap, with radiating points. The vault was again disturbed in 1868, when water that had penetrated there, and the previous desecration, had wrought great changes. The coffin plate of Farrington Stephens had been removed, and long lay loose in the vestry, but has since disappeared.[1]

It is impossible now to say when first the Chapel at Over Lypiatt was desecrated, but by 1740, when the inventory of furniture was made in view of the sale already mentioned, the inventory of the contents of the Chapel tells its own tale :—

" In the Chapple. One Clock.

One Cyder Mill.

One Grind stone.

Three Hen Cubs.

Two pair steps."

In 1744 Lypiatt House and farm land was let to Peter Leversage, by the mortgagees, Stephens, Hawker and Tayloe, for £140. John Stephens died in 1778, being buried at Stroud on March 24. It is thought that a very large coffin which was displaced in the vault when alterations were made to the old Church, was that of John Stephens. A plain marble tablet now on the east wall of the south transept near the monument of Thomas Stephens, commemorates this last representative of the family of Over Lypiatt.

" Sacred to the memory of John Stephens, Esq., of Over Lypiatt in this parish, the last of the Lypiatt branch of that ancient family, a gentleman universally esteemed for his integrity and benevolent disposition. He died March 19th, 1778, in the 81st year of his age."

John Stephens devised the manor and estates of Over Lypiatt, to his nephew, Thomas Baghott De la Bere, Esq., of Southam, Glos. In 1790, his rental shows that Peter Leversage was then chief tenant at a rent of £239 19s. 0d., and there were eleven other tenants. Thomas Baghott De la Bere, however, sold the residue, the mansion, Park,

[1] Fisher's Stroud.

etc., to Mr. Paul Wathen[1] of Woodchester, who in 1810 became high Sheriff of the county. He was knighted by the Prince Regent in order that he might stand proxy for Lord Strangford, who was absent as Ambassador at Lisbon, on the occasion of his creation as a Knight Grand Cross of the Order of the Bath. This event in the life of Sir Paul Wathen was commemorated by a life-size full length portrait of himself in his proxy dress of G.C.B., but bearing the mantle of the Order over his right arm to mark the distinction. The portrait is still to be seen in the dining room at Lypiatt. (Fontispiece). On 15 May, 1812, Sir Paul Wathen assumed the name of Baghott by Royal License.

Sir Paul Baghott made great changes, which will presently be noticed, in the mansion at Lypiatt. He was a collector of stained glass, and at the sale of Lypiatt Park on 31 August, 1820, some beautiful foreign glass of the early Renaissance period, was secured by the City Chamberlain of Bristol at a cost of £136 6s. 0d. for the east window in the Gaunt Chapel there. This fine collection of full length figures and scenes, probably of French origin, can be seen filling the principal lights of that window.

Lypiatt Park was mortgaged by Sir Paul Baghott to J. S. Jolliffe, Esq., and in 1823 passed into the possession of William Lewis, Esq., of Brimscombe, who also became temporarily Lord of the Manor of Bisley in 1801,[2] but fully so in 1824. Mr. Lewis resided at Lypiatt from 1825 to 1842, but on 8 January, of that year sold the estate to Samuel Baker, Esq. It adds an interest to the latter's short residence there to recall that his son, afterwards Sir Samuel White Baker, the great explorer who first discovered the Lake of Albert Nyanza in central Africa, passed part of his youth at Lypiatt.

Mr. Baker, on 25 February, 1847, sold the property to John Edward Dorington, Esq., who, in 1830, had married Susan, daughter of Joseph Godman of Park Hatch, Surrey, and Merton, Sussex.

---

[1] Mr. Rushforth states that Sir Samuel Wathen (of Stroud), was the purchaser of Lypiatt. See *B. G. A. S. Trans.*, xlix, 308.

[2] Bisley Court Roll, 24 December, 1801. Lypiatt MSS.

Mrs. Dorington died in 1866, having been pre-deceased by a younger son in 1863, to whose memory a stained glass window was erected in the Chancel of Bisley Church.

Mr. Dorington died 16 June, 1874, aged 88, a window in the south aisle of Bisley Church preserving his memory and that of his wife. He was succeeded at Lypiatt by his eldest son, John Edward Dorington, who was born in 1832 and who was created a Baronet (U. K.), 12 February, 1886. In 1859 he married Georgina, daughter of William Speke, of Jordans, Somerset, and sister of Capt. Speke, the African explorer, who in 1861 was travelling with Capt. Grant and shared with him the discovery of Lake Victoria Nyanza which they deemed to be the principal source of the Nile.

Sir John Dorington took an active share in many important public matters. He was J.P. and chairman of quarter Sessions for Gloucestershire, and chairman of the County Council : at one time he was Major in the Gloucestershire Yeomanry Cavalry, and was M.P. for Stroud in 1874, and for Tewkesbury Division of Gloucestershire from 1886 to 1906.

Sir John Dorington bore for arms,—Per fesse sable, and azure, three bugle horns argent, stringed gules, within a bordure invected argent. Crest,—a stag's head erased proper, charged with a bugle horn sable, stringed gules, in front thereof an arrow fesse-wise proper.

Sir John Dorington, besides taking an active part in parochial matters, was a kind and beneficent landlord, always engaged in improving the many estates which he acquired, including all the chief farms in the neighbourhood of Lypiatt. He died 5 April, 1911, and was buried in the Cemetery at Stroud. At the death of Lady Dorington, there being no direct heir, the property was devised to Thomas Philip Godman-Dorington, third son of Major-General R. Temple Godman of Highdean, Sussex, Major in the 1st Royal Dragoons, who was killed in action near Ypres, Belgium, in the Great War, on 12 November, 1914, aged 37. By this said occurrence, which is commemorated on a tablet in the north aisle of Bisley Church and which cut off one who was

deeply interested in the estate, the property passed to a
cousin of Major Godman-Dorington, who immediately sold
the whole to Mr. Bechely Crundall, representative of a
syndicate.   In 1919 the estate passed into the hands of
various purchasers, the Lordships of the manors of Lypiatt
and Bisley finding no purchasers.

, Lypiatt Park was acquired by W. J. Gwyn, Esq., and
became the residence of his brother-in-law, Judge Woodcock,
and Mrs. Woodcock.

THE MANSION OF LYPIATT PARK.

The name of Lypiatt which appears in various forms in
the preceding pages, is derived from the A.S. for a " leap-
gate," a term for a low gate in wooded areas, which whilst
allowing deer to leap over it, sufficed to keep sheep from
straying.

The approach to the mansion in former days was by way
of a road running close to the house and down Stancombe,
being the continuation of the ancient road which came from
Painswick, and which is now a lane running into the present
high road from Stroud to Bisley, near Fennell's Cottages,
and formerly entering the Park at the gateway still to be
seen in the Park wall.   This entrance was diverted to the
present drive entrance at the Bisley end of the Park by Mr.
Wathen, who planted the avenue of sycamores along the
highway, for the making of which an Act of Parliament
was obtained in 1823.   The sycamores, which had been
such a feature of beauty, were cut down after the sale of
1919.

The mansion occupies a commanding site at the edge of a
plateau which on its eastern side overlooks Stancombe,
with the Pear Hill at the turn of the valley leading down to
Bismore and Todsmore.   It is very much reduced in size
from its former appearance, for up to the time of Mr. Wathen
becoming its owner, Lypiatt on its north side had a gate-
house, with a long row of stables, about twenty yards in front
of the present entrance, forming a forecourt which, in its

exposed situation, was a great protection to the house. Many of the domestic buildings at the south side of the house were removed, and the front wall of the banqueting hall was taken down and rebuilt with only one large bay-window in the centre, reaching from the floor to the ceiling, and which was filled with foreign stained glass.

To the west of the hall Mr. Wathen built a square embattled tower, altered the windows in the apartments in that direction, and erected a passage from the tower towards the chapel, something like a cloister, of Gothic appearance. Coats of arms were carved plentifully on the cloister, and also under the eaves of the east side of the old building. The banqueting hall was considerably reduced in size by partitioning off the open gallery and passage. Its ceiling was adorned with a good copy of Guido's Aurora. Many coats of arms of families connected with the estate are painted on oak in the hall and in the old panelled room, now the study, which with the room above it dates from the early sixteenth century.

Further alterations were made by Mr. Lewis and Mr. Baker, and Mr. Dorington and his son Sir John enlarged the house considerably by the addition of rooms running south towards the garden. At this time an old staircase was brought from Grays and re-erected at Lypiatt, when that old house was destroyed. The appearance of the mansion has thus changed very considerably since J. Kip took his view of it for Sir Robert Atkyn's History of Gloucestershire about 1707. (see plate 10)

There is one unique building of much greater age than the mansion, namely the Granary, which is a most beautiful erection of the thirteenth century, in perfect preservation. It must have been built by one of the earliest of the tenants who have been enumerated. (see plate 14)

Two special features are to be noted, besides its perfect windows, namely the outstanding moulding which prevents rats having access to the upper floor, where grain was stored, and the funnel for passing the grain down to the ground level. This is in the form of an ox's head carved in stone. This building is alluded to in Green's " History of the English People."

R

The chapel, the dedication of which is unknown, was built about 1367 by Thomas Maunsell and John Clifford, and consists of a nave and chancel, separated by an arch, with a bell-turret. A cross surmounts the chancel and also the west end of the nave. The east window is formed of two pairs of lights, each headed by a quatrefoil light, and enclosed under its own moulding, with a quatrefoil light between the heads of the pairs, both of which are contained under a hood moulding finished by corbels bearing coats of arms. One would expect these to be the shields of the founders, but they now bear the arms of De la Bere to the south and Baghott to the north. These are—Azure, a bend argent between two cotises and six martletts or, for the former, and—Ermine, on a bend gules three spread eagles, or, for the latter.

The west window is similar to the east, and the side windows of chancel and nave are square-headed. On a stone below the chancel window at the north side may be seen incised a small Agnus Dei.

The chapel has for some years been empty except for the Roman anaglyphs and altars placed there by Sir John Dorington after being discovered in the tump which was destroyed at the making of the road from Bisley to Bussage.

The plateau on which the mansion stands has been terraced on the valley side in pseudo-gothic style.

At the time of the sale of Lypiatt in 1812, the mansion house and gardens were reckoned to cover seven and a half acres, and the Park, including plantations 187¾ acres.

The service of the water supply is mentioned as the " Cundite " in a copy of the Court rolls of 1610, and this appears to be still in use.

The ancient road which formerly ran through the Park dropped down into Stancombe, affording access to the Pear and other houses in that valley, and emerging at Bismore, passed on beside the Todsmore lake or fishpond, and so on to the Stroud valley. In an old map of Lypiatt estate this is marked as the road from London.

Bismore, formerly parcell of the manor of Ferris Court, and subject to Lypiatt, was conveyed by Codrington to John Throckmorton in 1598. There were several cottages scattered about along the narrow valley on the south side, the sites of which can still be traced, perhaps by a solitary fruit tree or obvious enclosure. An evil noteriety was attached to two of the cottages adjacent to Cuthams stile, one of the ancient monolithic stiles so common in the neighbourhood. A full account of the murder of William Wickes, who owned two cottages there, himself living in one of them, on 28 January, 1830, can be seen in Fisher's Notes on Stroud (pp. 206-8). It appears that for the sake of robbing him of two or three Bank bills (which proved to be worthless) one, Thomas Cox, a weaver of 67, with the connivance of Mrs. Warren, who was tenant of William Wicke's second cottage, brutally murdered him by striking him on the head with a hatchet. Thomas Cox suffered the penalty for his crime at Gloucester.

CHAPTER IX

PART 2

MIDDLE LYPIATT

The manorial rights of Over Lypiatt extended over the sub-manor of Nether Lypiatt which again exercised its rights over the tything of Nether Lypiatt reaching as far as Thrupp. As in the case of Over Lypiatt manor the scope of this history is more or less confined to the Lypiatts proper, and does not cover entirely the whole tything, nor Stroud, which have been fully dealt with by Fisher in his " Notes and Recollections of Stroud."

The manor of Nether Lypiatt became divided, one moiety being now known as Middle Lypiatt and the other as Nether Lypiatt. The earliest references in charters speak only of Nether Lypiatt as in that of 1359, when Philip de Rodburgh, John de Upare, and Thomas, parson of the Church of Notgrove granted and confirmed to Thomas de Rodborough and Alice his wife and to their heirs all their manor of Notgrove and all lands tenements and rents which they had in Rodborough, Nether Lippyate, in a certain place called Thrope, in Stonhouse, in a certain place called Ebbeslowe and Hereford in the county of Gloucester with fields and pastures, etc., pertaining which formerly they had by gift and feofment of the said Thomas de Rodbergh, etc. It is further provided that the manor shall descend to William de Rodborough, Philip de Rodborough and Gilbert Gamage, or their heirs and Assigns. W.—John Monemouthe, John in le Felde, Nicholas Spelman, Richard atte Stable, John Soleret and Alice. Given at Notgrove on Wednesday in the Feast of St. Dionysius 33 Ed. III.[1]

---

[1] B. M. Carta Sloan xxxiii, 40

Land in both Over and Nether Lypiatt is dealt with in a Fine levied between Lawrence Dolman and Roger Duryard in 1367. It concerns one messuage, one virgate and a half of land, four acres of meadow and seventeen acres of wood in Over Lypiatt and Nether Lypiatt which Laurence Dolman purchased from Roger Duryard for 100 marks.[1]

In 1397, John Clifford of Denneway held one knight's fee in Lower Lypiatt of Humphrey de Bohun, Earl of Essex, and died possessed of a messuage and one virgate of land held of the Duke of Hereford at a rent of 4s. per annum.[2]

The moiety of the manor of Nether Lypiatt now called Middle Lypiatt at some time unknown became the possession of the Knights Hospitallers of St. John of Jerusalem of Quenington Priory, but in the list of Knights' fees and advowsons belonging to Humphrey de Bohun Earl of Essex, Hereford and Northants. taken at Gloucester 2 March, 1373, the year of his death, besides one fee in Paganhulle, one fee in Lupegate Seupier which John de Clifford held worth 100s., one fee in Biselee and Wynston which Edmund Earl of March held, one fourth of a fee in Biselee which Hugh de Biselee held worth 25s., there was half a fee in Lower Lupe-vate, which the Abbot of Tewkesbury and the Prior of the Hospital of St. John and Roger Re (Reame) held, worth 50s.[3]

At the time of the Dissolution, the rental of free tenants was 14s. 4d. and one lb. of cummin ; of the customary tenants £4 8s. 10d.[4] There were growing about the situation of certain tenements there 120 oaks ashes and elms of 60 or 80 years' growth whereof 60 were reserved for housebote and hedgbote, as set forth in the request by John Pope to purchase the estate in 1545.

The same year that John Pope purchased the manor he obtained the Royal Licence to alienate a moiety of it to Richard Fowler, including certain messuages then in the tenure of John Smarte, Giles Davys, Alys Davys, Thomas

---

[1] P. R. O. Feet of Fines, Glouc., 466.
[2] Fosbroke's Hist. of Glos., Esc. 21 Richard II., no. 19.
[3] Index Library, Pt. VI, 69.
[4] P. R. O. Particulars for Grants 874. Hockaday's Eccl. File.

Freme and John Byg. The remaining moiety of the manor and messuages in the tenure of Thomas Sewell, John Shereman, John Bulkeley, and Thomas Freme, he alienated to William Savell, clothier, of Stroud.[1]

The Inquisition P. M. of Henry Fowler, who was probably the son of Richard Fowler, made in 1564-5, records that he died seised of part of the manor of Nether Lippiat, which was formerly owned by the priory of St. John of Jerusalem, and that he owned lands lately the property of John Smart, and that William Fowler is his brother and heir, aged 45.[2]

The Inquisition P. M. of Richard Fowler, gentleman,[3] made at Thornbury, 16 September, 1628, recites that his son Roger, who predeceased him in 1626 made his will 11 February of that year and bequeathed to his father all his lands, namely the messuage situate in Nether Lypiate in the parish of Bisley, then or late in the tenure of the said Richard Fowler, and two fulling mills, one grain mill and one Gygge Myll in Neather Lypiat, four closes of arable land or pasture there commonly called the Parke Closes, containing about thirty acres; one close of meadow called Hasell Meade, containing about one and a half acres, . . . (concerning land in Minchinhampton) . . . one messuage and one close of arable land thereto adjoining containing about four acres in Neather Lypiat then or late in the tenure of Margarie Griffin, widow. . . The said Richard Fowler was seised of all that close of arable land, curtilage, and garden called Uppingland, lying in Neather Lypiatt opposite a certain messuage called Bigges Place; all that parcel of land there called Michellacre, with all the houses built thereupon; two closes of arable land or pasture there called Preestes; four closes of pasture or arable land called Busshey Closes containing twenty acres one close of pasture and arable land called Rolles Croft, containing six acres, and one close of arable land or pasture called Wheate close containing four acres. The said messuage and all the said mills in Neather Lypiatt, the closes there called Parke Close, the close called

---

1 Hockaday's Eccl. File.
2 Gloucestershire Notes and Queries, 1, 225.
3 *B. G. A. S. Trans.*, Inq. P. M. 1625-42, p. 53.

Hasell Meade . . . the premisses in the tenure of the said Margerie Griffin . . . are held of the King by reason of the minority of Henry Lord Stafford, as of the Honour of Hereford, by knight's service and are worth per annum clear 20s. 3d. It is stated that Richard Fowler died at Calthroppe, parish of Standish 7 July, 1637, and that Henry Fowler, clerk, son and heir is aged 30 or more.

In the absence of old title deeds it is impossible to identify the land and mills specified, none of the names mentioned appearing in the tithe terrier. Possibly the mills and land of Roger Fowler may have been those in the Todsmore valley : the "land held by Margarie Griffin" is probably near Griffin's Mill at Thrupp. The Griffins appear to have inter-married with the Fowlers for in the will of John Griffin of 1626, and of Elizabeth his widow of 1627, sums of money are bequeathed to their daughter Margery Fowler and to the four children of Mr. Henry Fowler.

The manor of Nether Lypiatt extended to Brimscombe for according to the Inquisition of Giles Davis, 1638, late of Nether Lypiatt, he was seised of two messuages and thirty acres of land in Brimscombe in Nether Lypiatt, sometime parcel of the lands of John Betoway there, which are held of Henry Fowler, clerk, as of his manor of Nether Lypiatt, by fealty and yearly rent of 5s.

Fosbrooke states that William Fowler who inherited Middle Lypiatt from his brother, had licence to alienate the estate to Richard Stephens in 1567 (according to a deed in the then possession of Thomas White of Stonehouse, Esq.), who granted it again in lease to Daniel Fowler. It was purchased by the Leversage family with whom it remained till 1845, when Peter Leversage, Esq., barrister at law, grandson of Peter Leversage, who was living at Middle Lypiatt in 1799, and who was well known for his hospitaility, sold it to Henry Wyatt, Esq., of Farm Hill, Stroud, who dying in 1847, it passed to his daughters, and later was purchased by Sir John Dorington. At the sale of 1919 Middle Lypiatt estate, of 249 acres, was purchased by Mr. Vines of Standish.

The house at Middle Lypiatt, which is a stone gabled building in the Cotswold style of the Tudor period, must have been built shortly after the Dissolution of the monasteries. There is a reception room panelled with oak in the reign of William and Mary, at which time the large Tudor fireplace was covered over and a small aperture left for a more modern grate. The original fireplace has a shallow arch enclosed in a square frame of stone mantel and jambs with several orders of mouldings. There is also an alcove in the wall. There are two winding staircases, one being of stone hidden under wooden treads, and there are some remains of glass of the seventeenth century. The cellars with stone groined roof appear to be of a great age, and their sides are in places supported by stones of a remarkable size and shape. At one part of an inner cellar some of the stones employed appear to be mediaeval, and probably formed part of the ancient building of the Knights of St. John. A large building near the front door was formerly a malt-house, where beer was brewed by Mr. Peter Leversage until towards the end of the eighteenth century when he established the Stroud Brewery.

There is a very ancient well in the yard between the malt house and the front door.

The Sterts.

A portion of the estate of Middle Lypiatt lying below the farm called the Sterts, Stirts, or Strits, (O. E. Steort—a tongue of land) and projecting into the valley above Todsmore Lake, has a remarkable appearance when viewed from the other side of the valley, and looks as if in ancient times its shape had been largely formed by man, possibly as a camp. Its curved eastern end is now surrounded by a belt of trees, part of the wood which till recently covered its steep slope. Merestones, (the position of which are marked on the Ordnance Map) indicate the limit of the Middle Lypiatt estate in that direction. There are said to be initials carved on some of them.

The earliest evidence of the Sterts is found in the Lypiatt MS book, copied from the original deed, wherein Hugh de Byslye, son and heir of Richard de Byslye, remitted and quit-claimed to Henry de Clifford and Macilla his wife and to Henry their son, all claim that he had in half a virgate of land which he held in the vill of Over Lypiatt, called Sterte-lond, or to rent for the same for ever.   W. John de Mone-menweth, John atte Feld de Paganhull, Andrew Clavyle, Robert de Eggesworth, Richard de Clyvehale, Thomas Mody, Hugh Galon, William de Wyk, and others.   Given at Bislye on the eve of the Anunciation of Blessed Marie, 1349.

The next notice of the Sterts is to be found in the interesting will of Walter Butt, who resided somewhere in Over Lypiatt, possibly at the Pear.   The family of Butt had been settled in and about Bisley in Tudor times, for the names of Richard and John Butt appear in the Lay Subsidy rolls of 1522-3 and similar references are in the parish registers of the sixteenth and seventeenth centuries.

Walter Butt made his will[1] 15 July, 1625.   He describes himself as clothier, and after commending his soul to the Holy Trinity having full hope confidence and trust of pardon and forgiveness of sins and offences through his Lord and Saviour Jesus Christ he desires that his body be buried where it seems good to his executors.   To his sons Richard and William Butt all his messuages called the Stearts, with all lands, meadows, and grounds, belonging and lying in Over Lypiatt with Benjamin Decroc's Lease with the terms therein contained which is ordered in Chauncery that Benjamin Decroc should reassure him and his executors, etc., by lawful conveyance, he being paid as due to him.   To his son Thomas Butt all the grounds called by the name of the Sterts with the woods there to belonging lying in Nether Lypiatt to have and to hold the said grounds called the Sterts with the woods thereto belonging to the said Thomas Butt, etc.   To his daughters Mary and Jane £20 each.   To his son Benjaymyne Butt £20, also at 21, out of lands conveyed in trust by him to Nathaniel Coxwell, Esq.   To his sons and

---

[1] P. C. C. 45 Skynner.

daughters all such his goods and chattels which he left in trust with Mr. Richard Stephens of Sisiter, appearing in an inventory and in trust till required, to be equally divided at his death. To his children one B . . . pe which is in Mr. Stephens' Court which he lent him, worth £5, to be sold by his executors and the money divided amongst his children. To his son Benjaymyne Butt one silver Boule gilt with his name thereon ingraved, which bowl remains in the hands of Richard Talboyts to have and to enjoy the said Bowl to him and his assigns for ever. To his son Richard Butt one Marcer Boule parcel silver gilt and inamelde with his name engraven thereon which said bowl remains in the custody and possession of the said Nathaniel Coxwell. To his said Children one trunk remaining with his father-in-law Thomas Blisse and one Oryce Coverlette with a pair of silk curtains and vallence, one dozen needlework cushions one bason and ewer of pewter, a pewter candlesticks and three down pillows, one fair carpett in coustody of the widow Freame of Bisley, one feather bed and Boulster and one down pillow, one flock-bed and boulster, one pair of new blankets, two stamell rugs with one coverlet wrought with white, one great chest of spruce, one barrell, one washing tubb, one other basin of pewter and a pewter dish, two towels, one other pewter candlestick, one haye crooke and one brush in custody of John Skynner of Stroud, also two fair rugs one green the other orange colour, one fair coverlette wrought with birds and a cloak of broadcloth damson colour, the cape whereof is of russett velvett laid about with silversicke laces, and one great candlestick of brass remaining in the possession of Roger Fowler of Nether Lypiatt all of which are to be equally divided amongst his children. To his son John Butt £20 on his coming into England. To Richard and William Butt one silver bowl, one silver salt, and six silver spoons which are in the custody of Mr. Thomas Freame, they paying to him £4 borrowed from him on the said articles. All results from the sale of lands now in trust with Nathaniel Coxwell to be divided amongst his children, after his debts paid, etc. Executors,—his sons Richard and William Butt. Overseers, Thomas Freame, Esq., of Nether Lypiatt, Thomas Taylor of Bisley, yeoman, and Thomas Webb of Stroud, yeoman (each

20s.). W. Nicholas Sharpe, Edward Moore. Proved 7 April, 1627.

" The messuages called the Stearts " lying in Over Lypiatt are now lost sight of, but the Sterts in Nether Lypiatt are still known by that name.

A later will, of Richard Butt, dyer, of Chalford, 29 April, 1742, is probably that of a descendant of Walter Butt. He left to his grandson Richard Butt son of his late son Samuel Butt his messuage or dwelling-house in Chalford near to the house he then lives in and also all the stable and outhouse standing opposite to his then dwelling-house, together with the garden lying in Chalford near to the dwelling-house, now or late of one Elizabeth Hyde. To his granddaughter Sarah Butt, daughter of his aforesaid late son Samuel, all the two messuages or tenements situated in a place called Tankard Springs, now or late in the possession of William White and Hannah Hyde, and after her decease these to go to his grandson Nathaniel Butt, another son of the late Samuel Butt. £10 each to Caple Butt and the said Nathaniel, Elizabeth Ann and Mary Butt. To his grandchildren William Sevill, Sara Sevill, Mary Sevill, and Ann Sevill, son and daughters of William Sevill and Ann his wife (testator's daughter) £10 each. To his said grandson Richard Butt his mare and colt. To his granddaughter Ann Sevill his silver tankard. The residue to be equally divided between the said Ann and his grandson Richard Butt who are to be executors. W. Thomas Holliday, Richard Pinbury, Edmund Clutterbuck. Proved 6 July, 1744.[1]

The Butts are spoken of by Fosbrooke as " an opulent family " at Chalford. They later resided at Arle Court near Cheltenham.

[1] Glos P. R.

CHAPTER IX

PART 3

NETHER LYPIATT

Nether Lypiatt was for many generations the property of the Ream or Freame family. In 1349 John de Reom, together with the Prior of the Hospital of St. John of Jerusalem in England, held half a knight's fee, which William de Reom and the Prior formerly held.[1] William de Reom must therefore have been living at the end of the thirteenth century. Roger de Reem was witness of a charter of Thomas de Rodbergh to William and Agnes Hokkenale in 1350, together with Thomas de Monemouth, John atte Felde de Paganhulle, Richard le Clerkesson, Roger de Seymour, Henry le Duriard, Adam atte Fairok and others, at Strode on the feast of the Translation of St. Thomas Martyr. Thomas de Rodbergh confirmed to William and Agnes Hokkenale certain land which had been that of Richard atte Hull in Biseleye in the parish of Stroud, one croft called le Hinhale, which extended upon the road leading near Wisynsmill and another which lay next the mansion of Robert de Reem, rendering yearly 12s. rent.[2]

Roger Freame was holding a quarter of a knight's fee there in 1373. He died in 1386 or 7, for at the Court of Hugh de Bisley, held 11 January, 10 Ric. II (1387), Thomas atte Reome (his son) swore fealty and service in the place of Roger Freme.

At Hugh de Bisley's Court of 10 October, 1393, excuse was registered of John Reome, and at the Court of the Feoffees held at Bisley in May, 1413, he was presented by the Homage as owing sac and soc and making default.

---

[1] *B. G. A. S. Trans.*, Feudal Aids, X, 278.
[2] B. M. Carta Sloan, xxxiii., 36.

In the Court of 7 June, 1429, Roger and Edward Reme are mentioned.[1]

In the Minister's Accounts of 1447-8 Thomas Freme is stated to pay ½-lb. of wax for rent of one messuage and half a virgate of land called Shermans' This is increased to 1 lb. of wax in the following year. This same Thomas Freme at the Court of Lypiatt of 8 October, 1457, was fined 40d. because he had not made his hedge as ordered, but it continued to be greatly in defect as stated at the Court of Thomas Whittington, 11 October, 1458, the hedge being situated between the property of Thomas Freme and William Dolman at the place called Parkers Hill Combe. Another fine of 40d. was incurred the next year, 8 October, 1459, as Thomas Freme still defied the Court.[2] These fragmentary records of the Freame family are all that can be found until the sixteenth century brings fuller knowledge.

In the Lay Subsidy roll of 1522-3 Thomas Freme is assessed at 20s., and John Freme at 40s.

John Freme attended the Court of Robert Wye, Esq., of Over Lypiatt on 30 October, 1516, and took a messuage and lands formerly in the tenure of Hugh Dower, to hold during his and his wife Deny's lives, making annually all burdens and service and giving a fine for admission of 53s. 4d.

In the Bisley Parish registers the first mention of the Freme family is the marriage of Richard Lugg and Catherine Freme 10 October, 1554, and the burial that year on 14 November of Richard, son of Thomas Freame, gentleman. The registers continue such notices at intervals throughout that and the following century, but some members of the family were connected with Stroud parish church and are registered there. Jone Freame dated her will 5 December, 1541. By it she bequeathed her Sole to Almighty God, the Blessed Virgin Mary and all the Saints in heven. She desired to be buried in the Churchyard of All Sayntes in Bisley. Her month's mind to be kept the whole yere. Her son John Freame to be residuary legatee and sole executor. W. Syr

1 P. R. O. Court Rolls, Glos., 175.
2 Lypiatt Court Rolls in Lypiatt MS. Book.

John Tryvyllyan " my gostely father," Richard Cuffe and others. Proved at Framton 30 March, 1542.[1]

There is a will of John Freme, of 1546, who is probably the son named above, bequeathing " to our Lady survyce 12d., and to the mayntynans of the Church lyghte and the belles a boschell of whete."[2] The place of his residence is obliterated, and he may have been of Tunley, where one Richard Freame was living in 1528, as mentioned in the will of Thomas Marshall, Parson of St. Gabriel Fanchurche, London, of that date.

The will of Thomas Freme, gentleman, of Nether Lippiate, dated 29 April, 1572, gives detailed information about his family. It opens with " I besheese my mercifull lord creator and redeemer to forgive me my sinnes and upon hartie repentance to receive my soule unto his eternal glorye," his body to be buried in the churche of Stroude as near to his wife's body as can be. Amongst six of his sons the sum of £12 13s. 4d. yearly.

His house and medowes, landes, woods, tenements and mill called New House from which the said sum of £12 13s. 4d. is to be made but if that sum does not arise out of the house and lands, then the rent of Thomas Gryffyn's house and also the other . . . meade he had bought of Henry Serman was to be set to rent to make 31s. The sum of money to be paid to William Freme the elder, his son £3 4s. 0d. To Gyles Freme 40s. To Richard Freme 40s. To John Freme 40s. To William the younger, 40s. To Walter Freme 40s. Richard and John Freme are to be put to " myrsters " by his executors. His sons William junior and Walter Freme to be kept at school. He gives to his son Thomas £6 and the reason he gives him no annuity is that he gave him a purchase holden of our soveraigne lady the Queen of the manor of Bisley.

To his two sons, to William sen. and to Giles Freme £5 to buy a farm with. To John Freme £5 for one half year, and Richard Freme, after they leave masters. To William

[1] Hockaday's Eccl. File, G. P. R.
[2] Hockaday's Eccl. File, G. P. R. 101.

Freme, junr. £5. To Walter Freme £5. To Marjery, his daughter, £40. To Edye his daughter, £40.

To the poor folk of Bysley and Stroude four marks, to Bisley 13s. 4d. and to Stroude 40s. For his funeral 40s. For the opening of his grave in Stroude 11s. 8d. . . . The remainder to Robert Freame his son and heir, who is appointed executor. Thomas Dobbyns and Edward Chalford, overseers and assessors. Bequests follow to his son-in-law Thomas, and Katherine.

Amongst his debts.—To Here Stock Keper of the castell 26s. To John Whitinge of Bisleye £10 whereof he hath a portion in his custody, a goblet of plate and the fellow of him is to be forwarded and upon payment thereof to recover the said goblet. To Thomas Dobbyns his overseer £10 and to Edward Stratford his other overseer, 20s.

W. Richard Hale, Thomas Spearwell, John Chambers, and Richard Smart. (The writer hereof.)[1]

James Freame was appointed reeve of the Bisley manor 1 May, 1592, vice Richard Perrin, whose occupation as " practiser of physic " at Bisley probably made it impossible for him to act. At the Court of John Throckmorton, Esq., 6 November, 1589, it is found that Johan Freame, widow, who held of the Lord by copyhold one messuage, and certain land, had died since the last court, a heriot of 30s. being due. As Walter Fennell came and claimed the premises by copy for term of life, this may have been Fennell's farm.

Robert Freame having succeeded his father at Lypiatt made his will 29 May, 1599, being described as of Nether Lypiatt, Esq. After a pious preamble, " being in perfect healthe and good memorie thanks be to Almightie God which I beseech him of his gratious goodness to direct and governe to his divine will and pleasure, " etc. " I bequeath my bodie and soule into the hands of Almightie God to whose good government I referr the whole disposition of my life." Joan his wife, is to have her £30 by yeare appointed her for her jointure, his house and lands in the forrest and half part of his household stuff, bedding, linen, etc., except all plate,

[1] Glos. P. R.

and some part of the house at Lypiatt. To his four daughters £800. To the eldest, Anne, £100 down and £100 on marriage if with consent of her mother and overseers : if not it is to be divided amongst the other children.

To his second daughter Elizabeth £200 on the same conditions. The third daughter Julian, and the fourth daughter Alice each £200 on similar conditions.

To his son William £100, all the house and lands in the forest beforementioned, after the death of his wife. Failing his marriage and heirs, to his son Robert, failing whose heirs to Thomas Freame his sonne heire and overseer. If he refuse to act, then he is to pay £500 to his son William at the age of 21.

To his youngest son Robert £200 at twelve years of age, to increase as stock under his overseers till he is 21. To George Freame his son £40 and £10 on the day of marriage of his heir. Any inheritance not falling to these is to be divided amongst his wife and remaining children. Arrangements for education at school or otherwise are left to his wife during the infancy of Robert, Julian and Alice.

His son is to make an even reckoning with his cosen Robert Ellen and to apprentice him to some good place.

Thomas Freme his son is heir and executor.

His brothers Gyles Freame, Richard Freame, John and William Freame, his cosen Gyles Davis, James Skittermishe and Thomas Skittermish, overseers.[1]

Giles Freame married and had a son John, baptized at Bisley 18 April, 1624. His wife lived till 1667, being buried at Bisley 17 November, and Giles died in 1669, being buried at the same place on 4 October.

Thomas Freame who succeeded his father at Lypiatt, died in 1659. There was formerly a monument to his memory in Bisley Church with the inscription :—" Here lies the Body of Thomas Freame of Lypite, Esq., who departed this Life the 5th day of January, 1659,"—with the coat of arms,—a

[1] Glos. Pro. Reg.

cross moline between four ears of wheat, impaling,—on a fess between three martlets, three annulets.

His burial is entered in the registers of Bisley as taking place on 10 January, 1660. His wife Elizabeth Biggs had died in 1647 and was buried at Bisley 15 November.

Thomas Freame, Esq., of Lower Lypiatt, whose formerly ornate monument was in the chancel of Stroud parish Church, now deprived of the emblematical figures of Faith, Hope and Charity, Innocence, with Cherubs, and Death's head, etc., which once adorned it, and reduced to a tablet bearing the following inscription,—was a son of the last mentioned Thomas.

" Thomas Freame, Armiger, ex cohorte centurio, obiit 18 Aprilis, an. dni. 1664, aetatis suae 63.
Non cecidit Fraemus, licet hic cecidisse videtur,
Ad superas abijt, venerat unde, domos :
Viva fides, charitas, spes, mens sua firma manebant :
Caetera deposuit, mors meliora dedit.

Hic etiam Anna Fream Thomae quondom Uxor post XXX, viduitatis annos interum Viro conjuncta fuit. January 26^c, 1694."

Mr. Fisher translated the verses as follows :—

" Though here to have died he seemed, Freame did not die,
He went to (whence he came) his home on high
Hope, living faith, love, his firm mind, remain'd ;
The rest laid down, from death he better gained."

Thomas Freame had married Anne Query, whose arms— Argent, a chevron sable in chief a fess engrailed gules, were impaled with his own.

In addition to this monument there is beneath it one in memory of Thomas Clutterbuck, the son of Samuel Clutterbuck, great grandson of Thomas Freame, of Lower Lypiatt, Esq., who died 14 March, 1715, in the ninth year of his age. Another tablet commemorated Freame Clutterbuck, infant son of Freame Clutterbuck, 1711.

Captain Thomas Freame's younger brother William, married Mary, daughter of Thomas Pate of Cheltenham.

William Freame's monument which was formerly in the chancel at Bisley, but which is now destroyed, bore a portraiture of him in stone, holding a book, and dressed in the costume of the period, with his arms depicted namely— Argent, a chevron sable, in Chief a bar engrailed gules, for Freame, impaling a Chevron between three pellets, on a chief three crosses patee fichy, for Pates. The Freames appear to have borne two coats of arms, as it will be noted that these differ from those of 1659.

The inscription to William Freame was as follows :—

" M.S.
Gulielmi Freame, Generosi,
Thomae Freame de Lypiat, Armigeri, Minimi natu Filii,
Cujus in pauperes Charitas in Amicos suavitas,
In omnes benevolentia effecit, Ut tristissumum sui
desiderium reliquerit Annorum et vitae Satur February 12 mo,
Anno Aetatis suae 84, Domini 1696."

Sarah, daughter and co-heiress of Thomas Freame married Henry Windowe, of Lincoln's Inn, youngest son of William Windowe of Gloucester (to whom there is an inscription in St. Nicholas Church, Gloucester) on 14 April, 1673, at Bisley Church. Their marriage settlement, now in the possession of Lord Biddulph, is dated 16 January, 1672, and by it he settled on his intended wife the manors of Hullasey and Tarlton in the parish of Coates, left to him by his father in his will of 20 April, 1668. Henry Windowe their son, married Sarah daughter, and co-heir of John, second son of Thomas Stephens of Lypiatt. The arms of Window,—Az. a fess counter-embattled between three lions jambs erected and erased or, quartered with those of Freame and an escutcheon of pretence, for Stephens, are to be seen in Churchdown Church. Elizabeth, second daughter of Thomas Freame married Thomas Clutterbuck, of Stroud.

Ann, the eldest daughter married Thomas Chamberlayne of Wanborough Co. Wilts.[1] Their daughter Catherine married as his second wife Charles Coxe, son of John Coxe, of

---

[1] From MS. notes of the Freame family. Mr. J. D. Thorp in *B. G. A. S. Trans.*, 1, 179, gives a different version, but is doubtful about its correctness.

Tarlton, by his wife Deborah Driver of Avening. Charles Coxe, who came of a Rodmarton family of which place he was subsequently Lord of the Manor, was born in 1661 and matriculated at St. Edmund Hall, Oxford, 10 July, 1674. He was a barrister of Lincoln's Inn and had a distinguished career as puisne judge of sessions for Brecknock, Glamorgan and Radnor from 1702-4, and Chief Justice there from 1704 to 1714. He was M.P. for Cirencester from 1693 to 1705, and from 1708 to 1713, and for Gloucester till 1722.

Judge Coxe's wife, Catherine Chamberlayne brought to him the manor of Nether Lypiatt, the mansion of which he entirely rebuilt in 1717. He died in 1729 and by his will dated 9 October, 1728, he left Lypiatt to his eldest son John Coxe. He was buried at Rodmarton.

A portrait of Charles Coxe, recently in the possession of the Shephard family, has unfortunately been lost sight of.

Persistent tradition has attributed to Judge Coxe an act of a most unworthy nature had it any foundation in fact, namely, that the ornate ironwork of the gates and screen of the forecourt to Lower Lypiatt Hall having been made by a smith whom the Judge had tried and condemned for murder, he was reprieved by the same authority till he had finished them, and then was hanged. In reality the work is thought to be that of Warren a well-known artificer, who made many gates at that period, notably those of Trinity College, Cambridge, Eagle House, Clapton, the Little Cloisters, Westminster, and Burleigh House, Enfield, the gates of the latter closely resembling those of Lower Lypiatt.[1] As Judge Coxe was a Welsh judge his jurisdiction was in Wales and did not extend to Gloucester. His love for his horse prompted him to erect a monument to its memory, consisting of an obelisque twelve feet high raised up on a base three feet square by four feet in height, still standing in the wood below the Hall. There was formerly an iron tablet on the east face of the base, which was unfortunately taken away and lost, but its inscription, according to Mrs. Ridler, wife of a tenant of the farm, was :—

1 The Manor houses of England, Ditchfield, p. 35.

" My name was Wag, that rolled in green,
The oldest horse that ever was seen,
My years they numbered forty-two—
I served my master just and true."

John Coxe of Lincoln's Inn, born in 1696, succeeded to Nether Lypiatt and to the farm at Tarlton, Coates. He entered Magdalen College, Oxford, 23 January, 1712, at the age of 16, and was called to the bar 14 June, 1718. He was M.P. for Cirencester from 1749 to 1754. He was one of the Feoffees of Rodborough of land held by them in Bisley, but beyond one other witnessing of a deed his name is not found in connection with events at Bisley, so it is doubtful if he resided at Nether Lypiatt. He died 27 January, 1783.

John Coxe bequeathed Nether Lypiatt to his son Charles[1] who inherited various other estates from his grandfather. He married on 1 April, 1749, Elizabeth, daughter and eventually co-heir of Sir Robert Westley, lord Mayor of London in 1743. The date of his death is uncertain, but he was living in 1793. Charles Coxe's son, Charles Westley Coxe, of Kemble House, M.P. for N. Wilts., inherited several manors from his father and mother. He married on 10 December, 1789, Ann daughter of Robert Gordon of Auchendolly, their only child being a daughter, Elizabeth Anne, who succeeded to all her father's estates. Charles Westley Coxe died 10 March, 1806, and was buried at Kemble. His daughter Elizabeth Anne married her cousin Robert Gordon (who died 23 March, 1865), and left an only child, Anna, born 1809, who inherited a great number of manors,[2] Nether Lypiatt coming to her through her grandmother Elizabeth Coxe's will. This she gave about 1880 to a distant cousin, Philip Charles Sheppard, son of Philip Sheppard of Gatcombe, Esq., Lord of the Manor of Minchinhampton, thereby carrying out the provision of her grandmother's will in her lifetime, instead of waiting for her own decease, which occurred 21 December, 1884.

---

[1] Will proved 1783. P. C. C., 342 Cornwallis.

[2] See History of the Manor of Coates, by J. D. Thorp. *B. G. A. S. Trans.*, l., 179.

Meanwhile the mansion was tenanted by farmers, for some years by William Gardiner, of Scottish descent, who married Mary Capner of Bisley, 3 October, 1758, and died at Nether Lypiatt, 1812, aged 88, being buried at Bisley and leaving a large family, from whom is descended the Rev. E. Courtney Gardiner. William Gardiner was succeeded by the Ridler family, the marriage of a daughter of Robert Ridler to —. Ratcliffe continuing the tenancy. Elizabeth Jane Ratcliffe, his daughter, married William Thomas Wallis, after whose death Charles Pearson Wallis, his son, carried on the farming till 1915, when the connected tenancy was broken.

The property, being in the hands of mortgagees, was sold to Mr. Arthur William Stanton in 1914, but was quickly disposed of by him to Mr. Corbett W. Woodall, who having been a restorer of many ancient houses, gave Nether Lypiatt a complete and most satisfactory restoration, with the assistance of Mr. Morley Horder, architect, and in 1923, sold the house and estate to Gordon Woodhouse, Esq., the present owner.

The Hall of Nether Lypiatt.

Of the ancient mansion of the Freames nothing remains, save an old well and a few foundations. It was entirely destroyed by Judge Coxe when he erected the present building in the style of the Queen Anne period, influenced as it was by the classic style of Wren's successors.

Situated on the crown of the Lypiatt ridge with extensive woods below it, the house is a prominent object in the landscape, and goes popularly by the name of "the Haunted House," though nothing more formidable than the ghost of Judge Coxe's horse is said to haunt the staircase.

The house is approached through a gateway to the forecourt, the wrought iron-work of which has been already mentioned, as the work of Warren. The gates are hung on stone pillars, having moulded caps and urn-shaped terminals.

Their lock-rail of rich interlacing work is deemed to show German influence. There are " four small panels, each filled with four scrolls proceeding from a circle, united by vertical bars with a central panel formed of scrolls and water leaves. The horizontals are fringed with C scrolls, holding waved spikes, and the dog bars are arrow-pointed."[1]   The scroll work above has the name of Coxe in monogram interlaced in it.

The house being four square with uniformedly placed windows on all sides, was found to be very difficult of internal arrangement, a few of the windows having to be filled in with ashlar as the partitions of the rooms sometimes came in the centre of them.   The house is built of oolite stone said to be quarried at Bisley, and consists of a barrel vaulted cellar, a basement floor with entrances from north and south, with two stories of the chief rooms and an attic with a single-span hipped roof, which till 1848, when the house was practically re-roofed, had two dormer windows on every side, instead of on the east and west only.   The date 1717, which is that of the completion of the house, is to be seen on the gutter pipes of lead, with the Coxe crest, a crowing cock.

The front entrance is by a flight of ten steps, leading up to a porch, consisting of a segmental pediment, supported by fluted Ionic columns and pilasters, and leading directly into the hall.   This hall, which has a richly carved stone mantel-piece, is said to occupy a corner of the original dining room of the Freames.   The panelling of the rooms, being chiefly carried out in elm and ash, became very decayed, but the hall is now panelled with sound panelling from other parts of the house.   The present dining-room, on the ground floor, formerly the kitchen, and now panelled, was, on its restoration found to have a most interesting old fireplace, with a wide Tudor shaped arch.   The study retains its old panelling, relieved of coats of paint, and the smaller dining-room on the ground floor, has Elizabethan oak scratch panelling on three sides, and walnut panelling on the fourth.   This was all discovered under six coats of paper and one of canvas.[2]

[1] The Manor houses of England, by Ditchfield.
[2] See Mr. F. Morley Horder's paper in *Country Life*, March 24, 1923.

The staircase, with its twisted balusters, is of chestnut. One bedroom had its walls formerly covered with blue velvet panels separated by strips of white embroidered satin, and two state beds have survived, which were entirely covered with needlework of the early eighteenth century.

The drawing-room formerly was adorned with three fine pieces of tapestry, of late seventeenth century work, which Miss Gordon presented to the School of Art at Gloucester. Two pieces measure 14 ft. by 10 ft. and the third piece 10 ft. by 8 ft. The subjects of these tapestries are scenes from the book of Esther, that of the smaller being the calling forth of Mordecai by King Ahasuerus. The other two depict the horse on which Mordecai is to ride through the city, and his enthronement with a golden crown on his head. The figures are after the style of Raphael and Rubens, and possibly the tapestries were made at Mortlake after the Restoration.

Whilst the front and back windows are of Renaissance style, with sashes, the side windows have mullions, transoms and casements, and have the appearance of late Tudor work. The barns and stables also carry on the influence of that period. An iron fireback, once in the dining-room, but now relegated to one of the garden rooms, has the coat of arms of the Freames on it.

During the levelling of a portion of the garden by Mr. Woodall, for the construction of a tennis court, the workmen came upon human skeletons at a depth of two or three feet, thought to be those of men of about six feet in height, perfectly preserved and with their teeth white and sound. As no experts appear to have seen these remains, no details have been preserved as to the position in which they lay, neither were the bones preserved in a proper manner. The conclusion arrived at was that they were the remains of soldiers slain in the Civil War, and that they were not of pre-historic origin.[1] Whilst there was fighting at Over Lypiatt, there is no record of any at Nether Lypiatt, and if there had been, it was usual to give the slain Christian burial in a churchyard, unless it was a great battle.

[1] *Stroud News*, December 5, 1919.

A shield of arms in stone was found during the restoration of 1922, built into the wall of the fireplace in the dining-room, with its carved face inwards, and thought to be dated between 1631 and 1634. It is very roughly carved and heraldically incorrect. The Freame arms, a chevron and a bar engrailed are placed in quarters 1 and 3, with the arms of Bigge—a fess between 3 Martlets, as many annulets, in the second quarter, and for Query,—a dexter arm in mail, in the fourth quarter.

CHAPTER X

PART 1

THE TYTHING OF OAKRIDGE.

Of Oakridge, the sixth tything of Bisley, Bigland finds " nothing worthy of remark." Its name, varying from Ockridge to Okerinch and Oakridge indicates that oaktrees were a notable feature there. Though early history is lacking, Rudder points out that the Abbey of Cirencester owned lands here which at the Dissolution were granted to Thomas Stroud, Walter Earl, and James Paget in 1544. Particulars of the value of the lands belonging to the Abbey were set forth in 1539, and after mention of rents of customary tenants at Througham, 18s. 4d. at Westwode, (still marked by a farm in Edgeworth parish of that name) at 30s., the tenants at Tunley paid 5s., at Abbenese 4s., and Frampton 10s. The farm of a tenement and close of pasture called Trylles (now Trillies), and a small close adjacent in Okeruge in the parish of Bysseley, was demised to William Frome, and Isabel his wife, and William and Thomas Cockes, sons of the said Isabel at 13s. 4d. rent, 20 September, 1539.[1] Trillies still retains its name, and stands at the east end of Oakridge, overlooking the Holy Brook and Golden Valley. It later passed into the possession of William Lediard, who was named as a free tenant at the Court Baron of 1736, (who married Anne, granddaughter of Thomas Iles of Oakridge, died in 1741), and it was afterwards acquired by Henry Jayne of Bisley. In the latter's will of 1764 it is mentioned as " all his messuage and lands at Oakridge called Trilleys let to William Royatt at the rent of ten guineas to his sister Mary, wife of Peter Clissold of Bristol." Perhaps part of this

---

[1] P. R. O. Aug. Office Petition for Grant, 1373. Hockaday's File.

former Abbey estate may be concerned in the demise of all his interest in the wood called Oaklands Grove of seventeen acres more or less, and his interest in a piece of land called Herringate of one acre which he leaves to his sisters Mary Clissold and Catherine Saunders equally.[1]

That Cirencester Abbey had other lands in Oakridge besides Trillies seems to be indicated, but identification of the locality has not yet been established. The finding of a supposed monastic seal (now lost sight of) in the garden at Frampton's Place by the daughter of Mr. Charles Newth the then tenant, led to the supposition that that was monastic property. The Frampton mentioned in the above list of customary tenants' rents appears to refer to Frampton Mansell.

The Holywell in the garden of Lydays rather suggests a possible connection with Cirencester Abbey, and this suggestion is strengthened by the appearance of the foundation stones of the barn, some of which are of mediaeval date and ecclesiastical style. The title-deeds only go back to 1658, when Mrs. Janet Butler, widow of Nathaniell Butler, of Sapperton, Clerk, conveyed the property to Richard Lyday, senr. By the end of the seventeenth century Lydays farm had passed to George Smart and was by him sold to Samuel Damsell, a well-to-do broadweaver, who died 1712. His son Nathaniel mortgaged it to John Gurner, weaver, who again mortgaged it in 1730 to William Hancock, of Frampton, yeoman, with a close of one acre adjoining, together with lands in Battlescombe field near Lillygate, and a part near Litteridge Cross and near Twissel stone.

Samuel Damsell's will reveals that he owned several pieces of land in the Fields besides Lydays, a close, formerly three, called Stookey's Close held on lease from the Rodborough feoffees, land in Hawkley Combs and Westfield, also a woodland ground known as Gossen grove in the parish of Bisley.

By 1798 the Old House as it was called was pulled down, and William Gurner, junr., in 1838, mortgaged the whole property to John Tanner, whose son Isaac acquired it by

[1] Glos. Pro. Reg.

default of the Mortgagor in 1840. Mr. T. C. Driver of Lilly-horn, held it in 1881, and after passing into the possession of Mr. Alfred Powell, architect, Gurners Farm as it was then called, was leased to Mrs. Mabel Dearmer, wife of the Rev. Percy Dearmer, D.D., Vicar of St. Mary's, Primrose Hill, London, in 1914. It was subsequently bought by Dr. Dearmer, who sold it to Miss Beatrix Hornby in 1934. It is now known as Lyday Close.

Rudder, in his History of Gloucestershire, states that George Rawleigh, Esq., died seized of lands in Okerinch and Avenash 37 Hen. VIII (1545-6), and that Simon his son had livery thereof the same year. Fosbrooke says that the Raleighs succeeded to Edgeworth as heirs of the Helyoms, who were heirs of Thomas and Geoffry de Eggeworth. In 1349 John Rawleigh held part of a knight's fee at Edgeworth and Sir Edward Raleigh was Steward of Bisley Hundred in 1488.[1] In the Bisley Court rolls of 4 May 38 Hen. VIII, it is recorded that George Raksleygth, knight, held one tenement and three tofts in Tonneley. Simon Raughley, knight, attended the Court of the Hundred on 3 October, 1584, and on 25 September, 1599, it was presented at the Manor Court that George Raughley, Esq., was a free tenant of the Manor and had made default in service. At the Court of 1602 it is recorded that he held a parcel of land called Buriat in Edgeworly for one penny and had alienated the same to Sir Henry Poole. After this the connection of the Raleighs with Oakridge appears to have ceased.

An interesting find of an old iron fireback was made in the garden of Greycote Cottage, having on it an unidentified coat of arms, namely,—a chief, three mascles, quartering barry of six, having on the bars what appeared to be ermine, and for crest a demi-bear couped. The quarterings are indistinct.

There are several wills of former inhabitants of Oakridge preserved at Gloucester, which indicate that they were usually clothiers, broadweavers, or agriculturists. One of the principal clothiers was Roger Batt, whose will of 5 May, 1700, with its homely details, gives a picture of the simple

[1] Fosbrooke, Vol. I., 359.

surroundings of the period. After stating that he is a
cloathier, and a pious preamble, he gives to his brother
Thomas Batt the Grove or woodland ground he holds of the
feoffees of Bisley for ninety-nine years, or three lives. To his
son Thomas, his bedstead in the best chamber and the table
board and form in the Hall. To his sister Joan Smart £20,
his horse, side cuppbord in the best chamber and the bed and
bolster and one pair of sheets, one pair of blanketts and one
coverlett belonging to the same, the great brewing kettle,
two new dishes of pewter, and his best coat. To his sister
Jane George one cow called Colly. To his sister Anne Taylor
one cow called Cherry. To his kinsman Richard Smart, the
bed and bedstead in the middle Chamber, etc., and two
dishes of pewter, the second best kettle, one possnet, the
warming pan and one cow called Browning. To his kinsman
Joseph Smart, one heifer, one boyler, two ewes and lambs
and two joyned stools. To Rebecca Kirby one ewe lamb
and one spitt. To his kinsman Roger Kirby two ewes and
lambs and to William Kirby the same. To his unkle Giles
Batt his best sadle and great coat. To his kinsman Thomas
Batt his best pair of boots and to Roger Batt his second best
boots. To Mary, daughter of Roger Batt, his best flaggon and
pewter tankard. To Joseph Smart his best pair of breeches
and two shirts. The rest of his wearing apparel to Richard
Walker. To Mabel Restall one brass pan and one boyler one
skimmer and two pottingers. All the residue to Thomas
Batt his brother and executor. W. Samuel Pacy, John
Butler, Thomas Twissle. Proved 8 October, 1700.[1]

By his will of 4 June, 1707, Matthias Restall, of Bisley,
broadweaver, left to his nephew John Restall, son of his
brother John, his house and garden at Oakridge in the occupation of William Jeffries, his tenant, and a quantity of woodland ground lying under the side of Quanly, as lately marked
out. To his brother Edward Restall, the house at Oakridge
with garden and orchard now occupied by James Pincott,
junior. To his brothers Henry, John, Isaac and William,
and to Walter, son of his brother Henry, each £5. To John,
Walter and Henry Tyler, son of John Tyler, and to Mabel

1 Glos. Pro. Reg.

and Margaret, daughters of his brother Henry Restall, each 40s. His household goods to his nephews and nieces. Overseers, Matthias Baker and Thomas Haynes, 5s. each. W. Anthony Thurmey, William Pantin, John Panting. Proved 8 August, 1707.

It is not possible to say where in Oakridge the clothiers lived : there are many old cottages, but the house now the Post Office, together with the house next to it on the west side, both of which may be of late Tudor date, have the appearance of having been of some importance in former days, and are very possibly the residences of the well to do inhabitants concerned in the cloth industry.

For some years there was a small silk mill at Oakridge near the edge of the Common. This was built by one of the Jones family of Chalford, and worked by him, in order to provide employment at a time when there was great distress in the district, about sixty years ago. There is little trace of the mill building.

Between Oakridge Lynch and Far Oakridge lies the Pest House, a small house which was built about 1779, according to the Feoffees' deeds, when it was arranged that the gentlemen shall go and fix a place whereon to build a house for the small pox. This was to have been used for its original purpose in 1895, when a bad visitation of small pox broke out in Gloucester, and was brought to Stroud by a tramp, who had been seen to beg round Bussage. Feeling was very strong in Bisley against any such use being made of the Pest House for Stroud people, and a band of men attacked the conveyance bringing the first case, and turned it back to Stroud. Before the police could arrive they set fire to the house and its contents. The rioters, (two of whom were Bussage men) were convicted at the assizes held at Cheltenham and received sentences according to their deserts varying from one month to one year of prison. An isolation hospital was afterwards built near the Wittan Tree at Bisley.

East of the Pest House lies Waterlane, at the crossing of the Bisley to Cirencester road with that leading from Oakridge to Rookwoods, and at the edge of the former Common.

Watercombe House, lying sunk below Waterlane occupies a site of two or three dwellings known as Watercombs, where Henry Damsell was living as stated in the will of William Holliday in 1725, and John Brown, yeoman, in 1728.   This latter bequeathed all his freehold and leasehold messuages and lands in Bisley to his second son William, whilst his daughter Mary Pegler and eldest son John Brown received only 1s. each.   His two daughters, Jane and Ann Brown received £150, and his third son Robert £300 when twenty-one.   His wife Jane Brown, is residuary legate whilst remaining unmarried.   W. Samuel and Abraham Ridler and Edward Loggin Griffin.   Proved 1729.[1]

William Brown was at the Court of 1736 for Watercombe. From the will of Samuel Bidmead, yeoman, 5 February, 1830, it is to be gathered that he had an estate at Watercombe with a house which together with all his lands he bequeathed to his son James Bidmead for life, whilst his wife Anne Bidmead was to continue at his house at Litteridge during her widowhood, with one load of wood yearly and 1s. 6d. weekly.   W. Thomas Panting, Elizabeth Gardner and Richard Smith.

Waterlane has its own tradition of a large house which once stood near it, the home of one of the conspirators concerned in the Gunpowder Plot, who knowing the officers of the law to be seeking for him, after he had left Lypiatt House, had taken the precaution to reverse his horse's shoes, so that when pursued to his own home, and having retired to bed, he was able to convince the officers, from his window, that he was not the person they sought, as they could find no horse-tracks leading to his dwelling.[2]

---

[1] Glos. Pro. Reg.
[2] See Notes on the Local District, *Stroud News*, Jan. 11th, 1935.

The Church of Oakridge.

The Church, dedicated to St. Bartholomew, was erected in 1835, and consists of a chancel, nave and south porch in the Early English style, with an embattled tower at the west end with one bell. It was consecrated by the Bishop of Gloucester on 24 August, 1837, as a chapel of ease to the mother Church of Bisley. Oakridge was formed into a separate parish 10 August, 1849. Up to that time it had been served by a curate of Bisley, the Rev. Charles Raymond Barker, M.A., being licensed as curate of Oakridge Chapel, 17 June, 1838, with £40 stipend and glebe house. The Rev. Richard Champernowne was similarly licensed 19 December, 1841.

The east window was given in memory of the Rev. C. Raymond Barker, who died at Clifton, 19 November, 1875, and there are two other stained glass windows, the south-west one in memory of Agnes Mary Maude Plunket Birtwhistle, 12 January, 1913, and that at the south-east to Agnes Augusta Fergusson Birtwhistle, 6 January, 1908.

The National school was formerly in the Churchyard to the north-west of the tower. It was removed to the other side of the road above the Church about 1860.

Vicars of Oakridge.

ROBERT GREGORY, C.C.C. Oxford, B.A., 1843, M.A. 1846. Deacon 1843, priest 1844, (see Chapter VI, Part 2).

H. FARMER.

W. BUCKLE.

OLIVER HEYWOOD, T.C.D., B.A. 1856, M.A. 1860, Deacon 1856, priest 1857. Vicar of Oakridge 1860-74. Rector of Southwick, Sussex 1874-86.

THOMAS KERBY EATON, Gloucester College 1869. Deacon 1871, priest 1872. At Oakridge 1874-77. Then curate at Merriott, Som. 1877-79. Vicar of North Newton Som. 1879-93. Vicar of Pilton, Shepton Mallett 1893.

GEORGE THOMAS BAILEY ORMEROD. Balliol College, Oxford, B.A. 1867, M.A. 1879, Deacon 1872, Priest 1873. Formerly a Barrister at Law and Curate of Stroud 1872-4, and 1875-8. Vicar of Oakridge 1878-9.

ARTHUR PERCIVAL DOHERTY, T.C. Dublin. B.A. 1858, M.A. 1875. Deacon 1859, Priest 1860. After several appointments in North Ireland, Vicar of Oakridge, 1879.

ROBERT LINGARD SIMKIN, Hatfield Hall, Durham, L.Th., 1884, Deacon 1885, Priest 1886. Vicar of Oakridge till 1906.

FREDERIC PHILIP DE FREVILLE (formerly Green) Christs College, Cambridge, B.A. Jun. Opt. 1880, Deacon 1880, Priest 1882, Vicar of Balking Berks. 1886-9. Rector of Pusey, Berks. 1889-99. Curate of Painswick 1899-1906. Vicar of Oakridge 1906.

NONCONFORMIST MEETINGS.

In 1742 a certificate to the Bishop of Gloucester announced that some of His Majesty's Protestant subjects intended to hold a meeting for worship in the house of Giles Davis at Okeridge Lynch, called Wherr Corner, which they desire to be registered in the Bishop's Court according to an act of Parliament of I William and Mary. Wherr Corner is now remembered as Wear Farm and Little Wear, above and below the school. In 1744, Daniel Jew of Oakridge Lynch registered another meeting, and this was followed in 1784 by a certificate for holding a meeting in the house of Thomas Peacey at Oakridge. In 1809 a certificate of Protestant dissenters, William Restall, Thomas Crook, John Whiting, Reuben Phelps, James Blackwell, and William Cook, stated that a building erected in the village of Oakridge for the purpose, is to be used as a place of religious worship by them.[1]

There is a Wesleyan Chapel, built in 1874 and a small school built in 1864.

----

[1] Hockaday's Ecclesiastical File.

FRAMPTON'S PLACE.

This ancient site is one of the most interesting in Oakridge. Lying as it does on the extreme southern limit of the parish, and adjoining the parish of Frampton Mansell, it does not derive its name from any connection with that parish and manor, but being part of the ancient parish and manor of Bisley, its name, usually found in the genitive case, indicates that its former possessor was a " de Frompton." The fact that a small pair of thirteenth century windows exists, in what has been used as a cartshed, affords undoubted proof of the antiquity of the site. The present owner having investigated the setting of the little windows, and finding ancient oak beams forming the head of the recess they occupy, is convinced that they are in their original position, so that that end of the house, abutting on the old sunk lane appears to be the oldest. A large fireplace in the same building seems to bear out this theory. Of the present dwelling-house the centre part is said to be Elizabethan, but judging from its thick walls of five feet in places, it may well have formed part of the earliest building. It had been altered and adapted in the seventeenth century, and again by Thomas Baker in 1829, his initials and this date being on an outbuilding, at one time used as a dairy. The earliest record of the de Frompton family that I have found is in the Feet of Fines of 1301, a study of which leaves no doubt as to the identity of John de Frompton, in connection with Bisley, not with Frampton Mansell. The transaction lay between John, son of Robert and Isabella Benet, and John de Frompton, concerning a virgate of land and 4s. 3d. of rent in Bisley, which the latter conceded to the former for 40s.[1]

Towards the end of the fourteenth century the name is written Frampton, and a small deed amongst the Corpus Christi College, Oxford, muniments of lands at Chalford, preserves a note recording John Frampton's obligations " for a grove called Peletysmede and Frytheland," the latter being the Frith Wood.

[1] P. R. O. Feet of Fines, Glouc., 212. There may be a thirteenth century John de Frampton, " chevalier " who witnessed one of the C. C. C. deeds concerned with the Cowcombe property.

T

In 5 Hen. IV, (1402-3) William Chalford and Walter Tristram confirm to John Frampton and Marjorie his wife, three tenements at Chalkforde, called Chalkeforde tenement and all that tenement at Colcombe (Cowcombe) within the lordship of Minchinhampton.

The following year Walter Tristram released to John Frampton lands and a mill at Chalford. About the same time John Sherman released lands at Colcombe to John Frampton.

In 1405 John Frampton of Chalford placed all his lands and tenements within the Hundred of Bisley and lordship of Minchinhampton and all his goods and chattels in trust with John Lymerok, John Notelyn, William Scott of Lessebergh, Walter Hugges, and John Myllant. This was witnessed at Chalford 7 June by several of the notables of the district—Edward and Philip de Rodbergh, Walter de Longford, Robert de Monemouth, Robert Kingston and others. In 1424-5 John Frampton conceded lands at Chalford and Colcombe to John Wansford, vicar of Bisley (till 1430) and John Solers in trust (as appears by a deed of 1461) for his daughter Agnes, who had married Robert Olyff.

By 15 October, 1441, John Frampton has died and John Lymbrok and others granted letters of attorney to " his beloved in Christ " Thomas Fylde and Francis Halyday of the parish of Bysseleye, to deal on his behalf with lands, etc., of John Frampton according to the charter dated Tuesday, 4 October, 1441.

John Frampton, senior appears to have been succeeded by another John Frampton, who in 1441 gave and confirmed to Thomas Mull and Margerie, his wife all his lands tenements and fields, pasture, woods and Mill with waterways within the Hundred of Bisley, with Colcombe in the lordship of Minchinhampton with one toft called Vynysse. This was witnessed by Sir Maurice Berkeley, Giles Brugge (Bridge), and John Lymaryke. The mill mentioned is Chalford mill, which later became the property of Corpus Christi College.

At the Court Leet at Bisley 1468-9, the homage presented that John Frampton was seised of lands at Chalford and

Colcombe by rent to the Lady Cecily, Duchess of York in fees at 26s. 6d. There was considerable trouble over the trust for Agnes Olyff, her husband and heirs, regarding the land and tenements at Chalford owned by John Frampton her father, the remaining trustee John Solers, gentleman (after John Lymerok's renunciation) having died, and his son John Solers refusing possession of the premises which were stated to be three messuages, three mills, two ploughlands, ten acres of wood and sixteen acres of mede in Chalford and Colcombe. The latter charges Robert Olyff with subterfuge regarding his second marriage with another Agnes. By 1469, William Olyffe, son of Agnes, and grandson of John Frampton, had obtained possession of the property.[1]

From the above evidence it is clear that the Framptons were wealthy owners of an estate, who further acquired the mill at Chalford, and the property which for many centuires went with it, whilst they themselves were residing at Frampton's Place.

There is a short will of Walter Frampton 21 June, 1555, of Bysley, perhaps of Frampton Place, devoutly leaving his soul to to Almighty God and all the holy Company of Hevyn, and his body to be buryed in the Churchyard of Bisley. He left his son Roger a calf of one year, and to his other sons, John, Thomas and Walter, sheep, his overseers being Henry and John Pers (Pearce).[2]

At the Court of the Manor of Bisley 11 April, 1598, William Frampton, son of Robert Frampton, came and took one messuage in the same manner as the said Robert had held it at 10s. rent. This probably signifies Frampton Place. William Frampton also held an acre in Battlescombe field in 1656.[3]

The successors of the Framptons at Frampton's Place appear to have been the Twissel family, with whom the present title-deeds commence, but Robert Twyssel or Twisle, gentle-

---

[1] *B. G. A. S. Trans.*, li., 212-217.
[2] Glos. Pro. Reg.
[3] Bisley Court Rolls.

man, is stated in an Indenture of 7 Hen. VIII, 1516, to have been associated with John Gryme in sharing the Chalford estate before it was acquired by William Compton.

THE TWISSEL FAMILY.

Family tradition asserts that the first Twysel to settle at Frampton's Place came from Switzerland, in the reign of Queen Elizabeth. The Twissel family may have originated at King's Stanley where the Twessils had long resided. They may, perhaps, have been connected with the Framptons, and the Pers or Peerse family appear to have been mutual friends or connections.

The earliest recorded in Bisley registers is Robert Twissel, baptised in 1516. This does not corroborate the family tradition.

The will of William Twissell of 5 July, 1586, was made when he was sick in body, and by it he committed his soul to the hands of Almighty God his maker and only Saviour, and his body to Christian burial. To his son William be bequeathed a great brass pot, a long broche, a feather bed, a wayne sheet, a tablebord in the hawle with the formes there, which tablebord and formes he shall have after the decease of Jane his wife. To his daughter Mary, twenty marks. To his daughter Joan a cobert, a joyne bedstead and a flock bed. To Jane Pers, daughter of William Perss an heyfer and two sheep. All his apparel to Thomas Twissell, son of William Twissell, Junior. The rest to his wife Jane who is executrix. Overseers, Roger Fowler and William Pers Junr. of Bussrige (Bussage) and John Lightfoot, Vicar there.

Roger Fowler had married Elizabeth Twisle, 7 December, 1579. The Pers or Peerce family were living at Nashend in the sixteenth century, Henry Perse having married Alice, daughter of — and Alice Sturmye.[1]

In the Court rolls of 1584 it is stated that William Twissle had built a house on land adjacent to Coxlease.

[1] Bisley Registers.

Jane Twizell died in 1596, having made a short will that year.

The brass in Bisley Church at the west end of the south aisle in memory of the Twissel family, records that Thomas Twissel of Chalford, clothier, died 14 June, 1656, aged 40. He had married Isabel, daughter of Robert Hollow, of Great Witcombe. She died 1690, aged 78. The mill below Frampton's Place has been frequently called Twissel's Mill, so no doubt it was there that the clothier business was carried on.

Their son Thomas Twissel of Oakridge Farm, (which is another name for Frampton's Place), who was a Feoffee in 1727, and is described as yeoman, died 12 October, 1734, aged 87, having married Mary, daughter of Robert Ridler of Quarhouse, clothier, in 1690. She died 1702, aged 49. They lost two sons, named Robert in 1699. Of the other children recorded, William died 15 April, 1712, aged 24. The Rev Thomas Twissel, who was Rector of Wool Bedding, Sussex, died 23 August, 1734, aged 56.

John Twissel died 15 March, 1749, aged 77, and his sister Sarah, in 1762, aged 70.

John Twissel is mentioned as the owner of Millmead, and also at the Court of 1736, as free tenant for Frampton's Place. After his death Frampton's Place appears to have been occupied by farming tenants. It is sometimes called Frogmoor in the later Court rolls.

Elizabeth Stratford,[1] who made her will 27 February, 1781, is described as of Twissell's Farm, parish of Bisley, widow. She gives to her brother Thomas Merry, of Sandhurst, Glos., farmer, her sister Hannah Church, spinster, and Joseph Young, of Minchinhampton, butcher, all her household goods, ready money, mortgages, bonds, etc., stock of cattle, corn, and hay, and personal estate, in trust to sell at the best price and after debts paid, the remainder to her daughter

---

[1] Elizabeth Stratford was the widow of John Stratford, yeoman, who died 20 Dec., 1773, aged 57. Either he or his father attended the Court Baron of 1736 for Througham. He was buried at Bisley, his infant daughter, Mary, being commemorated on the same stone, died 1769.

Elizabeth Stratford, till twenty-one or marriage. W. Matthew Baker and Abraham Walbank.[1] The Bakers became possessed of Frampton's Place after the Twissels, Mathias Baker being mentioned in the Bisley Court roll of 1736 as admitted to a tenement called Frogmore on the death of his father John. This may only have been a portion of Frampton's Place, but that estate was in possession of Mr. Thomas Baker in 1841, when the tithe terrier was made, Charles Newth then being the tenant. From Thomas Baker it descended to Mr. Charles Driver. It has recently passed into the possession of Mr. H. Alexander Parsons, whose wife is a collateral descendant of the Twissel family. (see plate 15)

The house is said to have had a ghost at one time, which was however, effectually laid by the Vicar of Bisley with eleven of his brother priests who were called in to assist at the exorcism, at what date is not related.

It is said that John Masefield had Frampton's Place in his mind when he wrote the poem, " No man takes the farm ", in which in his peculiarly graphic manner he recounts a version (somewhat differing from the facts) of the tragic shooting of James Wyndham, tenant of Frampton's Place, by his son Frederic, at Baker's Barn, 19 October, 1893. Domestic trouble had urged the murderer to commit this dreadful deed, for which he paid the penalty at Gloucester gaol.[2]

---

[1] Glos. Pro. Reg.

[2] See Mr. F. Kirby's Notes on the Local District, *Stroud News*, 11 Jan., 1935.

CHAPTER X

PART 2

THE TYTHING OF AVENAGE.

Avenage, Aveniss, Avenesse, Avenash, Albenesse, or Abenesse, the eighth tything as enumerated by Bigland, extends from the west side of Oakridge as far as Abnash, including France Lynch and Chalford Hill. The fact that Aveniss is written in so many forms, including Abenesse, which is definitely the origin of Abnash, makes it difficult to determine whether what we now know as Aveniss, or Abnash, is being referred to. Mr. Houghton translates the name as " the ash-tree of a man named Ab(b)a." If the configuration of the land be examined the latter part of the word, ness, (A.S. naes, nose), may suggest a reference to a promontory of land. The way the whole tything, with its lynches, projects into the valley below, is very striking.

Avenis is found written Habenasse in 1270.[1]

Fosbrooke states that Robert of Malecote gave to Cirencester Abbey lands in Albenesse ; whilst John Achard, Richard of Albenesse, and Richard Duriarde gave Essemead meadow, which we now know as Ashmeads. (See Chapter XII.)

A part of the history of Aveniss has already been considered in Chapter VIII, under the head of Sturmye's Court, the property of the Bisley Feoffees.

Though there are several very old cottages both at or near Aveniss Green or Bourne's Green, any history of them is unobtainable. Tradition has clothed the Court House Inn at Aveniss Green with strange stories. It is obviously an ancient building, but unfortunately no old deeds are to be

---

[1] Glos. Corporation Records.

found. The title begins with a release 24 June, 1844, between Thomas Jones of Chalford, clothier, and Thomas Hall of Througham, yeoman (1) Esther Tyler of Rookwoods parish of Bisley, singlewoman (2), Nathaniel Tyler of Avenis Green, Timberdealer (3) and John Davis of Chalford Linc, weaver (4). From this it is gathered that it was then called Webb's Court House, and had been owned by William Tyler of Rookwoods, yeoman. By deed he had left it, with his property of Rookwoods and Westley in trust for his two daughters, Esther and Maria. All the properties were sold, Webb's Court House passing into the possession of Stroud Brewery Co. in 1885. Amongst the many Webbs of the parish of Bisley it is not possible with certainty to distinguish one who could have given his name to Webb's Court House. There is, however, a deed of 24 April, 1750, whereby Samuel Webb, of Aveniss, and his wife, leased to John Freeman, the Elder of Bisley, clothier, for one year, the close of pasture ground called Wood lease, with the coppice of wood adjoining of one and a half acres, which also adjoined a close of John Freeman's called Scabarne, two closes called Rydings and the other Wood Close, with the coppice of wood adjoining, which last pieces do adjoin on some parts to the woods of Mr. Sheppard and Mr. William Sevill, and contain about four acres, all situated at Aveniss.[1]

Samuel Webb, of Avenin, broadweaver, died in 1763, leaving to his wife Sarah, all his freehold Messuages, etc., of which he is possessed for life. After her death to his loving friends John Panting and Henry Stephens, both of the parish of Bisley, in trust for his daughter Mary Webb and her heirs.[2]

There are indications in the will of William Webb, broadweaver, 30 January, 1723 (pr. 1724) of relationship to the Tylers, for he leaves his gold ring to Hesther Tyler, daughter of his cousin James Tyler, with residue to his cousin John Webb, executor, and Samuel and John Panting are witnesses. It may reasonably be supposed that the Court House came

---

[1] Feoffees' Deeds.
[2] Glos. Pro. Reg.

to the Tyler family of Rookwoods through family connection, or by marriage with the Webbs.

Having thus, perhaps, accounted for the name of Webb's Court House, the fact that it was a Court House remains unexplained. With Sturmye's Court so near, it can hardly have been a rival court, but it may well have been the place where the tenants of Sturmye's Manor met. That it ever could have been the scene of hangings and summary justice is impossible, for within the Hundred of Bisley Painswick alone had a court where death sentence or the tumbril could be inflicted. It is difficult to account for the gruesome stories of executions in that part of the house now used as a beer cellar, where, the floor of the room above having been removed, the joists are pointed out as the "gallows" on which victims were supposed to have been hung. More interesting is the fact that when the large open fireplace was altered, old newssheets, and broken pottery were found, and unfortunately destroyed.

One of the most important estates in Aveniss is Lillyhorn, comprising House and farm, and covering the site of the Roman Villa from which possibly the name is derived. Apart from the interest excited by the discovery in the late seventeenth century of the remains of the villa, which were lost sight of and re-discovered in 1841, as described in Chapter I, there is no history to record. The Damsell family appears to have owned Lillyhorn in the eighteenth century, or perhaps part of it, for in his will Samuel Damsell, senior, of Bisley, broadweaver, 2 April, 1721, bequeathes to his well-beloved wife Anne, all that messuage situate at Lillyhorn with all closes, arrable land, etc., belonging for life, which he had bought of James Pearce and Joane his wife, Thomas Ally and Mary his wife. Also he left to his wife all the several closes he bought of Matthias Baker, Thomas Haynes and Henry Restall, in Aveniss, for life, and four acres of arrable land in Battlescombe field, bought of John Mayoe, for life. After her death to William Damsell his son, on condition that he pays 20s. per annum for ten years to his daughter Martha, and £40 to his daughter Anne. Amongst other bequests, to his son William Damsell, his chest that came

from Driftcombe, the combe below Sydenham's, in Steanbridge. This Samuel Damsell it appears probable, was the
son of Samuel Damsell, broadweaver, of Bisley, whose will
is dated 18 October, 1709, and who seems to have combined
a good deal of agriculture with his weaving, as he had acquired
besides cottages, lands in the Westfield of Bisley, parcells
of land purchased in Battlescomb field of Richard Lydaye of
Oakridge, lying near Lilleygate, also near Litteridge Cross and
near Twisselstone. Also he leaves to his son Nathaniel,
three closes in Bisley, formerly one, and called Stookey
close, held of the Rodborough parish trustees. Lands at
Hawkley Combs and Gossengrove are also mentioned.[1]

Nathaniel Damsell leased Sturmye's Court in 1714, till
1734, when he sold his interest to James Ponting. William
Damsell of Lillyhorn, was a mortgagee of Firwood estate,
Brownshill, in 1771; so the family continued there till then.
Since the beginning of the nineteenth century Lillyhorn
House has been inhabited by various families, John Roberts,
Esq., dying there in 1810,[2] and Samuel Clissold and his
wife in 1811.[3]

———

SMART'S FARM.

This farm in Aveniss lying just below the road leading
from France Lynch to Bournes Green was, according to the
earliest title deed, known as Solomon's Court. There appears
nothing to explain this name, except the fact that amongst
the deeds of Corpus Christi College regarding their land at
Colcombe, there is mention of " a tenement called Salemones
in Colcombe," released by William Trenhulle of Colcombe, to
William Chalkforde in 1359-60.[4] In Gloucestershire dialect
the o would become a. The house is said to be four hundred
years old and was formerly thatched, with a much steeper
roof than at present, as can be seen at the gable end of the
house. The windows retain their small square panes of old

[1] Glos. Pro. Reg.
[2] Brass at E. end of S. aisle.
[3] Brass in belfry.
[4] *B. G. A. S. Trans.*, li., 224.

glass. The sitting-room was renovated in the best early Queen Anne style (when the Smarts were residing there), the plaster ceiling being a particularly good example of that period. It is divided into large panels by mouldings ; in the centre of each there is a cross with fleur de lis ends. The beams supporting the ceiling are ornamented with scroll work of Jacobean period, but being heavily whitewashed it is not possible, to see whether they are carved or whether the design is in plaster work.

The fireplace end of the room with its mantelpiece is panelled in Queen Anne style, and a large alcove with a shell canopy is on one side of the fireplace and a door on the other side opens on to a spiral stone staircase leading to the bedroom above, and formed in the thickness of the wall.

There is little doubt that Smart's farm was owned by a member of the family at Througham, who had settled there. There is, however, only one will which can be assigned to a Smart of Aveniss, and that is that of Thomas Smart, 2 March, 1757.

He is described as of Evenis, yeoman, and he leaves to his nephew William Smart, all his messuage lands and tenements situate in the parish of Bisley and elsewhere in the County of Gloucester chargeable with his debts and legacies. To his sister-in-law Sarah Smart, widow, £10. To his nephew John Smart, brother of the said William Smart £10, and he to be executor.

W. Moses Smart, Nathaniel Restall, J. Heart. Proved 22 February, 1759.[1]

Thomas Smart is named amongst the free tenants at the Court Baron of 1736.

Another family of Smart owned Rydings Farm, the next farm due south of Smart's Farm, but whether there was any connection between the two families does not appear. Andrew Smart and Judith his wife, daughter of George Pearce of Bisley, broadweaver, were dwelling at and in possession of Rydings in 1697, but in that year they let the whole farm to

---

[1] Glos. Pro. Reg.

Thomas Sollar till 20 April, 1701. This included the pasture called Wheat Leaze, the barn close and little meadow called the Parish lagger and one called Niblett's Hill, and two other closes of pasture called Great and Little Bittcomb, Smart's meadow and four acres lying near a little cottage belonging to Andrew Smart, together with the holdings in the Westfield of Bisley. Andrew Smart had died before the marriage of his son John Smart to Mary Burrows, widow, in 1728, when the estate was settled upon his wife, his mother Judith being still alive.

In 1724 Judith Smart and her son had broken the entail concerning a messuage a little garden and orchard adjoining at Avenis called Well House, with a six acre meadow called Ashland, and several small pieces of land, but placed the estate in trust, two of the trustees being William Tayloe and Mary his wife.

John Smart died without issue by 1742 and his widow Mary, began to mortgage the properties, which finally passed into the possession of the Ballinger family, and so remained until the sale of 1897.[1]

Following Moon's Lane, Bournes Green is reached, and after a group of several old and picturesque cottages is passed, the gabled farm belonging to Mr. Oliver Rowles attracts attention, both for its situation and appearance, standing well above the lane, and with its approach through an avenue of elms, which were planted by Henry Rowles.

On the front of the house are the initials and date, on each side of a large and well-carved fleur-de-lis,— B   16
MM 99

The initials stand for Matthias and Mary Baker. There is a good oak staircase of the period, but beyond well-preserved oak beams and a little panelling round the windows and shutters, the interior is not remarkable.

The Baker family had long been settled in Bisley. The will of John Baker, dated 11 May, 1616, shows him wealthy enough to leave to his daughter Alice £60 and a score of sheep

---

[1] Title deeds of Rydings.

and two kine, which the executors are to put forth to the most advantage of his daughter. She is to lose the money if she marry without the consent of his overseers. His wife Alice, is to continue in their then dwelling-house with all the lands, if she remains unmarried, but if she marry she is to have £10 and two kyne, and so to depart from the said house. The household stuff to be divided between his wife and daughter, the residue to his son John.[1]

John Baker his son, of Bisley, yeoman, made his will 14 November, 1673, leaving to his wife Elizabeth two kine and eight score of his sheepe and the use of all his household goods which are to be divided between his daughters Elizabeth, Alse, and Sara, except table bords, cupbords, benches, shelfs, chairs, stolis, seftones, and tester bedsteads, which are to remain in the howse. His son John to have after his decease, his grove of wood above the meade. He gives to his daughters Alse and Sara all the tenement lying in Avening which he purchased of the lorde Winsor and his trustees. Also to them the inheritance of the broad close with the dwelling-house and garden therein which he purchased of William Bliss and Walter Restell, after his decease and Elizabeth's his daughter, and the remainder of his lease. The rest of his goods to his sons John and Matthias Baker. W. Henry Stephens, Edward Stephens, Mary Garner.[2]

The Avening here mentioned is the parish of that name, and not a corrupt form of Aveniss. The dwelling-house may have been a former one on the site of the present house built by Matthias, John Baker's son.

In the tower of Bisley Church are brasses to the memory of the Baker family. William Keane Baker of Aveness Farm, died 15 December, 1785, aged 49. Mary Shuring Baker, his wife, also three sons and four daughters.

Matthias Baker, of Bisley parish, gentleman, 31 May, 1794.

William, son of John Baker, gentleman, by Elizabeth his wife, died 28 February, 1791, in infancy.

[1] G. C. C. 66 Cope. Also Glos. Reg.
[2] Glos. Pro. Reg.

Marshall Rowles who entered into possession of this farm on the death of the last Baker owner, had married Elizabeth, daughter of John Davis, yeoman, of France Lynch and sister of Abraham Davis of Bussage farm. From family records of the Davis family it appears that Mr. Baker offered the farm one night to Abraham Davis if the latter would agree to pay him £40 per annum as long as he lived. Davis suggested that it would be well to wait to the morning to conclude the bargain, but Marshall Rowles, having heard the proposition, got Mr. Baker to sign a similar agreement in *his* favour that same night. As Mr. Baker only lived six months after this, the farm became the freehold of Marshall Rowles, who was succeeded by his son Henry, and grandson Oliver Rowles, the present owner.

The Rowles family were of long standing at Avenis. William Rowles who died in 1639, was a fuller and possessed lands and tenements. He was married to — Hillman, but died without issue, leaving his mother Katherine his sole executrix, and directing her to bring his body decently and comlie as may be thote fitte for his degree and cauling to his grave. Edward Smart was a witness of his will.[1]

Other inhabitants of Avenis in the seventeenth century were Edward Hartland, Clothier and husbandman, who died in 1663, and left all his goods, cattles, and chattels in County Gloucester and elsewhere for ever to his wife and two children.[1]

George Stephens who died 1663, appears to have been a very well-to-do broadweaver, with property at Cirencester and vested rights in the Starre Inn there, as also right to Rodborough wood, purchased from Robert Pearce. His wife was Joan Hauthon, and his son carried on his father's business.[1]

---

[1] Glos. Pro. Reg.

ABNASH.

The farm known by this name on the west border of Avenage Tything, is of ancient origin, occuring under the form of Abenesse or Abenashe. Set in the wall of a cottage just above the farm is a pair of thirteenth century windows, carved out of one stone, which very probably came from an older house on the site of the farm. An early mention of land in Abenesse is in the Court Rolls of 1401, when at the Court of Oswald Charlton and the Countess of March it is recorded that William Boun holds of the lord one messuage and one ferundal of land in Abenesse, formerly Whithed's. This must refer to Abnash, as being in the manor of Bisley, which Aveniss was not entirely.

Sir William Nottingham, in his will of 1483, states that he had bought lands in Abenashe as part endowment for his Almshouses in Cirencester and for a priest to pray for his soul,[1] but the knowledge of the locality of this gift has been effaced. One old will gives a picture of simple agricultural life, namely that of Wm. West, 2 September, 1562, of Abenesse, who bequeaths his soul to Almighty God and his body to be buried in the place appointed. To his son James, his great crock, great panne and the bedstead that he now lies upon. The cobbard, three of the best sheep, a coffer and the brode lome with apparell, paying to his brother Richard 16s. 8d., are to be delivered to him on the decease of his mother. To his son Richard twenty sheep, the second crock and second panne, the sheep to be delivered directly after his departure. To his son Thomas, four sheep. To his son John, 20s. To his daughter Margarett 20s., the great salte, one pott and one bedde. To his daughter Bridgett, 20s. To the sons of Henry Noonye eight sheepe or 25s. and four sheep for the encrease. The residue to Margrett his wife, who is sole executrix and overseer. W. William Gardiner, Thomas Davis, James Tocknell and others.[2]

The titledeeds of Abnash date from 1651, at which time it was sold to John Maysey (he and his brother William having

[1] *B. G. A. S. Trans.*, 1., 186.
[2] Glos Pro. Reg.

been tenants) by John Coxwell. The indenture of 22 March, 1651, reveals that John Coxwell's father Samuel, and grandfather John had possession of the property, the latter being summoned to the Court of the Hundred of 1584, because of this. The Coxwell family was well-known at Cirencester. a street there bearing their name, and they were related to the Coxwells of Ablington House, near Fairford. As their names do not appear in Bisley registers, it is unlikely that any of them, except probably the first John Coxwell, resided at Abnash.

John Maysey, who was a clothier, by his will of 25 January, 1682, gave to his wife Elizabeth £15 per annum out of his lands (of which some appear to have been in Wiltshire and probably came to him through his wife), and to his son John £100, and the Abnash estate. John Maysey's marriage with Hester, daughter of John Cripps of Cirencester, took place the next year, the marriage settlements being dated 30 March, 1683. Their happiness was of short duration for the brief inscription in Bisley Church to " Esther, the wife of John Maysey de Ibnarsh and daughter of John Cripps of Cirencester, died 9 March, 1685 " indicates the end of their married life of two years. By 1706, John Maysey was getting into financial difficulties, as did so many of the clothiers, and he began to mortgage Abnash. After raising money on it several times, John Maysey sold Abnash in December, 1712, to John Iles of Minchinhampton, clothier. Daniel Wyatt was tenant of Abnash for some years, dying there in September, 1783, aged 72.

John Iles, junr., becoming involved, mortaged Abnash in 1781, and after passing through several hands, Joseph Pitt became possessed of it in January, 1791, but in March of that year the property was acquired by Charles Ballinger, and remained in that family until the sale of 1897, Farmer Teakle being the then tenant. Abnash was purchased by Jaspar Gardiner, and having later passed into the possession of Mr. Apperley, it is now the property of Arthur Winterbotham, Esq., in so far as concerns the house garden and part of the barn.

The house, with its adjacent barns, suggests a farm settlement of great antiquity, the oldest part of the building being that at the south end, with its very ancient chimney and thick walls. The house was evidently much added to and rearranged in the early seventeenth century, when a fine staircase was constructed and the building extended towards the north. The early Jacobean oval windows at each end of the house are notable features. The fine barn is of the period of William and Mary, or early Queen Anne. The large balls on the entrance gate posts were not there in 1875, so are not of manorial significance.

A mortgage deed of the Abnash estate of 1781 gives the old names of the various fields. After mentioning the two orchards adjoining the house of 1¼ a., comes the close of meadows called Hawkins Mead 4 a., a close of pasture called Holy (? Holly) Bush Close 4 a., do. called Captain's Mead 2½ a., the inclosure of arable called Well Close 8 a., do. called the Wood Close 10 a., do. called Rea Rhode Close 12 a., do. Rhodeyate 2 a. and 10 a., and do. of 8 a., adjoining on the west to the Common of Bisley, also the Lime kiln Tyning 17 a., and the inclosure of arable land 3 a. lying at Hitches Bottom.

———

William Maysey, brother to John Maysey, of Abnash, dwelt in a messuage somewhere adjoining the farm, which was inherited by his son Richard Maysey and was described in the marriage Indenture on the occasion of his marriage with Rebecca Partridge, of Malmesbury, Wilts., who owned a considerable estate there. Besides the messuage and its quarter of an acre meadow, there was a parcel of wood called Haskins 1 a., a cottage and close of 3 a. called Gater Leys, alias Halls of the Wood, and a piece of arable land called Brockleys acre in the Westfield of Bisley.

In 1741, Rebecca Meysey, then a widow, exchanged Brockley's Acre with Richard Champion of Bristol, merchant, who had a piece in the same field.

Mrs. Rebecca Meysey had one daughter and heir, Rebecca, living at Painswick in 1754, when she placed these lands in trust on her marriage with her cousin Charles Partridge, senior, of Malmesbury, as his second wife. He having long survived her, parted with these lands to Charles Ballinger, retaining an annuity of twelve guineas therefrom for life. Thomas Russell was then tenant.

SKIVERALLS, OTHERWISE THE CORDERRIES.

Adjacent to Abnash is the estate now known as the Corderries, formerly Skiveralls, forming part of an area so named, the cottages to the east of Corderries and the wood below still bearing that name.

The origin of the name of Skiveralls is unknown. It is first found in the Bisley Court rolls of 5 April, 1586, when it is stated that the trees growing in Skeveralls wood were cut down within the half year. At the Court of 30 June, 1592, Philip Knight is said to hold one toft and one virgate of land and one messuage called Skeverells and one pasture lying in Nashend and one close lying in Callowe, which is probably meant for Chalford, then in the tenure of Thomas Farr. At the Court of 24 August, 1592, came Elizabeth Romney and took the messuage called Skeverells, the pasture and close, for her own life and those of Esais and Thomas Butt. Whether these entries refer to the Corderries or to the old cottage still called Skeveralls, is not clear.

The title deeds of the Corderries state that Richard Saunders, freemason, of Bisley, bought it from Daniel Webb on 7 November, 1665. Elizabeth Jeyne is stated to have lately dwelt there. She was daughter of Richard Jeyne, baptized 5 October, 1606, at Bisley Church and buried there 9 August, 1669, but it is not clear how these Jeynes were connected with those of Jaynes Court. Daniel Webb, at the Manor Court of 29 April, 1693, was admitted as tenant for Skiveralls ; this must have been for the old cottage called by that name, as on 15 October, 1680, Richard Saunders sold the Corderries to Jasper Corderoy of Hyde, Minchinhampton, clothier. He had married Anne Taylor, daughter of Robert Tayloe and baptized at Bisley 5 March, 1642, her marriage also taking place there in 1661. Robert Tayloe was son of Thomas Tayloe of Overcourt and in 1644 was rated for Skiverals at 4s. The Corderoys were a Hugenot family and according to Abel Wantner bore for arms—Gu. billetty or.

If one does not mistake the meaning of Thomas Tayloe's (III) will of 1685 and the Bisley Court rolls, the Corderries was at this time called Long Tunn (als. chimney) for Thomas Tayloe bequeathes to his cousin Ann Corderoy all that right he had in the house and land she and her husband live in, called Long Tunn. The Court roll of 23 April, 1690, records that Jaspar Corderoy was tenant by Alienacion from Richard Saunders of a tenement called the Long Tun and a little close of arable and a parcell of wood thereto belonging.

The will of Robert Tayloe of 18 February, 1666, although the name is written Taylor throughout, by its internal evidence is that of the father of Ann Corderoy. Being described in it as of Sciverells, he bequeathes to his beloved wife Alice £8 per annum during the life of his mother-in-law Jone Taylor, to be paid by his brother Thomas. Also he gives her the estate he bought of Mr. Thomas Master at Litteridge called Taylors, for the term of her life and after to his two sons Robert and Edward Taylor, to be equally divided.

To his eldest son Thomas his house and two grounds at Battlescombe called Bouncehorne and also Chelmeade, after the life of his wife, " Provided that if he shall have and enjoy so much of my father's farm (that he have bequeathed in his will to my brother Thomas) as the value of that estate, he shall give to my daughter Ann Corderoy £20 and to my daughters Mary Taylor, Elizabeth, Jane, Sarah and Rebecca Taylor each £20."

To his daughter Mary £40, as also to Elizabeth, Sarah, and Rebecca, each £40 at twenty-one. To his grandchildren John Corderoy and Sarah Corderoy each 20s. His wife Alice to be executrix. W. Thomas Taylor, John Handcocke. Proved 4 March, 1666.

By 1701 Jaspar Corderoy had died and Ann his widow handed over the Corderries to his eldest son John on condition that he paid his father's debts.

Jaspar Corderoy had two sons besides John, namely Robert, baptized at Bisley 5 November, 1665 and Edward, and six daughters, Mary, baptized 23 February, 1668, Anne, 2 April, 1670, Jane 20 December, 1672, as also Sarah, Ellen, and Elizabeth who married — Whitehead. These three last are mentioned in the will of their brother Robert Corderoy, clothworker, who bequeathed to each £5 per annum. John Corderoy died a bachelor in 1745.

Edward Corderoy, gentleman, succeeded his brother at the Corderries. He forsook the Church and joined the Baptist body, for in 1747 he furnished a certificate to the Bishop of Gloucester that he intended to hold meetings for worship at his house " near the wood originally known by the name of Brillings Freith, or now the Coppice Gate, in the parish of Bisley." It is probably Edward Corderoy's aunt whose headstone on the north side of Bisley Churchyard records the death of Sarah Corderoy 18 November, 1717, aged 81.

Edward Corderoy died unmarried, his will being dated 16 October, 1754. He bequeathed the Corderries to his cousin William Tayloe of Minchinhampton, clothier, and £50 apiece to his cousin John Blackwell, of the City of Gloucester, to Thomas Wetmore of Stroud, clothworker, and his two brothers, Robert and William, to the three brothers of his cousin William Tayloe, namely Thomas, Edward and John Tayloe, to Samuel Trotman of the parish of Bisley, cloth-worker, to Mary Morris wife of Peter Morris, late Mary Butt, spinster, to Ann Wetmore, to Elizabeth Clissold, wife of John Clissold, clothworker, to Elizabeth Trotman, widow of his cousin Edward Trotman, all being his cousins, and £20 to the poor of Bisley. W. Edmund Clutterbuck, Abraham Walbank, Edward Castleman. (Thomas Trotman had married Mary, daughter of Robert Tayloe 1 September, 1667, at Bisley).

William Tayloe, of Minchinhampton, who inherited Corderries from his cousin Edward Corderoy, came to reside at Chalford Lynch and died there in 1778, being buried at Bisley 24 November, outside the south porch. Administration of his estate was granted to his wife Sarah (Tombs) who survived him till 8 March, 1787.

Their son William Tayloe, of Chalford Hill, gentleman, made his will 22 November, 1798, and died two days afterwards, aged 53, being buried with his parents. He bequeathed his freehold messuage, etc., in the parish of Bisley in trust to Benjamin Glazebrook, of Far Hill, Stroud, junior, and Joseph Glazebrook, also of Stroud, to pay to his wife Betty (Bidmead), £20 per annum, and to his eldest sister Elizabeth Hopton, £10 per annum out of it. The rest of his rents and profits were to go to the clothing and education of his two daughters Elizabeth and Sarah Tayloe, till twenty-one, and then the estates were to be conveyed to them. He orders timber trees to be cut down in Skiveralls wood and to be disposed of. W. Henry Clarke, John Beams, Sarah Burrows.

Mrs. Betty Tayloe and her two daughters went to live at Fairford, as did also Elizabeth Hopton in her widowhood. By a feoffment of 25 March, 1806, between the above and their trustees, and John Webb, of Chalford Hill, clothier, and William Winn of Brownshill (his trustee), John Webb bought Skeverells wood containing six acres, and heretofore in the tenure of John Isles, bounded on the east partly by Bisley Common and by a wood now in the possession of John Webb, on the west by a wood belonging to Mr. Arthur Blackwell, on the north by lands of John Isles, which wood was purchased by William Tayloe of John Isles 27 July, 1770.

John Webb proceeded to mortgage Skeveralls to William Lambert of Chalford, for £300. Mention is made in the deed of " the newly erected building situate near the premises and used as a stove or drying-house."

In 1811 John Webb having become bankrupt, the estate was put up to auction at the Red Lion Hotel, Chalford, on 15 April, 1811, and it was bought by Charles Innell on 29 September of that year. He mortgaged the same to Mr. John Paine, of Stroud, and having left Chalford, in 1825, he sold " Skiverells, now more commonly called Corderoys " to Jacob Bath, of Chalford, Esq., together with the pew allotted to the property in Bisley Church. From Jacob Bath the estate went to his niece Rebecca (Morse), wife of Benjamin Thomas, of Nailsworth. Her sister Mary married John

Garlic Ball, of Minchinhampton, and when his three sons succeeded him they conveyed the Corderries to Benjamin Crawthorne in 1881. Meanwhile it had been tenanted by Henry Crundall. Dr. Crawthorne resided there and was the first doctor in a series of medical men who owned it. Dr. Crawthorne sold it to Dr. F. C. Palmer in 1885. In 1890 Dr. Edward Brown bought it and he was succeeded in the medical practise by Drs. Hamsden, J. M. Rogers-Tillstone and Charles Derwent Edwards, who resided at the Corderries as tenants, till it passed into the hands of Dr. Marcus Graham Dill. After being owned for a short period by Mr. Warren Hastings, it is now the property of Dr. George Western. The oldest part of the house dates from the seventeenth century. The wool-store or drying house of the late eighteenth century was used as a dispensary by the various medical owners, and the drawing room and room over it were enlarged by Dr. Brown.

———

There are many old houses and cottages in France Lynch and Chalford Lynch, which appear to have been erected in the seventeenth and early eighteenth centuries.

The house now known as Grey Cot, formerly Gordon House, is of the early seventeenth century, and had been occupied by Huguenot weavers at that time. On a pane of glass on the staircase leading to the weaving room is scratched in handwriting of that century the legend :—" Est une folie, toute ma vie—Graham."

The title deeds of this house only begin in 1673, with the conveyance of the house and shop and piece of ground of a quarter of an acre above it by Philip Davis broadweaver, to his son William Davis also a broadweaver, who sold it in 1797 to Joseph Elburow, of Bisley, yeoman. After passing through the hands of Thomas Cornwall Gardner of France Lynch, weaver, and James Bidmead of France Lynch, clothier, Joseph Wear of Hyde, clothier, and Thomas Smart of Chalford Hill, shopkeeper, with various mortgages, Gordon House became the property of Mrs. Patience Rebecca Hancox, wife of Henry Edward Hancox, and daughter of Mr. M. G. Camm. It was acquired by Mr. Mark Fryer, in 1912, and is now the property of his daughter.

Of Rodney House there is no known history, but its substantial early Georgian front covers a building of much greater age, judging from the thickness of its walls. It was at one time a public house, but has now again become a private residence.

The modern house now known as the Limes has behind it a cottage dated " I. F. 1697."

THE CHURCH OF ST. JOHN BAPTIST, FRANCE LYNCH.

This Church was erected in 1857 as a chapel of ease to Bisley Church, being served by a curate of that parish. It was mainly through the efforts of the Rev. Edward Pyddoke, the first curate-in-charge, that the Church and school were built. He gave the ground for the churchyard and besides contributing largely himself, he collected the necessary funds, Mr. Swayne being the largest contributor.

The basis of the style chosen for the Church was that of the Decorated period in a modernized form, and with some beauty of detail. The building consists of a chancel and organ chamber and nave of four bays and North aisle, with a South porch, and a bell-cot for a single bell. The font is of polished Devonshire marble, and the capitals of the nave pillars and the corbels of the chancel arches are well carved.

France Lynch Church was the first complete Church designed by Bodley, the Architect, who was a friend and protégé of Mr. Keble.

The Churchyard cross was erected in 1907 in thanksgiving for fifty years of Church life, 1857-1907, and in memory of Edward Pyddoke, founder and first priest of the Church. The cross was dedicated by the Right Rev. Edmund Smyth, then Bishop of Lebombo.

PRIESTS IN CHARGE AND VICARS OF FRANCE LYNCH.

1857. EDWARD PYDDOKE, M.A., the founder, was born in 1808, being the fifth son and tenth child of the fifteen children of Henry Piddock Whately and Frances (Barker) his wife, at Oxhill, Handsworth, Staffs. Henry Piddock Whately was the son of John Whately who had married Mary Piddock, the heiress and last of the Piddocks of the Austins, Handsworth, an estate possessed by that family for over three hundred years.

H. P. Whately, most of whose income came from Birmingham Small Arms found that on the cessation of the war in 1815, it was necessary to economise, so accordingly in that year, with his wife and children, he sailed in an open boat from Exmouth to France, for a time residing at Boulogne, and then at Tours. In 1849 he was able to return to England, settling at Cheltenham where he died in 1853.

Austins was left to four of the unmarried daughters of H. P. Whately, and they adopted the youngest son, Edward (whose name was changed to Pyddoke) as their heir, sending him to Rugby and to Trinity College, Cambridge, where he took his B.A. degree in 1832. Being called to the Bar and finding it impossible to make a living at home, he went to Australia, where members of the English Bar were in demand.

Owing to the expressed wish of his parents he hastened to start home again, and then began a series of hardships which must have told on his health. The quickest way back at the moment was by cargo boat to America and thence to Europe, but unfortunately he was wrecked on the coast of Australia, and nearly starved, water-melons being the only food he and his fellow-survivors could find during the fortnight's tramp north to the nearest port. From there he got a ship to Chili, and through the kindness and hospitality of Spanish settlers and the loan of a horse, he was able at length to reach the West Indies, and there to embark for England.

Edward Pyddoke finally decided to enter Holy Orders, and after taking his M.A. degree in 1842, he was ordained deacon in 1843 and priest in 1846, his first curacy being at Badgworth, under the then vicar, the Rev. John Christie, who was an old Rugby friend and a supporter of the Oxford movement. For the last part of the time he was priest in charge of Shurdington, and in 1847 became curate of Bisley, under the Rev. Thomas Keble, sen. His fellow curates were Robert Gregory (afterwards Dean of St. Paul's), Mr. Jeffreys (later Canon), R. G. Swayne (later Canon and Chancellor of Salisbury) and Robert Suckling.

During 1855 and 1856 Edward Pyddoke volunteered as S.P.G. chaplain with the Forces in the Crimea, spending most of his time at the hospitals of Scutari. In 1857 he was at France Lynch, building the Church, and in 1862 he married Georgiana, daughter of Edward Cookson, Rector of Kirby Thore, Westmorland (her mother being a Strickland).

Owing to ill-health Edward Pyddoke gave up regular work in 1875, but was able to help his friend Mr. Hopton of Canon Frome, Herefordshire, that winter. In 1876 he finally left France Lynch for Cheltenham, residing there till 1894, when a move was made to Abbey House, Tewkesbury, where he died on 22 August of that year. He was buried at France Lynch. When first at Bisley, Edward Pyddoke resided at Overcourt, and later at a small house where his sister Miss Antonia Whately lived (now Trinity Lodge). This house was burnt to the ground and he lost all his library. One of Mr. Sucking's kind acts was to send him some valuable volumes from his own library, as recorded in the Rev. Isaac Williams' Memoir of the latter.[1]

1875. CHARLES MUNRO.

1878. PITT EYKYN, of Chichester College. Deacon 1877, Priest 1878. Afterwards Vicar of Ashton Gate, Bristol, 1883-6. Vicar of Mayo W. Redwick, Mon., 1886-90. Vicar of St. Augustine's, Bristol, 1890.

1884. GILBERT WHITE.

1885. J. W. REYNOLDS.

1885. JOHN CHARLES KERRY, Chichester College, 1876. Deacon 1878, Priest 1879. Curate of St. Jude, Bristol, 1878-84.

[1] From information supplied by Miss Mary Pyddoke.

1892. WALTER GARNETT LYON, B.A., Down. College, Cambridge, 1884, Wells Theological College 1884. Deacon 1885, Priest 1886. Curate of Bisley from 1885 to 1887, when he worked for S.P.G. in Canada till 1892, in which year he returned to Bisley as curate-in-charge of France Lynch.

In 1895 France Lynch having been constituted a separate parish, Mr. Lyon became its first Vicar.

1895. GERALD SAMPSON.

1897. CHARLES HANMER STRUDWICK. University College, Durham, L. Th., 1892. Deacon 1893, Curate of Blyth Notts, 1893-4. Curate of Ilkeston 1894-7. Vicar of France Lynch 1897-1901. Curate of All Saints, Cheltenham, 1901-3, of St. Augustine's, Kilburn, to 1905, of Thorpe Malsor to 1912. Vicar of Whetstone, Leicester, 1912-26. Rector of Glooston 1926-31, and Vicar of Slawston from 1926.

1901. JOHN GRIFFIN. Gloucester College, 1887. Deacon 1889. Priest 1898. Curate of Bourton-on-the-Water, 1889-92. Of Gillingham in 1892. Vicar of Deerhurst 1912-22. Of Newland w. Redbrook 1922.

1903. GEORGE W. PHILIPS.

1909. ARTHUR WADE WADE EVANS. Jesus College, Oxon, B.A., 1896. Deacon 1898. Priest 1899. Curate of St. Stephen, Ealing, 1898-1900. Of St. Matthew, Oakley Square, London, 1900-2, St. Mary, Paddington Green, 1902-6, St. Andrew, Cardiff 1907-8, English and Welsh Bicknor 1908-9, Vicar of France Lynch 1909-26. Since leaving France Lynch Mr. Wade Evans has been Vicar of Pottersbury, and Rector of Wrabness. Distinguished as a Welsh scholar, he is the author of " Welsh Mediaeval Law," A " Life of St. David " and " Welsh Christian Origins."

1927. KENNETH KEBLE EVAN RICHARDS. St. David's College, Lampeter, B.A. 1904. Deacon 1905. Priest 1906. Curate of St. Paul, Grangetown, Cardiff 1905-7. Of Melksham 1907-11, Sheepscombe 1911-15, and Vicar there in 1915 till his appointment to France Lynch.

The Vicarage adjoins the Churchyard, the back part of it being older than the front, which is of Queen Anne period.

When the Rev. E. Pyddoke first rented it (from Mrs. Baker), there used to be a school in the oldest part, reached by steps from the road to a door, now blocked up. An interesting relic of the past was found behind the fireplace by Mr. Lyon, when the drawing room was being renovated, namely a bill " for a mulberry coloured coat " for Dr. Wheeler, who lived there at one time.

Nonconformist Meetings.

Amongst the many Nonconformist meeting houses in France Lynch and Chalford, that known as France Meeting is the oldest.

In 1695 a paddock which formed part of Starry Hill, was acquired and placed in the hands of trustees, for the use of " his Majesty's Protestant subjects dissenting from the Church of England." A round building was erected thereon, called the Old Vestry, and the surrounding ground was used as a graveyard.

In 1776 another paddock near the Old Vestry was acquired, the site of the present France Chapel and minister's house, the Old Vestry being used as a schoolroom, till it was pulled down in the nineteenth century. The trustees of both properties amalgamated and there seems to have been some confusion as to the particular sect for which the meeting was provided, for in the deed of 1776 the Presbyterian Meeting is named, but in 1795 and 1808 the new Trustees denominated the Meeting " Calvinistic Independents," but later on in the deed of 1872 which recites the previous deeds, the Society is said to be commonly known by the name of " Paedobaptists " with Calvinistic doctrine.

That the small body of Nonconformists who by the Act of Uniformity of 1662 and the Conventicle and Five Mile Acts of 1664 and 1665, were prohibited from meeting together for worship, and had had to hold secret meetings for that purpose in Westley and Cowcombe woods, should have been able to develop the meeting houses mentioned, was due to the fact that they were supported by many of the wealthy clothier families, or others in prosperous industries.

The list of trustees of the Starry Hill paddock of 1728 include Thomas Beale, senior and junior, the Harmers, the Fowns, John Webb of Chalford, Cordwainer, William Pool and others, while the Indenture of 1798 includes the names of the Harmers, Ballinger, Innell, and William Tayloe and his sons, James and Edward.

Amongst the tombs preserved in the Old Vestry graveyard there is a large square of six vaults marked J. Innell, 1806. There is a tomb to the memory of Robert, son of John and Esther Tayloe, died 9 June, 1794, aged 25, with the following inscription characteristic of the period :—

" Dear friend farewel, your mournful sighs asswage
Though Death have crop'd me in the flow'r of age
Lament me not, more welcome scenes appear,
Unmixed with grief, unblended with a tear,
For now I'm wafted to a happier shore
Where pain and sorrow shall have place no more."

Two stones commemorate tragedies,—that to Miss Emily Reap, 26 September, 1828, aged 40, " whose death was occasioned by the over-turning of a stage coach at Wootton," the other in memory of two aged people Aaron and Mary Lord, who were both burnt to death in the night of 12-13 January, 1795.

Some of the older inscriptions now in France Meeting (built in 1819) were brought from the Old Vestry. Amongst these is one of the first pastor of France, " Theodorus Westmacott, Obyt 31st August, 1728." In 1719 he had leased for 99 years from the Feoffees the west part of their Common wood ground known as Church Hill in Aveniss, of six acres, lately in the occupation of John Sevill deceased, and a cottage sometime since built on the said common wood in the occupation of Peter Clissold. After Theodore Westmacott's death his widow assigned her interest therein to Gabriel Clissold.

Other pastors of the eighteenth century were Silk, Morriston, Ingram, Miller, Evans, Pearcey, Hiscock, Thomas Jones, who becoming pastor of the Old Vestry in 1781, died in 1820, since which date there have been sixteen successors.

There are several tablets in France Meeting to the memory of the Ballinger and Innell families.

CHAPTER X

PART 3.

THE TYTHING OF CHALFORD

Of the tything of Chalford in ancient times little history has survived. Its name is found as Chalkford, or Chawford, and signified the Calf's ford, the ancient British cattle way which dropping down from the heights of France Lynch to Chalford Bottom, crosses the river Frome and proceeds up Hyde Hill. Chalford, now a populous village of about 2000 inhabitants, situated in a narrow valley, and called by Bigland "a very Alpine hamlet," is a vastly different place to what it was before the development of the clothing industry, the making of the canal in 1775, the construction of the turnpike road in 1814, and the opening of the Great Western Railway in 1845. Formerly the only means of access was by way of the pack-horse lanes, still traceable up and down the steep hillsides, and eminently unsuitable for the coach and carriage transport which came into fashion with the rising fortunes of the wealthy clothier families.

Whilst the mills lie in the bottom of the valley, beside the river Frome, whose waters are specially excellent for the production of the scarlet cloth for which the village was once so famous, the houses of the inhabitants are scattered along the terraced sides of the valley, mainly on the northern side, reminding one of the villages of North Italy.

Chalford has preserved much of its rural beauty in spite of its industrial activities, and in that part of it which passes into the Golden Valley, where modern mills cease, and only those of old time add beauty and interest to their surroundings, the scenery is unsurpassed in the Cotswolds. This name of the Golden Valley is not a modern description, for it is found in a will of the late seventeenth century, and again in a

Reeve's rate account of 1784, when Mr. Winn of Brownshill, Thomas Gregory, William Hopton, of Corderys, Mr. Charles Balinger and William Hall for Pontings, are rated under the heading " the part from the Bourn to the Goulden Valley."

Year by year Nature justifies this name when the trees of the vale are clothed with their glorious autumn tints ; but whether arising from this poetic source, or from the fortunes made by the numerous clothiers of the valley, remains a moot point.

The earliest reference to Chalford in the Bisley Court Rolls is the attendance of William Chalkforde at the Court held 15 Ric. II, 1391.

We owe to the fortunate preservation of the title-deeds of the property of Corpus Christi College, Oxford, such information as is available about Chalford, and from these we gather that the oldest and most important point in the valley was that known as Chalford Place, now the site of the Company's Arms, and the adjacent Tudor Mill. It would be the home of the De Chalkfordes, Robert de Chalkeford being mentioned in the Feet of Fines of 1240 as paying 5s. of rent to Thomas de Biselegh's wife Hawisia, for his tenement in that manor, and Elias de Chaleford being mentioned in a deed respecting Colcombe property, together with John and William of Chaleford (witnesses) of the late thirteenth century.

William de Chalkforde granted to Richard the Combare of Chalford all his dwelling place at Chaleford which the said Combare held of him, and the stream which bounds his garden on the west, with the water and the way which extends from his court as far as Borne, for one mark of silver. John the Comber released the " certain mansion " and curtilage in Chalford to William, son of William Chalford in 1354.[1]

A glimpse of further development at Chalford Place is afforded by the Fines executed by William Chalford to Thomas Sethcombe, chaplain, of all his lands and tenements in Chalford, Frethhouse, and Pathcumbe, 17 May, 1361. This was witnessed by Hugh de Bysleye, Robert Stonhenge,

[1] *B. G. A. S. Trans.*, li., 222 *et seq.*

(the Feoffees' house at Brownshill), and Walter Bysrugge (Bussage).

The same day Thomas Sethcombe returned the said lands and tenements, with mills, waters and ponds that are by the watercourses of the said mill, to William de Chalford and Alice his wife, whose heirs are William, Thomas and Walter.

It has already been stated in Chapter III that Mary de Bohun co-heiress of Humphry de Bohun, granted to William de la Fripe of Chalford, the whole field called Fripeland (Frith land) that William of Chalkeford held of Bisslye, which lies in the wood of Bysrugge (Bussage), for 5s. per annum, circa 1373. The witnesses of this charter were Henry le Eyr of Byssleye, Reginald of Troham (Througham) Richard of Budefield (Bidfield) Radulphus Ferre (Ferris), Richard of Albenesse (? Abnash), and Walter of Pagenille.

The Inspeximus of this document is a grant by Maria de Boun between 1373 and 1380, to William of the Frithe of Chalkford, for his homage and service, All that land of " largesse " (or gift) which is called Le Frithlond, which to William de Chalkford is well known, and which the said William formerly held in the holding of Byssleye, which lies in the wood of Bysrugge, for rent of five shillings of silver. The witnesses were William of Pagenille, Richard of Clissale, John of Chalkforde, William of Tonlye, John, clerk, of Frampton, and Walter Sered.

It appears from this and some of the rather earlier documents which are dated, that the Frithland extended not only over the present Frith wood, but covered the area leading down from it to Chalford Place, in the combe then called Pepcumbe or Pathcombe.

An undated charter of Ralph Mortimer granted to William son of Hugh of Chalford, for his suit and service, all the land pertaining to him in Chalford, together with his mills and all pertaining to them, for the annual rent of 16s. There is a copy of this deed witnessed by Philip Mortimer, but it has not been possible to assign a date to either.

It is evident from a series of deeds relating to the Colcombe property of the College, which lay in the manor of Minchinhampton on the south side of the river Frome, that the Chalkford family remained in possession and residence at Chalford. Unfortunately several of the deeds are not dated, but are possibly of the thirteenth century.

Elias de Chalforde exchanged with Walter of Colcombe one acre of his land lying at Rudgborne, for land in the valley " called of me Repe," next the wood of Westleye, his witnesses being John and William of Chalforde, John Faber (of Bussage), and John Frampton (of Frampton's Place).

John of Chalforde above-mentioned released a messuage to Henry Atte Mapele, at one mark per annum rent in 1291-2 subject to the court of the Abbess de Cadarno (Caen), of Mynchenehampton . . . Henry of Chalkforde, probably son of John of Chalford, confirmed certain land in Colcombe which Ellis, son of William de la Frithe, of Chalkforde, some-time held, to his son William, as a marriage portion on his marriage with Agnes, daughter of Richard Kynne of Minchinhampton.

William Chalford further acquired lands from Katherin of Tymberhulle, and a tenement called Salemone's (Solomon) in Colcombe from William Trenhulle in 1359-60.

Then his son William and Alice, his wife, acquire from Walter Tristram lands called Mapeldenemead, in the parish of Minchinhampton in 1370.

The last of the Colcombe deeds, dated 18 Ric. II, 1394-5, is an indenture between William Chalford and Alice his wife, and Walter Tristram and Isabella his wife, conceding to the latter lands and tenements and a mill, etc. in the vill of Byseley and Hampton Moniale, mentioning the dovecot and house, and that the said Walter and his wife are to have all the croft called the Longecroft, with a field called Pikatteshey, and a croft called le Stonyruydonge and le Soweruydyngge, and le Hale and two acres of land in the field of Bysseley. Walter Tristram and his wife have a hall (aulam) with garden and six acres of land. The rent of the lands is 31s. per annum, and Hugh of Byseley, Richard Monmouth, and Thomas Freem are witnesses on Monday before the feast of Blessed Mary 1394-5.

In all probability Walter Tristram and his wife were relations of the de Chalfords, whose real name never transpires, but who were presumably of Norman origin and dependants of the Norman Lord of the Manor.

With a charter of 1403-4, whereby William Chalford and Walter Tristram confirmed to John Frampton and Margerie his wife, the Chalkford and Colcombe tenements, (see Chapter X, Part 1, Frampton's Place), the Chalford family disappear. There is a long charter of 1461, reciting the passing of the Chalford estate from William Chalkford to Walter Tristram, who enfeoffed John Frampton, of the same, William Chalkford being called " sometime lord of Chalkeford," but there is no trace of Chalford ever having been a separate manor.

In 1441, John Frampton confirmed to Thomas Mull and Marjorie his wife for life, all his Chalford estate, valued at 60s. per annum, with Colcombe at 13s. 4d., and one toft called Vynnyse. This was again confirmed in 1456. Thomas Mull was son of John Mull, of Harescombe, Esq. He petitioned the Duke of York, then Lord of the manor of Bisley, about his holding of Chalford Mill at 16s. per annum rent, because of late the Duke's officers had charged him a black ewe and a black lamb for the use of the waters thereto belonging, and a further eighteen pence for not closing a hedge in Bisley Grove. He asks that the matter may be committed to the Duke's " lernyd counsell."

Thomas Mull died in 1460, his son William Mull, knight, inheriting the lease of these estates. He was attainted for treason and his lands were taken into the hands of King Edward IV, who bestowed them upon Thomas Herbert, one of his esquires of the body, in 1465.

The Chalford estate was then described as a messuage, a water mill, two fulling mills, and meadows, feedings, pastures, and wood called Chalfordes, a tenement, 40 acres of land, 100 acres of meadow, 10 acres of pasture and 6 of wood in Longeney, and three tofts, two virgates of land, 20 acres of meadow and 20 of pasture in Colcombe.

Thomas Herbert died and his son Thomas, inheriting, died without heirs, and the King then granted Chalford to

v

Sir Richard Beauchamp in 1474. His connection with Chalford did not last long for at this date Reginald Mull, youngest son of Thomas Mulle began to lay claim to the same, and demanded justice.

Meanwhile work at the mill in 1448 and the three following years was carried on by Walter Butt, sub-tenant. By 1461 John Frampton being dead and Agnes his daughter and heiress being married to Robert Olyff of Shipton Oliffe, dying, the Chalford estate being in the hands of John Solers, junr. as son of John Solers, senr., a trustee, (John Wansford, Vicar of Bisley having been the other), there was considerable trouble about it, Robert Olyff having married again another Agnes. It was finally settled that William Olyff, son and heir of Agnes, first wife of Robert Oliffe, should be in possession of Chalford, subject to the rent of 26s. 6d. due to the Duchess Cecily of York, as Lady of the Manor.

On 7 August, 1469, William Oliffe granted all his rights in the lands and fields in Chalford and Colcombe to John Mody, Esq., and Agnes his wife. The witnesses that day at Chalford included Thomas Brugge (Bridge), Esq., William Whityngton, Esq., John Gyse, Esq., Thomas Lymryk, for one deed, and Thomas Whytyngton, John Bowman, Richard Benet, John Castleman and John Butte for the other.

John Mody of Colleborne having obtained full possession of Chalford and Colcombe messuages, toft, mill, dovecot and land in 1470, leased the same to Edward More, formerly of Rodborough in 1474, at a yearly rent of 43s. 3d. (with 26s. 3d. due to the Lord of Bysselegh and 5s. 6d. to the lord of Minchinhampton).

John Gryme later became tenant under John Mody (then of Malmesbury) a tokyng mill and a grist mill being then specified, and by 1483 he had defaulted in payment of his rent to the amount of £22 5s. 0d.

John Gryme in 1448 was paying 8d. rent for a parcel of the water course called Burnewater "a ley flodeyates usque Molin" called Strodemylle.[1] He died in 1509-10, his will

---

[1] P. R. O. Ministers' Accounts.

being proved 14 February.[1]   He was buried in the churchyard
of Bisley and left 3s. to the Church, 12d. to the torches and
20d. to the service of the chantry of St. Mary of Bisley.

In 1485-6 a court was held before Thomas Whytyngton and
Thomas Baynan, custos J.P., when it was stated that John
Mody, Esq., of Malmesbury and Edmund Mody, gentleman,
formerly of the same place, had expelled Edward Mull from
the Chalford property. It is not explained how Edward
Mull was there, in spite of the Modys being legal tenants. A
complaint was made by the Modys that several malefactors,
robbers, and unknown disturbers of the king's peace came
with swords, bows and arrows, shields, jakkes, salettes and
other arms of defense on Tuesday after the feast of Corpus
Christi in 1486, to Edmund Mull at Chalford, and killed two,
and took three of Walter Sherman's shears of the value of
30s., of the goods and chatells of Edmund Mull.

Apparently the parties agreed to settle their differences by
arbitration, the result of which is not recorded.

In 1516 Richard Fox, Bishop of Winchester, acquired the
Chalford and Colcombe estate as part endowment for his
newly founded College of Corpus Christi, Oxford. Sir Lionel
Norreys and Anne his wife, were holding it at that time, but
whether they acquired it by inheritance or purchase is not
shown. But on 26 February, 1516, they granted a lease
of the premises to William Compton and Elizabeth his wife,
and Walter his son, stating that they had lately been held
by John Gryme and Robert Twyssel, gentleman.

On 4 October, 1524, the above lease has terminated and the
President and scholars of the College granted a fresh lease to
William Compton of Bysleigh, clothworker, of a mese with
a place called Challyford place and a fullyng Mylle, a grist
myll, and lands appertaining, for 70 years, at a rent of
£3 6s. 8d. Amongst the conditions it is stipulated that
William Compton and his successors shall gather yearly and
receive the rents, fines, etc., due to the President and Scholars
in Over and Nether Donnyborne, Longney, Bysley, Mynchin-
hampton and Chalford, and shall pay them in at the two terms

[1] P. C. C. Bunnett 25.

at Ladyday and St. Michael's, and shall make true accounts thereof once in the yere at the feast of St. Martin in November in the College of Corpus Christi, in Oxford at his own cost and charges, save only meat and drink at the cost of the President and Scholars.

William Compton's annual ride to Oxford across the bleak Cotswolds in November weather to present his accounts must have been a trying experience. On 1 July, 1546, he obtained license from the College authorities to assign his lease to Thomas Wymar, his servant, for 20 years, probably on account of his failure in health, as he died before 3 November of that year.

William Compton has already been mentioned in Chapter V. as owner of Througham Manor. He was of the family of the Earls of Northampton, his arms being—Sa. a lion passant guardant or, betw. three helmets arg. garnished or ; but though probably connected with the Hartpury Comptons, this connection cannot be established with absolute certainty.

Fosbrooke relates that Walter Compton acquired the manor of Hartpury from Sir W. Herbert, K.G., to whom it had been granted at the Dissolution. He states that Walter Compton's grandfather was John Compton, of Wilts., and his father was William Compton, who married Elizabeth, daughter of . . . Showell (or Shewell, ? of Ferris Court). He further states that Walter married Alice, daughter of John Lytley of Co. Warwick, and had issue,—Francis, John, Anne who married W. Rogers, . . . wife of Wm. Cecill, Elizabeth wife of W. Smyth and William of Hartpury, with whom the pedigree of the baronetage commences. If the accompanying pedigree, constructed from the Bisley registers and wills be examined, it will be found that the Christian names of the wives of William and Walter Compton correspond with those named by Fosbrooke, and also that of Francis Compton.

It must have been during the time of William Compton's occupancy of Chalford Place that the Tudor mill still standing by the bridge over the canal was built. He was a friend of Thomas Marshall (of the Cirencester family of that name), Parson of St. Gabriel, Fenchurch, London, and also of

Sapperton, for in the will of the latter, 7 July, 1528, he bequeaths " To my Churche of Sapperton in the Countie of Gloucestr tenne pounds which £10 Will'm Compton Cloth-maker dwelling in Chalford in the parish of Bysley hath in keping and to have at both my Churches dirige and masse for me."[1]

William Compton, who died 4 September, 1546, made his will as follows. After the usual committal of his soul, he desired to be buried on the south yelde of the parish Church of All Hallows of Byseley.

To the high altar for tithing forgotten if any be 10s. To the maintenance and reparation of the church of Mynchin-hampton 10s., the church of Biseley 20s., and £6 for the poor of Biseley. To every godchild alive 3s. 4d. To every child of his son-in-law Edmonde Webbe and " to my daughter his wife £3 6s. 8d. to be paid to every of them at their marriage. To Alice Heskynnes my daughter £20 to be delivered her at the time of her need as it shall be thought convenient by executors. Also to her a gilte saulte with a cover the which was bought of her husband or else the price of it shall be praised by a goldsmith if she outlive her husband." Also to her £5 yearly to be taken from lands And if it be unpaid by the space of two months then the said Alice can distrain.

To Elizabeth Bennet £6 13s. 4d. and her apparel convenient for a servant besides her wages.

To every manservant, if they be married out of the testator's house 6s. 8d. and to every woman servant 10s.

To his son Water all plate after his mother's departing, or, if he die, to his children.

To Elizabeth, testator's wife all holdings which he has both by copy and indenture for her life, with remainder to Water, the son, with the residue of goods, not bequeathed, to her and to Water, who are made executors, provided she has them for life and Water after her death. And if Water die before his mother then the goods are to be divided between

---

[1] P. C. C. Jankyn 25.

his children and the children of the said Edmond Webb and daughter Margery his wife, by even portions.

To Water his lands in Gloucestershire and Worcestershire and elsewhere. And that Elizabeth his wife shall receive the rents thereof for her life and after her death then the goods he has are to go to his children.

Supervisors. Richard Halyday and Edmonde Webb who are to have 40s. each. W. Richard Gravenor, clerk, Walter Butt, Anthony Wyllye, Thomas Wymar, William Butt and John Adams.[1] Walter Compton proved his father's will 3 November, 1546.

In the Fine roll of 1 Ed. VI, 1547, it is recorded that general livery in Gloucester was made for Walter Compton, aged 38, as son and heir of William Compton of Chalforde, " clothyer " who died 4 September, 38 Hen. VIII, seised of the manor of Througham and lands in Througham, Clyssale, Westwood, Tonley, Frampton and Okeruge, a yearly rent of 4s. in Througham, and a cottage and two enclosures in Abbenesse in Bisseley parish, a toft or park and a " skar " hill called Sebarnes in Abbenasse, two acres of arable called Swynesley at Haygrove in Minchinhampton, a croft at Box in the same parish, a close of pasture and two acres of land called Tymbercombe in Bysseley and a yearly rent of 8s. from lands of Thomas Coke in Colcombe, of which premises the manor of Througham is held of the King in Chief.[2]

In 1548 Walter Compton, gentleman, then residing at Avening obtained license to assign his lease of Chalford Place for twenty years to his son Francis Compton, gentleman, then of Chalford.

Abel Wantner states that Walter Compton was High Sheriff of Gloucester in 1576. He appears to have been a very different character from his father William, whose devotion to the Church is evident in his will. Walter Compton on the other hand was continually enriching himself out of Church property, and we have seen in Chapter VI, part I, how he

---

[1] P. C. C. Alen fo. 19.
[2] P. R. O. Ap. I, Mtr. 11.

acquired the rectorial moiety of Bisley tithe, and the revenue of the Chantry (Chapter VII, part II). And that there was little care for the Church is evidenced by his neglect to keep the Chancel in repair, an obligation laid on him as lay Rector. (Chapter VI, part I). It is, perhaps, not surprising that moral deterioration manifested itself shortly after his father's death. The records of the Gloucester Consistory Court of 1547 notify that in that year Walter Compton brought an action before it against Francis Holyday of Minchinhampton and Elinor Balle of Avening for defamation of character, they having accused him publicly between June and October of various grave lapses from morality. The result of this is not recorded, but in 1551-2, his wife Alice sought a decree of divorce in the Consistory Court. He was excommunicated for not appearing, when cited, but after a few days was restored on appearing, and the Judge admonished him to produce as witnesses Sir Nicholas Poyntz, Thomas Throckmorton, Esq. and others. Unfortunately the conclusion is not recorded.

Though for some time Walter Compton was living at Avening, (as in 1550-2) he had apparently returned to live at Bisley, probably in the Rectory house which he had rebuilt. He died and was buried at Bisley 17 August, 1585.

Francis Compton his son, who had taken over the lease of Chalford Place in 1548, obtained license from the President and scholars of Corpus Christi College to assign it to William Hopton, of Leonard Stanley in 1563. He had been residing first at Chalford, and then at Bisley, where he lost two sons, William buried 12 February, 1562, and John buried 9 February, 1563. Possibly the death of these two sons was the cause of his assigning the remainder of the lease, which ran till 1594, to William Hopton. He died before his father.

Francis Compton's son Henry, who survived him, was residing at Bisley at the time of his death in 1593. He had married Joan, daughter of Henry Bridges, Esq., of Avening, who was already related to the Comptons, he having married Alice Compton at Bisley on 21 May, 1586. Alice Compton was the widow of Walter Compton, who had died the previous year. Her second husband was the son of John Lord Chandos, of Sudeley Castle. His monument in Avening Church, on which he is represented kneeling on a cushion in prayer, has this inscription :—" Here lyeth the body of Henry Brydges, Esquoir, son of John Lord Chandos, Baron of Shewdley, who departed this life the 24th day of Januari, Anno Dom., 1615."

This pious monument marks the close of an eventful life, for Henry Bridges had been a notorious highwayman, who had terrorized the country side, and according to Mrs. Dent, in her " Annals of Winchcombe and Sudeley " during his career as a free-booter had indulged in " deeds of lawlessness and robbery almost surpassing our modern powers of belief." He had also been a privateer and had equipped two ships in 1580-1, the "Salamander " and the " Mary Grace " with which to carry on his piracy. The Danish ship " Whalefishe " which he had attacked and robbed of her cargo, was the cause of his cessation from these evil ways, for the ship's owner was successful in his application of the law, and Bridges was bound over to keep the peace, and receiving a pardon from James I retired to live and die at Avening.

Henry Compton had a son Brydges, baptized at Bisley, 26 February, 1587, and two daughters who were left to his wife to breed up and educate, one of them, Mary, having been baptized at Avening 10 January, 1584. His will has been already given in Chapter VI, part I, and though his wife Joan lived on at the Rectoryhouse till 1607, all other connection with Bisley or Chalford, of the Comptons, appears to have ceased.

After William Hopton had taken over the lease of Chalford Place, information as to later tenants has not been available, except that on 5 April, 1794, the authorities of Corpus Christi College let it with the fulling and corn mill and lands, etc., belonging to it and the Colcomb estate (late in the tenure of Anne Ridler) to William Hunt Prinn, Esq., of Charlton, Glos., for twenty years, at the yearly rent of 44s. 2d. and 15 bushels of sweet wheat, and two quarters of sweet malt on 10 October and 5 April, or in lieu of the said corn, so much money as the same should be sold in the Market of Oxford the next market day before the said corn should be due.

Under-letting was sanctioned and Charles Ballinger became the sub-tenant.

At some subsequent date Chalford Place was divorced from the mills and became an Inn, which still bears the name of the Company's Arms, signifying The East India Co. The formation of the canal, the turnpike road and the railway, split up the grounds of Chalford Place and left its eighteenth century stables stranded near the foot of Hyde Hill. In 1872 the Company's Arms and the Old House (which formed part of the Colcombe estate) with eleven acres of pasture garden or building land, were sold by the College authorities, and the Old House has since been pulled down.

The Company's Arms, as we now know Chalford Place, is seen to be older at the north side than at the former front on the south. The northern part of the house is of Tudor date, the southern is an admirable example of the William and Mary period, but unfortunately that front has been sadly defaced by the erection of a hideous building against part of it in the late nineteenth century. It was doubtless a residential house for some years, after its enlargement in the late seventeenth century, the excellence of the work being manifested in the still sound oak beams and tiling. The front door is surmounted by a tablet which, however, bears no design. An oak-panelled alcove in one of the rooms is to be noted.

A doorway which led underground may have been the means of access to a cellar, or store, or even to a place of detention, for it was here that prisoners on their way to Horsley goal were allowed to rest awhile.

The College still retains part of its property, stretching up Pathcombe on the west side of the ancient road which runs up past Millswood, crossing the present highroad and continuing on just opposite Old Neighbourhood to Frith wood.

An ancient cottage, called College Cottage, the front gable of which is early sixteenth century, stands just above this last-mentioned path, and below it, sunk beside the highroad, is an old spring and trough. In digging out the road the workmen of 130 years ago, or so, came upon several bottles, sealed and full of some liquid, of which the nature is not recorded. On digging further they came to a wall, in which, in a bricked up recess, was the skeleton of a young girl. No tradition has survived of the ancient tragedy here evidenced, but doubtless a murder had been committed which has escaped earthly justice.[1]

College Cottage was leased to Charles Ballinger, junior, for twenty years in 1864. The premises which comprise 35a. 2r. 15p. after a fine of £120 were let at a rent of 8s. 6d. and 17 gallons and 2 quarters of good clean wheat and 16 gallons of malt, or their value, per annum.

To complete the survey of the College lands, it has already been shown that the Frith wood, (a Saxon name meaning a wooded enclosure) or Bysrug wood, is a prominent feature in the earlier deeds. Though these deeds are amongst the College muniments, there is nothing to show how and when the wood ceased to go with the Chalford property. It may have gone by the name of Brillings or Bullins Frith, described in 1747 as near the house of Edward Corderoy and then called Coppice gate, or as in the Bisley Court of 1681, when Walter Seavell (Savell), was amerced for enclosing the common adjoining Bullins frith 40s. The only evidence now available is a release dated 2 and 3 January 1775, between Ralph Randell, of Chalford, clothier (1), Abraham Walbank of Chalford, gentleman, and John Randell, of Sapperton (brother of Ralph Randell) carpenter (2), Charles Ballinger (3), and John Innell of Chalford (4), when for the sum of £1500 Ralph Randell conveyed to Charles Ballinger and John Innell his trustee, all the grove of wood called the Frith of 33 acres, and also the Barn and seven acres of arable adjoining, then in possession of Ralph Randell, having been bequeathed to him by Joseph Bennett, late of Bisley, clothier.

––––––

[1] From information given by Mrs. Ballinger.

OLD NEIGHBOURHOOD, OR OLD NEIGHBOURING.

Close to the College Cottage property of Corpus Christi College though on the opposite side of the road, stands the picturesque gabled Tudor house known indifferently by the above names.

Though of recent years it has lost much of its beauty through the removal of the ancient stone Cotswold tiles, and through being divided up into tenements, its front over-looking Pathcombe gives some idea of its former appearance when it was a single residence of importance. Unfortunately no deeds earlier than an Indenture of 25 December, 1772, are forthcoming to show its remoter history. It was then the property of William Hall of Theescombe, Malster, and it had close beside it, " all that new erected Tenement or Dwelling-house near adjoining to the said Messuage and now used as a workhouse,"[1] Of this building there is now no trace or tradition, though from the appearance of the court-yard one would suppose it had stood on the upper side. Doubtless it would be demolished after the formation of the Stroud Union Workhouse in 1837.

The oldest part of the house is Tudor, and there is a large mullioned window, which is of doubtful date. The house at one time was used as a vicarage for Chalford.

Included in the Old Neighbouring property was a piece of land which lies at the fork of the old lane leading past College Cottage, called the Orchard, having on it a stable : also the cottage above Old Neighbouring, with its old wool-store reached by steps beside the road, and then in the tenancy of Robert Lugg, and also " a pew in the parish Church of Bisley, containing four seat places being the third seat or pew on the Gallery next the North door of the said Church." All these premises were bought by William Hall from Ralph Randle of Chalford, Clothier, the then owner of Frith Wood, who died 17 June, 1778, being buried at Bisley.

The whole of this property was in 1772 mortgaged to John Tayloe of Chalford, Clothier, and William Tayloe of Chalford

---

[1] In 1808 Bisley Vestry agreed that a house of Industry should be erected on Chalford Common as near Chalford as convenient.

Hill, Clothier, for a short period, John Tayloe (described as coal-merchant in 1801), being resident at Old Neighbouring in 1792, and William Tayloe in 1801.

Meanwhile William Hall had released the property to his brother John Hall of Coates, yeoman, in 1779, who by his will of 1792 bequeathed the same to his nephew William Hall, junior, of Througham, gentleman.

In 1801 and 1808 further mortgages placed the property in the hands of William Toghill, of Chalford, Clothier, taylor, and chapman, who for some years busied himself with acquiring properties, including Bussage House, Thanet House, Chalford, (now the property of Mr. Frederick Hammond, but then in the occupation of Charles Toghill)[1] and the adjoining house, then occupied by Joseph Franklin. By 1827 William Toghill was bankrupt, and James Hodges of Cirencester, victualler, having been an assignee of his estate, himself became bankrupt, when the Old Neighbourhood property was put up for sale, and was purchased by Robert Parker Pelly, of Hyde Court, Minchinhampton. In 1847, Mr. Pelly (then of Cheltenham), sold Old Neighbourhood to Samuel Hook, silk Throwster, of Millswood, Chalford. The house, which had formerly been occupied by William Toghill, had also had as tenant the Rev. Charles Hutton, followed by Mr. Nathaniel Jones, and later by Miles Whiting and Henry Brown. In 1851, the Old Neighbourhood property was sold to Charles Ballinger, of Skaites Hill House, and remained in that family till the sale of 1909.

————

Millswood, lying below Old Neighbourhood beside the old road up Pathcombe, is a site of some antiquity, the present house dating from the seventeenth century. In the Bisley Court roll of 20 April, 1599, it was ordained that the scholars of Corpus Christi College in Oxon should place a fence in the

---

[1] NOTE.—One, Richard Togyll is mentioned in Ministers' Accounts of 1448-9, as paying new rent for a certain fishery of water in a place called le Firth next Robert Frampton's Mill, as far as the bridge called Stevenensbrugge. This bridge, which is still known as Stephens Bridge is below Valley Corner.

way in the wood called Mileswoode, as far as Chalford brook by the first day of June. It is found written Mullswood, and probably obtained its name from Thomas Mulle, otherwise Mill, when renting Chalford Place.

A building near the road with pseudo-gothic doorways was erected in the nineteenth century as a place of worship for certain people said to be Swedenborgians.

Amongst the many occupiers of Millswood has been John Trotman, clothier, who died there 3 October, 1802, aged 69, and was buried at Bisley.

———

CHRIST CHURCH, CHALFORD.

There is no indication of any special spiritual provision for Chalford in mediaeval times, though if it be the case that a chapel existed at Brownshill, doubtless that would supply the needs of the houses in the valley. In Rudder's days (1779) the population of Chalford was reckoned to be about 2000, living nearly three miles from their parish Church of Bisley.

In 1725, during the incumbency of the Rev. Stephen Phillips, senior, the inhabitants of Chalford erected a "neat chapel" which we now see as the nave of the present Church, with a very small apse at the east end. In 1841 the chapel was enlarged and altered, the north aisle being added, with an arcade of tall circular shafts and semi-circular arches, springing from square unmoulded capitals, opening from the nave and admitting of a long gallery. The tower with a small broche spire was erected and a larger square-ended sanctuary, divided from the nave by a three-centred arch, and having three windows of the same style as those of the nave. The Church with its burial ground was consecrated on 15 September, 1841, by the Right Rev. James Henry Conk, Bishop of Gloucester and Bristol. In 1880 the greater part of the gallery was pulled down, a small portion at the east end being left for an organ loft.

A large sum of money was spent in 1890 and at the beginning of the present century in an endeavour to beautify the very plain interior of the Church.

One of the most distinguished men born at Chalford is commemorated by a small figure of Charity which formerly stood in a niche in the Sanctuary, but is now placed over the south door. This was the work of John Thomas, a famous sculptor and architectural draughtsman, born in 1813, the son of William Thomas, an innkeeper of Chalford vale, and was placed by him as a memorial of his brother, Richard Selby Thomas and his family. John Thomas was fortunate in coming under the notice of Sir Charles Barry, who perceiving him to be a most capable sculptor engaged him to supervise the elaborate work carried out on the Houses of Parliament. This led to his employment at Windsor Castle, in Edinburgh, and on various well-known buildings in London, till the time of his death in 1862.

There are several tablets in Chalford Church amongst which the following are commemmorated :—John Lowe, Esq., of Sevillowes, died 1894 aet. 90 : Nathaniel Jones of Green Court died 7 March, 1873 aet. 79, and his wife Hannah (nee Hinton), died 1876 : John Ballinger, Esq., of Skaits Hill, " a man who feared God and walked with him," died 1848 aet. 72, and Maria his wife, died 1877, aet. 62 : and in the nave, Henry Ballinger.

Chalford shares in the charities of Bisley and owes part of the endowment of the vicarage to Mrs. Hester Tayloe, who by her will of 5 August, 1788[1] bequeathed to seven trustees, namely to John Roberts, Walter Tayloe, John Trotman and Charles Ballinger, both clothiers of Chalford, Archer Blackwell of Chalford, gentleman, Walter Sevill the Younger, of Chalford, Woolstapler, and Richard Gobb of Stroud, clothier, the sum of £850 the interest of which was " to be paid to the Minister or Clergyman for the time being who shall officiate and do and perform Divine Service in the Chapel of Chalford aforesaid, for that purpose twice every Lord's Day, that is to say prayers according to the Litany of the

---

[1] P. C. C. Bishop, 266.

Church of England, provided always and my will is that if the Nomination or appointment of a minister to officiate and perform Divine Service at the said Chalford Chapel shall be at any time vested in the Bishops of Gloucester or the Vicar of Bisley, or the chapel be suffered to run to decay, or Divine Service shall be discontinued for twelve calendar months, then the above sum is to be paid to the dissenting Meeting House at France Lynch."

Mrs. Tayloe, like so many of the clothier families wavered strangely between the Church and Dissent, and her prejudice against the patronage of either the Bishop of Gloucester or the Vicar of Bisley, has had to be met by placing it in the hands of the Archdeacon of Gloucester.

CURATES AND VICARS OF CHALFORD.

1764, 30 May. Subscription to the Thirty-nine Articles, and to three in Canon 36, by WILLIAM PITT, B.A., licensed as curate in the parish Church of Chalford.[1]

1766, 16 August. Subscription as above by WILLAIM PITT, curate, to be ordained priest on 17 August, by the Bishop of Gloucester.[1] Subscription as above by JOHN JONES, Clerk, as curate of the free chapel of Chalford.[1]

1827, 15 November. Subscription of CHARLES JAMES HUTTON, B.A., licensed to the perpetual Curacy of Chalford Parish Church.[1]

1837, 6 July. HENRY BOLTON, M.A., Licensed to read prayers and preach in a certain chapel or building (unconsecrated) called Chalford Chapel, the Rev. Thomas Keble, Vicar of Bisley consenting and trustees of the chapel having nominated.[1]

1841. SOLOMON (or SAMUEL) GOMPERTZ, B.A., on the nomination of the Rev. Matthew Blagden, Charles Whateley and William Pye, patrons.[1]

[1] Hockaday's Eccles. File.

1862. HAMILTON KINGSFORD, B.A., Worcester College, Oxford. Deacon 1856, Priest 1857, Curate of Chalfont St. Peter 1865. Vicar of Stoulton Worcestershire, 1867.

1864. WILLIAM STANLEY DE COURCY IRELAND, B.A., 1852, M.A. 1858, Trinity College Dublin, Deacon 1853, Priest 1854. Formerly curate of Crewe Green and Chaplain at Crewe Hall 1853-5, Curate of Lever Bridge, Lancs. 1855-7, Incumbent of St. Mary, Montrose 1857-60, Curate of Dursley 1860-64. Died at Chalford 1900.

1900. FRANCIS WHITNEY DREWE. Gloucester College, 1887. Deacon 1889, Priest 1890. Curate of St. Francis Ashton Gate, Bristol 1889-93. Of Bourton on the Water with Lower Slaughter 1894-1900.

1903. ALBERT EDWARD ADDENBROOKE, M.A., St. Edmund Hall, Oxford. Dock Chaplain at Sharpness 1890-8. Diocesan Missioner 1898-1903. Vicar of Chalford 1903-21, Vicar of Chipping Sodbury 1921-6, and of St. Stephen's, Cheltenham 1926-35, when he resigned.

1922. AUSTIN JOHN HODSON, M.A., Christ Church, Oxford. (1904). Curate of All Saints, Cheltenham, 1906-11. Assistant Diocesan Missioner of Gloucester 1911-15. Curate-in-Charge of Leckhampton 1915-21 and Chaplain to the Forces 1918-20. Vicar of Chalford 1921-24, of Wotton-under-Edge, 1924-34. Archdeacon of Gloucester 1933.

1924. WALTER JOHN CARDER, M.A., Keble College, Oxford, 1914. Deacon 1912, Priest 1913. Curate of All Saints, Cheltenham, 1914-24.

———

There is an inscription on the gallery of Chalford Church which, after recording the building of the Church in 1725, and its consecration in 1841, sets forth the charities connected with it, mention being made of the endowment contributed by Mrs. Hester Tayloe, Mr. Thomas Batt, Mrs. Martha Trotman, and the Rev. Dr. Warneford, £1115 15s. 3d. three per cent. Consols.

Mrs. Trotman desired a sermon to be preached every Epiphany. There is a fund of £139 9s. 3d. three per cent. Consols for the repair of the Church. A piece of land at Bourne was given by Mr. Richard Gabb for the use of the minister, subject to a charge of 6s. 4½d. to the organist. Mr. Henry Ballinger's bequest is also recorded.

THE GROVE, CHALFORD.

This estate, with its imposing residence at the foot of Marle Hill, like the other good houses in Chalford has been the home of successive clothiers, the back part of the house being the original structure to which the present front rooms with their classical exterior and pediment were added in more prosperous days. Within is a double-height hall, supported by classic columns and pilasters adorned with moulded plaster frieze. It was formerly called the " Blackhouse " and it was possessed by the Blackwell family, of whom Fosbrooke states that they had for ages a very ornamental residence here, of striking effect. Archer Blackwell possessed a charter dated 1399, which mentioned John atte Blackwelle of Chalford, then called Chalkford. Richard Blackwell was at the Hundred Court of 1584 and Nicholas Blackwell is named amongst the free tenants of Bisley manor at the Court of 29 April, 1591, and again in 1599, when he made default of service and was fined 4d. John, son of Humfrey Blackwell received a legacy under the will of Thomas Phillipps of the parish of Bisley, 23 December, 1619, of all the land he had bought of John Shewell of Ferris Court of ten acres. Nicholas, Thomas and Humphrey Blackwell and Agnes Leith, daughter of Humphrey Blackwell, senr., received each £4. The Blackwell and Phillipps families were probably related, and two more of the former, Henry and Edmond, received bequests of houses at Grismont under the same will.

Archer Blackwell, whose name appears in many contemporary deeds, carried on the business of a clothier, and left at his death in 1785, by his wife Katherine (Webb) a son John, who succeeded his father, and died in 1771, leaving two

W

children, Catherine, wife of Henry Bengh, Esq., of Stanley
Park and Archer Blackwell, who resided at the Grove, but
sold the estate in 1803 to William Toghill and retired to
Barton End, Horsley, until his death in 1836.

William Toghill, who was also a clothier at Smart's Mill
(now Mr. P. Waal's) sold the Grove in 1808 to John Ballinger,
who in course of time bequeathed it to his brother, Charles
Ballinger, of Skaites Hill House.　Charles Ballinger, sold it
two years later to John William Jones (eldest son of Nathaniel
Jones of Green Court) who was in business at Seville's and
Oakridge mills.　He died a young man in 1860, leaving a
widow Mary Morland (Jeens) and three daughters.　Mrs.
Jones remarried, her second husband being Charles Rudolph
de Bary, who was then on a visit to his friend, William
Trotman Lambert (Lawyer Lambert) of Marle Hill House.

The trustees of J. W. Jones sold the Grove estate to Charles
W. Smith of Chalford, who re-sold to Richard Daniel Jones,
(brother-in-law to Mr. W. Dangerfield of Bliss Mills) who
resided there till his death in 1913.　A year later it passed by
sale to F. J. de Courcy Dashwood, who re-sold it during the
Great War to R. M. Osborn, and it was let for officers of the
local Australian Aerodrome.　In 1919 the Grove was
purchased by Walter Benjamin Gardiner, of Barry Dock,
and sold by him in 1923 to Mrs. Sheppard, the present owner.

During the course of years there were occasionally tenants
in occupation of the Grove.　The Rev. Sir George Prevost,
Bart., later Archdeacon of Gloucester, was resident there
during John Ballinger's ownership, while Mrs. Wilberforce
Heelas was tenant in 1884.　At a later period a member of
the Grist family lived there, and enhanced the beauty of
the surroundings by keeping peacocks in the adjacent
stabling.

Before the cutting of the canal (1789) and the road from
Stroud to the White Horse Inn (1815), the Grove stood upon
the edge of a meadow which was the property of Corpus
Christi College, Oxford, stretching across to Spring Mills and
Bliss Mills.　The construction of the canal and road cut
up this meadow, so that a strip of land was left between the

road and the frontage of the Grove, which was made into a lawn, but not incorporated into the Grove estate till many years later.

———

Near to the Grove is Marle Hill House, standing near the foot of that hill.   Over the front door is a device carved in stone resembling a spinning wheel, with the initials " T. M. 1712." These probably stand for Thomas Matthews, who was a clothier of Chalford, and is buried at Bisley. The kitchen and wash-house are of much earlier date, and a heavily moulded fireplace, moved from the kitchen to the dining-room, is reckoned to be three hundred years old.

———

GREEN COURT

The site of this house has been occupied for many centuries, there being enclosed between a modern front and a seventeenth century back, a Tudor building, evidence of which can be seen in the doorway of a bedroom of that date.   It has been the home of many of the clothiers, the earliest record showing that it had been in the possession of Edward Smart, clothier, (probably buried at Bisley, 13 April, 1654), who sold the estate to Richard Batt, who resided there.   It would appear that he made his will 22 December, 1618, being of Stenbridge (al. Stevensbridge), parish of Bisley.   To his wife Johan Batt (nee Hancox) the use of the messuage with $1\frac{1}{4}$ acres and twenty of errable land then in the occupation of William Dangerfield, and adjoining to the messuage he then inhabited, to have after his decease till such time as his eldest daughter Katherine Batt shall be married or full eighteen years when the said Katherine shall have the said messuage for the rest of the term unexpired, together with £50 to be paid at marriage or when eighteen.   To his wife Johan Batt the use and occupation of all his mille with all houses, etc. and profits belonging for such time as Jane and Maria Batt, his daughters if either is eighteen or married, in which case the said daughters are to have the mill.   To each £30.   To his daughter Elizabeth Bridge £3.   The residue to his well-beloved wife Johan Batt, who is sole executrix. To his son Richard Batt his middle rack and his least Platt vats. Overseers, his well-beloved Jerome Orkeld, gentleman, Thomas Badger and his brother Roger Batt, 10s. each in token of his love. W., John Boorne, Thomas Bridge. Proved, 16 January.

Of Richard Batt's several children only two daughters, Jane wife of William Watkins, and Mary (or Maria) wife of Walter Seville surived. Jane died without issue, leaving her moiety in the estate and mills to her nephew, John Seville, son and heir of the above Walter Seville and Mary Batt. In course of time John Seville also inherited the moiety of his mother and so became the full possessor. He sold the mills but retained Green Court and it eventually came to Mary, wife of Edward Bliss, as great granddaughter of Richard Batt.

The estate had been mortgaged after a marriage settlement in 1758, when Green Court was settled upon Thomas Bliss (son of the above Edward) upon his marriage to Ann Insall of Chipping Norton. A further charge was made to Joseph Cripps of Cirencester and Green Court was then offered for sale, but there being no bidding, it was assigned to William Turner a trustee for J. Cripps. Joseph Cripps died in 1782, after which it was conveyed by his executors to John Innell (1784). This John Innell died there 27 October, 1808 (see his monumental inscription in France Congregational Chapel), leaving his house (after provision for life for his wife (Mary Ballinger) to James Innell, his son, and after his decease to his grandson John, who married Mary Washbourn in April, 1816.

In 1823 James and John Innell were bankrupt and after repeated mortgages of everything they possessed, the family had to earn its living as grocers and innkeepers.

Green Court was sold by assignees to Nathaniel Jones, who was living there as tenant, and there he died in 1875, since which time it has passed through many hands.[1]

---

[1] I am indebted to Mr. Frederick Hammond for the main part of the history of the Grove and Green Court, also for much valuable information concerning the Tayloe and other clothier families of Chalford.

THE TAYLOE FAMILY OF CHALFORD.

In the preceding pages the Tayloes of Chalford and district have been frequently mentioned. The Overcourt Tayloes died out in 1720, but younger branches had settled in the neighbourhood, at Chalford, Brownshill and Minchinhampton, and though it has not been possible to establish their relationship to the Overcourt family, there is no doubt that they were descended from it. There are numerous registers of Tayloes at Bisley, but seeing that three Thomas Tayloes of Bisley married within a few months of one another, and named their children with recurrent family Christian names, with no indication of their mother's name, or of their place of residence, it is impossible to identify most of them.

We are, however, on sure ground with Thomas Tayloe who married Margery Hone at Bisley, 29 September, 1654, as his second wife, and appears to have owned the mill and lands at Chalford, which descended to the two William Tayloes, his son and grandson. This mill had been in the Hone family for some years, the Court roll of the Manor of 1600 stating that Robert Hone held of the Queen by Indenture the tenement and Mill called Chalford, parcell of the manor of Bissley, and a certain close called le Park close in Byssley. He died in 1655, his will, which gives an interesting insight into a yeoman's household, being dated 10 December, 1653. He is described as of Chauford, yeoman, and he left his wife Joan all the stuff and implements which she brought with her at her marriage. To his daughter Sarah, one flockbedd and bedstedd in the yearne chamber, two coverletts, one pair of blanketts, one boulster. To his daughter Mary, wife of Samuel Beard, one bolster, one coffer that came from Hyde that was his uncle's Walter Hones the least of two, one table board in the kitchen. To his daughter Margery (who later married Thomas Tayloe) his best bed and a dowlas bolster, two coverletts, one pair of blanketts, one chilve beddsheet, one other coffer that came from his uncle Hone at Hyde the best of two, the short tableboards in the Hall with the frame and one tableboard in the little hall with the frame, one wainscote chest and two joyne stools, also all his linen, brass, pewter, broches, and irons, and drinke vessels undisposed

of that were his before his marriage that now is he gives to
his three daughters.[1]

Thomas Tayloe made his will 20 August, 1667, bequeathing
to his brother-in-law, William Hone, all haye and cattle of
all sorts.   To his son Henry Tayloe £5, and all working tools,
etc., belonging to cloth dressing.   To his son William Tayloe
his dyeing furnace and fattes and all presse and papers for
pressing of cloth.   His executrix was to have the use of all
till his son William is twenty-two, and she shall take care for
the breeding of him up.   To his daughter Sarah Tayloe £14.
To his daughter Elizabeth Tayloe £40, also to his daughter
Lettice £40.   To his daughter Mary Stone, all his goods,
etc., and she to be sole executrix.   Overseer, Thomas Taylor,
of Biseley.   The will was proved 8 October, Thomas
Tayloe having died in September and he was buried at Bisley
on 12 September, 1667.[1]

William Tayloe (I.), son of Thomas Tayloe, clothier, was
baptised at Bisley 2 August, 1657.   His half-sister Mary,
married William Stone of Chalford, yeoman, in 1659.   If she
was baptised on 17 May, 1642, she was then about seventeen
and by the marriage settlement of 13 August, 1659, the toft
and two closes of land called Woolrings and one toft and a
messuage and half yard of land, a fulling mill, then in the
occupation of William Stone, were placed in trust with
Nathaniel Ridler of Chalford, clothier, and Richard Blake of
Bisley, gentleman, for the use of William Stone for life and
for Mary his wife for life, but provision was made for William
Tayloe's entry into possession on coming of age.

Exception was made of the house and Dyehouse near and
the orchard adjoining unto part of the Rackhill, and part of
a meadow ground called Belcher's Mead, then in the occupation of Sarah Hunt, widow.

On 16 March, 1683, an Indenture was signed between
William and Mary Stone and William Tayloe, and Ann
Fletcher, of Northwick, daughter of Edward Fletcher,
deceased, with whom William Tayloe was about to contract

---

1 Glos. Pro. Reg.

a marriage, the trustees being Thomas Fletcher of Northwick, yeoman, and Thomas Trotman of Chalford, clothier. On 10 May, 1708, a payment of 4s. by William Tayloe to Samuel Webb secured the use of the seat place near the west end of the Church at Bisley, where the said Tayloe did always sit, having a seat of Daniel Webb on the west and of Pettitt on the east. William Tayloe's (I.) wife Ann died in 1730 being buried at Bisley 15 April. Her husband followed her in 1735, aged 78, his burial being on 20 January. His only son William (II), baptised at Bisley 1 September, 1684, married on 12 May, 1739, at Bisley Hester Roberts of Cirencester, with whom he received a marriage portion of £1000, and on whom he settled the house at Chalford in which he lived (now called Wickham Grange) as well as four messuages then let to tenants and the fulling Mills containing two stocks and one Gig Mill, the half yard land and arable called Woolrings, formerly the estate and inheritance of William Stone, gentleman, and also certain hereditaments in Worcestershire, inherited from his mother.

William Tayloe (II.) had presented himself at the Court Baron of 23 October, 1736, to be admitted tenant of the Chalford property at the rent of £1 9s. 2d. per annum, it being noted that it had been granted by deed of 18 March, 1620, by George Lord Marquess and Earl of Buckingham then Lord of the Manor of Bisley to Robert Hone, from whom it had descended to William Tayloe's father.

William Tayloe's (I.) only daughter Mary married Thomas Keble of Brownshill, and had died before 1740.

William Tayloe (II.) was High Sheriff of the County in 1742, and was an acting Justice of the Peace, as stated on the monument, formerly over the south door, but now in the belfry at Bisley Church. He died 30 May, 1749, aged 64. He left an only son, William, baptised 4 September, 1746, aged only three at his father's death. The same monument tells all that is known of him :—

" Adjoining to the same grave in a new Vault lie deposited the Remains of William Tayloe, of Hert. Coll. Oxon, only son and Heir of the said William Tayloe, by Hester his wife.

He died the 24th of October, in the Year 1773, Aged 27 years.

Greatly regretted, being a Gentleman of the most promising Hopes and Expectation and highly esteemed by his Neighbours and Acquaintance. The said Hester Tayloe, his disconsolate mother out of Pious Regard to her husband and son erected this Monument."

The arms of the Tayloe family, namely a sword in pale between two Lions rampant adorsed, surmount the monument.

By his will William Tayloe (III) described as of Pall Mall, in the parish of St. James Westminster, bookseller, devised all his messuages and lands to his mother, Hester Tayloe.

Mrs. Hester Tayloe, who was popularly known as Madame Tayloe, sold all her Chalford property to Charles Ballinger in 1778. She died 17 February, 1790. Her will, a portion of which relating to Chalford Church endowment has already been quoted, was dated 5 August, 1788, and by it she bequeathed her messuages and lands at Little Compton, Glos., to her nephew John Roberts. All her lands and tenements at Draycott, in the parish of Blockley, Worcs. to the said John Roberts and Peter Leversage, junior, of Lypiatt in the parish of Stroud, gentleman, in trust for her kinsman Charles Tayloe Phillips, grandson of her late brother-in-law Stephen Phillips, Clerk,[1] for life and then in succession to his five sons.

The Blockley estate is charged with the sum of £600 to her kinswoman Mary Phillips, sister of the said Charles Tayloe Phillips when twenty-four.

To Sarah, wife of Daniel Mills of the parish of Bisley, weaver, formerly Sarah Webb, daughter of Samuel Webb and Elizabeth his wife, who was one of the daughters of Thomas Keble, all that cottage at Chalford Lynch then in possession of Daniel Mills, for her life, and after to William Mills, their son. To Thomas Tyler, son of John Tyler by Martha his wife, another daughter of Thomas Keble, the sum of £200. To her said nephew John Roberts and to Walter Tayloe of

---

[1] Vicar of Bisley, second of that name.

Chalford, clothier, (son of Mr. Edward Tayloe), the sum of £340 in trust to pay Samuel Ridler, William Ridler and Hannah Ridler, sons and daughter of Mary Ridler, late wife of Nathaniel Ridler, one of the daughters of the said John Tyler by Martha his wife, in proportions specified.[1]

The will was proved by John Roberts[2] 12 May, 1790, Mrs. Hester Tayloe having been buried at Bisley on 11 March.

SKAITESHILL.

The origin of this name is unknown, but it is first found in the Bisley Court rolls in 1693, when James Dowell was amerced 1s. for digging stones in Scaites hill, and in 1695, when Samuel Taylor was amerced 2s. 6d. for breaking the ground and setting up a rack in Skaites hill.

The site of the present house of Skaites hill is of ancient occupation, and the road between it and the Paganshill or Firwood estate, is of great antiquity. A pair of mediaeval stone gate-posts marks the entrance to the grove and fields where the farm cottage lies.

There are no old deeds to be found, but an indenture of 27 and 28 May, 1800, concerns the purchase of the Skaites hill property by Charles Ballinger from William Sevill, yeoman, of Chalford and Frances his wife, and it is there stated that it had been the property of William Sevill of Sydenhams, gentleman, and had been devised by his will of 7 December, 1798, in trust to Thomas Packer Butt of Chalford, clothier, and William Tayloe also of Chalford, clothier, for his widow Hester Sevill, to receive £50 per annum therefrom. It had been in the tenure of Richard Millard, but was then in the possession of Charles Ballinger, who on acquiring it added part of the present house on to the original cottage, traces of which can still be seen. The farm cottage mentioned

---

[1] P. C. C. Bishop, 266.

[2] John Roberts lived at Lilly Horn and died there 2 Sept., 1810, aet. 64, according to his tombstone in Bisley Churchyard.

above was the scene of a murder in the early eighteenth century, the memory of which was preserved by Daniel Ware, senior, who was living in the cottage about 1820, and who was the first person to be buried in Chalford Churchyard. He related to Mrs. Ballinger, when he was a great age, that a boy who was a Chalford Parish apprentice, living with his master at the cottage, suddenly disappeared, his master saying he had run away. In the year above-mentioned Daniel Ware, junior, was digging in the garden and he came upon a stone of unusual size, which being unable to lift, he rolled partly down the hill, on which he observed part of a skull adhering to the stone. This led him to dig further down, when he found the skeleton of a boy, the bones of which had crumbled almost to dust.[1]

The Ballinger family which rose to considerable prominence in the cloth industry of Chalford came from Chedworth, where they held a small property, in the seventeenth century, Elizabeth Ballinger, widow, being the earliest mentioned in the Bisley registers, as buried 8 December, 1641.

Henry Ballinger, son of Charles Ballinger of Duntisborne Abbots, who married Anne Jotham of Chedworth, was born in 1702, and was the first of the family to settle at Chalford and to engage in the cloth industry. He married Deborah Burrows at Bisley 29 December, 1729, and died in 1785, being buried at France Meeting. His eldest daughter, Mary (born 28 October, 1730) married John Innell of Chalford, clothier, at Bisley, 6 April, 1752.

Charles Ballinger, his elder son, born 1740, carried on his father's business successfully and in 1773 married Elizabeth, daughter of . . . Webb of Avening, clothier, by whom he had two sons and two daughters. He died in 1798 and was buried in the old burial ground of France Meeting on 2 July. By his will he left two shares in Stroud Navigation Co. in trust, the profits to be divided equally between the Church-wardens of Bisley and Chedworth, and the minister that may perform Divine Service at France Meeting in the parish of

---

[1] Recounted by Mrs. Ballinger, senr. in 1865, to Miss Anna Maria Suckling, afterwards Mother Superior of All Saints Community, Margaret Street, London.

Bisley, the said Minister being a Protestant Dissenting minister and no Baptist or Methodist, and in case there be no Divine Service performed at the said Meeting house at least once a month the said profits to be equally divided between the aforesaid Churchwardens till services are continued. The said money to be used for clothing the poor, not being in the Workhouse or house of Industry. John Trotman, of Millswood, and William Tayloe, son of Edward Tayloe, clothier, of Chalford, to be trustees. He left his mills, etc., in trust to his son Charles for life, and failing heirs, to his son John, who also inherited the Chedworth estate. His daughter Elizabeth, was to have his property in Sapperton and his leases in Stroud.

The house in which Charles Ballinger lived is that at the foot of Dark Lane, now known as Wickham Grange, bought from Mrs. Hester Tayloe in 1778. Included with his purchase were the fulling mills with Stock and Gigg mill belonging, known as Woolings, and one cottage adjoining, used as a workshop, five pieces of land called Upper Leasows (30 acres) in the possession of Thomas Gregory, the Grove of wood of 20 acres, a meadow called Belcher's Mead 13 acres (then in the possession of Edward Tayloe), the leasow of three acres called Rack Hill, the Lowermead leasow, three acres, and another called the Moors, two acres, the last two being in the possession of Abraham Walbank, and one pasture ground of two acres called Freame's Hill, or Little Rack Hill, and one acre of arable land called the Lyes, in the possession of Thomas Gregory.

Charles Ballinger, son of the above Charles, was baptized at Bisley, 2 June, 1774. He married Sarah daughter of . . . Jones, and resided at Glewstone, Herefordshire, at one time.

John Ballinger, the other son married first Elizabeth, daughter of Simon Woodall, by whom he had three sons, Charles, Henry and Walter. She died in October, 1824, and was buried at France Meeting. He married secondly Maria, (? Bishop) who long survived her husband, dying in 1877, aged 91.

John Ballinger died 9 December, 1848, being buried at
Christ Church, Chalford, and by his will dated 1 October, 1846,
he bequeathed to his son Charles, Abnash farm then in the
occupation of Charles Ratcliffe, and Maysey's Grove in his
own holding, and all the land held under Corpus Christi
College near Old Neighbourhood and Frith Wood, and the
cottage in the occupation of Charles Cox and all Copse wood
in his own holding, Seaburns ground and houses and lands at
Abnash in the occupation of William Tayloe and Thomas
Morgan.   Also two cottages at France Lynch, then in the
occupation of Thomas Cox and William Gubbins.

To his son Henry, all the messuage with garden, etc., at
Chalford in the occupation of Samuel Wright, and the
carpenter's workshop and timberyard and close near thereto
but divided from it by the Turnpike road and lying between
it and the Canal.   Also six several houses with the Mercer's
shop in the valley of Chalford near the said premises.   Also
the land called Old hills and cottages at Ashmeads and the
lands called Oatlands woods in his own holding.   Also four
fields called Windmill Tynings, then in the occupation of
Jasper Gardner.   Also all the mill called Iles Mill with land
adjoining, then in the occupation of Thomas Jones.   Also all
woods and lands called Westleys and Penny Hill wood.
Benefits were left on trust for his son Walter Ballinger, of
Bridstow, Herefordshire, who married but died 28 November,
1852, aged 30, being buried at Christ Church, Chalford.

Henry Ballinger lived at the Grove, Chalford, and died a
bachelor 31 March, 1855.   By his will he left £100 to the
County Infirmary of Gloucester, £100 to the Casualty Hospital
at Stroud, £600 to the Minister and Churchwardens of Chalford
Church, to be invested as to half to be spent in coal for the
poor of Chalford, and the other half for the benefit of the
National School there.   £200 to Brompton Hospital, and
£400 to the Rev. Solomon Gompertz, who was sole executor.

Charles Ballinger, of Skaites Hill House, married Mary,
daughter of John Mills, of Miserden House, and died s.p.,
5 February, 1884.   Amongst other charitable bequests he
left £1000 to the Minister and Churchwardens of Chalford, to

be invested, and half the interest to be used for the purchase of coals for the poor of the district Church of Chalford, and the other half to the support of the National school master.

Charles Ballinger was buried at Christ Church, Chalford. His widow, Mrs. Mary Ballinger, survived him for twenty five years, dying 8 March, 1909, aged 89.

———

FIRWOOD.

On ascending the hill past Skaiteshill House, and crossing the top of Mutton Lane, the estate of Firwood is reached. Its earlier name of Paggonshill Farm suggests an historic connection with Fitzpaine of Painswick, or with Paganhill, Stroud, but of this there is no proof.

The titledeeds of Firwood only begin in the middle of the seventeenth century, when the estate belonged to Thomas Mayo (1746), woolscribbler, and was left by him to his wife Hester for life, and then to his son, John Mayo, who in 1767 mortgaged it to John Jenkins, of St. Cloe Green, Minchinhampton. In 1770, the property being put up for sale at Cirencester, was bought by Joseph Mayo, yeoman, of Brownshill, and mortgaged by him and Thomas Clutterbuck, of Avening, in 1771, to Sir Joseph Mawbey, bart. and John Mawbey, his brother. The property is called the messuage tenement and farm commonly known by the name of " Paggonshill, otherwise Brownshill " with gardens, barns, stables and orchards, etc., of thirty acres.

It was immediately mortgaged to William Damsell, of Lilyhorn, yeoman, E. Clutterbuck sharing in the proceeding. Cottages which went with the property, formerly belonging to John Maysey, were sold by John Mayo and John Jenkins to Joseph Cullerne, who had acquired possession of the Feoffees' estate at Brownshill, as well as of Paggonshill farm. He became bankrupt in 1794, the Commissioners finding that he did for six previous years last past, carry on and follow the business of a Surgeon and Apothecary, and during such time did seek and endeavour to get his living by buying drugs, compounding and dispensing of medicines, and selling the same, and by so doing endeavoured to get a livelihood and maintenance, as others carrying on the same trade and business are accustomed to do." The whole property appears to have been mortgaged to Samuel Beale, of Upton-on-Severn, and mention is made in a deed of 1795 of John Beale, clothier, of Brownshill, and Miles Beale of Hyde Court, parish of Minchinhampton, clothier. John Beale mortgaged the whole property to Edward Beale, of Fenchurch Street, London, in 1796, and in 1799, to Wakeman Long, Esq. John Beale had married Jane, daughter and co-heiress of Thomas Evans, late of St. Katherine's Tower, London, distiller. As his widow she retained the property till 1813, when she sold it to John Perrin, son of John Perrin, of Iron Mills, Minchinhampton, gentleman, and Thomas Howell,[1] of Griffin Mill, Stroud, (son-in-law of John Perrin). John Perrin, junior, died in 1822, leaving the estate in trust with John Ballinger, Thomas Howell, and Stephen Blackwell, junior, of Nailsworth, clothier, for Thomas Perrin Howell, his great-nephew, till he was 21.

Firwood, as it came to be called, was continued in its uneasy state of mortgages, and in 1839 came to the hands of his uncle Thomas Brown, of Coln St. Aldwins, gentleman, who, dying intestate in 1852, the estate reverted to his nephew T. P. Howell, and his sister Mrs. Price, as joint heirs. T. P. Howell had been residing at Firwood but ultimately went to the United States. Lord Teynham, who is still remembered as a strict Plymouth brother, occupied Firwood for some years, and in 1891 it was purchased by the Rev. Christopher Smyth, on his retirement from the vicarage of Bussage.

The back portion of the house is the oldest, and of seventeenth century date, the front having been added about 1830. Mr. Smyth built a private chapel, of the Good Shepherd, which was later duly licensed by Bishop Ellicott to be used as a chapel of ease for Chalford. On his death in 1900, Firwood passed into the possession of his two daughters,

---

[1] He was of Brownshill. In a vault in Bisley Churchyard lie the remains of Emma Maria, his daughter, and those of his wife, Anna Maria, died 1831, aged 26.

and is now the residence of Miss Smyth and of her elder brother, the Right Reverend Edmund Smyth, (M.A., King's College, Cambridge, and M.D.) who was consecrated first Bishop of Lebombo in 1893, and has spent the best part of his life in the South African mission field.

BROWNSHILL.

The history of certain parts of Brownshill has already been considered in Chapter VIII, " The estate of Stonehing or Stonehouse " belonging to the Feoffees, and also Brownshill House under the heading of " The Tything of Bussage." How Brownshill obtained its name is unknown, but its earliest mention as such is in the Court roll of 14 October, 1586, when Richard Fowler is recorded to have broken the ground of the lord at Brownshill within the Custom wood there, and dug for stone. There are a few other references to this small hamlet in the Court rolls. On 31 March, 1681, John Coxwell, gentleman (probably connected with Abnash), was to attend the Court to be taken tenant for Brownshill. Otherwise " breaking the ground " seems to have been the only excitement in Brownshill, as was done by Richard Holliday, in 1683, and Francis Franklin, who also dug holes in 1704. Giles Whittenye was amerced for not fencing the Quarr dug by him in Nashend Wood, near the way leading from Brownshill to Stevens bridge.

That there was at one time a windmill at Brownshill seems likely, from the existence of two mill-stones, one at Tanglewood, and one at Huntley Cottage. There appear to be indications of its site on the raised ground on the hill directly north of Tanglewood.

An indication of a Roman occupation of this hamlet is afforded by the finding of a coin of Hadrian in a garden just below the suggested site of the windmill, now occupied by Mr. Fred Roberts.

CHAPTER X

PART 4

THE TYTHING OF BUSSAGE.

The name of Bussage has suffered many changes in the course of its development, from the Bysrugg of 1304. It is found as Byserugge in 1354, Bussrige in 1586, Byssridge in 1598, Bissridge in 1601, Bussage in 1685, Bussridge in 1707, Bisseridge in 1727, Bushage in 1729, and Bussige in 1722.

The meaning of the name was translated by the late Mr. G. J. Wood, F.S.A., as " the ridge of the does," but modern experts would probably explain it as the ridge of Bissa. In view of the numerous place names of the Cotswold district of old times indicating the animals of field or wood, perhaps many will accept the first interpretation.

The tything of Bussage included Eastcombe (Isscombe or Esscombe, the combe of the ash-tree), and stretched south-wards as far as Black Ness to the Stroud valley. Bisley Common extended to Brownshill and bounded the tything on the east, and the Todsmore stream marked the western side. It was possible to drive the whole way to Bisley along the Common before its enclosure in 1865, when the upper road, dipping down to north Bussage near the Ram, and then running on to Bisley above Eastcombe, was made.

Of ancient history there is none, but the woods of Bysrugge, of which the Frith wood is a fragmentary and ancient site, are mentioned in charters of Corpus Christi College, Oxford, in connection with their Chalford property.[1]

[1] *B. G. A. S. Trans.*, li., 211 *et. seq.*

Perhaps the earliest mention of a Bussage inhabitant is the name of William of Bysrug, a juror at the Inquisition P. M. of Edmund Mortimer, in 1304. Then in the Court Roll of 1354 John Byserugge is stated to have paid XIId. for all services to the Lord of the Manor, and 4d. for one wood, formerly John Sered's. The woods of Ocrugg (Oakridge)and Bysrugge are the concern of the woodward in 1361, and in 1382 John Knight, clerk, was elected Woodward for Bisrug wood.

The only names that emerge from the past of Bussage are found as witnesses to the Corpus Christi documents, such as Peter Faber (the smith) of Biserige, Ellis Faber of Bysrige, Walter Bysrugge (1359 and 1361).

Sir William Nottingham acquired land in Bysrugge and Abenashe (as well as in other places in Gloucestershire) which by his will of 1 September, 1483, he directed should be set aside to provide a priest to pray at the altar of St. Thomas in Cirencester Church, for his own soul and those of his parents and two wives, and also for the upkeep of four poor men in the house he had built for them in Batell Street (now Thomas Street) at Cirencester. These lands were long ago alienated from their sacred purpose.

It is not till the Manor Court of Queen Elizabeth, 10 October, 1589, that one gathers the name of any property in Bussage, when it is stated that Richard Pope came to take one messuage and one ferendall called Horshalles, which was in the tenure of Thomas Pope his father. Thomas Pope came and surrendered Horshalls, lying in Busridge in 1597, paying a heriot of one cow worth 26s. 8d., and on 21 July, 1597, William Smith came to take the same messuage and one ferendall of land for his life, that of Henry, his son, and of Jocose, his wife. So late as 1736, at the Court Baron of Bisley Manor of John Stephens, Esq., of 23 October, amongst the names of the free tenants there is that of William Winne for Horshalls, but the knowledge of its locality has passed away. Possibly the site of an ancient homestead and garden which can be traced in the field at the back of Bussage Vicarage, or Glebe House, at one time allotments, may represent Horshalls.

x

The Popes held seven acres of land at Lypiatt, adjoining Colliers near Copsgrove, and this was bought by John Stephens in 1684. Whether any of this family was connected with John Pope who speculated in the manor of Nether Lypiatt in 1545, or not, is unknown. Richard Pope of the parish of Bisley, clothier, exchanged his three acres of land in Stancombe field with Walter Shewell in 1656, and in 1669 he devised his three acres in Nottingham Corner to Peter Clissold, blacksmith, for the remainder of his 900 years. The parish registers contain several entries regarding the Popes from 1560 to 1579. Members of the Rogers family, related to Rogers of Catswood, were living at Bussage. Mary Rogers made her will 18 March, 1707, describing herself as of Bussridge, spinster, then very sick and weak of body but of perfect memory (thanks be to Almighty God). First being heartily sorry for her sins past, most humbly desiring forgiveness for the same, she commits her soul to the hands of Almighty God, hoping to be saved through the merits of Jesus Christ, And her body to be buried at the discretion of her executor. After debts paid, to her brother Samuel Rogers 1s. To her cousin Richard Rogers that lives with her all her right and title and interest in her estate lying and being at Bussridge wherein she now dwells. He to be her executor. W. Susanna Rogers, Ambrose Cox, Thomas Keble. Inv. £41 10s. 0d. Proved 9 November, 1709.

Richard Rogers made his will 11 April, 1729, being of the parish of Bisley, yeoman. He bequeaths to his brother-in-law Samuel Rogers all that messuage wherein he now dwells at Bushage with all barns, stables, outhouses, etc., closes of arrable and pasture ground. To his brother Thomas Rogers 20s. To his sister Martha Horwood £3. To his sister Katharine Wallis 20s. To his sister Elizabeth, wife of Thomas Collins 20s. The residue to his said brother Samuel Rogers, who is sole executor. W. Nathan Cox, Thomas Tiler, John Panting. Proved 17 September, 1730.[1]

Thomas Rogers, of Bussige, mentioned in this will was assessed at 3s. 9d. for poor rate in 1722 and later. His will

1 Glos. Pro. Reg.

made 3 July, 1737, was proved in 1741. He was a cloth-worker and left to Mary, his wife, all the messuage where he lives, with the outhouses, gardens, close of pasture ground, lands, etc., and also the Cottage tenement near to the said messuage with its garden and outhouses, and all other lands and tenements whatsoever, the last mentioned cottage being in the possession of Jonathan Stephens. W. Edmund Clutterbuck, James Tyler, Thomas Tyler.[1]

Richard Rogers, of Bussige, 1722 and 1723, was living at Todsmore in 1738, his wife Ann having died 13 August, 1727, aged 46.[2]

Samuel Rogers, brother to Thomas Rogers, was assessed for Poor rate in 1678 (or Mrs. Rogers, Bussige) at 19s. 10d., which indicates a substantial holding. George Rogers of Bussage, Clothier, died 27 March, 1737, aged 37, as recorded on a brass now in the tower of Bisley Church. Possibly he worked the Todsmore Mill.

From certain documents referred to under the head of Todsmore, the connection of the Rogers family with that locality is established. It was evidently the oldest part of Bussage, though it is now looked upon as a hamlet only to Bussage village on the hill above.

With very little of any great antiquity to be seen at Bussage, stones of ancient working may be observed built into the walls of the older cottages, and in many instances the original home of many of the cottagers of eighty or ninety years ago may be seen in what is now used as an outhouse, or which has attached to it enlarged buildings of more recent date. Some of these very small cottages doubtless represent successful encroachments on the edge of the Common before its enclosure in 1865.

The principal house at Bussage, Bussage House, was enlarged by Mr. William Davis, popularly known as Squire Davis. When first erected, the road, now diverted outside the walls and running down beside the Church yard, originally

<hr/>

[1] Glos. Pro. Reg.
[2] Bigland's His. of Glos.

passed in front of the house, out at the large gate to the north, now walled up, across the grounds of Applegarth, then an orchard, and out of the north gate, up the lane and into the field below the Vicarage. It crossed the former allotments there, and entering Vatch Lane, passed up it and into the field where a track to Bisley can be traced across the fields to Eastcombe and Sheephouse.

Up to the beginning of the nineteenth century there were several cottages more or less along this track, remains of which may be seen built into some of the field walls.

Of Bussage House before it was acquired by William Davis, little is known, but a mortgage of this and other premises in 1826 shows that William Toghill, the then owner, had purchased Bussage House from John Yale, and that John Drew was the then tenant. It was mortgaged to James Hodges, of Cirencester, victualler.

Squire Davis removed a couple of cottages from his grounds within the upper gate. He added the large room at the back of the house and used it as a meeting house in opposition to the Church, and provided it with an organ, which later was placed in the Baptist Chapel at Eastcombe. Bussage House afterwards passed into the possession of Mr. John Sibree, who established a boys' school there, and added on largely to the house. This continued to the beginning of the present century, when the house became a private residence for some years. In 1912 it was acquired by Miss Dorothea Beale, and till 1937 was a girls' school.

Squire Davis was also the owner of the house known as Woodlands, and of the orchard below it, now the site of Applegarth. Woodlands, which dates from the early years of the nineteenth century, was formerly two cottages, one being a Dame School, at one time. Later Mrs. Suckling, widow of the first Vicar rented it, it having been turned into one dwelling-house, since which time, with the exception of its use as a Sanatorium for the boys' school, it has been used as a residence.

Squire Davis also acquired the property known as St. Michael's Cottage, formerly Bussage Villa. It was originally a farm house, probably of the eighteenth century, to which was added a new front in the style of George IV's time.

The piece of garden ground which goes with this house was formerly called Perks.

One of the few dated houses at Bussage is the Old House, on which is inscribed over the front door " H.I.C. 1704 "— which stands for Henry Collins and his wife. From the title deeds of this property it appears that Henry Collins, broadweaver, acquired the land that year from his father Samuel Collins of Bisley, carpenter, for £20 10s. 0d. It is described as " a certain close " of arable land, pasture and woodground called by the name of the Calves Close on the south west, part of the said Close next adjoining at the east end and south side thereof to the Custome wood or Common of Bisley and near unto certain quarrs called Bussage quarrs being for the most part wood or woodland ground, and to contain one full acre to be measured and accounted at the rate of 18 feet to the Lugg, rod or perch, to extend from the uppermost of the said Calves Close eastward down westward towards a place called Todsmore Bottom, and next adjoining to the Custome wood on the south side thereof, to hold of the Chiefe Lord of the fee under the yearly rent of three pence.

Thomas Collins who married Elizabeth Rogers, sister of Richard Rogers succeeded his father and in 1725 mortgaged the estate and finally sold it to William Long, from whom through a series of mortgages it came to the possession of James Tyler of Todsmore, Millwright, only son and heir of Thomas Tyler of Todsmore, Broadweaver, and was by him assigned to Samuel Rogers of Bussage, victualler, in 1816. The Old House is then described as having a shop thereunto adjoining, formerly built by the said James Tyler, Millwright, for his own use and now converted into a dwelling-house, and also all that parcel of arable land lying near of one and a quarter acres together with the cottage sometime since converted into a dwelling-house. All which premises are situated at Bussage and were late in the tenure of William Workman as tenant to James Tyler, and since that in the tenure of William Workman, Thomas Bingle, and Elizabeth

Watkins, but are now in the several tenures of Thomas Bingle, Mary Workman, Samuel Lewis, and George Ridler.

Thomas Russell, carrier, appears to have purchased the Old House as well as the house known as the Haven, and to have left the two properties to his nephew, Nathan Edmund Pincott. The Old House was for many years in an absolutely ruinous state and was used as a cowhouse, till it was taken on lease by the late Miss Evelyn Whish and restored by her as a residence. It has recently become the property of Mrs. Wilson.

The Haven, mentioned above, is of about the same date as the Old House, and contained good specimens of local ironwork. In one fireplace the four seasons were represented and in another the fireback had a ship in full sail.

The outhouse, originally a cottage, attached to the Grange is dated 1799.

The Ram Inn, which was rebuilt in 1900, was formerly a picturesque old cottage covered with creepers, bearing the date 1800, which is still over the Inn door.

There was formerly an old cottage in the upper vegetable garden of Bussage Vicarage, some of the stone of its roof-ridge still edging the paths. This was bought from Samuel Gurner by William Toghill, and at the time of his mortgaging it in 1826, it was occupied by Richard Jeffries. Later, the Armstrong family were living there.

The water supply for this house and the Ram Inn was pumped from a well, now closed, but situated in the semi-circular recess in the wall of the garden of the Vicarage, which is still visible, though the pump no longer is there.

THE CHURCH AND PARISH OF BUSSAGE.

We owe the foundation of our parish of Bussage and the building of the Church of St. Michael and All Angels, to the piety of twenty undergraduates of Oxford, who met at

Christ Church on 28 May, 1839, and there undertook to lay aside £20 each per annum for five years, in order to build a Church which should be substantial, beautiful, and handsomely adorned, in a place to be decided on when the funds allowed. The offer of the results of their self-denying efforts was made to the Rev. Thomas Keble, Vicar of Bisley, in 1842, and the hamlet of Bussage was selected as the place in his large parish most needing a Church.

The first site chosen for the erection of the Church was below the field leading from Bussage to the House of Mercy, now a garden ; but this was abandoned as being too near the line of occasional landslips. The existence of several yew trees, (most of which have been cut down within recent years), below Bussage House, decided the founders to select that most beautiful but somewhat inconvenient spot. There the foundation stone was laid on 21 November, 1844. On it was carved the following inscription, which though not now visible, was last seen when the South Aisle was being built.—

" In Honorem Dei

Mortuorum et vivorum Domini
Et in curam pauperum in Christo
Haec Ecclesia fundata est
Cal XI Dec. A. S. MDCCCXLIV.

Suis impensis aedificant viginti
Academiae Oxoniensis alumni
Ignoti quidem his locis sed Deo noti."

This inscription has been thus translated :—

To the Honour of God

The Lord both of the dead and living
And in pious care for the poor in Christ,
The Foundation Stone of this Church is laid
on the 21st day of November in the Year of Salvation, 1844.

Built at the sole expense of twenty Scholars of the University of Oxford.

Unknown in this place, but known of God.

The site chosen proving to be not quite so stable as desired, the foundations of the north wall were strengthened by oak piles, driven into the hill-side. The Church, as first built, consisted of a Chancel with vestry, nave and tower at the west end, and South porch, in the style of the Decorated period. The need for further room in order to seat the inmates of the Bussage House of Mercy soon led to the addition of a south aisle opening into the nave by an arcade of three bays, designed by Bodley. The chancel was furnished with return stalls for the priests, similar to a College chapel, but this was later altered to the usual north and south situations. The altar slab is of Purbeck marble, but as it was found to be too small and low, a larger top was laid over it during the incumbency of the Rev. C. Smyth. The bays of the arch-braced roof of the nave are supported by demi-figures of angels with hands folded in prayer.

The Church was consecrated on 6 October, 1846, the Rev. R. A. Suckling, then being Priest in charge. Many of the Oxford Tractarians, friends of Mr. Keble, gathered round him on this occasion, and a procession of forty-four priests accompanied the Bishop from the Ram Inn, where they vested, to the Church. The sermon was preached by the Rev. Mr. Ridler.

The churchyard was also consecrated by the Bishop, but it was then smaller than it is now, for a portion of ground was added at a later date extending from the yew tree[1] near the large gate and round the upper side to the South-east. This was never consecrated.

The furnishing of the Church was carried out in the best manner possible, and in the opening years of this century it had the reputation of being the most richly appointed village Church in the diocese. The bell was cast at the celebrated Whitechapel foundry ; the plate was provided by the twenty founders and consists of a chalice and patten silver gilt, the former more recently jewelled, a small silver chalice and patten for sick communions, a silver gilt flagon,

---

1 This yewtree has been recently destroyed.

an alms basin of copper gilt and one of silver gilt,[1] and a pair of candlesticks of brass. Other candlesticks have been added to the ornaments, as well as a Sanctuary lamp, given in memory of Father Suckling, of St. Alban's, Holborn, who himself presented, in memory of a brother who was born at Bussage, a silver gilt set of cruets on a tray, with lavabo and wafer bowls. Every other necessary adjunct for the full ritual of the Church, which has obtained for many years, has been added from time to time. The screen, originally given by Mr. Arnott, was enriched with a cresting and rood as the War Memorial.

By the will of John Edmund Wallis, who died 14 May, 1931, a sum of £100 was bequeathed to the Vicar and Parochial Church Council to be invested in the Gloucester Diocesan Trust, the interest thereon to be applied to the up-keep of Bussage Churchyard, and another £50 was bequeathed to the Vicar and Churchwardens to be similarly invested and the interest to be paid to a deserving person who will tend the Wallis grave.[2]

FORMATION OF THE PARISH OF BUSSAGE.

The Parish was not legally constituted till 1848, when the Queen granted an Order in Council dated 29 August, 1848, at the Court held at Osborne House, Isle of Wight, defining the boundaries of the new Chapelry District of Bussage, and assigning only a small portion of the tything for the purpose, and so omitting both Eastcombe and Brownshill.

" The chapelry district of Bussage is bounded on the north-west and west by the parish of Stroud : on the south and south-east by the Chalford district as far as the north west corner of Frith Wood ; and on the east and north east by the remaining part of the parish of Bisley from which it is separated by a line drawn in a northerly direction from the said north west corner of Frith Wood, across Bisley

---

[1] Strangely enough both these alms-dishes have been described in the inventories as brass.

[2] These bequests are to be known as " the Wallis Bequest."

Common to the footpath leading from the said Common to Daniel's Farm, along which said footpath the boundary line then proceeds north easterly up the middle of the latter footpath, as far as Cuckoo Lane ; and then proceeds north westerly, northerly, and again north westerly, up the middle of that lane and crossing Bismore Bridge meets the boundary of the before-mentioned parish of Stroud, as such proposed chapelry district of Bussage," etc. The population was then said to be 400, but it has since fallen to 320.

The living is in the gift of the Bishop of Gloucester.

The Rev. Isaac Williams published a Memoir of the first Vicar of Bussage in 1852, and this gives some interesting details about the work of the parish in its early days. He also edited a volume of Mr. Suckling's sermons.

The Church School was built on land given by Miss Anna Gordon in 1848. Mr. William Davis conveyed the top portion of the copse and of the Churchyard to the Vicar and Churchwardens in 1854, stating that a certain portion had already been used as a schoolyard.

Vicars, otherwise Perpetual Curates, of Bussage.

1. ROBERT ALFRED SUCKLING, M.A., Caius College, Cambridge. Deacon 1842, Priest 1844. Appointed to Bussage 24 June, 1847.

Mr. Suckling, born in 1818 came of the ancient family of that name of Woodton, Norfolk, and was heir to that estate. He entered the Royal Navy in 1831, and continued at sea till 1839, when the call came to him, after two severe illnesses, to prepare himself for Holy Orders. After his marriage to Anna Maria, daughter of Dr. Yelloly, of Cavendish Hall, Suffolk, 22 April, 1840, he took up his residence at Cambridge in 1841, and in September, 1843, was ordained deacon at Gloucester to the title of the curacy of Kemerton, offered him by Archdeacon Thorp. In 1846, the Rev. Thomas Keble asked him to undertake the charge of the newly built church of Bussage, and when he first did so, he resided at Brownshill House for a short time. It was found impossible to work the parish satisfactorily so far from the Church, so in 1850, after the death of Abraham Davis who occupied what was then known as Bussage Farm, that property was bought for the Vicarage and glebe. It was then only a cottage, but the front was removed and suitable rooms were added. The old part, dating from the early eighteenth century, can still be distinguished at the back of the house.

During his short incumbency Robert Suckling did a great work amongst his poor parishioners, (how poor they were may be gathered from the Rev. Isaac Williams' poem in "Thoughts in Past Years," entitled "A Bussage Family ") and also amongst those in the Stroud Union. His health had been undermined by fever during his naval career, so that when suddenly stricken down by illness on All Saints Day 1857, he succumbed three days later. His body rests in Bussage Churchyard.

2. ROBERT GEORGE SWAYNE, B.A., Wadham College, Oxford, Deacon 1844, Priest 1845. At Bussage from 1852-59. He was afterwards Rector of St. Edmunds Sarum from 1863-77, Prebendary of Gillingham Major in Sarum Cathedral 1870-77, and was Canon and Chancellor of that Cathedral. He died 22 April, 1901.

3. WILLIAM MAUNDER HITCHCOCK, B.A., Wadham College, Oxford, Deacon 1858, Priest 1859. At Bussage from 1859-61. He was Perpetual Curate of Shildon, Co. Durham, 1862-6, Rector of Whitburn 1866-81, Vicar of Romford 1881-88, and Vicar of East Farleigh, Kent, 1888-93.

4. ALEXANDER POOLE, M.A., St. John's College, Cambridge, Deacon 1855, Priest 1856. At Bussage 1861 for a few months only as he was appointed Minor Canon, Precentor, and Sacrist of Bristol Cathedral that year. He was Vicar of Ryde, Isle of Wight 1868-91, when he became Rector of West Meon. He was an honorary Canon of Winchester, and died in April, 1899.

5. EDMUND NELSON DEAN, M.A., Pembroke College, Oxford, Deacon 1827, Priest 1828. At Bussage 1861-78.

Entered into rest 24 September, 1878, and is interred at Bussage.

6.　JOHN SMITH.　At Bussage 1878-81.

7.　HENRY ARNOTT.　University of London 1860. Chichester College 1876.　Deacon 1878, Priest 1879.　Before his ordination he was Assistant Surgeon at St. Thomas' Hospital, London.　After serving as curate of Beckenham 1878-81, he was appointed to Bussage and remained there till 1885.　In his time a great deal was done to adorn the Church and he enlarged the Vicarage by the addition of a spacious dining room and room over it on the north side of the house. He subsequently became Rector of Beckenham in 1885 and a Canon of Rochester.

8.　IRVINE KEMPT ANDERSON.　Chichester College, Deacon 1883, Priest 1884.　At Bussage from 1885-86.

9.　CHRISTOPHER SMYTH, M.A., Jesus College, Cambridge. Deacon 1851, Priest 1852.　Was Curate of Great Yarmouth 1851-6, Rector of Woodford, Northants, 1857-84.　He was Vicar of Bussage from 1886-91.　After his resignation of Bussage, he bought Firwood at Brownshill and there built a private chapel, which was subsequently licensed as a chapel of ease for that district.　Mr. Smyth was the father of the Right Rev. Bishop Smyth, Bishop of Lebombo 1893.　Mr. Christopher Smyth resided at Firwood till his death in 1900 when he was laid to rest at Bussage.

10.　WILLIAM BARKER DRAWBRIDGE, LL.B., Caius College, Cambridge.　Deacon 1855, Priest 1856.　He was Chaplain in India till 1883, and after three curacies in England was Vicar of Bussage 1891-5.

11.　NORMAN DONALD MACLEOD, M.A., Jesus College, Cambridge.　Deacon 1881, Priest 1883, after training at Ely Theological College.　Curate of Roath, Cardiff, 1881-91, of All Saints, Clifton, 1891-4, when he was appointed to Bussage. It was during his incumbency, viz., in January 1899, that unwelcome attention was paid to the Church services by a Protestant emissary and correspondent of the " Record " newspaper, who attended the Sunday sung Eucharist for the purpose of collecting data for his articles entitled " Lawlessness in the Church." A Similar visitation was made by two other busy Protestant agitators in July 1904,—the Rev. the Hon. W. E. Bowen, of Barkston Gardens, S.W., and Mr. W. G. Johnson, of Putney, who gave evidence before the Royal Commission on Ecclesiastical Discipline in 1905. The Vicar was only notified of their evidence by the Commissioners, and in his letter acknowledging their missives he writes,— " Without pledging myself to all the details, I have to say that the ceremonial used in this Church is that ordered expressly or by implication by the Ornaments Rubric, to the provisions of which I consider myself bound to conform." Nothing resulted from this outside interference, and when, during the incumbency of the Rev. H. F. Hayward, the Wycliffe Preachers' Van arrived and an endeavour was made to stir up strife, the men of the village signified their intention of dealing with the van if it was not removed. The Preachers found it advisable to move on. The Rev. N. D. Macleod on leaving Bussage in 1905 became Rector of Narborough, Leicester, which living he exchanged three years later for that of Denbury, Devon, and after three years there he accepted the Chaplaincy of St. Barnabas Home, Torquay, which he resigned in 1930. He was appointed a Licensed Preacher for the Diocese of Exeter, and died at Torquay 18 June, 1934.

12. HERBERT FINZEL HAYWARD, M.A., Hatfield Hall, Durham (1893). Deacon 1891, Priest 1893. He was successively curate of Wareham 1891-2, of St. John Baptist, Newport, Mon., and of Coleford, Glos. He was Vicar of Bussage from 1905 to 1921, when he resigned and became Vicar of St. Marks', Gloucester.

13. HERBERT PULMAN BARCHARD, B.A., Brase-nose College, Oxford, 1887. At Ely College 1892. Deacon 1894, Priest 1895, Curate of East Retford 1894, of Tunstall, Staffs. (Ch. Ch.) 1901-7.

He succeeded the Rev. H. Sawyer as Chaplain of the House of Mercy, Bussage, in 1907, and became Vicar of Bussage also in 1921.

Note on Bussage Vicarage, from a Memorandum by Miss A. M. Suckling. " In this it is stated that in 1848 a little house on the site of the present Vicarage was established as a Parsonage. About 1849 some additional rooms were built on, and that new part is now the old part of the present Vicarage. The Rev. R. G. Swayne during his incumbency, pulled down the original little house and built the vicarage as it now is."

BUSSAGE HOUSE OF MERCY.

An important event connected with the ecclesiastical life of the new parish, was the foundation of the House of Mercy in 1851, which though not within the actual limits of the parish, lies within those of the tything. Mr. Suckling in his ministrations at the Workhouse had felt the want of some House of Refuge for the sad cases he encountered there, so when he received a letter from Mr. Armstrong (afterwards Bishop of Grahamstown) inviting him to attend a committee at Gloucester to forward a scheme for a Diocesan Penitentiary which the Bishop proposed should be at Bussage, he gladly furthered the plan and consented to be the first Chaplain.

The House of Mercy was begun in Kirby's Cottage, which lies near the grounds of Brownshill House, and on Church Hill, and which is now incorporated in the building of the House, designed for twenty-five inmates with staff and Sisters, a chapel dedicated to St. Michael and All Angels, and a laundry.

There the good work began under the supervision of Mrs. Grace Anne Poole, who, with her husband, James Poole, Esq., had come to reside at Brownshill House. She was the eldest daughter of the Rev. John Hopton, of Canon Frome Court, Co. Hereford, and as the brass tablet erected to her memory (and to that of the Rev. Robert Suckling and of Bishop Armstrong) in Bussage Church states, she was Foundress and first Mother Superior of the Community of St. Michael and All Angels, which undertook the work of the House of Mercy.[1]   After the death of the Foundress in her 91st year, when her body was laid to rest in Bussage Churchyard, 24 January, 1920, the small Community somewhat languished, and became unable to carry on the Penitentiary work, which was ultimately committed to the care of the Community of St. Mary the Virgin, Wantage, and so continues.

Amongst the old houses of Bussage tything, Brownshill House is to be noted, as its oldest part, originally a small farmstead, is of the early seventeenth century, with an eighteenth century addition, to which again was added a nineteenth century block. Sometime in the seventeenth century it became the property of a member of the Poole family of Sapperton, Thomas Poole, in 1641 and 1642 being rated for Brownshill at £2 2s. 0d.   It was later the residence of Robert Poole, lawyer, whose monument, formerly in the chancel of Bisley Church, is now in the tower.   Beneath the Poole arms, namely,—Per fess azure, semy of fleur de lys or, a lion rampant argent, impaling,—a chevron between three spear-heads (for Crump) is the following inscription :—

" Juxta hunc lapidem Requiescit quod mortale est Roberti Poole, de Browns Hill, Jurisperiti, Qui vitam hanc demigravit, Quinto die Martii, Anno Dom. MDCCXX.   Aetatis suae LXXX.   Piæ Memoriæ Chari ejus Soceri Sara Crump de Newnham Generosa.

Hoc posuit Monumentum."

For some years after this date Brownshill House became the home of the clothier family of Nash, as appears from several memorials at Bisley.   On a brass let into a stone outside the west end of the north aisle of the Church is the inscription :—

" To the happy memory of Mary, wife of John Nash, of Browns Hill in this parish, Clothier, who Dyed ye 10 day of Decembr, 1737, Aged 79 years.

" Also Sarah their daughter and wife of William Parham, of Chalford, Clothier, Dyed the 2nd day of May, 1734.

[1] The title has been recently changed to " St. Michael's Home."

" Isaac Nash, their son, Dyed ye 2nd of July, 1736."

Near this is " In memory of Elizabeth Witt the daughter of John Nash of Brownshill in this Parish, Clothier, who died May the 22nd, 1761. Aged 62 years."

Within the tower a brass plate records,—" John, son of John Nash, of Browns Hill, clothier, died 7 February, 1741, aged 62." Another brass plate is to " John Nash, clothier, of this parish, died 30 November, 1716, aged 61. And William his son, Clothier, died 17 September, 1700, aged 16."

The clothier family of Wynn, or Winn, appear to have succeeded the Nashes at Brownshill House, though whether this was the case at the first mention in connection with Brownshill of William Winn in 1754, or not till later, is not stated. William Winn died 20 December, 1758, his wife Mary living to be 83, and dying 16 January, 1788. Their son John Winn, clothier, died 7 March, 1789, aged 60, his wife Mary pre-deceasing him 10 May, 1775, aged 26. Having lost two children in infancy, their son William Winn lived till 2 May, 1816, having married Sarah, daughter of John and Mary Aland. She died at the age of 28, on 18 June, 1803, leaving her husband with a family, of whom Sarah died 14 March, 1807, and William the youngest son died in the October after his father, aged 17. They are all buried on the south side of Bisley Church.

Miss A. M. Suckling states in a note on Brownshill House, that it was a cottage added on to by a Mr. Wynn in the reign of William IV. He wanted a good room for music ; hence the large drawing-room. Mr. Wynn's son sold it to a Mr. Gardiner, a wealthy man, who sold it in his turn to the Rev. Richard Champernowne (son-in-law of the Rev. Thomas Keble, senior) for a Parsonage for Bussage. However, the house proved to be inconveniently distant from the Church, school, and village.

As already stated Brownshill House was the residence of Mrs. Poole during her married life, but when she became a widow she resided at the House of Mercy as Mother Superior, till her death, and Brownshill House became the home of the various chaplains of the Community. In 1856 it passed into the possession of the Rev. William Parsons Hopton, of Bishop Frome, Co. Hereford. With its plantations and three closes of land the estate consisted of 7 acres, 3 roods, 11 perches. It is now the property of the House of Mercy.

At the foot of the Church Hill, below the House of Mercy, lies a cluster of ancient cottages, reached by a deeply sunk lane, the former pack-horse road from Stroud. This hamlet, called Black Ness, or Neass, as in the will of William Grime, 1701, ends the tything of Bussage to the south.

TODSMORE.

Below Bussage village lies the beautiful valley of Todsmore, with three ancient mills, besides modern ones, lying on the banks of its stream which flows down from Bisley through Bismore and the Fishpond, to join the Frome at Bourne.

The name of Todsmore, now corrupted to Toadsmore, probably signifies " the moor of the young foxes," a name still most suitable for it.

A treasured tradition connected with Todsmore, and one perpetuated by Sir Robert Atkyns, is that the middle mill (formerly a corn mill) next below Selwyn's Flock Mill, was the birthplace of Roger Bacon, the discoverer of gunpowder, about 1214. This is disputed by those who hold that he was born near Ilchester, Somerset (of which there is no proof). Tradition further asserts that he was educated at St. Mary's Mill, where at that time there was a chapel, etc., belonging later to the nuns of Sion. Certain ruinous rooms are pointed out as his study and cell, and though no doubt ancient, they can hardly claim to be of the thirteenth century.

Part of Todsmore (including the Fishpond) lay within the Manor of Over Lypiatt, and at the Court Baron of Mrs. Anne Stephens, held at Over Lypiatt 13 October, 1724, it was presented that " that part of Todsmore bottom lying north west and adjoyning to Mr. Shepherd's Woods strait from Bismore Bridge to a Merestone lying below Cuthams, and

Y

from there strait over the Common to a Merestone pitched in William Watkin's Garden Wall is within the Manor of Over Lupiatt."

The Common at Todsmore was formerly 17 acres and 19 perches in area, with 15 acres 3 roods 3 perches of More, and 5 acres, 3 roods 38 perches at Bismore. The field now known as Holly field is still called the Common by old inhabitants, but only represents a portion of its former extent. Encroachments upon the Common took place there as elsewhere, and in 1693 Anthony Snowe was fined 10s., for enclosing common at "Toadsmore" bottom. Cutham's is still commemorated in "Cutham's stile," beyond the north end of the Fishpond.

It is interesting to find that a trade of over a hundred years continuance in the same family, is still carried on in a workshop on the east side of the Fishpond, below the Common, where corks are being cut by hand in the same way that the artificer's father did before him. In the early days of this work the corks were carried by the maker in a sack on his back for sale at Bristol.

The earliest mention of the mill at Todsmore which I take to be that now known as Todsmore or Selwyn's mill, is in the Bisley Court Rolls, of 24 August, 1592, when it was ordained that the tenants of Bysridge and Nashend and the tenant and occupier of the Mill, should scour the watercourse in Todsmore before the feast of St. Michael.

At the Bisley Manor Court of 25 October, 1690, William Hayward on the decease of Giles Nurse and alienation from him, desires to be admitted tenant to a messuage, mill and lands in Todsmore, called Snow's Mill. Giles Nurse or Nourse was either a relation or friend of the Snowes. He was at the Court Baron of 1675. In the Poor rates assessment of 1728, Hayward's Upper Mill is rated at £1 10s. 0d., and his Lower Mill at 10s. 0s. The field adjoining the east side of the Fishpond is known as Snow's orchard.

The Snow Family of Bisley were either clothiers or yeomen, and are found mentioned in the Lay Subsidy rolls of 1522-3, when Thomas Snowe is assessed at twelve pence on 40s., and Richard Snowe at 2s. on £4. In the roll of 1549 John Snowe is assessed at 30s. on £30 and is described as a tucker, and in 1593-4 William Snowe at 8s. on £3. The assessment was laid on the value of goods or lands.

John Snowe of Bisley, clothier, made his will 1 April, 1584, bequeathing to his daughter Joan £100 at 21, and to his son Ferdinand £100 in like order. To the poor to be distributed at his burial £3 6s. 8d. The rest to his wife Alice. Overseers—Richard Smart, James Broughton and William Snowe.

W. William Evans. John Whything, Thomas Rogers and John Lightfoot, vycar.

Ferdinand or Ferdinando Snowe became possessed of the old house opposite the Wells in Bisley in which a pair of thirteenth century windows is to be noted.

Another John Snowe was an inhabitant of Overcourt at the time of its purchase by Thomas Tayloe in 1621. Richard Snow, of Bussage, yeoman, was numbered amongst the Bisley Feoffees in 1688, as was also Edward Snow, fuller, in the same year and in 1664.

In 1827, there were three people working the Upper Mill at Todsmore, namely, Mr. A. Evans, John Lock, and Mr. Winn. The latter was residing at Brownshill House at that time. For some years Todsmore mill, then a flock mill, was owned and worked by Mr. William Selwyn, since whose death it has been in the hands of a company. The Selwyns came of an ancient family, widely spread in Gloucestershire. The first, perhaps, in this neighbourhood is Robert Selwyn a juror at the Inq. p.m. of Edmund Mortimer in 1304.

Todsmore seems to have had a number of residents in the seventeenth and eighteenth centuries, some of whose cottages still remain, the largest being those just above Todsmore Mill. Some of the names of former inhabitants are known through the Lypiatt MSS. On 19 April, 1701, Thomas Stephens, Esq., granted to Daniell Witts a house place called Woodfalls and a plot of garden ground and orchard belonging,

lying in Todsmore Bottom of a quarter acre and adjoining
Deptcombe Wood, having a tenement of the said Thomas
Stephens in possession of Henry Pinall to the north, and a
tenement in the possession of Mary Gay and now of Mary
Davis on the south, the Lessee to build a house and keep it
in repair. For 99 years at 5s. and suit of court.

On 29 September, 1708, Thomas Stephens granted to Sarah
Davis, widow, a tenement and garden in Deptcombe adjoining
to a house in possession of Daniel Witts and next a highway
that leads out of Deptcombe woods into Todsmore Bottom.
For 90 years on three lives, 10s. per annum and a covenant
to build a shop and keep it in repair.

By Indenture of 9 September, 1709, Thomas Stephens
leased to William Watkins, for 99 years, the hilly plot of
pasture or wood-ground of eight acres adjoining the dwelling-
house of William Watkins and abutting upon Toadsmore
on the south, and the land of Mr. Freame on the west, to land
of William Rogers called the Stirts on the north and to a
certain grove of the said Thomas Stephens called Woodfalls[1]
or Deptcombe Grove on the east, situate in the parish of
Stroud at 10s. rent.

There was formerly a fulling or grist mill standing on land
called Wiselands, which by 1801, had fallen into decay.
This land with a cottage, then called Wyesland, and perhaps,
so named from having been owned by the Wyes of Lypiatt,
is mentioned in the Court Roll of Bisley Manor, 22 September,
1598, as lying in Byssridge. It was surrendered at that date
by Thomas Shewell, senior, with a heriot of 20s., and taken
by John Dyer for the lives of John and William Shewell,
son of Thomas and Elizabeth Shewell. This site can be
identified as lying between Todsmore Mill and the Fishpond, for the evidences of the cottage properties situated on
either side of the lane leading down to the Fishpond from
Bussage indicate that Richard Rogers was holding a cottage
and cowpen, the Old and the Young Orchard, the Home Close

---

[1] John Woodfall had held his tenement for 6s. 8d. per aunnm and two
capons and a heriott in 1613. Deptcombe is the combe running west from the
north end of the Fishpond.

and a fulling mill called Wiseland, with Mill Grove, then called Rogers Wood, during the eighteenth century. George Rogers of Picking House, and William Rogers each occupied adjoining cottages. These were all bought by John Stephens, of Lypiatt, from John Rogers, together with a piece of pasture called Scrubbins Orchard, 29 perches, and were later acquired by Charles Ractliffe (als. Ratcliffe). The two upper cottages are now the property of Mrs. Piper and Miss Mabel Wallis, his granddaughters.

The Richard Rogers above-mentioned married Margaret Oatridge in 1739, his marriage settlement being alluded to in the cottage evidences. His only son and heir was Joseph Rogers, of Avening, in 1763.

EASTCOMBE.

In the hamlet of Eastcombe there are some old cottages to be seen amongst a good many modern ones, one at the north end of the village being of the time of William III.

The earliest allusion in documents to the name of Esscombe or Iscombe, is in the Bisley Court rolls of 1361, when the death of Walter Iscombe, in October, is noted, and a heriot of one ox and one cow falls to the Lord (at that time the Bishop of Winchester) and Felicia his widow enters on his holding. In 1586 at the April Court the same Iscombe is mentioned as the place where James Field had held of the Queen one toft and one ferendell of land.

The Manor Farm which was built by Sir John Dorington after the enclosure of the Common, happened to be placed on a site of considerable interest, as besides the many flints of the later Bronze Age which are frequently found in two of the fields and also the finding of a bronze knife on the site of the water tank, there was the mysterious find of the remains of two rapiers of the reign of James I. It was on the occasion of a hole being dug to renew a gatepost behind the house that the workman came upon the remains of these weapons, one being almost rusted away, but the other being in better condition. The leather handles of both with silver wire attachments lay in fragments which were not preserved, but the blade of the rapier which was rescued had on both sides of its blade the following inscription :—

" Jacobus Mag.   Defensor Fidei
   Britannici   Pacis q Amator."

There is a small shield with a bordure and a rose engraved, surmounted by an orb and cross, and a larger orb and cross ends the inscription. This rapier is now in the Stroud Museum.

Unfortunately no expert was called in before the place where the rapiers were found was filled in, again burying the remains of the second weapon and the leather handles, and no further investigation was made to see if there were any human remains near. It has been suggested that there may have been a skirmish here during the Civil War, but more likely a duel may have taken place which demanded secrecy and the hiding of weapons.

In 1681 Feidges or Fidges, which lies on Fidge Lane is bequeathed in the will of Robert Cooke, to his brother John Cooke, provided that he pays £50 in money to his brother Richard Cooke. The executor of his will is his uncle Thomas Tayloe of Bisley. To his master, Thomas Trotman[1] all his " wearing aparel."

Another will, that of James Holliday, 1712, disposes of his fields, meads and house and Little Fidges to his son William, while the lengthy will of Samuel Munden, yeoman, 4 September, 1723, gives interesting topographical details of the neighbourhood of Eastcombe. After the pious bequest of his soul, etc., he bequeaths to his son Samuel Munden his messuage in the parish of Bisley near the Custom Wood and

---

[1] Glos. Pro. R. The Trotmans were clothiers for several generations and connected with the Tayloes and Corderoys. There are several tombs to their memory in Bisley Churchyard, notably that of Thomas Trotman, of Bisley, clothier, died 1803, and John Trotman, of Mills Wood (Chalford), clothier, died 1802 ; Sarah, wife of Robert Trotman, yeoman, and daughter of William and Sarah Clissold, of Bisley, died 1851 ; Robert Trotman, of Myra Villa, Bisley, late of Down Farm, Stroud, died 1884, and his wife, Elizabeth, died 1891.

known as Goathouse, with garden, etc., then in possession of Daniel Snow; also one broad loom now in the said messuage and £10, his best Great Coat, Close bodyed Coat, wastcoat and breeches. To his daughter Hannah Munden his messuage wherein he now dwells, his two best beds and bedsteads and two best ruggs, his great pott and great kettle and two best pewter platters, and all his tubbs and trendles, two of the best Barrells, his largest Chest, one box and one warming pan, one largest coffer, three chairs, etc., one malt mill and one Oatmeal Mill and £10. To his son William Munden his messuage orchard and garden situated at Workmans' Hill in the parish of Bisley, purchased of Nathaniel Workman, also £10 and his chattels. To his daughter Elizabeth Munden his new-erected messuage he built in the place where there was an old house which he pulled down, together with an orchard and garden, etc., situate at Escombs near a place called the Wells and which old house and garden he purchased of Richard Rogers, and sundry chattels and £10. To his daughter Margaret Munden sundry chattels and one Spinning Tourne. To his trusty friend and brother-in-law John Fabian of Nettleton Co. Wilts, yeoman, the close of meadow called Dowers[1] of four acres with Grove adjoining upon trust for the use of his two children, Thomas and Margaret Munden, Mem. He gives to the said John Fabian a rick of hay now standing in the backside belonging to the house he dwells in and also two horses to be sold by him to his own use, for his trouble. W. Robert Dark, junior, John Chester, William Holliday. Proved 27 March, 1725.

The inhabitants of Eastcombe were frequently amerced at the Bisley Manor Courts for various misdemeanours.—William Howell on October 27, 1688, for annoying the watering place at Eastcombs Well, was ordered to repair it by 5 November, on pain of £5.

In 1693, John Young, William Hill, John Holliday, Richard and William Davis and Nathaniel Ridler were amerced for enclosing the Common near Escomb, 10s. each.

---

[1] The Dowers, for some generations, held Slatters and Hawkins, two tenements in Over Lypiatt, somewhere near Fennell's Farm.

31 October, 1706, Anthony Cox, junior, and William Davis were amerced 10s. each for building a wall upon a highway between Eskcombs and Busidge. William Davis was further fined in 1708, for digging a quar in the Custom Wood near the way leading through Eastcombe to Bisley and not filling it up again. In 1704 John Nullis was fined 10s. for enclosing the Common and adjoining it to his free land near Fidges.

A windmill formerly stood, within the memory of old inhabitants, on the upper part of Eastcombe in the enclosure called Little Hoar-stone (427, T.M.)

At the end of the eighteenth century Eastcombe had its annual fair, held on part of what is now chapel property. The inhabitants were very rough and ignorant and the standard of morals and general conduct was very low. The distance from the parish church and from the school had conduced to this condition. It was not till 1868 that Canon Keble provided a Church school at Eastcombe, which was also used for Church services for some years. Later he procured an iron Church, that of St. Augustine, with the further intention of building a permanent Church, but after his death, the Church school having been given up, the building was set apart as a place of worship, the iron building being now used for secular purposes. The altar now in use is that formerly in Miserden Church.

Till Canon Keble made provision for Church worship at Eastcombe, the hamlet was, spiritually, in a very neglected state. It is not surprising to find that some of the inhabitants had begun to provide some sort of religion for themselves, and as far back as 1742 James Young certified to the Bishop of Gloucester (as required by law) that he intended to hold a meeting at his house for worship. This was probably the result of John Wesley's preaching in the neighbourhood, and other Non-conformist bodies tried to establish themselves at Eastcombe. It was, however, the Baptists who prevailed, and one of their preachers, Thomas Williams, who came there in 1799, was instrumental in procuring the erection of a chapel, which was opened in 1801. This building was practically rebuilt and enlarged, with the addition of a turret and clock in 1860, and in 1863 the organ from Bussage House was loaned to the congregation for a term of years by Mr. William Davis, on whose death in 1873 it was purchased, and still remains in use. The graveyard opposite the Chapel was secured after the enclosure of the Common. A British school was started in 1877, and a school building was erected.

CHAPTER X.

PART 5

BIDFIELD AND STEANBRIDGE TYTHINGS.

BIDFIELD.

Bidfield was one of the tythings of Bisley, though it was not allowed to be a separate manor.[1] The earliest record of Bidfield or Budefield, so far discovered, is an agreement made 22 Ed. I. (1293-4) between Maria le Blunde (or fair-haired) and Master Thomas de Sodynton, and Richard le Matherune (or Malherum) de Wishanger, about sixty-six acres of land, two of meadow, and the half of 3s. rent, and two parts of a messuage in Budefield, which were conveyed to Maria le Blunde and Thomas de Sodynton for the sum of £20.[2]

Rudder states that Owen de Roderick was seised of Bidfield, consisting of a messuage and a carucate and a half of land with three acres of wood, eighteen of meadow, and 36s. of rent from tenants, held of the Earl of Hereford, in Ed. III.'s reign, but that on being attainted for treason, having joined with the French, the estate was granted to Mary Hervey, widow of William Hervey, in 1373-4. In 1445 William Golding and Joan his wife held some land in Bidfield. Later Bidfield was in the possession of Thomas Butler and Maud his wife, then in that of John Baker 1465-6, of Thomas Gilbert in 1472-3, and of Edward Pye, in 1476-7. In 1500, July 28, Edmund Mylle had a grant for twenty years of the keeping of the farm of Bidfield in the Hundred of Bysseley at a rent of £5 14s. 4d.[3]

---

[1] Bigland's History of Glos.
[2] P. R. O. Feet of Fines, Gloucs., 183.
[3] P. R. O. Cal. Pat. Rolls.

Henry VIII. granted the farm of Bydfelde to Thomas Heneage, Lord Willoughby, and this grant was confirmed in 1548 by Ed. VI., granting also the profits leased with it to William Kingeston, Knight, deceased.[1] The following year it is noted that James Gunter and William Gunter, gentlemen, were licensed to grant their farm of Bidfield and lands leased to William Kyngeston, Knight, deceased to William Graye, Knight, Lord Grey de Wilton and his heirs.

In 1516 Sir Henry Poole acquired certain rights over Bidfield, such as fairs, markets, views of frankpledge, customs, etc., when he purchased the Manor and Hundred of Cirencester and its seven hundreds.

Richard Chew was tenant of the farm in 1675, making his will there on 16 January, in which he described himself as of Bidfield Farm, yeoman, bequeathing to his beloved daughter Mary Chew £200 at 21 or on marriage, the increase to be used for her good education. If she should marry without his overseers' consent, then she is to have 12 pence. His kinsman, Richard Cardy's sons to be heirs next after his daughter. £5 to his beloved mother Anne Chew, and his wife Mary to be sole executrix. His brother Michaell and his loving friend Henry Partrige of Wishanger, gentlemen, Richard Townsend and John Cull to be overseers, 20s. each. W. John Cull, Thomas Clements. Proved June 25, 1677.

The house of Bidfield Farm had the date 1604 over the front door. The large barn is dated D.M. 1731, and the stable E. 1799 B. The farm buildings are very extensive.

Bidfield was cut off from the parish of Bisley in the nineteenth century and is now part of the parish of Miserden.

STEANBRIDGE.

The tything of Steanbridge " lies on the lower slope of the north side of Stroud Hill, between the tithing of Upper Lypiatt and the river Slade, and extends from Badbrook on

[1] P. R. O. Grants, 4 Ed. VI, Pt. 2.

the west, to its extremity, in the rural hamlet of Elcombe on the east."[1]

Of this tything the County historians find nothing to record yet evidences of great antiquity remain at Steanbridge Slad farm, with its two pairs of thirteenth century windows, one pair being of the early part of the century, the other of the latter part, and having within the original winding stone staircase which it illuminates. Also in the valley Steanbridge Farm is notable for its fine Jacobean front. It, however, is over-shadowed by the New Mills Court, with its former Mills and ponds, stretching across the valley. This house was built in 1766 by Thomas Baylis, who at that time owned the adjacent mills and estate. It descended to his son Daniel Baylis, who sold the property in 1810. For some years William and Mashiter Helme owned the mills, and some of the estate, enlarging the house, which afterwards passed into the possession of Mr. Libby, and later to Mr. Gilbert Jones. There are two wills which give the names of a few of the inhabitants of Steanbridge. That of William Alredge 17 March, 1561," of the Limitation of Strode within the parish of Bisley " bequeaths a large number of cattle to his children Richard Cannon, William, Anthony, and Elizabeth. To Thomas his son and heir, his two wains with two iron bands and other farm implements when twenty-one. Annis, his wife, is to have the keeping and custody of the premises unless she marry again. She is to have his house where he now dwells in Steanbrigstheslad, with all houses and dowes, leasowes and arable landes for the maintenance of his children and to be sole executrix. To the poor 2s. Overseers.—Thomas Freme, gentleman, Henry Williams, William Flayse, Thomas Marysand, and Robert Allredge (his brother). W. Thomas Loveday, John Alrygg, Thomas Freme, Kristopher and John Pesyne and others. Proved 15 January, 1561-2.

Thomas Clissold, senior, of Steanbridge Slad, in the parish of Stroud, yeoman, made his will 14 May, 1616, bequeathing to the children of his son John, Thomas and Julyan, when

---

[1] Fisher's Stroud.

twenty-one, £10 equally divided.   His wife was to share the house with his son John.   W. Robert Clyssold, Giles Carter. Overseers,—William Clyssold and Edward Snow (5s. each).[1]

The great event with which Steanbridge is connected in the seventeenth century is the passage of King Charles I's army through it on his way from Bristol to the seige of Gloucester. On the 8th of August, 1643, the army had marched from Bristol to Tetbury, where the King had dined and afterwards proceeded to Cirencester to rest the night at Sir William Masters.   On the 9th August they came along the Minchin-hampton road, and descended to Brimscombe, where they crossed the river Frome, and went up the north side of the Stroud valley via Quarhouse and past Nether Lypiatt, from whence they passed down the north side of the hill, towards Steanbridge, where they crossed the river Slade.   They next climbed up Wickeridge Hill, and passing over the ridge at Bull's Cross, they dropped down into Greenhouse Lane and up Tibbywell Lane into Painswick.

The following September 5 saw the army back again in Painswick, where it encamped on Spoonbed Hill, within the ancient entrenchments, but it was in retreat after the abortive siege of Gloucester.[2]

Beyond the Court Baron of 1724, when the death of Thomas Clissold of Steanbridge Slad who held a messuage there which his son John claimed, and in 1736 when William Townsend held Ridings Lease and part of Millons in the same place, Thomas Gryffin was holding Stroud-house there and Thomas Aldridge a house and land, there is nothing more to be gleaned from the manorial records.

The large Driver vault in Bisley churchyard was built in November, 1811, by Nathaniel Driver of Steanbridge.

---

[1] Glos. Pro. Reg.
[2] Fisher's Stroud.

CHAPTER XI.

Old Sayings about Bisley. The Common. Field Names.
The Prison. The Pound. Market and Fairs. Roads.
The Wells. Agriculture. Wool Industry. Old
Customs. Some Former Residents. Two Bisley
Doctors. Surnames.

" And further see old Bisley Spire
Which rises quite as high or higher
Than most in Gloucestershire.
And thousands round that ancient pile
Lie mouldering till the Seventh Vial
Is poured upon the air."

" Bisley gates are open." (When the wind blows from the
   north).

" These poor sheep have nothing to shelter them but Bisley
   Spire." (A saying at Stow-on-the-Wold.)

" Beggarly Bisley, Strutting Stroud,
Mincing Hampton, Painswick proud."

" Where do you come from ? Bisley, God help us."

BISLEY COMMON

In the preceding chapters of this book reference has been
made frequently to the Common of Bisley, which played an
important part in the life of the people down to the time
of its enclosure in 1863-5. Abel Wantner states that "In the
reign of Edward II, Roger Mortimer, Earl of March, gave to

the poor of Bisley for ever all that great carique or Parcell of ground called Bisile Common, containing 1200 acres, wherein is contained twelve Customain woods, viz., Barneage, Blackfrith, Boltonfrith, Calfway, Cattswood, Dignishfrith, Frelands frith, Litteredge Wood, and Timbercombe." The Common is said to have originally covered about 2000 acres, but the various encroachments, attempts at which were a constant source of trouble to the Lords of the Manor, had reduced it to 1032 in the year in which the following note was made and entered in the Reeve's Rate book for 1727, though the actual entry is undated :—

" The number of Acres in ye Comns of Bisley as ye year.

	A.	R.	P.
Nashend, with 3 Inclosures 488a. 3rp. 333.			
but net	479	3	0
Skaitehill	13	3	09
Stephensbridge hill	9	3	08
Todmore	17	0	19
More	15	3	03
Bismore	5	3	38
Avenis Green	1	3	35
Bourns Green	8	0	33
Okeridge about	372	0	0
Plaisters about	79	0	0
Nottingham about	—		
Swifts Hill	9	0	0
TOTALL	1032	1	29"

In 1707 the Commons were called woods, generally Customs woods, though not all timbered at that time. Probably they were so named because their acres had been more wooded in olden times.

Attempts were made in 1733 and again in 1815 to enclose the Common, but the enclosure was not effected till 1863-5. It, of course, was felt to be a great grievance to the poor, but each freeholder got a piece of land in proportion to his holding, only this worked out as very large allotments for the larger landholders. Not only was profitable cultivation greatly increased, but lawlessness abated. Deeds of violence were often committed by the rougher inhabitants of the hamlets round the open Common, escaping discovery and consequent punishment. One specially dangerous spot was at the Cottage near the Frith wood, behind Primrose Mount, which in 1717 was a pothouse surrounded by trees. About 1817 there were found buried in the outhouse of this cottage two skeletons of remarkable size, having nails six inches long run into the back of their heads. The skeletons were re-buried in the same place. Daniel Ware, the first to be buried in Chalford Churchyard, at the age of 91, remembered hearing of the disappearance of two well-known pedlars, both men of remarkable size ; it was a matter much talked-of at the time, there being no way of accounting for their disappearance. They used to go on regular rounds for their business and suddenly ceased, the murder taking place about 1717.[1]

Evidence of a similar tragedy was unearthed about the year 1899, when the road leading from Frith wood north to the cross-road was being widened, adjoining Primrose Mount and the cottage already mentioned, for a human skeleton, with a shattered skull was discovered buried under the hedge, it having obviously lain there for many years. This, again, is said to have been the murder of a pedlar who had a long round, and was often entrusted by farmers to carry money for the settlement of their accounts with other farmers whom the pedlar visited on his journeys, and this became known in the neighbourhood. On one occasion the pedlar was traced to the old pothouse of sinister reputation and then disappeared, no doubt murdered and robbed, and hastily disposed of under the hedge, where his body was found. After the inquest in 1899, it was at length laid to rest with Christian rites.

It is difficult now to picture the Common as it was before the enclosure, when it was possible to drive from Brownshill to Bisley by the road still traceable along the top of the ridge as a footpath ; but study of the Tythe map and Terrier

---

[1] Related by Mrs. Ballinger, senr.

enables the student to locate much of the former Common, and the open " fields," the names of which—Bisley, West-field, Stancombe, Battlescombe, and Througham, occur frequently in the deeds preserved at Lypiatt Park. The strips of land attached to various properties in the " fields " were constantly changing hands, and their position is described, so that it is possible in some case to identify them with present enclosures, particularly as several mere-stones still remain, marked on the Ordnance Map, together with fields com-memorating former boundary stones, such as Hoar Stone, and Twizzlestones (678-9-80), besides many fields still retaining the names of former owners. Hayhedge Lane probably marks the site of the Bisley field laid down for hay, and Rye Corner in Battlescombe field, Hempland and Sainfoin ground (779-781), denote their former crops as also Clover Ground (792-3, 796).

For the management of the manor, the Lord's Steward generally presided over the courts, and collected the rents, etc., assisted by a reeve, chosen annually, one or two haywards, one or two woodwards, two sheeptellers, and a shepherd. The reeves were appointed from amongst the freeholders in succession, and if unable to serve they had to provide a deputy. The shepherd's times for attendance on the Common were from four to ten a.m., and from two to eight p.m. The breeding of the Cotswold sheep, noted for their size and heavy wool, formed an important part of the agricultural life of Bisley, and it will have been noted in preceding pages how frequently sheep are bequeathed by will. Provision for daughters, deemed to be ample, often consisted of a bedstead with its furniture, and two sheep. With free pasture on the Common and wise husbandry, no doubt the two sheep often developed into a flock, and would be a source of considerable profit.

Consideration of some of the names attached to fields is enlightening as to the former appearance of the country. Windmill Tyneing (684)[1] near the Holloway, indicates a windmill there, whilst others were probably in view from that

---

[1] The numbers given are those on the Tithe Map.

z

high ground at France Lynch (near Windmill Cottage on the Calfway) at Eastcombe and at Brownshill.

It has been stated that a wayside cross, called St. Mary's formerly stood at the corner of the Cross field near the original highway through Lypiatt Park. Possibly two other wayside crosses may have existed, for the field behind Nashend Farm is called " Nashend Cross " (651), and a field near Litteridge wood is called " Litteridge Cross " (935), and " Against Litteridge Cross " (936). It is possible that this simply means a cross cut on a wall stone as a boundary mark, but more probably there were wayside crosses at these points, remains of which may some day perhaps be found built into some wall or barn.

It must be remembered that the Commons extended originally over the sites of Oakridge, Chalford Hill, Brownshill and Bussage, and the strange meanderings of the lanes in those villages are said to have originated in the tracks made by sheep and adopted by man.

Some of the names of fields preserved in the Tithe Terrier give us glimpses of a far-off past. Auger Stone piece (1380) and Langstone (1454) may indicate pre-historic monuments. Roman Camp piece (1378) speaks for itself, while Chestergate piece (527-8 and 521) suggests a Roman Castrum near Bisley, and at no great distance from the Roman well which existed, indications of which may be seen in the plantation on Lime-kiln Lane. On the opposite side of the lane, one field away, near the ruins of a seventeenth century cottage called Starveall in the O.M., but otherwise called Sterwell or Starwell in a seventeenth century terrier, there is an ancient well, reputed to be fully 450 ft. deep, which probably was connected with the Roman Well, and both would flow into the stream in Battlescombe. Candlemas Croft (28), Holywell (454-5), Parson's Close (529), and the Poor Ground (822) suggest connection with the Church. Deer Park (295), the Cockshoot (haunt of woodcock, 577), Coffin Ground (948), Great Snakes hole (744), Crab orchard (662), the Vineyard (338-648), and the Wineyards (1337), to mention a few of the names that have come down to us, all stir up visions of the past life of the people.

The Court rolls record the transgressions against the laws of the manor, and the fines inflicted, besides affording much information as to the transit of land, the succession and deaths of tenants, etc., from 1335 onwards. Instances of some of the business transacted are as follows :—

In 1401-2 the homage presented that the house and barn of William Tymberhulle were burnt by his own negligence, and the court ordered him to rebuild them or forfeit all his oxen. In 1445 the customary tenants presented John Benet for not enclosing his hedges at the times due by the ancient customs of the manor. He was fined a sheep and lamb, worth 1s. 6d. It was agreed in 1598 that Litteridge (one of the Bisley fields) should be opened on Trinity day, and the corn carried within thirteen days, and no one was to put in beasts till the last stack was carried.

There were frequent encroachments by the building of cottages on the Common, chiefly by the " Carders, Spinners and Weavers " ; sometimes they were ordered to be pulled down, but more often they were permitted to stand on the payment of a fine.

At Bisley tenants were fined for building a " Piggis cot " on the Common, and in 1688 John Standley had erected a " Piggs Coat " upon the Lord's waste," " annoying the highway," (a practise continued to this day).

The pilfering of wood from the Queen's Woods and the perpetual digging of quarrs, or not fencing them when dug, neglect of waterways, and setting up of rack-places without license, kept the Court busy.

Abel Wantner says the town of Bisley was governed by a Constable and his assistant. The Blind House, dated 1824, a lock-up with two cells, standing in the Feoffees' premises, next the Old Bear, is the successor of a prison which existed in mediaeval times, there being mention of a prison at Bisley in 1302, when pardon was granted to Richard Wroth in consideration of his services in Scotland, for receiving Richard and John de Matle indicted for robberies in Co. Hereford, and for breaking the prison of Bisley, Co. Glos., and of his own outlawry for the same.[1]

Though Bisley gave its name to the Hundred, it did not have the right to gallows or tumbril, which could only be used at Painswick. There was, however, a pillory, the stone stump of which may be seen in the path against the wall near the Blind House. The last person who was exposed in the stocks, which stood on the opposite side of the road, it is said, was a marine who had fought under Nelson at the battle of Trafalgar, and who occupied this position about 1863.

The standard of morality at Bisley and its hamlets has never been high, but evidently deterioration had culminated in 1791, when the vestry on 13 October, meeting in the Church ordained,—" That all Lewd Women that shall have a Bastard Child or Bastard Children in this Parish and shall become Chargeable, shall be dealt with according to the Statute in that Case Made and provided, that is to have them committed to the Common Goale to be punished and Set to hard Labour During the Terme of One whole Year. And it is agreed that no Examination or Warrants shall be paid for Bastardy any more unless ordered for."

On 23 August, 1781, the Churchwardens agreed to have it mentioned in Church the next Sunday, that no Beer shall be sold in the Town of Bisley on any Sunday Evening after six o'clock, under Penalty of their being presented.

The pound lies beside the Old Bear and opposite the new Bear Inn, but it is not now kept in order for impounding stray cattle. As regards the Market, James II. had in 1687 granted a weekly market, on Thursdays with Court of Pie-powder belonging, to the people of Bisley, and Sir Robert Atkyns, Lord of the Manor in the reign of Charles II. obtained a Charter of Privilege. The market and fair rights had been farmed out to John Edridge, innkeeper, who in 1713 sold his interests therein to Thomas Parker, of Sapperton, yeoman.

An undated paper,[2] probably late eighteenth century, contains a complaint from Thomas Smith, who had acquired

1 Cal. of Pat. Rolls.
2 Lypiatt MSS.

the rights to all tolls and profits from Fairs and Markets at Bisley, from John Stephens, Lord of the Manor, for 99 years, and " to cub sheep on the Lord's waste land there." Samuel Clissold had pulled down two cottages adjoining the street and made the ground with a wall round a cubbing for sheep there, to Smith's loss.

The Market house stood where the present Court House now is. It could only have been a very small building, finished in 1735, and supported on round pillars, which were secured by Sir John Dorington on its removal, and used by him in the barn at the Manor Farm, Eastcombe. In 1829 the market house was in a dangerous state, requiring immediate repair.[1]

The Court House ceased to be required for its original purpose and was allowed to be used as a reading room, till in 1920, it was bought by the Feoffees ; the upper room is now let to the County Council for technical classes, and the lower room is used for a Reading Room.

Two fairs were granted by James II. yearly, namely, on or about St. George's and All Hallows days, or on May 4 and November 12. (See Appendix I.) The sheep fairs were important events, for the farmers came in from all the country round and the sheep were penned at the corner between Bear Pitch and the New Inn, in what was then the New Inn yard, as well as up the Bear Pitch. Possibly the introduction of railways took away the usefulness of the Fairs, or changes in the cloth industry, but by degrees they were less and less frequented and becoming useless as sheep fairs, pigs were substituted, but even this failed to keep the fairs going, and they were gradually dropped.

Reference has been made to various old roads and tracks, or pack horse lanes within the parish, and to the new road from Stroud to Chalford. From Chalford Church the present road to Bisley was made at the same time, (the original track past Millswood being now used as a footpath), and the Turnpike Cottage still stands, under the name of Catchpike, at the

---

[1] Bisley Court Rolls.

junction of this road with that going up to Brownshill. It is said that the toll-keeper had difficulty with carters and others who sought to evade the tollgate by trying to drive up the old track, and accordingly he had a small window made by which he could spy out any attempt of that sort.

The road from Stroud to Cirencester and London originally passed up High Street, Silver Street and the Hill, through Bisley, across Oakridge Common to Waterlane, Tunley and Henwood, through the river Frome, to Park Corner, and along the north side of Oakley Wood and Lord Bathurst's Park, to Cecily Hill and Cirencester. About 1751 the highway from Cirencester to Minchinhampton and Rodborough and Stroud was repaired and made a more convenient road to Cirencester, so that the Bisley road ceased to be used for through traffic. In the nineteenth century the new road to Bisley was made, from Nelson Street, past the Workhouse and the north side of Lypiatt Park to Stancombe Ash, where the toll-house stands.[1]   The road continued to Bisley High Street, and passing on to Oakridge another toll-house is seen at its junction with the new road to Bussage, Joiners' Lane and Holloway.

A notable feature of Bisley is the public water supply at the Seven Springs in Well Road. Originally only five water spouts filled the troughs, but when the present well-head was erected in 1863 the spouts were increased to seven. The original five are supplied from a spring from under the Church-yard, and the two new ones from a spring in the Inakers field.

Though Bisley parish is well supplied with springs and wells, the water at Bisley itself is not universally good, and standing as it does at a height of 784 ft., to lead water to it presents considerable difficulty.

The dressing of the Wells on Ascension Day, and their blessing by the Vicar each year, is a custom established in 1863 by the Rev. Thomas Keble after the restoration of the Well-head. This picturesque event when the children and parishioners carry flowers to deck the springs, is attended

1 Fisher's Stroud, p. 145.

annually by a large number of spectators from the country-side.

Bobblewell is a name encountered in the district for a spring and there are two in the parish, one near Ferris Court, and one at Chalford.

There are two streams within the parish of Bisley, that which flows from the Bisley Wells down to Todsmore valley, feeding the Fishpond there, and emptying itself into the River Frome, which forms the southern boundary of the parish, at Bourne. The other is the Holy Brook, which rising at Whiteway, flows through Wishanger and Honeycombe Farm, feeds a fishpond near Grays, and continuing down the valley past Tunley, reaches the Frome below Denway, its course being marked by romantic beauty of vale and wood.

Before the rise of the Clothiers in Elizabethan days, agriculture was the principal occupation of Bisley, though one finds in the wills of the sixteenth century that husbandry was frequently combined with weaving. A few examples are of interest.

Richard Restall, of the parish of Bisley, weever, 24 February, 1550, to be buried in Christian burial in the Church-yard of Bisley.[1] To Agnes, his daughter, four ewes and four hoggs. To Thomas Hues, his son-in-law, two ewes with their lambs, etc. To William, his son, one of his brode weeving lummes which he shall enjoy in his house as long as he and his mother agree, but if they disagree, the said William is to have one lumme with all manner of harness belonging. To John Restall, his son, one other loom after the decease of his mother at her gentlynes and discretion. To Agnes Towesyer, his goddaughter, one chylmer lamb and to William Hunt, his godson, one other chylmer lamb, both to be set to some honest man to the profit of the said children. To James his son, one cowe at twenty-one. He owns he owes to the parish of Bisley 33s. 4d. which he binds Margyt his wife to pay ; his alms to the poor of Bisley at the discretion of his

---

[1] The direction as to burial in Edward VI's reign should be contrasted with that in Queen Mary's of the ensuing will.

wife and overseers, John Whytynge and John Hues, his neighbour.[1]

Thomas Peers, husbandman, whose will is dated 7 March, 1554, after bequeathing his soul to Allmighty God, to the blessed Virgyn Mary, and to the celestiall companie of hevyn and his body to be buried in the churchyard of Bisley, left to Water Perse his son, his brode lome, his coferer, his brazen morter and his brazen Judde, and a yerenbare and his betond pane. To Edythe Felpe his furryd gowne. To William Pers his son, his great and beaste brass pane, and a canstyle. John Perse, his son, shall have his tenement of Bysley, paying 6s. 8d. to bere towards the harryatt, and his wife Kathryn to bere the rest. W. John Tomson, clericus, John Grymy Richard Cuff.[1]

The Restall family seemed to combine husbandry and weaving to the end of the century, for Edward Restall, 29 January, 1597, after pious commendation of his soul, " In which holy Trinity of persons united and to be worshipped in the unities he puts his whole trust for his salvation " bequeaths a loom each to his sons, William and Walter, but a ewe and a lamb to various other relations and friends.

The will of Thomas Workman, 25 July, 1579, acquaints us with a well-stocked Elizabethan farm at Bisley, but unfortunately with no indication of which one he occupied. The will is evidently drawn up by John Lightfoot, his vicar, as the wording of the commendation of his soul into the hands of Almighty God, his only Maker and Saviour, is his usual formula, and he is a witness.

He bequeaths to Thomas his son, one corn wayne with his appture, a plow with shere and culter, a payr of dytpes, two yoke and two stryngs, a drey, a dreybryddle, an oxe, the eldest horse, and half an acre of wheat beyond Calfoys. To his daughter Anne Hawkens, a quarter of barley and two bushels of wheat. To his son Robert two store pigges and two bushells of wheat. To William his son, a sow pygge, four sheep, a quarter of barley and a stawle of Bees. To his son

---

[1] Glos. Pro. Reg.

Richard 20s. in money, a calf, four sheep, a store pigge, etc. To Elizabeth his daughter a floke bed . . . a quarter of barley, an ewe and a lame, a platter and a great caudren. To his daughter Joan a flock bed, a pealing, a caudren and a yelte pigge. To his daughter Katherine a quarter of barley, three bushells of wheat, two sheep, a black panox, a stawle of Bees, and two store piggs, one of the bygge sort and one of the other lesser sort. To his brother James four bushells of barley and two bushells of wheat. To Roger Stewes an heyffr great in calf and two lambs. To Elizabeth, his wife's cossen a cow if she lives, and if she dye, then the cowe to be equally devided amongst his children. To William Hyll two sheep. The rest of all his beasts and his pewter to Joan, Elizabeth and Katharine his daughters, to be equally divided. All other his goods, cartell and chattells to Joan his wife, who is executrix. Overseers, Richard Smart and James Keysser. W. Richard Hyll and John Lightfoot, vicar.

The custom of using oxen for the plough continued in the Cotswold district down to the middle nineteenth century in some places. The breast plough, which was laboriously pushed by the ploughman over the very hilly part of the Cotswolds, ceased to be used after the early part of last century.

The feudal system which compelled a farmer to work for the owner of the land at fixed terms, was commuted in many cases in Edward III's reign for rent paid in money, or by purchase of freedom. This new-found liberty was disturbed by the Black Death of 1348, which robbed England of half its population of 4,000,000. Labour becoming scarce after this visitation, agricultural labourers demanded double wages, and their demand ended in the Peasant's revolt all over England, the villeins joining with the labourers in refusing to work for the landlords, who gradually gave up their demands of service and let their lands to leasehold tenants, and so by the time of the Dissolution in 1540, all labour services had ceased, and payment of rent in money had taken its place.

With the changes wrought in Bisley through the rise of the great clothier families, who took the place of the old aristocracy, there was a fair amount of prosperity for the people who combined agriculture with home weaving. But when the clothing industry failed and machinery came into use, the sufferings of the poor were very great, owing to the low wages, often only 7s. a week, with bread at 1s. a quartern loaf, as it was in 1830 onwards. The acme of misery was reached one year when the wheat " growed " and consequently loaves would not bake, and the sound of the looms, which habitually filled the Chalford valley and villages round, ceased, trade having failed. Then about 1835-6 influenza devastated Bisley, and Mr. Jeffreys (a curate) used to go round the village to feed people with toast dipped in port wine." Mrs. Keble had a shop in the study at the Vicarage where she sold rice and food at half-price.[1]

It is not surprising that in 1837 a great emigration of 68 persons from Bisley was arranged, and on 31 August they were placed on a steam vessel at Bristol, to join their ship lying at King's Road. Bisley had to borrow the money to defray the cost of this move. Clothing, etc., cost £1 10s. 8¾d. per head, including Bibles and Prayer Books, etc., and the two waggons and a cart which conveyed the party to Bristol, their victuals on leaving, and on the road, and breakfast at Bristol cost £24 13s. 6d., and one day's victuals, the first day on board the steam packet £2. It is good to know that they were accompanied by Dr. Rogers, the emigrant surgeon, and that success attended this venture in the New World.

<hr />

THE WOOL INDUSTRY

The wool trade of the Cotswolds went hand in hand with agriculture through the centuries, for the breeding of Cotswold sheep for their valuable fleeces became the chief interest of the farmers, as the export of wool to the Continent was a lucrative business. Whilst spinning and weaving went on in the cottages and farms for home needs, the principal manufacture of woollen goods was in Flanders. Edward III.

[1] From information supplied by Miss Keble (Sister Cordelia).

had prohibited the export of wool and had encouraged Flemish weavers to settle in England in the hope of increasing home manufacture. The prohibition remained in force till Queen Elizabeth removed it, and she encouraged the Flemish Huguenot weavers to come to England after Alva's persecutions. The export of wool was again forbidden from 1660 to 1825.

Towards the end of Henry VI's reign a new form of short lease for three or four lives of mill streams in Stroud and Bisley, indicates that the use of water power for mill purposes was recognized, and fulling mills began to be frequently mentioned. Todsmore valley claims to have had the earliest tuck-mill in the district, and at Bobblewell, Chalford, in 1586, a fresh mill with two rack places and a dyehouse, was erected.

Most of the weaving was done in the cottages or in the house of a masterweaver who had space to employ several hands on the looms in the long attic rooms still to be seen in many of the larger cottages in Chalford and Chalford Hill and elsewhere. The fulling and finishing of the cloth was conducted at the mills, and all English wool was used till the end of the seventeenth century.

The remarkable prosperity of some of the clothier families of the seventeenth and eighteenth centuries recorded in previous chapters, as well as their frequent failures and bankruptcy towards the end of the eighteenth and beginning of the nineteenth centuries, is an index to the course of the trade, in which the weavers' lot was cast. In 1728 the Justices of Quarter Sessions had appointed Inspectors of cloth and fixed wages at Bisley and other places, but in 1756 they lowered wages by fifty per cent. and made regulations as to the length of the chain on the bar. However, a petition from the weavers of Bisley and other places sets forth complaints that the masters neglected the regulations, and had lengthened the chain from 600 threads to 900, so that a weaver could only earn four pence by sixteen hours' labour, and with his whole family working the miserable pittance which they earned seems incredible in these days. How the clothiers could regard it with equanimity is incomprehensible.

With the introduction of machinery in the mills about 1838, the cottage weaving ceased.   After a period of prosperity for the mills the cloth trade in Stroud valley declined in 1875, largely owing to the unwillingness or inability of the mill-owners to meet the changes of fashion in cloth materials with new machinery and designs.

Two of the most notable clothier families of the district, the Clutterbucks and Playnes, were of Huguenot origin.

In the nineteenth century as many as twenty silk mills existed in Stroud and Nailsworth valleys, but they nearly all closed down by the end of the century.

In common with most of the Cotswold villages Bisley had its Christmas mummers, who enacted the play introducing Father Christmas, St. George, Robin Hood, the Doctor and other characters as usual in the district,[1] in their own version. It was kept up till 1913, when the Great War caused it to cease, and it has not been revived.

There is a tradition that in the days when " Dog-Whippers " held office in the Church that it was the duty of the sexton to keep men awake during the sermon with a wand, the other end of which was furnished with a fox's brush which was applied to slumbering women's faces.

A peculiarity of Bisley burials was in the shape of the coffins, called " fish-tail " coffins, because, a special division was made for each foot.   This custom has died out.

Many of the mediaeval families are represented still in Bisley by descendants, though new names were continuously introduced by the marriage of daughters.   Occasionally members of well-known County families came to reside for a short period at Bisley, of whom the only remembrance is to be found in the parish registers.

[1] The Gloucestershire Country Side, vol. ii, 4, pp. 62-4.

" 1547. 26 September. Sir Edmond Huscrofte, Knight of the Rodes, a Dorsetshire man, died in the P'ish and was here buried." Perhaps he was only a temporary sojourner.

The Masters family resided at Bisley in the seventeenth century, being related to Thomas Masters, D.D., who became Lord of the Manor in James I's reign. Between 1605 and 1611 the registers show there were four daughters born to Walter Masters, gentleman, and one son, William, in 1606. On 15 December, 1637, Henry, son of Thomas Masters, who was Lord of the Manor, was baptized at Bisley, and his son Thomas 29 March, 1657. He himself died in 1670, and was buried at Bisley, 5 October. The place of his abode is not known, but possibly it may have been Nowell House. In 1679 Henry Masters was appointed Reeve, but nominated Roger Batt as his proxy, Sir Robert Atkyns being then Lord of the Manor.

Edmund Kingston, Esq., connected with the family of Miserden, appears to have been a resident at 5 February, 1606, when his son Charles was baptized (his daughter Elizabeth's baptism at Miserden 9 December, 1604, being recorded in the Bisley register), his daughter Bridged's 13 December, 1608, and his son Thomas Kingston's 15 May, 1610, baptisms showing he was residing at that time. After that date there is no further notice of him, but Culpersandy, daughter of Walter Kingston, gentleman, was baptized at his house, 25 February, 1624.

Samuel Sheppard, gentleman, who probably resided at Sturmy's Court (see Chapter VIII.), had a daughter Isabel baptized 19 December, 1635 (buried 21 December), his daughter Ann 29 January, 1639, and on the 12 June of that same year his son Samuel was buried at Bisley.

Other entries in the registers of the seventeenth century are of people strangers to the district, of whom nothing is known.

23 March, 1614. Giles, son of John Hitchman, gentleman, baptized.

5 July, 1614. The wyfe of Richard Platt, gentleman, buried.

3 September, 1640.　William Monmouth, gentleman, buried.

21 July, 1655.　Elinor, wife of Thomas Bigges, Esquior, buried.

11 April, 1672.　William Stitchell, gentleman, buried.

Bisley does not seem to have attracted residents from the outside world much at that time, and besides the families at the Lypiatts, the clergy and the doctors, there were few gentry.

The names of two of the seventeenth century doctors have come down to us.　One, Robert Tomlins, Doctor of Medicine and M.A., was buried at Bisley 24 February, 1635.

Of the other, Richard Perryn, more is known.　He was the son of Richard Perryn, a devout person, who died at Bisley in 1548, and bequeathed gifts to the Church (see Chapter VI., pt. 2.)　Richard Perryn, junior, made an interesting will, 2 March, 1605.　He describes himself as practiser of physic, and after bequeathing his soul to the hands of Almighty God his only Saviour and Redeemer, and his body to Christian burial, he gives to his daughter Uriall all his books of phisick and sergery and the coffer by his beddsyde wherin are part of his books, one flock bed, one yeallow coverlet and pair of blankets, one pair of sheets, one boulster and to pillows.

To his daughter Catherine Townsend 20s. to be paid one year after his decease.　To Rychard Townsend and Poriander Townsend his daughter's sons 10s. in money each, and a book of psalms in prose, with the principles of Christian religion and Cattechisms, to be kept by some person of trust till such time as the said children come to twenty-one years.　To Mary Townsend, daughter of the said Charles 10s.　To Elizabeth Robingson, his daughter, his Bible and psalm book, with the Cattechism.　To William Robingson, her son 10s., and a Psalm book, and to Elizabeth 10s. and a psalm book, to be kept for them as above, till twenty-one.　Remainder to Margaret his wife, who is executrix.　He appoints his well beloved frynde Mr. Walter Maisters, John Theyer, and

William Snow, overseers. Signed Richard Peray, alias Peryn,[1] He was buried on 13 December, and his daughter Uriall did not live to profit by his bequests, as her death followed closely on her father's, and she was buried three days after his funeral. It is to be hoped that his " well beloved frynde, Mr. Walter Ma(i)sters " helped the bereaved wife and mother through this trial.

The name of Perryn did not continue at Bisley, but was known later in the Stroud valley.

The native inhabitants of the parish of Bisley are a mixed race, for there are to be traced in them descendants of the populations mentioned in the early chapters of this book, as well as an intermixture of Welsh, French Huguenots, and gipsy blood from people who have found their way hither and contributed their characteristics to the inhabitants.

In an interesting memorandum addressed to Sir John Dorington in 1866 on the numerous surnames in Bisley Parish, the following are mentioned :—

Gardiner, 90, chiefly in Oakridge, and Chalford Tythings.

Davis 57, the majority in Bussage Tything.

Whiting 28, mostly in Chalford Tything.

The Davises, having many of them the same Christian names, were formerly divided into tribes in order to distinguish them, each tribe being known by a nickname, such as :—

Crows, Buck, Rawpost, Gnawpost, Curly poll, Ragged head, Twilt, Twolt, Rocka. An early mention of a Davis at Bisley is in connection with the marriage of Thomas Davis, 1550, to one of the Mason family. Those bearing the name at the present day are not all descended from the same stock.

[1] Glos. Pro. Reg.

APPENDIX I.

James II., by the Grace of God, king of England, Scotland,
Ireland and France, Defender of the Faith, etc., to all to
whom these present letters shall come, greeting.

Since it was discovered by a certain Inquisition taken at
Birdlip in our county of Gloucester on the 23rd of March
lately past before Thomas Cann (? Caun), Knight and Sheriff
of the County aforesaid, in virtue of a Brief directed to the
same Sheriff, upon the oath of good and law-abiding men of the
same County :—

That it will not be to the hurt or prejudice of Ourselves
or others, nor to the hurt of neighbours, merchants or pedlars,
if we granted to ROBERT ATKINS, Junior, Knight, to his
heirs and assigns one Market to be held in Bisley in the
county aforesaid on any Thursday in any week in the year,
for ever, for the buying and selling of fish and flesh, and of
other provisions of whatever kind.—

And further, it was discovered that it would not be to the
loss or hurt of Ourselves or others or to the damage of neighbours whether merchants or pedlars if we were to grant to
the same Robert Atkins, to his heirs and assigns for ever two
Fairs or markets to be held in Bisley aforesaid, one of them
to be held on St. George's Day each year, the other to be held
on All Saints' Day yearly for the buying and selling of all
kinds of beasts, goods and merchandise of whatsoever kind,
as the more plainly and fully recorded remains in our Court
of Chancery by means of the same Inquisition—

Know ye that We of Our special favour, by Our mere
motion and certain knowledge, have given and granted—
and by these presents do give and grant for Ourselves, Our

heirs and successors for ever—to the aforesaid ROBERT ATKINS and his heirs, free and lawful power, licence and authority, that he and his heirs have keep and guard—and be strong and able to have keep and guard—one Market in Bisley aforesaid on any Thursday in any week in the year for ever for the buying and selling of all kinds of fish, flesh and provisions of what kind soever :—

And also of two fairs or markets, one of them to be held upon St. George's Day each year for ever, the other to be held upon All Saints' Day for ever yearly, together with a Court of Pied Powder (*i.e.*, Dusty Feet)—and all liberties, free customs and customary powers of Stallage Pictage (?), Theolonia (? Felony), and other conveniences regarding and pertaining to these kinds of Markets, Fairs, Sales, and Courts of Pied Powder.

Providing That there exists express mention of the annual value and certitude of the foregoing or any one of them, made by Us, Our Progenitors or Predecessors, or of gifts or concessions made by us to the same Robert Atkins, Knight, previously, and not mentioned in the presents : any other provision, Act, Statute, ordinance or restriction formerly made, held or published, ordained or provided, or any other matter or cause in any respect notwithstanding.

In witness whereof I have caused, with myself as testimony, these letters patent to be made at Westminster, 9th July in the IIIrd year of our reign.

By a Brief of the Privy Seal :

PIGGOTT.

The original of this Charter is now in Stroud Museum, and I am indebted to Mr. C. J. Gardiner, Curator, for the above translation.

A1

CHAPTER XII

NOTES ON SOME OLD FARMS, FAMILIES AND HOUSES.

RECTORY FARM

This was the property of the Rectors of Bisley, the fine eighteenth century barn being a prominent object in that part of the farm lying in Hayhedge Lane. The farm residence which is notable for its Georgian frontage immediately on the entrance to Bisley at the south-east, is now strangely detached from its farm buildings, as other buildings and a road intervene. At one time the Rectory Farm was the residence of Edward Aldridge, a Justice Quorum, who is said to have dispensed justice on occasions from his bedroom window, overlooking the street. He died in 1836, a memorial brass being at the west end of the south aisle in the Church. Immediately behind the house lies an ancient dwelling, known as the Old Red Lion, and having cellars beneath it of great antiquity. A large late Georgian room at the back has been used as the Court room.

ROOKWOODS.

This seventeenth century gabled building (see plate 15) Fig. 2) lies hidden in a romantic little valley on the Holy Brook near Waterlane. It doubtless takes its name from the numerous rooks of the surrounding woods, for which Bisley is famous, and as Rocwude, appears first in 1190 (Feet of Fines) and as Rocwode in 1327. Amongst the documents relating to the Cistercian monastery of St. Mary Kingswood, Co. Wilts., at one time in the possession of Mr. F. F. Fox, of Yate House, is the following charter :—[1]

[1] The same charter or a copy, is noted as in the possession of V. R. Cholmondeley, Esq., in the Record Comn. Reports on Historical MSS. House of Lord's Calendar.

" Let present and future know that I, John del Egge, have given and granted and by the present charter have confirmed to God and the Church of the Blessed Mary of Kingswode and the monks there serving God all my land which Gillebert my father held and which descended to me by hereditary right with wood and all its appurtenances at Le Egge in the manor of Symundshale in perpetual exchange of all the land which the said monks had at La Rocwode in the parish of Byseleye with the wood and all appurtenances. To have and to hold, etc. . . But if we should not be able to warrant the whole of the aforesaid land of Rocwode with woods and all appurtenances the said monks shall freely seize it again without any contradiction from me or my heirs or assigns And that this my gift and grant may remain ratified and stable, I have appended my seal to this writing. W. Peter de Eggeworth, Oliver de Berkeley, William dn Troham (Througham), Richard de Abbenesse, Robert de Mulecote, Henry de la Stride, Roger Petifer and others."

This charter is said to be of 1243.

Adam de Rokwode was one of the jurors at the Inquisition P. M. of Theobald de Verdun taken at Bisley in 1309.

The Butlers appear to have resided at Rookwoods for several generations and probably came to Bisley by reason of intermarriage with the Corderoys and Tayloes in the seventeenth century as they are not named in the lay Subsidy rolls of the previous century. John Butler was one of the Feoffees in 1688, in which year his son Thomas died, as recorded on a brass plate formerly affixed to a pillar in the Church. " In memory of Thomas Butler, son of John Butler, of Rockwood, clothier, who departed this life the 2nd Day of March, Anno Dom. 1688, and his body resteth in the Middle alley of this Church near this place. He gave to this Parish 30s. per Ann. for ever, that is to say, to the Minister for preaching a Sermon on Easter Monday, and 20s. to the Poor, to be disposed of in small Bread according to the Discretion of the Churchwardens the same Day, yearly."

John Butler's death was presented at the Court Baron of 13 October, 1724, as he held of the manor of Bisley land in

Nashend called Lugg's land, which his son Thomas, the second of that name, inherited.

John Butler's long will is dated 1716. After describing himself as of Rockwoods, parish of Bisley, he commits his soul to Almighty God, etc. To his beloved wife Sarah, during her life all lands and tenements in Oakridge, and his messuage or tenement in Chalford, and after her decease to such uses as are already arranged. To his wife the ground called Ashmeads for life, after her death to his executors for the rest of the term of the lease. To his said wife Sarah £100 due to him from Mr. John Jones, jnr., of South Cerney, with the bond for the same, etc. His wife to have the use of his house and goods for life, and after her death to his two sons, John and Richard Butler, equally. To his son Richard all his Upper Coppice wood with ground there lying in Calfeway wood subject to payment of 30s. yearly and every year. . . (Here follows the clause already quoted in Chapter VIII, under the head of Bisley Charities) Which same sum is the same his son Thomas Butler deceased did in his sickness desire him to give in this manner. On failure of payment the Churchwardens are to distrain upon Coppice Wood. " Item my will and desire is that the messuage lands and tenements in the said parish of Bisley, called the Chantry which I bought of one John Webb shall remain according to the settlement thereof made upon the marriage of my said son Richard with his present wife." He forgives all sums of money his said son owes him. To Elizabeth and Mary Butler, daughters of his son Richard Butler each £10 at 18. To his grandson John, son of John Butler £40. To Elizabeth, daughter of his grandson Richard, son of John Butler one gold guinea. To his grandson Thomas Butler and his heirs all his messuage or house and mill with the little house adjoining at the Combes in Nashend in the said parish of Bisley and the meadow and pasture grounds belonging. For want of such issue then to his grandson James Butler one other son of his son John Butler and to his heirs. To his said son John Butler his close of meadow called Lugg's Leaze in the parish of Bisley for the rest of the term of the lease and after his decease to his said grandson Thomas

Butler and heirs, failing whom to his grandson James Butler. To his grandson Thomas Butler £40. To his son John Butler all his lower Coppice wood and ground at Calfway Wood for life, and after his decease to his grandson Thomas Butler. To his grandson James Butler, son of John Butler, £150 at 24. To his granddaughters Anne and Elinor Butler, daughters of his son John Butler £300 to be divided equally between them at 21 or marriage. To his cousins Robert Corderye, Sarah Cordery, Robert Tayloe and William Poole one gold guinea each. To his said kinsman Robert Tayloe his best great coat and best suite of clothes. To his cousin John Butler of Oakridge 10s. To his cousin Mary Holland 20s. To his cousin Mary Spenser daughter of John Spenser one guinea, etc.

W. Charles Holland, jun., Rachell Timbull, Thomas Abell and Charles Holland, sen. Proved 12 October, 1716.[1]

The Luggs mentioned in the will were living at Nashend in the sixteenth and seventeenth centuries and held land and wood in the Common fields to which their name was attached. The Mill in Nashend Combes must have been that now called Cricketty Mill.

By 1752 Mr. Richard Butler was living at the Chantry. (See Chapter VII, Pt. 2. X.)

A dispute about a faculty to appropriate a seat in the gallery in the south aisle of Bisley Church to Thomas Townsend of Bisley, gentleman, in 1741, elicits the statement from John Butler, junior, that his grandfather had built the said pew and he prayed for it to be allotted to his messuage of Rookwoods.

ILES FARM.

This farm at Iles' Green, Far Oakridge, is of ancient origin, as testified by the finding of a pair of thirteenth century windows, now built into the barn wall.[2] The present building in typical Cotswold style is dated 1614, but

---

[1] Glos. Pro. Reg.

[2] Information given by a mason who moved the windows.

in recent years has been adapted as a private residence by Sir Wm. Rothenstein, and it is now the property of William M. Hornby, Esq. The name of Iles first appears in the parish registers on 20 November, 1606 when Margaret, daughter of Richard Iles was baptized. The name has been considered to be Huguenot, and if so, its proper pronunciation has been preserved in the baptismal register of Richard, son of John Eeles, 6 April, 1640. They were one of the well-to-do clothier families, and owned the mill at Chalford still called by their name, lying between Bliss Mill and St. Mary's Mill.

Thomas Iles' will, dated 22 March, 1713-4, describes him as of Oakridge, clothier, and after pious commendation of his soul and body he refers to £350 to be paid to his son-in-law John Barnfield, after his own and his wife's decease, according to the marriage settlements with his daughter Anne Iles. To his daughter Martha Batt, wife of Roger Batt £140 for her own proper use, and after her death to her children equally, except to her eldest son. To his daughter Katharine, wife of William Jones £100 and his stock of cattle. To his brother-in-law Joseph Jones £45 in consideration of money formerly borrowed of him by his son John Iles, deceased. To his son-in-law John Barnfield all his household goods except one silver tankard, and also one broad loom, furnace, and one dungcart, in consideration of £40 to be paid to the children of his daughter Martha Batt. To . . . eldest son of the said Martha Batt, his silver tankard. All this disposing of goods is not to take place till after the decease of Eleanor his wife. The residue to John Barnfield, sole executor. W. Samuel Swisse, Samuel Pacy, Samuel Winstone. Proved 26 February, 1714.[1]

A flat stone in the Church had the following inscription :—

" Thomas Iles of Oakridge, who died March 28, 1714, aged 77. Also in memory of Anne, the wife of William Lediard and granddaughter of Thomas Iles of this parish who died the 9th of January, 1741, aged 39.[2]

[1] Glos. Pro. Reg.
[2] Bigland's History of Glos.

John Iles, Esq., was present at the Court Baron of 21 October, 1736, for his holding of land at Abnash and elsewhere. This is Skiverells Wood at Abnash, consisting of six acres, bounded on the east partly by Bisley Common and by a wood in the possession of John Webb, on the west by a wood belonging to Mr. Arthur Blackwell, on the north by the lands of the said John Isles (as described in a deed of 1806) which the then John Iles sold to William Tayloe of Chalford Hill 27-8 July, 1770.[1]

The same John Iles held land in Battlescombe field in 1789. In 1754 the rate for John Iles, Esq., for Abnash was £3 18s. 9d., and in 1762 £2 16s. 3d. In 1758 Mrs. Sarah Iles was rated at 9s. 2d. for Goathouse ground.

Some of the Iles family went to live at Minchinhampton, where in the Church there is a monument to John Iles of Chalford, died 1727, and Mary his wife, 1737. The arms depicted are :—Argent, a fess engrailed, and in chief three fleurs-de-lis sable.

SHEEPHOUSE.

Sheephouse is a small farm lying on the ancient track between Bisley and Eastcombe. It is mentioned in the will of Edward Townsend, of the parish of Bisley, baker, 7 May, 1680, being left by him to his son John, who appears to have leased it to Mary Pettet, of Stroud, for in her will of 20 August, 1701, she leaves her lease of the house and ground called Sheephouse to her son William Pettet.[2] John Townsend's death was presented at the Court Baron of 1724, he having held of the manor of Bisley a messuage and lands in Nashend called Webb's House. Thomas Townsend, his brother, held the estate.

LOWER NASHEND FARM.

Around this ancient farm on the edge of the Common there is a small group of old cottages. Undoubted evidence of

---

[1] Title-deeds of Corderries.

[2] Glos. Pro. Reg.

the antiquity of the farm is to be seen in the fine pair of thirteenth century windows, now fixed in the gable of the garage, but which were for some years lost sight of, having been removed by a contractor and built into an inner wall. (see plate 16). The farmhouse itself has an interesting kitchen, adapted from a barn, but thought to possess a Norman pillar. The house and buildings were restored by Mr. Albert Rothenstein.

Although there are frequent entries about inhabitants of Nashend in the Court rolls, there is nothing to indicate which of them lived at Nashend farm. John Wynchcombe als. Whytynge, held of the Lord of the Manor, Thomas Wye of Lypiatt, from 20 January, 1530, one messuage in Nashend for lives of himself, his wife Alice and son James. In 1558 the Court censured him for keeping a sub-tenant in his tenement without the leave of the Lord, and so he forfeited his holding. On 28 October, 1597, came James Keene to the Court (Lypiatt) and took one messuage and half a virgate of land called Paynes in Nashend on lives of himself and sons James and Thomas.

The death of Richard Lugge of Nashend, in 1589, is notified at the Court, and that John Lugge has sold his land to John Cook.

On 7 December, 1622, William Lugge, of Nashend, tailor, made his will and bequeathed to his son William " during the tearme of yeares yett unexpired that part of my meadow which Richard Smart doth rent of me with that rent of housing about to be billt at my howse end and the fower ackers of land near unto Litteredge, and after the decease of Margrett my now living wife with the rest of the wholl tenement if the said William shall happen to survive his mother." To his son Robert to be paid at the time he shall be forthe of his prenticeshipp in money 40s. To his son John to help him to a schoolmaster 20s., etc. W.—Henry Broughton, Nicolas Eversley, Annes Edgerley, and Annis Davies. Proved, 15 November, 1623.[1]

---

[1] Glos. Pro. Reg.

In the last cottage on the right hand side ascending from Bisley, on the fireplace beam of oak is carved " Henry Smart, 1674." Possibly he was son of Henry, baptized 12 March, 1648.

DANIEL'S FARM

This farm, now known as Rodways, is notable for possessing a pair of mediaeval stone gateposts to the farm yard, and a round chimney, built by a former Irish employee, in imitation of the chimneys of his native land.

BRATTONS

There is nothing to indicate the origin of the name of this small farm, but its antiquity may be assumed if the pair of thirteenth century windows it possesses are in their original setting. It seems likely that they were moved to this cottage from the Chantry, which was first built in that century.

No record of the cottage under its present name is to be found until 1814, when it is mentioned in an Indenture between Sir Paul Baghott and John Mansfield and others. The latter acquired Brattons at the same time as Jaynes Court for his son the Rev. Edward Mansfield. In 1935 Brattons was considerably enlarged and altered by Mrs. Johnson, the present owner.

COPSGROVE.

The earliest record of Copsgrove in the Bisley Court rolls is in that of 25 October, 1369, when Simon Taillo took from the Lord one toft which Agnes Coppesgrave formerly held, and another toft and one acre of land in another field which Seth Tristram formerly held, for the life of himself, Johanne his wife and Edward his son. In 1452-3 twelve pence of farm of one toft with curtilage and two acres of land, formerly of Walter Stonehenge, but now of Agnes Coppesgrave.[1]

---

[1] P. R. O. Ministers' Accounts, 31 Henry VI.

A toft is a place where a building once stood. A curtilage is a piece of land near a house.

Another record of Copsgrove is in 1400, when the Homage presented that Richard atte Grenehull, who held of the Lord one messuage and one ferendell of land, formerly Stancomb, and one toft and one ferendell of land called Nether Coppegrove, died in the month of September, Alice being his relict, and Richard and John his sons. A heriot of two oxen was due in place of XXXIs. VIIId.

In a deed of 10 March, 1620, George Marquis of Buckingham recites that King James I on 5 August, 1619, had granted a messuage called Colliers and eight acres of arable belonging (four being in Over Lypiatt Field and four in Stancombe Field) and a cottage called Coppesgrove with its appurtenances in Bisley, to be held of the manor of East Greenwich in soccage, by yearly rent of £53 16s. 6¾d. The Marquis, for £80 grants these estates, then in the tenure of Edward Stephens of Lypiatt, by virtue of demise from Queen Elizabeth, 24 January, 1593, to George and Thomas Throckmorton and Anthony Willie, for 16s. per annum and suit of court, and twopence upon every discent or alienation. This was followed on 6 May, 1621, by the sale for £15 of the Marquis' rights in a Little Grove in Copsgrove, to Edward Stephens, this having been bought lately from John Davys.

Colliers, mentioned above, is now represented by a small plantation so named, lying on the east slope of Stancombe opposite Lypiatt Park. The cottage was shortly after decayed.

An Indenture of 14 January, 1623, between John Davis, senior, and Edward Stephens, declares that George Marquis of Buckingham, by an indenture of 1 March, 1621, had granted to William Trapp a tenement called Copsgrove, which the said William Trapp had since granted to John Davis and heir. For £20 John Davys granted to Edward Stephens two meadows, with a piece of woodground belonging to Copsgrove, one containing four acres shoots down towards the Weare, and adjoins Highmeads,[1] the other a Lagger of one acre adjoining.

---

[1] Highmeads wood lies on the east slope of Stancombe.

By 15 May, 1669, Obadiah Sedgwick, of London, grocer, and Susannah, his wife, sell to Thomas Stephens the messuage and tenement with one yard land, called Copsgrove, containing five closes adjoining to the manor of Lypiatt, two closes of meadow, one of pasture and of arable, one acre in Stancombe field and three acres in the same, and all houses, paying the Crown and fee farm rents.

On 11 September of that year John Davis, son of John Davis deceased, released all his right in Copsgrove to Thomas Stephens. Copsgrove appears to have been divided, part being called Smart's Copsgrove, and part Davis' Copsgrove. John Davis of " Coxsgrove " or Copsgrove, who was descended from Robert Davis to whom in 1559-60 was granted the Hundred of Bisley, which he held till 1566-7, made his will 28 March, 1624, leaving his tenement at Coxsgrove to his son William. This line of Davises, yeomen or clothiers, migrated to France Lynch, and from them descended Abraham Davis of Bussage Farm, now the Vicarage, or Glebe house.[1]

Once the Copsgrove and Colliers estates were acquired by the owners of Lypiatt, they have ever since passed with that estate.

STANCOMBE.

Stancombe, otherwise Stone combe, the combe dividing Bisley from Lypiatt, gave its name to the Common Field above it and to the farmhouse at its head. This, though now a modern building, has been the site of a farmhouse for many centuries. At the Court of the Manor of Bisley of 1400 it was presented that Richard atte Grenehulle had held one messuage and one farendell of land formerly Robert Stancombe's. His widow Alice and son John, sought permission to rebuild and construct at their own cost one house for their hall and one grange. Thomas Stancombe in 1441, and with John Stancombe in 1461, was witness to deeds connected with Chalford, evidently being in friendship with John

---

[1] From information supplied by Mrs. Brimfield, a descendant, who owns the old house at France Lynch belonging to her ancestors.

Lymbrok (or Limbrick, whose farm of that name is at Water-lane), and of John Frampton.

Stancombe Ash, from which another farm is named, had a notable ashtree which was a landmark on the edge of the Common on the road to Stroud.

Bisley wills have frequent reference to land in Stancombe field, but not to Stancombe farm.

FENNELL'S FARM.

Fennells is a site of great antiquity, a pair of small Saxon windows being built into a compartment of the great barn (see plate 7) ····   and a pair of thirteenth century windows lighting the attic of the ancient farmhouse. A fourteenth century window in the outhouse in the garden is thought to have been brought from Gray's by Sir John Dorington.

In the Lypiatt MS. book it is recorded that Fennells' house was purchased by Mrs. Stephens, Mr. William Hall and Edward Manwaring in 1614, for £240 fine paid to Hall. In 1609 Fennells had been demised to Robert Nicholls, alias Fennell, for 900 years. This Robert Nicholls appears to have been descended from another of that name who on 24 April, 1516, attended the Court of Robert Wye at Lypiatt, in which Manor it lies, and took two messuages on his own life, that of Margerie his wife, and of John his son. His father Walter Nicholls had married Agnes, daughter of Edward Freame, deceased. She came to Thomas Wye's Court, 25 August, 1573 and returned to the Lord of Lypiatt the reversion of a messuage which formerly she took when unmarried, with garden and orchard, with pasture, meadow, and sixteen acres of land in the Fields, which had been in the tenure of Joan Freame her mother. Walter Nicholls alias Fennell, husband to Agnes, came and took these premises on three lives, their own and their son Robert's, after the decease of Joan Freame.

Robert Nicholls had passed on his tenure to one Smart, who assigned it to William Hall, of whom, as recorded above, Elizabeth Stephens bought it in 1614.

At the valuation of Fennell's in 1796, it was reported to consist of forty acres—Frith two acres, Lower Frith formerly arable, Tumpy ground, Kilminster Mead, Crab orchard, Nodlings, Axton, Lower, Middle and Upper Axtons, Stephens Ground (Barn and Court) formerly arable, ten acres, Ferney Ground, Mowing Mead, Crossfield, Great Mead, Little Mead, Lower Easton's Croft, Upper ditto, formerly arable, four acres, and Holtocks, twenty acres.

The Crossfield here mentioned was formerly the Lower Field of Over Lypiatt, and being a common field of $23\frac{3}{4}$ acres, was in the hands of several tenants. It was so called from having the Cross of St. Mary at its corner, at the junction of the roads to Bisley and Lypiatt Park. It would seem, judging from an Indenture of 1669, that four ashes also marked this junction.

Great and Little Meads have been added to Fennell's with other closes belonging to two Messuages which had been pulled down by 1725, called Slatters and Hawkins, and which in 1558 had been the homes of Richard Dower, and his son Robert with his family. The area of the farm suffered many changes, and parts were let separately, Thomas Clissold having a lease for three lives in 1612, and John Clissold in 1646.

Thomas Clissold appears to have acted as attorney for the Marquis of Buckingham in 1662 at the time of the sale of Overcourt to Thomas Tayloe. He was a trusted overseer for the wills of several of his friends.

Fennell's Farm continued till 1919 in the ownership of the Lords of Lypiatt Manor.

CATSWOOD.

This ancient farm, held of the manor of Bisley is mentioned in Ministers' Accounts, 29 Henry VI, 1450-1. " In Cattwode, of trees and roots in Tymbercombe sold to William Clerke." The present house, said to have been built in the time of the Protector Cromwell, is approached through a gateway, the pillars of which are remarkable for being crowned with miniature steeples.

The Rogers family first appears in the registers in 1598 and continues through the seventeenth and eighteenth centuries, probably an offshoot of the Rogers of Dowdeswell and elsewhere in the county of Gloucester. It is most likely that Thomas Rogers built the house at Catswood, but in the absence of old deeds this cannot be positively asserted. It seems that in 1699 ten acres of land called Coxland piece were sold and acquired by Mr. Rogers of Catswood. At the Court Baron of 1736 Thomas Rogers, an infant, appeared for Cattwood and Coxeland. Amongst the brasses in the Church tower at Bisley is one to " Thomas Rogers of Cattswood in the parish of Bisley, Gentleman, died 14 February, 1759, aged 35." His aunt, " Anna Brown, widow and relict of Mr. Robert Brown, late of Stroud, Apothecary, and daughter of Thomas Rogers, of Cattswood, in this parish, Gentleman, died 9 June, 1760, aged 74." Nathaniel Rogers of Catswood, was a Foeffee in 1782.

In the opening years of the nineteenth century the Rogers were no longer at Catswood, as Thomas Shill, yeoman was then in possession, dying there 3 March, 1829, aged 84, as recorded on a tombstone on the north side of Bisley Church.

ANSTEAD'S OR HANSTEADS FARM.

This farm for many centuries, has been the property of the Feoffees of Rodborough, having been granted to them by one of the Rodborough family for the parishioners of the hamlet in order to help them to provide a priest to minister to them there, they being two and a half miles from their parish Church of Minchinhampton. There was a case, not dated, in Early Chancery Proceedings respecting the unlawful withholding of profits from the land, etc., by one, John Payne, of Rodborough, a churchwarden ; unfortunately, the document recording it is so mutilated that information is obscured. It is, however, stated that there were two messuages in Bysley, sixty acres of land, meadow and pasture called Handstets and other acres of land, and 60s. of rent yearly with appurtenances.[1] That the farm was known as

---

[1] Hockaday's Ecclesiastical File, Rodborough. P. R. O. E. C. Pro., 1005 and 1008.

Hanastie or Hanestie in the fourteenth century appears from the charter of William de la Pere (see Chapter III) in which Robert de Hanestie and Radulf de Hanestie are mentioned as having land in the Common fields, namely in Stancombe field. Certain of this land was in dispute in 1654, as to whether it was part and parcel of Over Lypiatt manor or of Hanstead Farm.

Ashmead

Ashmead in Abenash in Bisley as we have already seen in Chapter X, part 2, was owned by Cirencester Abbey. In 1564-5 it was held by Walter Blisse, yeoman, who died seized of part of a wood, etc., in Bisley (held of the manor of Sapperton), of a capital messuage and lands called Ffaderweke, held by 9d. rent, of a messuage called a barne and close annexed and thirty-two acres and better of arable land and mead called Ashmead, held by knight service, Thomas being his son and heir.[1]

Ashmead was in the possession of William Fream of Bisley, dyer, when he made his will 15 August, 1651, bequeathing thereby to his daughter Sarah his mead called by the name of Ayshmeade, after his wife Sarah's decease, and his two houses in the parish of Frampton he gives to his daughter Sarah after his wife's decease for life, and after the said Sarah's decease his two houses which be in the parish of Minchinhampton to William Sevill, his daughter's son. Also he gives to Sarah Sevill his daughter's child, his meadow ground which is called by the name of Ashmeads, lying in the parish of Bisley, All that part of the meadow ground which lies above William Stone's house and all that part of meadow ground he gives to Mary Sevill, his daughter's child, as lies below William Stevens' house.[2]

---

[1] Escheats 7 Eliz. Fosbrooke. Thomas Blisse is mentioned at the Court of the, Hundred 3 October 1584, and Richard Blisse was Reeve in 1589. The name has been continued in Bliss Mill at Chalford.

[2] P. C. C. Alchin, fo. 82.

DRAKE'S HOUSE, BISLEY

Drake's House lies next the modern Court House in High Street. Part of the house was pulled down when this new building replaced the old market house. The date L. 1682 F. can be seen on the chimney and the remarkable carvings round the doorway will be noted. Thomas Drake was in possession of the house in 1782, according to a deed of 1 August of that year, whereby John Butler and his family assigned to Mr. Edward Aldridge their interest in the leasehold property for the rest of the term of 440 years. It is stated that one John Stanley preceded Thomas Drake in possession.[1]

About 1822 Moses Woodfield was living at Drake's house. In 1934 it was restored after being in a ruinous condition.

MAGNET HOUSE, BISLEY

This ancient house in Well Road, Bisley, has been referred to in Chapter X, part 4, when Ferdinando Snow is mentioned as the owner. That it is one of the most ancient in Bisley is evident from the pair of thirteenth century windows it possesses, and also from the discovery of a mediaeval interior wall made of clay and cut grass. This wall collapsed during the recent restoration, when its nature was revealed.

Ferdinando Snow let off part of the house to Robert Boulton, the lease being dated 15 February, 1637.

THE BEAR INN

This inn as we know it, was formerly the Court House and Assembly room of Bisley, the inn of that name at that time being the house on the opposite side of the road, the property of the Feoffees. (see plate 16)

The picturesque facade of the Bear Inn, with its portico supported by late Jacobean pillars, covers an enlargement of that period which was added to the Tudor building lying behind it, a doorway of that date appearing on the north side of the house. The interior has been altered since the time it

---

[1] Deed in possession of Mr. Wilfrid Randall, the present owner.

was used for assemblies, but in the tap-room there remains a remarkable seventeenth century fireplace, complete with its old ironwork and jack.   A ratebook of 1777 assesses Thomas Clissold for the New Bear, as well as for the Old Bear, but it is to be gathered from the Bisley Court roll of 20 December, 1766, that the old Court House had become the Bear Inn that year, as for the first time it is recorded that the Court of John Stephens was to be holden at the House of the widow Driver, known by the sign of the Bear Inn in Bisley. and so the statement of the same place of meeting continues down to 1838 (when the rolls cease) with the names of the various inn-holders (who appear to have changed frequently) noted.

The old Bear Inn was leased by the Feoffees to John Eldridge in 1751, and to Sarah, widow of Richard Driver, innholder, deceased, in 1760.   She appears to have transferred the inn business to the Court House in 1766.

An Indenture of 6 March, 1781, between the then Feoffees, namely—Thomas Baghott Delabere, Esq., Thomas Hancox, William Turner, William Sevill, senior and junior, Matthias Baker, John Jones, John Wynn and Nathaniel Rogers, gentleman, and Thomas Clissold, of Bisley, gentleman, states that the latter stood legally possessed of the Beare by purchase from Charles Driver, of Toadsmore, deceased, and that for £2 10s. 0d. per annum, the Feoffees let to him the tenement known as the Beare with all buildings, barns, stables, gardens, etc., and one close of meadow of half an acre, and half an acre of arable adjoining the garden, the said premises being then in the occupation of William Bishop and William Driver, brother of John and Charles Driver, deceased, under tenants, to hold for three lives, doing and performing suit or service in the court of the said Feoffees for the Manor of Sturmies in Aveniss.

Thomas Clissold died the following March, 1782.

THE BELL INN

The deeds of this old leasehold house only date from 1735, when it was in the possession of the Townsend family, but it is stated to have belonged to Richard Fernley, mercer,

before 1723. It had been divided into two tenements, one
of which was occupied by Richard Townsend, baker, whose
son Samuel succeeded, but it passed through many hands,
owing to incessant mortgaging, till in 1750 it was acquired
by Joseph Clissold, who died in 1796, bequeathing the Bell
Inn to his son John Clissold. John Clissold died about 1806,
leaving his wife Ann and two sons, Joseph and Peter. By
1826 Joseph Clissold was carrying on the business, but
mortgaged the premises that year to George Playne of
Forwood, gentleman, and after further similar dealings, the
property was finally acquired by Mr. Wilfrid Randall, and
has ceased to be an inn.

BOURNE HOUSE

The estate at Bourne, which till recently had preserved its
park-like amenity, was the site of an ancient house, remains
of which are built into the wall bounding the north side of
the grounds. Abel Wantner, writing in 1704, describes the
Todsmoor stream as passing " under the Bourne House
Court millpond, and there falleth into Stroud water."

William Hopton, clothier, who we have already seen in
Chapter X, Pt. 1, took over the lease of Chalford Mill from
Francis Compton in 1568, and came from Leonard Stanley,
lived at Chalford, and appears, from his widow's will, to have
had a lease of Bourne House. He made his will 20 September,
1590, and after pious commendation, touching his house at
Chalford, his son Thomas is to have the same by an obligation,
or else £200, of which he had received a great part. His wife,
who knows of it can make up the part and retain the house.
His son Ferdinand is to have the farm at Dunsborne. He
requires his wife Johan Hopton to have a special care of
Samuel Hopton and Jane, their two children, being un-
provided for at present. His wife to be sole executrix. His
son-in-law John Bowcher and Thomas Tailor (Tailoe) overseers. William Hopton was too ill that day to set his hand
or seal to his will, but heard all which was read to him and
would have nothing altered. W. Leonard Tailour, John
Shewell, Esq., sen., Robert Englefielde.

His will was proved in London 8 March, 1591, and **two** days after, his widow, Joan Hopton, made her will, in which she says, touching the lease of Holliday's house, she gives it to her brother Henry Bearde, with one cow. To her son, Samuel Hopton, the lease of the Overmill and the lease of the Boorne house, with ten acres of wheat in Hampton feilde. To her daughter, Joan Hopton, the lease of Wakenhill, with all her wearing apparel, a diaper borde cloth and one diaper towel, one dozen diaper napkins, one holland towel, one pair of best pillow dowes, and the best cubborde clothe and payre of three leaved sheets.

To Marget Bearde one bedstead with three beds, two pairs of sheets, two pairs of blankets, two coverletts, and two pillows and two bolsters, ten pieces of pewter and one cow.

To Jane Ridler one smock and one apron. To Elizabeth Simons in respect of a petticoat clothe she owes her one smock and a petticoat. To Alice Tayloe's three boys each a chilver sheep. To the poor £2. The residue to Samuel and Joan Hopton. Overseers, Thomas Taylowe, and John Burgher, two sheep each. W. Thomas Taylowe, John Robins, Joane Hopton.[1]

Joan Hopton only survived her husband a very short time, for she died in April, 1591, and was buried at Bisley on the 9th.

Ferdinand Hopton, William's son by his first wife, made his will 18 February, 1614, and is described as of the Born, parish of Stroud, and Tithing of Nether Lippeat. He desired to be buried in the Church of Bisley. To his son Humphrey, his copyhold at Hyde after his wife's decease, one gilt salt and one bed with its appurtenances, and one grey colte about four years.

To his son Thomas £20 at 21 or marriage and one bed and one cow. To his son William £20, one bed, one cow, and a gilt cup. To his son Henry £20, one bed, one cow and a silver cup. To his son Samuel £20, one bed, one cow. To his daughter Mary £20, one bed with furniture, one dozen

[1] P. C. C. 28 St. Barbe.

silver spoons, and one heifer, to be paid at 21 or marriage.
To his wife Margery, the house he then dwells in during the
term.   The residue to his wife, who is executrix.   Overseers,
John Robbins of Matson, Samuel Hopton, W. Roger Fowler,
John Robbyns, Anthony Grime, Daniel Hopton.[1]

Ferdinand Hopton was buried as he desired at Bisley, on
20 February, 1615.

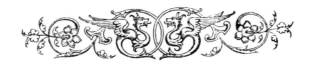

1 P. C. C. 41 Rudd.

APPENDIX II

List of residents in the parish of Bisley whose names appear in the Index Library of Gloucestershire Wills.

(Many of the names given especially in the eighteenth century refer to Administrations only).

WILLS PROVED IN THE PREROGATIVE COURT OF CANTERBURY.

Arundell, John, clothier, 1655.
Arundell, Richard, Stroud-water, 1601.
Baker, John, yeoman, 1616.
Bisley, Hugh, also of Sand-hurst, Berks., 1415.
Broughton, Henry, 1581.
Brudge, George, 1587.
Butt, Walter, clothier, Over Lypiatt, 1627.
Clayfield, Samuel, clothier, 1628.
Compton, William, 1546, Chaweford.
Eckley, Thomas, 1591.
Fowler, Roger, 1541.
Fream, William, 1654, dyer.
Grainger, Richard, 1655.
Griffin, John, 1627.
Griffin, Elizabeth, 1628.
Gryme, John, 1509.
Hone, Robert, 1655, yeoman, Chaulford.
Hopton, Ferdinand, 1615, Bourn, N. Lypiatt.

Hopton, Joan, 1591.
Hopton, William, 1590, Chal-ford.
Mason, John, 1654, yeoman.
Master, Richard, Esq., one of the ordinarie phisitians of the Queen, Silver Street, London, Bysley, Glos., and Wilts., 1588.
Maysey, Ann, 1651.
Phelps, Andrew, 1597.
Phillipps, Thomas, yeoman, 1624.
Risby, John, 1654, Millwright.
Tayloe, Thomas, 1602, Strowde.
Taylor, Richard, 1585.
Turner, John, 1609, yeoman, Througham.
Tyler, Richard, 1655, mercer.
Whytington, Thomas, Esq., 1491, Lupegate.
Wye, Robert, Esq., 1520, Over Lypiatt.
Wye, Thomas, Esq., 1581.

WILLS PROVED IN THE CONSISTORY COURT OF THE BISHOPS OF GLOUCESTER.

Adams, Ursula, 1763.
Ainsley, John, 1680.
Alder, Jeremiah, 1689.

Aldridge, Mary, 1749.
Aldridge, Thomas, 1616, Stroud.
Aldridge, William, 1765.

Alredge, William, 1561.
Allen, Ferdinand, 1693.
Allen, Samuel, 1734.
Allen, William, 1726.
Allen, William, 1731.
Ansloe, or Anslow, Edward, 1705.
Ansloe, Eleanor, 1712.
Ansloe, George, 1684.
Ansloe, Roger, 1691.
Ansloe, Roger, 1712.
Ansloe, Thomas, 1723.
Ansloe, Thomas, 1726.
Ansloe, William, 1716.
Ansloe, Thomas and William, 1717.
Archer, Margaret, 1697.
Arthur, Francis, 1757.
Arundell, John, 1573.
Arundell, John, 1666, Over Lypiatt.
Attwood, Pacy, 1692.
Badger, John, 1713.
Bagliss, Thomas, 1722.
Bailey, William, 1763.
Baker, John, 1616.
Baker, John, 1675.
Baker, John, 1766.
Baker, Matthias, 1794.
Baker, Susannah, 1768.
Baldwin, William, sen., 1764.
Ball (als. Jayne), Joseph, 1685.
Ball, Thomas, 1688.
Barksdale, Mary Barbara, 1758.
Barnfield, Joseph, 1728.
Barrow, Robert, 1708.
Bartlett, Henry, 1747.
Bartlett, John, 1769.
Bartlett, Thomas, 1782.
Batt, Elizabeth, 1723.
Batt, Johanna, 1706.
Batt, Richard, 1618.
Batt, Richard, 1700.
Batt, Richard, 1740.
Batt, Thomas, 1618.
Batt, William, 1707.
Bennett, Henry, 1545.
Bennett, John, 1618.
Bennett, John, 1631.

Bennett, Joseph, 1755.
Berryman, Nicholas, 1685.
Berryman, Richard, 1737.
Berryman, Sarah, 1737.
Bidmead, Anthony, 1754.
Bidmead, Daniel, 1723.
Bidmead, John, 1753.
Bidmead, Martha, 1699.
Bidmead, Richard, 1742.
Bidmead, Samuel, 1730.
Bignell, Timothy, 1736.
Blakeney, Daniel (als. King), 1704.
Blanch, Thomas, 1792.
Blandford, Charles, 1741.
Blisse, Sarah, 1768.
Blisse, William, 1645.
Blisse, William, 1700.
Borne, George, 1612.
Borne, John, 1620.
Boulton, Robert, 1676.
Boulton, Thomas, 1608.
Bowman, Joseph, 1768.
Bowton, Elizabeth, 1564.
Bowton, Thomas, 1563.
Bowton, Thomas, 1605.
Bridge, Richard, 1713, Thrupp.
Brion, Thomas, 1736.
Britton, Richard, 1680.
Broughton, Christopher, 1578.
Broughton, Hanna, 1719.
Broughton, James, 1611.
Broughton, William, 1685.
Brown, John, 1729.
Browne, John, 1797.
Browning, Thomas, 1790.
Browning, William, 1684.
Browning, William, 1771.
Brunden, Richard, 1740.
Brunson, William, 1690.
Bucknell, Samuel, 1790.
Burdock, Ann, 1779.
Burdock, Sarah, 1700.
Burdock, Thomas, 1701.
Burroughs, John, 1719.
Burrowe, James, 1620.
Burrows, James, 1727.
Butcher, Daniel, 1800.
Butler, James, 1726.

Butler, John, 1716.
Butler, John, 1723.
Butt, John, 1737.
Butt, Richard, 1744, Chalford.
Capenor, Elizabeth, 1781.
Capenor, Mary, 1745.
Chambers, James, 1600.
Chapman, Jane, 1759.
Chapman, Thomas, 1759.
Chapman, Thomas, 1769.
Cherrington, John, 1698.
Chester, John, 1740.
Chew, Richard, 1677.
Chew, Richard, 1745.
Child, Ann, 1783, Chalford.
Child, Mary, 1783.
Child, Richard, 1744.
Churches, John, 1560.
Claffield, Elizabeth, 1559.
Clarke, Elizabeth, 1544.
Clissale, Richard, 1553.
Clissall, Nathaniel, 1677.
Clissold, Ann, 1693.
Clissold, Elizabeth, 1784.
Clissold, John, 1687.
Clissold, John, 1766.
Clissold, Joseph, 1701.
Clissold, Joseph, 1796.
Clissold, Mary, 1714.
Clissold, Peter, 1700.
Clissold, Peter, 1759.
Clissold, Susanna, 1766.
Clissold, Thomas, 1616.
Clissold, Thomas, 1782.
Clyssold, Richard, 1577.
Clutterbuck, William, 1673.
Coates, Thomas, 1735.
Collins, Henry, 1725.
Compton, Henry, gent., 1593.
Cook(e), John, 1698.
Cook, John, 1734, Chalford.
Cook, Margery, 1725.
Cook, Nathaniel, 1761.
Cook, Richard, 1724.
Cook, Robert, 1681.
Cook, Thomas, 1750.
Cook, William, 1622.
Cook, William, 1702.
Cook, William, 1727.

Corderoy, Edward, 1758.
Corderoy, Eleanor, 1750.
Cox, Anthony, 1664.
Cox, Betty, 1773.
Cox, John, 1736.
Cox, John, 1769.
Cox, Matthew, 1717.
Cripts, Oakridge Henry, 1727.
Crook, Martin, 1756.
Currier, Robert, 1618.
Damsell, Elizabeth, 1729.
Damsell, Henry, 1731.
Damsell, Nathaniel, 1740.
Damsell, Samuel, 1712.
Damsell, Samuel, 1741.
Damsell, Thomas, 1795.
Damsell, William, 1787.
Damsell, William, 1796.
Daniel, Francis, 1709.
Daniel, John, 1712.
Daniel, Richard, 1719.
Daniel, Richard, 1744.
Daniel, Samuel, 1721.
Daniel, Thomas, 1746.
Davis, John, 1624.
Davis, Joseph, 1745.
Davis, Robert, 1631.
Davis, Robert, 1684.
Davis, Roger, 1784.
Davis, Thomas, 1765.
Davis, als. Etkins, Thomas, 1766.
Denton, Richard, 1704.
Dobbs, James, 1674.
Dower, Katherine, 1588.
Dower, John, 1558.
Dowman, James, 1714.
Driver, John, 1780.
Driver, Richard, 1763.
Dudbridge, Thomas, 1692.
Dudbridge, William, 1670.
Dudbridge, William, 1689, Over Lypiatt.
Dudbridge, William, 1693.
Dyer, Thomas, 1591.
Eacut, John, 1738, Catswood.
Edgerley, John, 1756.
Edgerley, Nicholas, 1613.

Edgerley, Roger, 1631,
  Nashend.
Edgerley, Thomas, 1545.
Edgeloe, William, 1766.
Egles, Thomas, 1583.
Elcher, William, 1696.
Eldridge, John, 1738.
Evans, Jonathan, 1734.
Farner, John, 1743.
Feeld, Sybil, 1568.
Field, Anthony, 1629.
Frampton, Walter, 1557.
Franklin, Francis, 1712.
Franklin, Francis, 1714.
Franklin, Francis, 1766,
  Chalford.
Franklin, Joseph, 1754.
Freame, Giles, 1670.
Freame, Robert, Esq., 1599,
  Lower Lypiatt.
Freame, Robert, 1684.
Free, John, 1545.
Free, John, 1685.
Freeman, Anne, 1766.
Freeman, Anthony, 1732.
Freeman, John, 1763.
Freeman, William, 1738,
  Chalford.
Fry, John, 1766.
Fry, Robert, 1736.
Fry, William, 1725.
Gardner, Daniel, 1729.
Gardner, Giles, 1650.
Gardner, Isaac, 1685.
Gardner, James, 1755.
Gardner, Job, 1749.
Gardner, Joseph, 1740.
Gardner, Richard, 1717.
Gardner, Richard, 1778.
Gardner, Samuel, 1759.
Gardner, William, 1731.
Gardner, William, 1764.
Garner, John, 1582.
Gator, William, 1618.
Gingell, James, 1712.
Goddyn, Thomas, 1559, Lypiatt
Gootheridge, Arthur, 1578.
Gregory, Thomas, 1787.
Griffin, James, 1613.

Griffin, Richard, 1620.
Griffin, William, 1591, Stroud.
Griffin, William, 1592.
Grimes, William, 1702.
Gryme, Richard, sen., 1548,
  Stroud.
Gurner, Martha, 1763.
Gurner, William, 1735.
Gurner, William, 1755.
Gyngell, Henry, 1715.
Hall, Andrew, 1613.
Hall, John, 1712.
Hall, William, 1769.
Halliday, William, 1727.
Hancox, Alice, 1625.
Hancox, Henry, 1625.
Hancox, John, 1620.
Hancox, John, 1691.
Hancox, John, 1753.
Hancox, Mary, 1771.
Hancox, Nathaniel, 1729.
Hancox, Thomas, 1793.
Hancox, Walter, 1743.
Hancox, William, 1708.
Hanley, Sarah, 1733.
Harbord, Edward, 1684.
Harmer, Richard, 1729,
  Chalford.
Harmer, Thomas, 1784.
Hartland, Edward, 1663.
Hartland, Joan, 1675.
Haydon, Anthony, 1783.
Hayley, William, 1792.
Haynes, Thomas, 1729.
Hayward, Thomas, 1690.
Henley, Thomas, 1728.
Herbert, William, 1684.
Hews, Sarah, 1708.
Hill, Edward, 1754.
Hill, Hester, 1754.
Hill, Solomon, 1721.
Hone, Robert, 1603.
Hone, William, 1697.
Holliday, John, 1619.
Holliday, John, 1712.
Holliday, Richard, 1668.
Holliday, Samuel, 1775.
Hook, Henry, 1774.
Hook, Joan, 1793.

Hooper, Josiah, 1739.
Horston, Mary, 1705.
Hoskins, Richard, 1611.
Humphrey, Walter, 1598.
Hunt, John, 1799.
Hunt, Thomas, 1577.
Hunt, William, 1560.
Hunt, William, 1642.
Hurden, Thomas, 1705.
Hurne, Thomas, 1692.
Hurne, Thomas, 1711.
Iles, Thomas, 1703.
Iles, Thomas, 1714, Oakridge.
Ireland, Eleanor, 1615.
Jayne, Henry, 1765.
Jeffreys, Alice, 1622.
Jeffereyes, Hugh, 1615.
Keeble, Mary, 1740.
Keen, Deborah, 1766.
Keen, Isaac, 1772.
Keen, Jaspar, 1701.
Keen, John, 1617.
Keen, John, 1722.
Keen, John, 1797.
Keen, Mary, 1778.
Keen, Sarah, 1778.
Keen, Thomas, 1667.
Keen, Thomas, 1752.
Keen, William, 1686.
Kerby, Rebecca, 1731.
King, Edward, 1567.
King, Edward, 1760.
King, James, 1696.
King, John, 1689.
King, John, 1737.
King, Sarah, 1724.
King, Stephen, 1735.
King, Thomas, 1718, Painswick.
Kynge, John, 1585.
Lea, Alexander, 1778, Lypiatt.
Lediard, William, 1769.
Lewis, Henry, 1750, Chalford.
Lewis, John, 1721.
Lewis, William, 1717.
Looker, John, 1579.
Lovell, James, 1716, Lypiatt.
Lugg, Elizabeth, 1593.
Lugg, Richard, 1587.
Lugg, William, 1622.

Lyday, Richard, 1680.
March, John, 1714.
March, Jonathan, 1731.
Marsh, Jonathan, 1793.
Marsh, William, 1778.
Marle, John, 1748.
Mason, Anne, 1627.
Mason, Charles, 1778.
Mason, Charles, 1793.
Mason, George, 1793.
Mason, Henry, 1767.
Mayson, William, 1574.
Masters, Henry, 1694.
Masters, Thomas, 1674.
Matthews, Thomas, 1710.
Matthews, William, 1713,
    Chalford.
Maynard, Sarah, 1763,
    Chalford.
Mayo, Arthur, 1747.
Mayo, John, 1625.
Mayo, John, 1797.
Mayor, Richard, 1733.
Mayowe, William, 1555.
Maysey, James, 1728.
Maysey, Richard, 1727.
Maysey, William, 1639.
Milliard, Joseph, 1772.
Millard, Mary, 1749.
Mill, John, 1586.
Mills, Paul, 1778.
Morgan, Jonathan, 1739.
Morgan, Samuel, 1776.
Morton, John, 1724.
Mose, John, 1754.
Moss, Robert, 1743.
Munden, Jeremiah, 1701.
Munden, Samuel, 1725.
Munden, Thomas, 1794.
Nash, John, 1741.
Neal, Benjamin, 1776.
Neal, Sarah, 1726.
Niblett, Daniel, 1660-1.
Niblett, James, 1724.
Niblett, James, 1737.
Niblett, Thomas, 1717.
Niblett, Thomas, 1740.
Niblett, William, 1722.
Nicholls, Alice, 1607.

Nicholls, Robert, 1630.
Nicholls, Thomas, 1558.
Nurse, Giles, 1689.
Olney, Giles, 1594.
Orpan, John, 1625.
Pacy, Beata, 1690.
Pacy, Samuel, 1732.
Panting, Hannah, 1770.
Panting, James, 1766.
Panting, John, 1729.
Panting, Margaret, 1724.
Panting, Sarah, 1769.
Panting, Thomas, 1758.
Panting, William, 1713.
Panting, William, 1716.
Panting, William, 1768.
Parker, Richard, 1760.
Parker, William, 1709.
Partridge, Richard, 1694.
Parsons, George, 1709.
Parsons, George, 1740.
Parsons, James, 1733.
Parsons, Thomas, 1696.
Parsons, Thomas, 1714.
Passloe, Elizabeth, 1700.
Payton, Benjamin, 1726.
Payton, Charles, 1729.
Payton, Philip, 1668.
Payton, Thomas, 1717.
Payton, William, 1665.
Pearce, George, 1735.
Pearce, James, 1721.
Pearce, Richard, 1631.
Pearce, Susannah, 1762.
Pearce, William, 1698.
Pearce, William, 1750.
Pearce, William, 1762.
Peerse, Henry, 1559.
Peerse, Henry, 1609, Avenes.
Peerse, John, 1597.
Peerse, Thomas, 1555.
Pegler, James, 1797.
Pegler, Richard, 1693.
Pegler, Richard, 1708.
Pegler, Richard, 1719.
Pegler, Richard, 1796.
Pegler, Sarah, 1800.
Pegler, Solomon, 1723.
Peirce, George, 1663.

Peirse, William, 1626.
Perryn, Richard, 1548.
Perryn, Richard, 1605.
Pettat or Pettit, James, 1598.
Pettat, John, 1581.
Pettat, Hannah, 1777.
Pettat, Richard, 1574.
Pettat, Thomas, 1707.
Pettat, Thomas, 1775.
Peyton, Caroline, 1778.
Phillipps, Thomas, 1624.
Phelps, John, 1738.
Phelps, Nathaniel, 1729.
Phelps, Sara, 1720.
Phelps, William, 1729.
Pincott, James, 1713.
Pincott, Thomas, 1793.
Polson, Richard, 1796.
Poulson, Richard, 1767.
Price, Thomas, 1783.
Priest, Elizabeth, 1770.
Priest, Francis, 1768.
Priest, Isaac, 1765.
Priest, Martha, 1686.
Priest, Simon, 1715.
Prior, Thomas, 1552.
Quarrell, Jane, 1643.
Randle or Randell, Mary, 1697.
Randell, Thomas, 1687.
Randell, William, 1775.
Rannels, John, 1735.
Restall, Ann, 1767.
Restall, Edward, 1597.
Restall, Giles, 1714.
Restall, Henry, 1665.
Restall, Henry, 1724.
Restall, Isaac, 1716.
Restall, Isaac, 1795.
Restall, Isaac, 1799.
Restall, Matthew, 1707.
Restall, Richard, 1550.
Restall, Walter, 1754.
Roberts, William, 1778.
Robinson, Elizabeth, 1792.
Rogers, Mary, 1709.
Rogers, Richard, 1730.
Rogers, Thomas, 1741.
Rotten, Timothy, 1784.
Rowland, Ann, 1712.

Rowland, Henry, 1712.
Rowland, Mary, 1712.
Rowles, Elinor, 1741.
Rowles, Jeremiah, 1728.
Rowles, James, 1719.
Rydler, Christopher, 1591.
Sadler, Oliver, 1787.
Sanders, Richard, 1707.
Sanders, Daniel, 1724.
Saniger, John, 1598.
Sansome, Richard, 1616.
Savage, Robert, 1605.
Seed, Brice, 1709.
Seed, Edward, 1764, Chalford Lynch.
Sellars, Alice, 1607.
Sevill, Jeremiah, 1700.
Sevill, John, 1719.
Sevill, Samuel, 1678.
Sevill, Samuel, 1753.
Sevill, Walter, 1708, Chalford.
Sevill, William and Mary, 1713.
Sewell, John, 1625.
Sewell, John, 1646.
Sewell, Mary, 1716.
Sewell, Thomas, 1632.
Sewell, Thomas, 1694.
Sewell, Walter, 1593.
Sewell, Walter, 1665.
Shewell, John, 1684, Nether Lypiatt.
Shewell, Walter, 1639.
Shewell, William, 1582.
Shewell, William, 1627.
Shewell, William, 1708.
Showell, Margery, 1612.
Shuring, Anthony, 1708.
Sims, Bisley, 1724.
Smart, Alice, 1578.
Smart, Alice, 1694.
Smart, Alice, 1697.
Smart, Edward, 1694.
Smart, Eleanor, 1713.
Smart, George, 1673.
Smart, George, 1708.
Smart, Henry, 1709.
Smart, James, 1706.
Smart, John, 1706.
Smart, John, 1736.

Smart, John, 1799.
Smart, Moses, 1724.
Smart, Obadiah, 1724.
Smart, Richard, 1684.
Smart, Richard, 1760.
Smart, Richard, 1774.
Smart, Richard, 1776, Greys.
Smart, Thomas, 1561.
Smart, Thomas, 1747, Greys.
Smart, Thomas, 1752, Greys.
Smart, Thomas, 1759.
Smart, Thomas, 1764.
Smart, William, 1558.
Smart, William, 1751.
Smith, Anna, 1750.
Smith, George, 1719.
Smith, Jane, 1706.
Smith, John, 1582.
Smith, Mary, 1758, Chalford.
Smith, Richard, 1697.
Snow, Daniel, 1677.
Snow, Daniel, 1745.
Snow, Joseph, 1584.
Snow, Richard, 1584.
Snow, Richard, 1596.
Snow, Samuel, 1731.
Snow, William, 1692.
Stankes, William, 1727.
Stanley, James, 1712.
Stanley, John, 1703.
Stephens, George, 1663.
Stephens, Henry, 1633.
Stephens, Henry, 1757.
Stephens, Isaac, 1780.
Stephens, John, 1545.
Stephens, Richard, 1621.
Stephens, Richard, 1639.
Stephens, Richard, 1650.
Stephens, Richard, 1694.
Stephens, Richard, 1699.
Stephens, Robert, 1718.
Stephens, Samuel, 1800.
Stephens, Thomas, 1708, Over Lypiatt.
Stephens, Thomas, 1726, Randwick.
Stephens, William, 1684.
Stratford, Elizabeth, 1781.
Stratford, John, 1776.

Stratford, Richard, 1612, Stroud.
Stringer, John, 1606.
Sturmye, Alice, 1604.
Sturmye, Henry, sen., 1599.
Sturmye, Henry, 1600.
Tailor, Robert, 1666.
Tanner, John, 1701.
Tanner, Nathaniel, 1770.
Taylee, Thomas, 1720.
Tayler, Edmund, 1687.
Tayler, Henry, 1621.
Tayler, John, 1574, Stroud.
Tayler, John, 1710, Stroud.
Tayler, Maud, 1573.
Tayler, Richard, 1569.
Tayler, Richard, 1585.
Tayler, Richard, 1682.
Tayloe, Henry, 1681.
Tayloe, Thomas, 1667.
Taylor, Joan, 1673.
Taylor, Nathaniel, 1669.
Taylor, Thomas, 1666.
Taylor, Thomas, 1679.
Taylor, Thomas, 1685.
Teal, James, 1746, Chalford.
Teal, James, 1781.
Test, Robert, 1754.
Tomlins, Robert, 1683.
Torner, William, 1552.
Townsend, Edward, 1681.
Townsend, Henry, 1660-1.
Townsend, Martha, 1763.
Townsend, Mary, 1798.
Townsend, Samuel, 1728.
Townsend, Thomas, 1742.
Trotman, John, 1729.
Turner, Edward, 1727, Througham.
Turner, Elizabeth, 1776.
Turner, Henry, 1599.
Turner, Henry, 1664.
Turner, Henry, 1729.
Turner, John, 1615.
Turner, John, 1681.
Turner, William, 1715.
Tweest, William, 1616.
Tweezle, William, 1616.
Twissell or Twizell, Ann, 1686, Lypiatt.

Twissell, Catherine, 1717.
Twissell, George, 1690.
Twissell, Jane, 1596.
Twissell, John, 1717.
Twissell, John, 1760.
Twissell, Samuel, 1733.
Twissell, Thomas, 1734.
Twissell, William, 1586.
Tyler, James, 1794.
Tyler, John, 1784.
Tyler, Matthew, 1726.
Underwood, Ann, 1770.
Underwood, Thomas, 1723.
Underwood, Thomas, 1776.
Vaizey, Ann, 1799.
Vallender, William, 1730.
Vaughan, Thomas, 1770.
Verinder, Richard, 1597.
Verinder, William, 1711.
Walker, James, 1596.
Walker, John, 1798, Chalford.
Walker, Richard, 1598.
Walker, William, 1733.
Warren, Thomas, 1666.
Wathen, Matthew, 1669.
Weaver, Tristram, 1610.
Webb, Edward, 1559, Stroud in Bisley.
Webb, James, 1669.
Webb, James, 1702.
Webb, James, 1727.
Webb, John, 1719.
Webb, Nathaniel, 1733.
Webb, Sarah, 1748, Chalford.
Webb, Samuel, 1712.
Webb, Samuel, 1762.
Webb, Samuel, 1763.
Webb, William, 1724.
Welch, William, 1787.
Welch, Simon, 1791.
West, William, 1562.
West, William, 1721.
Westrippe, William, 1604.
Wheatley, Samuel, 1723.
Whiteing, Giles, 1721.
Whiteing, William, 1711.
Wight, Richard, 1638.
Wilkins, Deborah, 1729.
Wilie, Anthony, 1565.

Wilie, Anthony, 1610.
Windle, Christopher, 1625.
Winn, Hannah, 1740.
Witts, Frances, 1747.
Witts, Henry, 1737.
Witts, Susan, 1684.
Witts, William, 1686.
Wood, Thomas, 1712.
Woodfield, John, 1741.
Woodfield, Samuel, 1713.
Woodfield, Samuel, 1730.
Woodward, Thomas, 1610.
Workman, Richard, 1721.
Workman, Thomas, 1579.
Wyatt, Ann, 1783.
Wyatt, Daniel, 1790.

Wyatt, Eleanor, 1629.
Wyatt, Samuel, 1783.
Wyatt, Susan, 1738.
Wyatt, William, 1783.
Wynchcombe, Alice, 1591.
Wynchcombe, Mary, 1585.
Yarington, John, 1574.
Yarnton, Margaret, 1589.
Yonge, or Young, Edward, 1638.
Young, Edward, 1650.
Young, Elizabeth, 1723.
Young, Hannah, 1795.
Young, James, 1724.
Young, James, 1764.
Young, John, 1777.
Young, Nathaniel, 1752.

INDEX

Abbenesse, 312. Richard de, 389.
Abnash, 289-292.
 Farm, 334.
Abell, Mrs. George, 52.
 Thomas, 391.
Acchard, John, 281, Thomas 27, 133.
Achrad, Robert, 65.
Adams, John, 312.
Addenbrooke, Rev. A. E., 322.
Adey, Jane, 233.
Agnus Dei at Chantry, 193.
Aland, John, Mary, Sarah, 354.
Albenesse, Richard of, 305.
Aldridge or Alredge. Edward 97, 198,
 388, 402.
 Richard, 55.
 William, 366 (will).
Alexander, chaplain, 18.
All Saints, Bisley, 22.
Alspath (or Alspach) Edmund de 90.
 Gerard de, 31-2.
 John de, 20, 32, 90.
Allen, Samuel, 108-9, 206.
Allesley, Warwick, 236.
Ally, Mary and Thomas, 283.
Alveton, Staffs., 30.
Amener, William, clk., 194.
Anderson, Rev. I. K., 350.
Anne, Queen, 38.
Anstead's farm, 400-1.
Armonde, Robert, vicar, 146.
Armstrong, Bishop, 352.
Arnott, Rev. H., 347, 350.
Arragon, Katharine of, 37.
Arthur, Prince of Wales, 37.
Arundell, John, 102.
 Richard, 231.
 Robert, 49.
Ashmeads, 86, 281, 334, 390, 401.
Astley, Sir Jacob, 232.
Atkyns, Sir Robert, 38, 100, 374, 386.
Avenage Tything, 281-302.
Avening farm, 126.
Avery (or Uphaven) clk., 117, 130, 133.

Bacon, Roger, 355.
Bacoun, John, clk., 119, 138.
Badger, Thomas, 326.
Badlesmere, Bartholomew, 32,
 Elizabeth, 32.
Baghott, arms of 244.
 Sir Paul, 58.
 William, 237.

Baker, John, 280, 287 (will), 364.
 Mary, 286.
 Matthias, 271, 280, 283, 287.
 Matthew, 280.
 Thomas, 275, 280.
Baker, Sir Samuel, 240.
Baldwin, John and Thomas, 95.
Barksdale, Mrs. Mary, 206.
Ball, Henry, clk, 166.
 John Garlic, 296.
 Robert, 228.
Balle Eleanor, 313.
Ballinger, Charles, 198, 206-7, 290, 292,
 315-6, 318, 323-4, 326, 331-2, 333
 (will) 334, 335 (will).
 Henry, 320, 332, 334 (will).
 John, 320, 324, 333-4 (will).
 Maria, 320.
 Mary, 335.
 Walter, 334.
Ballinger family, 286, 331-5.
Barchard, Rev. H. P., 351.
Bardoe, Marmaduke, 74.
Barker, James, 76.
Barker, Rev. C. Raymond, 273.
Barnfield, John, 392.
Barrow, Robert, 83.
Barrows.
 Bourne's Green, 1.
 Camp, 1.
 Giant Stone, 1.
 Long Barrow, 1.
 Money Tump, 2.
 Througham, 2.
Barry, Sir Charles, 320.
Bath, Jacob, 295.
Bathurst, Earl, 98-9.
Batt, John, 325.
 Katharine, 325-6.
 Martha, 392.
 Richard, 325 (will) 326.
 Roger, 269-270 (will), 326, 392.
 Thomas, 322.
Baude, Richard le, 121.
Baylis, Daniel and Thomas, 366.
Baynan, Thomas, 309.
Beale, Dorothea, 342.
 Edward, 336.
 John, 336.
 Miles, 336.
 Samuel, 336.
 Thomas, 204, 302.
Bear Inn, 402-3.

Beard, Mary and Samuel, 327.
Bearde, Henry and Margaret, 405
Beauchamp, Sir Richard, 66, 308.
Beaufort, Joanna, 36.
Bell Inn, 403-4.
Bell-ringing, 185.
Bells, inscriptions on, 185.
Bengh, Catherine and Henry, 324.
Bennet, Elizabeth, 83, 311.
Bennett, Giles, 82.
    Isabella, 275.
    John, 67, 275, 373.
    Joseph, 316.
    Robert, 275.
    Richard, 35, 308.
Bentham, 223.
Berkeley, Sir Maurice, 20, 276.
    Oliver de, 389.
    Thomas, 20.
Berkhamstead, 36.
Berryman, 98.
Betway, John, 249.
Bibury, Bisley piece at, 140.
Biddulph, Lord, 260.
Bidfield, 364-5.
    Richard of, 305.
Bidmead, Anne, 272.
    Betty, 295.
    James, 272, 296.
    Mr. 98.
    Samuel, 272.
    Sarah, 79.
Bigge, arms of, 266.
    Elinor, 384.
Biggs, Elizabeth, 259.
Byg, John, 248.
Bigges, Thomas, 384.
Bigges Place, 248.
Bingle, Thomas, 343.
Birt, William, 106.
Birtwhistle, 273.
Bishop, John, 50.
    Maria, 333.
    Mary, 50-1.
    Sarah, 79.
    William, 403.
Bisley, Hundred of, 36-7.
Bisley (or Bysseley), John, 17, 166.
    Margaret, 16.
    Richard, le Eyr, 16.
    Robert, 166.
    Thomas le Eyr, 16.
    Thomas, 22-3.
Bisley, Boy, fable, 53.
Bisley, Church, seat in, 329.
Bisley Common, 368-373.
Bisley Court House, 375.
Bisley Fair, 374-5, 386-7.
Bisley Market, 374-5, 386-7.
    Pillory at, 374.
    Pound at, 373.
    Prison at, 373.

Bisley Schools, 207-9.
    Spelling of, 5.
    Wells, dressing of, 376.
Bismore, 17, 85, 101, 233.
    Murder at, 245.
Bisrugge, Highway to, 18.
Black death, 379.
Black Ness, 355.
Blackwell, Archer, 198, 323-4.
    Arthur, 295, 393.
    Catherine, 79.
    James, 274.
    John, 79, 294.
    Family, 323.
Blake, Richard, 151, 153, 207, 328.
    William, 127.
Blockley, 330.
Blind House, 373.
Bliss or Blysse, Edward, 326.
    Mary, 326.
    Richard, 143.
    Thomas, 252, 326, 401
    (n) Walter, 401.
    William, 287.
Blue School, 207-8.
Blunde, Maria le, 364.
Bobblewell, 377, 381.
Bodley, architect, 297.
Bolinbroke, Henry, 24.
Bolton, Rev. Henry, 321.
Boningham, 76.
Born, or Burne, 104-5.
Boorne, John, 326.
Bordon, Walter, 116.
Boskenels, William, 135.
Botiller, John, 140, 142.
Boulton, Robert, 97.
Boun, William, 289.
Bourne, 108, 132, 235.
Bourne, House, 404.
Bowcher, John, 404.
Bowman, John, 308.
Bowton, Elizabeth, 146, 196.
    Roger, 196.
    Thomas, 196.
Box, 312.
Bradley, Kathrin, 105.
    William, 109.
Bradwell, Wilts., 225.
Brainford, 147.
Braose, William de, 26.
Brattons, 58-9, 395.
Brewery, Stroud, 250.
Bridges, or Bridge, Alice, 126.
    Elizabeth, 325.
    Giles, 276.
    George, 93-4.
    Henry, 126, 313-4.
    Thomas, 308, 326.
Bridstow, 334.
Brimsfield, 34, 37.
Britton, Camanuel, 152.

Britton, Richard, 150, 160.
　Sarah, 150.
Britton, Richard, Complaint of, 151-2.
Bromwich, Edward, 88, 91, 101.
　Margaret, 88, 91.
Broughton, James, 357.
　Henry, 54, 70, 394.
　William, 106.
Brown, Dr. E., 296.
Browne, Grace, 232.
　James, 103.
　John, 42, 232, 272.
　Thomas, 83, 94, 336.
Browns Hill, 154.
　Chapel at, 114.
　House, 349, 353, 355.
　Windmill at, 337.
Bruce, Miss, 100.
Bryan, Bishop, 123, 135.
Buckingham, Earl and Marquis, 38, 109,
　329, 396.
Bulkeley, John, 85.
　Hon. Thomas Coventry, 128.
Burgess, John, 166.
Burgeys, Robert, vicar, 135-7.
Burgh, John de, 31.
Burnewater, 220, 308.
Buck, Alice, 81.
Buckle, Rev. W., 273.
Burdocke, Alice, 110.
Burdon, Archdeacon, 131.
Burne, John, 24.
Burroughs, or Burrows, Deborah, 332.
　James, 85.
　John, 85.
　Mary, 286.
　Robert, 82, 85.
　Sarah, 295.
　William, 56.
Bussage, 305.
　Church, 344-7.
　Curate of, 159.
　Farm, 349.
　House, 318, 341-2.
　House of Mercy, 352.
　Parish boundaries, 347-8.
　Protestant attack of, 350-1.
　Tything of, 338-363.
　Vicarage of, 352.
　Woods, 338-9.
Butcher, Samuel, 69.
Butt, Alice, 231.
　Jane, 45.
　John, 24, 308.
　Richard, 86, 253 (will).
　Thomas, 251, 292.
　Thomas Packer, 198, 331.
　Walter, 251-2 (will), 308, 312.
　William, 231, 312.
Buttle, Rev. W. Francis, 128.
Butler, Jane, 268.
　John, 196, 389, 391 (will), 402.

Butler, Maud, 364.
　Nathaniel, clk., 268.
　Richard, 155.
　Thomas, 364.
　Bequest, 390.
Byan, William, vicar, 139.
Byrde, Richard, 126.
Bysrugge, John of, 339.
　Walter of, 305, 339.
　William of, 27, 133, 339.

Caldecote, Hugh de, 134.
Calf, William, vicar, 130, 133.
Calfway farm, 110.
Calfway wood, 45, 390.
Camm, M. G., 297.
Canon Frome, 352.
Caperoun, Robert, vicar, 135.
Capner, Mary, 263.
Carder, Rev. W. J., 322.
Carpenter Bishop, 120.
Carpenter, Roger, vicar, 139.
Castle at Stroud, 257.
Castleman, Edward, 294.
　John, 308.
Catchpike, Chalford, 375-6.
Catesbye, Robert, 227.
Catswood, 399-400.
Cavendish Hall, Suffolk, 348.
Cawdwell, 76.
Cecill, William, 310.
Chalford, 253.
Chalford or Chalkford, Edward, 257.
　Elias, 304, 306.
　Henry de, 16.
　Hugh de, 305.
　Richard, 166.
　Robert, 15.
　William, 23, 26, 33, 276, 284, 304-7.
Chalford, Church, 319-321.
　Estate, 307.
　Mill, 309-310.
　Place, 304, 309.
　Riot at, 309.
　Tything, 303.
　Workhouse, 317.
Chamber, William, 104.
Chamberlayne, Ann and Thomas, 260.
Champernowne, Rev. R., 168, 273, 354.
Champion, Richard, 49, 210, 291.
Champneys, Henry and Margaret, 90-1.
Chapman, Rev. J., 79.
　Mr., 98.
Chandos, Lord John, 313.
Chantry of Our Lady, 143-4.
　Crucifix from, 195.
　Foundation of, 190-1.
　House, 195.
　Land, 196-7.
　Tenants, 197.
Chapel of the Good Shepherd, Browns-
　hill, 336.

Charities of Bisley, 205-7.
Charleton, Robert de, 123, 192.
Charlton, Oswald, 34, 289.
Chedworth. 332-3.
  Thomas, 66.
Chester, Earls of. Hugh, 9, 10, 64, 212.
  Charter of, 11.
  Randolph, 10, 12.
  Richard, 10.
Cheyney, Bishop of Gloucester, 145.
Chew, Richard, 365 (will).
Child, Sir William, 234.
Chircheheye, Nicholas atte.
Church, chest, 188.
  Neglect of, 145.
  Plate, 186.
  Restoration, 158.
  Wardens' accounts, 187-9.
Church, Hannah, 279.
Churchdown, Church, 260.
Church Hill, Aveniss, 201-2.
  Brownshill, 202.
Cirencester Abbey, 144, 267-8.
  St. John, 221.
  St. Thomas, 339.
  Star Inn, 288. ,
Clappen, John, 97.
Clare, Arms of, 174.
  Eleanor de, 31.
  Elizabeth de, 31.
  Gilbert de, 28, 31.
  Richard de, 14, 121.
  Thomas de, 32.
Clarence, Lionel, Duke of, 33.
Clarke, Rev. G., 157.
  Elizabeth, 56.
  Henry, 295.
  Lionel, 87.
  Richard, 35, 54.
  William, 70, 399.
Claville, Andrew, 90, 251.
  Richard de, clk., 123, 134-5.
Clay, Rev. W. J., 160.
Clements, Thomas, 365.
Clifford, Henry de, 21, 89, 90, 101, 251.
  James, 22.
  John, 22-3, 32, 85, 99-100, 218, 244, 247.
Cliffisale, 66, 70-72.
Clinton, John de, 32, 35.
Clissale, Richard, 23, 70-1. (will), 74, 305.
  Thomas, 66-7.
Clissold, Gabriel and Hugh, 207.
  Henry, 67.
  John, 294, 404.
  Peter, 44, 48, 56, 267, 302.
  Samuel, 284, 375.
  Thomas, 42, 107, 231, 366-7, 403.
  William, 366-7 (will).
Clopton, Alice, 225.
  William, 226.

Clutterbuck, 253.
  Edmund, 50, 210, 294, 341.
  Samuel, 259.
  Thomas, 259, 260, 335.
  William, 151-3, 167.
Clyveshale, Henry de, 65.
  Richard de, 16, 19, 32, 66, 70, 90, 193, 251.
Cobham, Bishop, 117.
Cockes, Thomas and William, 68.
Codrington, Francis, 85, 101.
  Giles, Richard and William, 101.
Coffin lids, incised, 182.
Coffins, fishtail, 382.
Coke, Thomas, 312.
Colcombe (Cowcombe), 276, 306.
  Walter of, 276.
College Cottage, 315-7.
Coles, Hugh, 59.
Collins, Henry, 343.
  Thomas, 340, 343.
Coln St. Aldwyns, 226.
Combare, Richard, the, 304.
Company's Arms, Chalford, 315.
Composition, Exemplifications of, 141-2.
Compton, Arms of, 310.
  Alice, 312.
  Elizabeth, 309.
  Francis, 312, 404.
  Henry, 105, 125, 126 (will), 312.
  Joan, 127, 314.
  John, 60.
  Walter, 38, 60, 68, 125, 127, 146, 196, 309-313.
  William, 309, 311 (will).
Condon, David, vicar, 144.
Conisborough, Richard de, Earl of Cambridge, 34.
Cook, or Cooke, John, 360, 394.
  Robert, 360 (will).
  Thomas, 83, 104.
  William, 274.
Cookson, Rev. E., 299.
Cooper, Mrs. V. M., 52.
Cope, Anthony, 196.
Copsgrove, 224, 228.
Copsgrove, Agnes, 41, 395-7.
  William de, 18.
Cork cutting, 356.
Cornish, Rev. C., 159.
Corpus Christi College, 309, 324, 334, 338-9.
Corse, 223.
Corbels, Portrait heads, 176.
  Saxon King, 180.
Corbet, Joan, 20, 30.
  Peter, 16, 29, 30.
  Robert, 12.
Cordell, Sir William, 226.
Cotes, Robert de, 100.
Court House Inn, 281-3.
Court rolls at Lypiatt, 39.

Coventry, Lord and Lady, 128, 151.
Cockes, Thomas and William, 267.
Cox(e), Anthony, 150, 362.
  Ambrose, 340.
  Charles, 203, 260, 334, 356.
  Judge, 261, 263.
  Charles Westley, 262.
  John, 262.
  Nathan, 340.
  Thomas, 245, 334, 340.
Coxwell, John, 290, 337.
  Nathaniel, 251, 252.
Corderoy, arms of, 293.
  Ann, 45, 293.
  Edward, 294 (will).
  Jasper, 292.
  John, 293.
  Robert, 294, 391.
Corderries, 292-6.
Cricketty Mill, 391.
Cripps, Charles, 59.
  Hester, 290.
  John, 290.
  Joseph, 326.
Cronste, Robert, 89.
Crook, Thomas, 274.
Crosses, 372.
Cross of Mary, 215.
Croxdon Abbey, 30.
Crundall, Bechely, 242.
  Henry, 296.
Cuffe, Richard, 256.
Culham, Thomas, clk., 93.
Cull, Hester, 47.
  John, 48, 365.
  Stephen, 48.
Cullerne, Joseph, 205, 325-6.
Cummins, William, 79.
Currier, Jane, 88.
Cussy, John, 67.

Daglingworth, 79.
Damsell, Henry, 272.
  John, 33.
  Nathaniel, 200, 268, 284.
  Samuel, 268, 283-4 (will).
  William, 335.
Dangerfield, W., 98, 324.
Daniel's farm, 395.
Dashwood, F. J. de Courcy, 324.
Daubeney, General, 63.
Davis or Davys, Abraham, 288, 349, 396-7.
  Family, 385.
  Giles, 247, 249 (I.P.M.), 258, 274.
  Handey, 59.
  John, 288, 397 (will).
  Philip, 296.
  Rebecca, 235.
  Richard, 361.
  Thomas, 289.
  William, 201, 342-3, 348, 362, 396.

Dawes, Mrs. M. K., 52.
Dean, Beds., 236.
Dean, Rev. E. N., 349, 350.
  Mrs., 52.
Deane, Clutterbuck, 61.
Dearmer, Mrs. Mabel, and Dr. Percy, 269.
De Bary, Charles Rudolph, 324.
Deboneyr, Henry le and Laetitia, 16.
De Belmis, Philip, 12.
De Bisley, Arms of, 15.
  Emma, 66.
  Hawisia, 15, 304.
  Henry, 20, 165.
  Hugh, 16, 17, 19, 22, 40, 89, 91, 123, 218, 247, 251, 254, 304, 306.
  John, 33, 165.
  Philip, 13, 15.
  Rades, 165.
  Ralph, clk., 164-5.
  Richard, 15-7. 19-21, 29-30, 89, 165, 190, 251.
  Roesia, 15.
  Roger, 19.
  Robert, vicar, 130.
  Sodewigius, 12, 15.
  Thomas, 15-7, 19, 304.
  Walter, 89.
  William, 21, 66, 165.
De Bohun, Eleanor, 23.
  Henry, 28, 217.
  Humphrey, 11, 13, 21, 23, 28, 123, 212-215.
  Grant of, 215-7, 247.
  Joan, 212.
  Mary, 23, 24, 88, 305.
  William, 33.
Decroc, Benjamin, 251.
De Freville, Rev. F. P., 274.
De la Bere, Arms of, 244.
  Anne, 232.
  John, 232.
  Kinard, 234, 236.
  William Baghott, 237-9.
De Laci, Roger, 10.
De la Strode, Henry, 15.
De Maisi, William, 13.
Denman, Thomas, 83.
Denton, Richard, 20, 110.
Denway, 88-91.
  House, 98.
  Oratory at, 89.
Deptcombe Grove, 358.
Despencer, Hugh le, 28-9, 31.
De Tilleul, Robert, 9.
De Verdun, Theobald, 16.
Dill, Dr. M. G., 296.
Dog Whipper, 189, 382.
Doherty, Rev. A. P., 274.
Dolman, Lawrence, 247.
  Thomas, 140.
  William, 255.

Domesday Book, 9-13.
Donecan, Thomas, clk., 34, 120, 139, 193.
Dorington, Arms of, 241.
   Sir John, 39, 69, 74, 103, 241, 249, 398.
   John Edward, 240.
   Windows to, 185-6.
Dowell, Chrycham, 76.
   James, 331.
Dower, Denys, 255.
   Hugh, 255.
   John, 145.
   Richard, 399.
   Robert, 399.
Down and Connor, Bishop of, 140.
Downton, William, 71.
Draycott, 334.
Drake's House, 402.
Drawbridge, Rev. W. B., 350.
Drew, John, 342.
Drewe, Rev. F. W., 322.
Driftcombe, 284.
Driver, Charles, 280, 403.
   Deborah, 261.
   Family, 87.
   Nathaniel, 367.
   Richard, 49, 56, 403.
   T. C., 269.
   Widow, 403.
Duck, Abigail, 152.
Dudbrigge, Isabella and John, 66.
Duntisbourne, 79.
   Alexander de, 212.
   Abbots, 332.
   Rous, 78.
Duriard, Henry le, 254.
   Roger, 247.
   Richard, 281.
Duryste, 223.
Dyer, John, 105.
Dyryse, 75.
Dyson, Reginald J., 52.

Eales, Thomas, 146.
Earl, or Erle, Walter, 67, 267.
Eastcombe, 338, 359-363.
   Baptist Chapel at, 342, 362-3.
   Church and school, 362.
   Manor Farm, 114, 359, 360.
   Windmill at, 362.
Eaton, Rev. Thomas K., 273.
Eccles, Thomas, 145.
Eckold, Thomas, 44.
Edgeworth, Peter de, 389.
   Thomas of, 133.
Edridge, John, 374.
Edward, Black Prince, 20.
Edward IV., 36.
Edward, John, vicar, 138, 192.
Edwards, Dr. C. D., 296.
   John, priest, 166, 220, 224.

Edwards, Thomas, 234.
Effigy outside Church, 172-3.
Egerley, John, 144.
Egge, John del, 389.
Eggeworth, Geoffry, 100n.
   Robert de, 90.
   Thomas de, 27, 100n.
Elburow, Joseph, 296.
Elcombe, Edmund de, vicar, 118, 135.
   Grange, 135.
Eldridge, William, 46-7.
Eleanor, Queen, 27.
Elizabeth, Princess, 37.
   Queen, 37, 40.
Ellen, Robert, 258.
Elshawe, Henry, 88.
Emigration from Bisley, 380.
Endowment of Stroud, 130-3.
Epidemics, 147, 155.
Estrick, Reginald, 19.
Essex, Earl of, 217.
Ethelbald, charter of, 8.
Evans, Rev. A. W., 300.
   Thomas, 336.
   William, 357.
Everard, William, 220.
Evreux, John of, 117.
Ewyas Lacy, 30.

Faber, Ellis, 339.
   John, 306.
   Peter, 339.
   William, 16, 30.
Fabian, John, 361.
Fairford, 295.
Farmer, Rev. H., 273.
Farr, Thomas, 292.
Fawkes, 226.
Felde, John atte, 30, 54, 90, 251.
Felpe, Edythe, 378.
Fenchurch, St. Gabriel, 256.
Fennell's farm, 398-9.
Fennell Walter, 257.
Fenny Ditton, 123.
Feoffees, Bisley, 198-9.
Ferre, Radulphus, 19, 305.
Ferrers, Isabel de, 26.
Ferris Court, 101-112.
Ferneley, Jane, 152.
   Richard, 403.
Fettiplace, Jane, 45.
Field, Anthony, 230.
   Giles, 231.
   James, 359.
   John, 246.
   Thomas, 231.
Fiennes, Sir William, 27.
Firwood, Brownshill, 205, 284, 335-7, 350.
Fishpond, 213, 355.
Fitzalan, John, 26.
Flaxley, Abbot of, 220.

Fletcher, Ann and Edward, 328.
Font, Norman, 172, 178-9.
Forestario, Thomas, 19.
Fotheringay Castle, 36.
Fowler, Ann, 96-7.
  Daniel, 249.
  Henry, clk., 248 (I.P.M.), 249.
  John, 96-7, 144 (vicar).
  Richard, 248, (I.P.M.) 249, 337.
  Roger, 43, 143, 252, 278, 406.
  William, 249.
Fox, Bishop of Winchester, 309.
Frampton, (or Frompton), John, 30, 33, 36, 139, 275-7, 306-7, 398.
  Walter, 277 (will).
Frampton's Place, 268-275-8.
France Lynch Church, 297.
  Meeting, 301-2, 332-3.
  Pastors of, 302.
  Old Vestry, 302.
  Vicarage, 300-1.
Franceys, Edmund, 22.
Franklin, Francis, 337.
  Joseph, 318.
Freame or Freme, Arms of, 259, 260, 266.
  Anne, 398.
  Catherine, 253.
  Edward, 398.
  Giles, 258.
  James, 257.
  Joan, 143, 253 (will) 398.
  John, 256 (will).
  Richard, 256.
  Robert, 257-8 (will).
  Thomas, 85 (will), 104, 106, 219, 248, 252, 255-9, 306, 366.
  William, 85, 104, 133, 221, 260, 401 (will).
  Widow, 252.
Freeman, John, 282.
Fresco in Church, 178.
Friars of Gloucester, 220.
Fripe, William de la (Frith), 23, 305.
Frith Wood, 316.
Frome, Isabel and William, 68, 267.
Frost, William, 66.
Fryer, Mark, 297.
Fulk, William, son, of, 65.
Fust, Edward, 235-6.
  Sir John, 235.

Gabb, Richard, 323.
Galon, Hugh, 90.
Gamage, Gilbert, 246.
Gardiner, Rev. E. C., 263.
  Jasper, 290, 334.
  Mr., 354.
  Thomas C., 296.
  William, 263, 289.
  William B., 324.
Gathorne, John, 168.

Gatley, Margaret, 147.
Gaunt, John of, 36.
Gaveston, Peter de, 28.
Gawde, Thomas, 120.
May, Mary, 358.
Gegge, Thomas, 83.
Geneworth, Henry de, 89.
George, Hugh, 38.
  Jane, 270.
Gerard, chaplain, 164.
Gerveys, John, 66.
Giffard, Bishop, 115.
Gilbert, Thomas, 364.
Glazebrook, Benjamin and Joseph, 295.
Glebe land, 161.
Glewstone, 333.
Gloucester and Bristol, Bishop of, 319.
Gloucester, St. Bartholomew Hospital, 17, 221.
  St. Margaret's Hospital, 17.
Goathouse, 361.
Goddard, George, 51.
Godman, George, 51.
  Joseph and Susan, 240.
Godman Dorington, Major, 241.
Golden Valley, 303-4.
Golding, Joan and William, 364.
Gompertz, Rev. Samuel, 321.
Goodlake, Thomas Mills, 69, 128.
Gordon, Ann, 262.
  Anna, 348.
  John, General, 51-2.
  Robert, 262.
  Sarah, M. S., 52.
Gordon House, France Lynch, 296-7.
Grange, The, Bussage, 344.
Graunger, John, vicar, 138, 193.
Gravener, Richard, clk., 104, 167, 312.
Grazebrook, Joseph and Hester, 58, 156.
Greenwich, East, manor of, 37.
Greer, Joan, 100.
Gregory, Edward, 204-5.
  Rev. Robert, 169, 273.
  Thomas, 204-5 (will), 333.
  William, 51.
Green Court, Chalford, 325.
Green, John, 167.
Greenhull, Richard atte., 396.
Greville, William, 221.
Grey de Wilton, Lord, 365.
Greycote Cottage, Oakridge, 269.
Greys, The, 73-4, 78-9.
Griffin, Elizabeth, 249.
  John, 249.
  Rev. John, 300.
  Margerie, 248.
  Thomas, 256, 365.
Griffin's Mill, 249, 336.
Grismont, 333.
Grime, Anthony, 406.
  John, 278, 308, 309 (will).
  William, 109, 355.

Grymes, John, 143, 194 (will).
Grove, The, Chalford, 323-5.
Gubbins, William, 334.
Guisborough, Bishop, 133.
Gunter, James and William, 365.
Gurner, John, 268.
  Samuel, 344.
Gwyn, W. J., 242.
Gyse, Sir Anselm de, 16.
  John, 308.

Hakborn, Walter, clk., 119.
Haklut, John, clk., 117, 134.
Hale, Richard, 231.
Hall, John, 318.
  Thomas, 50, 282.
  William, 317-8, 398.
Hallyday, Francis, 276.
  Richard, 312.
Hammond, Frederick, 318, 326n.
Hamsden, Dr., 296.
Hamstead, Capt. John, 57-8.
Hancox, Arms of, 92.
  Family, 91-8.
  Alice, 93-4 (will).
  Edward, 297.
  Henry, 95 (will), 297.
  Henry William, tragedy of, 98.
  John, 92 (will), 99.
  Marjorie, 105.
  Nathaniel, 96 (will), 97, 198.
  Patience, 296.
  Peter, 88.
  Robert, 70.
  Sara, 43, 45.
  Walter, 97 (will), 104.
  William, 95, 96 (will), 268.
Hanestie, Robert de, 18.
Harrison, Rev. George, 167.
Hartland, Edward, 288.
  John, clk., 167.
Harvey, Charles, 69.
  Henry de, clk., 123.
  Sir William, 74.
Hastings, Warren, 296.
Hathaway, John, 66.
Hauchell, Sir Ralph, 143, 166.
Haven, The, Bussage, 344.
Hauthon, Joan, 288.
Hawker, Samuel, 238.
Hawkins, Anne, 378.
  Edward, vicar, 156.
  Margaret, 94.
Haynes, Edward, 80, 82.
  Thomas, 283.
Hayward, Rev. H. F., 351.
  William, 356.
Heaven, John, 107.
Heelas, Mrs. Wilberforce, 324.
Helme, William M., 366.
Helyom of Edgeworth, 100n., 269.
  Sir Walter, 16.

Herbert, Joan, 94.
  Thomas, 307.
  Sir W., 310.
Here, John, 70.
Hereford, Duke of, 91, 100.
Heron, Sir William, 22.
Hervey, Henry, clk., 117.
  Mary and William, 364.
Heskynnes, Alice, 311.
Heywood, Oliver, vicar, 273.
Hidde, Richard, clk., 120.
Hiett, Richard, 226.
Higgins Court, 54, 95.
Higons, Thomas, 54.
Hikcokkes, John, 22.
Hildeberwerth, 117.
Hill, Rev. Erroll, 168.
  Robert, 91, 99.
  William, 228.
Hill House, 92, 94, 99.
Hipkyne, Robert, clk., 194.
Hitchcock, Rev. W. M., 349.
Hitcham, Giles, and John, 383.
Hodges, James, 318, 342.
Hodson, Rev. A. J., 322.
Hokkenale, William, 254.
Holford, Thomas, 221.
Holland, Alianora, 34.
  Mary, 391.
  Thomas, Duke of Kent, 34.
Holyday, Francis, 313.
  James, 360 (will).
  John, 361.
  Richard, 312, 337.
  Thomas, 253.
  William, 361, 272.
Holywell, Oakridge, 268.
Hone, Margery, 327.
  Robert, 329.
Hook, Samuel, 318.
Hop, family, 76.
Hopton, Elizabeth, 295.
  Ferdinand, 404-6.
  Henry, 405.
  Humphrey, 405.
  Joan (will), 405.
  Rev. John, 352.
  Richard, 47, 61.
  Samuel, 405 (will).
  William, 313-4, 404 (will).
  Rev. William P., 355.
Hornby, Miss B.. 269.
  William M., 392.
Horston, Richard, 167.
Horwood, Martha, 340.
Hospital of St. John, Prior of, 23.
Housman, Rev. Thomas, 168.
Houghton, F. T. 5.
How, William, 166.
Howell, Thomas, 366.
  Thomas Perrin, 336.
  William, 361.

Hoylon, John, 123.
Hues, Thomas, 377.
Hughes, Joan, 80.
Hullasey, Manor of, 260.
Hullavington, 139.
Hulle, John, vicar, 138.
Hundred Court, 37.
Hunt, Robert, 70-1.
   Sarah, 328.
   William, 377.
Hunting of vermin, 116.
Huntley Cottage, 337.
Hurdon, Thomas, 208.
Huscrofte, Sir Edmond, 383.
Hutton, Rev. C. J., 318, 321.
Hyde, Elizabeth, 253.
   Gloucester, 17.
   Minchinhampton, 317, 336.
Hyde Court, 317.
Hywyssh, 138.

Icombe, 224.
Iles, arms of, 393.
   Ann, 267.
   John, 290, 295.
   Thomas, 267, 392 (will).
   Farm, 391-3.
   Mill, 334.
Innell, Charles, 209, 295.
   James, 326.
   John, 316, 326, 332.
   Tomb, 302.
Insell, Ann, 326.
Interdict on Bisley Churchyard, 140.
Ireland, William, 146.
   Rev. William, S. de Courcy, 322.
Isabella, Queen, 28.
Iscombe, Felicia and Walter, 359.

James I., 38.
Jayne, or Jeyne, Arms of, 57.
   Catherine, 93.
   Elizabeth, 292.
   Henry, 55 (will), 267, (will).
   Richard, 292.
   Thomas, 54, 56-7, 95-6.
   Thomas Tyndall, 55, 57.
   Walter, 95.
   William, 55-6, 93.
Jaynes Court, 14, 38, 54, 60.
   Cockpit at, 60.
Jeffries, Richard, 344.
   William, 270.
Jeffry, Rev. H. A., 51, 168.
Jenkins, John, 335.
Jennings, Mrs. Mary, 79.
Jew, Daniel, 174.
Joiners, 210.
Jolliffe, J. S., 240.
Jones, David, 140.
   Gilbert, 366.
   Rev. John, 167.

Jones, Joseph, 392.
   J. W., 321.
   Nathaniel, 318, 320, 326.
   Sir Robert, 143.
   Sir Roger, 194-5.
   Sarah, 333.
   Thomas, 282, 334.
   William, 392.
Jotham, Anne, 332.
Jurdan, Reginald, 27, 133.

Kearsey, Woodroffe, 51.
Keble, Rev. John, 157.
   Mary, 329.
   Thomas, 203-4, 329, 330, 340.
   Rev. Thomas, senr., 156-8, 209.
   Rev. Thomas, junr., 159-160, 299.
   Window to, 185.
Kelston, Som., 156.
Kemble, 226.
Kemerton, 348.
Keene, James, 210, 394.
Kene, Edmund, 146.
Kerry, Rev. J. C., 299.
King, Robert and Thomas, 108.
Kingscotte, Thomas, 67.
Kingsford, Rev. H., 322.
Kingston family, 383.
   Robert, 276.
   Sir William, 365.
Kingswood, Abbot of, 221.
   Abbey of, 388.
Kirby, Rebecca and Roger, 270.
Kirby's Cottage, 352.
Knight, John, clk., 82, 167, 339.
   Philip, 292.
Knights Hospitallers, 144, 247.
Kynge, Matthew, 68-9.
Kynne, Agnes, and Richard, 306.
   Robert, 67.

Labanus, Bartholomew, 215.
Lacy, Mary de, 30.
   Peter de, 117-9, 135-6, 138.
   Roger de, 64.
   Walter de, 30, 118.
Lady, statue of Our, 183.
Lambert, 69, 295.
   William T., 324.
Lambe, Sir John, 149.
Lastyrie, Marquise de, 128, 164.
Latymer Master, 224.
Lawford, Daniel, vicar, 149.
Le Bret, Nicholla, Richard and William, 217.
Leghe, William de, vicar, 134.
Le Eyr, Henry (de Bisley) 134, 305.
   Hugh and Richard, 134.
   Robert, 130.
Leckhampton, 23.
Lediard, Mrs. 51.

Lediard, William, 267.
Legrove, Old Sodbury, 236.
Leversage, Peter, 78, 103, 238-9, 249, 330.
Lewis, Samuel, 344.
  William, 196, 240.
Llewellin, Prince of Wales, 26.
Lewnod, 64.
Lisle, Viscount, 229.
Libby, Mr. 336.
Litteridge, Roger of, 16.
Litteridge, Cross, 268, 284.
  Way, 112.
Lightfoot, John, vicar, 71, 77, 146-7, 357, 378-9.
Lilyhorn, 4, 5, 283-4, 335.
Llanthony, Prior of, 118.
Limes, The, cottage at, 297.
Lippiatt, meaning of, 7.
Lodge, Joseph, vicar, 153.
Long, William de, clk., 89, 343.
Longford, Walter de, 276.
Long, Tunn, 45, 293.
Looker, John, 70-1 (will).
Lord, Aaron, and Mary, 302.
  William, clk., 167.
Lord's Stone, Stancombe, 213-5.
Lowder, Rev. W., 51, 169, 175.
Lowe, James, vicar, 143, 194.
  John, 320.
Lugg, John, 394.
  Richard, 255, 394.
  Robert, 317.
  William, 394 (will).
Lupeyeat, Henry de, 212, 215-7.
Lutrugge, 18.
Lyday, Farm, 268.
  Richard, 268, 284.
Lymbrick, John, 276, 397-8.
  Thomas, 308.
Lynthon, Richard de, clk., 116, 191.
Lyon, Rev. W. G., 300.
Lypiatt, John, Nicholas and Thomas, 165.
  Philip, 166.
Lypiatt (Over), Capture of, 232.
  Chapel, 3, 90, 138, 218, 230, 235, 239, 244.
  Cundite, 244.
  Granary, 243.
  Manor, 23, 212-245.
  Mansion, 243.
Lypiatt (Middle), 245-250.
Lypiatt (Nether), 23, 254-263.
  Gates, 261.
  Hall, 263-5.
  Mills at, 248.
  Monument, 261-2.
  Skeletons at, 265.
  Tapestries, 265.
Lytley, Alice and John, 310.

Macleod, Rev. N. D., 350-1.
Magee, J., 93.
Magnet House, Bisley, 402.
Malecote, Robert of, 281.
Malmesbury, Roger, clk., 120.
Malthouse (Overcourt), 52.
Mansfield, Rev. Edward, vicar, 58, 156, 395.
  Hester, 59-61.
  Sir James, 156.
Mansion, The, 62-3.
Manwaring, Edward, 228, 398.
March, Edmund, Earl of, 247.
  Countess of, 289.
Marle Hill House, 324-5.
Marshall, Thomas, 256, 310-1.
Martelye, Walter de, clk., 165.
Martyn, William, 104.
Masefield, John, poem of, 280.
Mason, Grace, 80.
  Richard, 97.
Massey, Col., 232.
Masters, Family, 383.
  Thomas, 38, 293.
  Walter, 94, 384.
Matherune, Richard le, 364.
Matthews, 200, 325.
Maunsell, Arms of, 218.
  John, 165, 217.
  Margaret, 217.
  Nicholas, 90.
  Philip, 218-9.
  Thomas, 90, 218, 244.
  William, 212-3 (I.P.M.), 218.
Mawbey, Sir James, 335.
Mawer, Professor, 6.
Maydeston, Bishop Walter, 174.
Mayo, Henry, 229.
  Hester, 335.
  James, 209.
  John, 283, 335.
Maysey, John, 289-290 (will), 291-2, 335.
  Richard, 291-2.
  William, 81, 291-2.
Medeford, Richard de, clk., 119.
  Walter de, clk., 119, 138-9, 193.
Meriet, Robert, vicar, 138, 193.
Merlymond, Oliver de, 25.
Merry, Thomas, 279.
Meyrick, Rev. T., 179.
Miers, F. R., 59.
Mill, John, 154.
  Mary, 109.
Millard, Richard, 331.
Mills, Daniel, 330.
  Deborah, 210.
  John, 210, 334.
  Mary, 334.
  Sarah, 330.
Mills, William Yarnton, 57, 128, 164.
Millswood, 318-9.

Minchinhampton, Gilles, 221.
Mapelenemead, 306.
Muggemore, 104.
Miserden House, 334.
Mody, Agnes, 308.
Edmund, 309.
John, 308-9.
Thomas, 21, 89, 90, 220.
Monmouth, Henry de, 131.
John de, 23, 90, 246, 251.
Richard de, 22, 306.
Robert de, 276.
Thomas de, 254, 384.
Montacute, William, Earl of Salisbury, 33.
Philippa, 33.
More, Edward, 308.
Richard, clk., 193.
Morris, Mary and Peter, 294.
Mortimer, Anne 34.
Edmund, 27, 31, 33-4, 88, 116, 120-1, 133.
Hugh, Parson of Bisley, 18-9, 26, 116-7, 121, 190.
Hugh (Earl), 26-7.
Matilda, 31, 116.
Philip, 12, 26, 305.
Ralph, 25-7, 305.
Roger, 11, 25-8, 31-4, 115, 117, 123, 135, 368-9.
Mortimer's Farm, 56, 61, 76, 95.
Moulson, Thomas, 232.
Mounteagle, Lord, letter from, 227.
Mummers, 382.
Munden, John, 95.
Samuel, 360-1 (will).
Munro, Rev. Charles, 299.
Mutton Lane, 335.
Mull, Edmund, 364.
Edward, 309.
John, 307.
Marjorie, 276, 307.
Reginald, 308.
Thomas, 276, 307, 319.
Sir William, 307.
Murders. 13

NAMES OF FIELDS AND OTHER
   LOCALITIES :—
Ashland, 286.
Baldwins, 56.
Barnhegge, 24.
Battlescombefield, 108, 277.
Belchers Mead, 328, 333.
Bidcombes, 201.
Bittcombe, Great and Little, 286.
Blacks, 24.
Blackwells, 56, Grove, 88, 109.
Bouncehorn, 293.
Brillings Frith, 316.
Brockleys Acre, 291.
Buriat, 269.
Bushley, 19.

NAMES OF FIELDS AND OTHER
   LOCALITIES :—
Busshey Closes, 248.
Chefrudinge, 18.
Chelmarsh, 293.
Church Grove, 204.
Church Piece, 4, 170.
Clissold's Glade, 70.
Colliers, 228, 231-3, 396.
Cook's Hill, 59.
Coppice Wood, 390.
Countermead Grove, 97.
Coventry Lands, 128.
Coxlease, 278.
Crockelporne, 18.
Crossfield, 399.
Customs Scrubbs, 3.
Cuthams, 355-6.
Dagnash Wood, 233.
Davis Copsgrove, 230.
Dimallsdale, 201.
Dowers, 224.
Dowrie, Le, 47.
Ekins, 108.
Etheridge Wood, 112.
Far Hill, 58.
Ferres, Little, 102.
Fidges, 360.
Flagghey Meadow, 106.
Freame's Hill, 333.
Frithlond, Le, 305.
Frogmoor, 279.
Frythland, 27.
Fuerin Mead, 105.
Gater Leys, 291.
Goathouse Ground, 393.
Gossengrove, 268, 284.
Gratton Grounds, 111.
Hale, The, 106, 300.
Halhymediche, 18.
Hardings, 108-9.
Hasell Meade, 248.
Haskins Wood, 291.
Hawerugge, 220.
Hawkins, 399.
Hawkley Combe, 284.
Hawkley Wood, 128, 268.
Hayhedge, 153n.
Herringate, 56, 112, 268.
Highmead, 88, 109, 233, 109.
Holbrooke, 110.
Horshalles, 339.
Huckwills Cort, 106-7.
Hurhelyate, 18.
Innock, 57.
Kirbys, 55.
Litteridge Wood, 49.
Lilygate, 268.
Longney, 81.
Losemore, 223.
Lugg's Frith, 49, Leaze, 390.
Luterage, 24.

Names of Fields and other
  Localities :—
Lyes, The, 333.
Mayseys Grove, 334.
Millmead, 279.
Newman's Close, 97.
North Ekins, 92.
Nottingham Corner, 340.
Ockfields Mead, 95.
Oldhills, 334.
Otesland, 56.
Parkers Hill Combe, 255, Leaze, 82.
Parsons Meade, 108-9.
Pathcombe, 21, 305.
Patts, 152n, 153.
Paynes (Nashend), 394.
Peletys Mede, 275.
Perks, 343.
Perelond, 21, 89.
Peweslond, 89.
Peyntenesfryth, 24.
Piketteshey, 306.
Pirleyehulle, 18.
Priests, 154, 248.
Pyerhyncumbe, 223.
Quanly, 270.
Rea Rhode Close, 291.
Redes, 108-9.
Rhodegate, 291.
Ridings, 44, 75, 86.
Rogers Wood, 359.
Rolles Croft, 248.
Rudgeborne, 306.
Rudge Hill, 67.
Sackeritch, 94.
Sadwells, 106.
Salemons, 306.
Seabarnes, 282, 312, 334.
Sheephouse Close, 81.
Shermans, 255.
Sidnams Way, 111.
Slatters, 399.
Sowmead, 83.
Soweruydyngge, 306.
Stancombe, 17.
Ash, 398.
Starry Hill, 302.
Sterts, 215, 217, 250-1, 358.
Sterteland, 89.
Stonyruydonge, 306.
Stookeys Close, 268, 284.
Stubby Close, 106.
Swynesley, 312.
Symundshale, 389.
Tagonheggo, 24.
Taylors, 293.
Tomlines, 72.
Twissel Stone, 268, 284.
Tymbercombe, 24, 312.
Tymberhulle, 18.
Vynnyse, 276, 307.
Westfield, 268.

Names of Fields and other
  Localities :—
Westley, 223, 282, 334, Wood, 306.
Wherr Corner, 274.
Wilkyns House, 76.
Windmill Tyning, 371-2.
Wiselands, 358.
Woodfalls, 357, 358n.
Woolrings, 328-9, 333.
Worlands, 137.
Wyesland, 105.
Nash, John, 102, 353-4.
  Mary, 353-4.
  Mathew, 103.
  William, 103.
Nashend, 390.
  Lower Farm, 393-4.
  Wood, 337.
Neal, Anne, 236.
  John, 236.
  William, 238.
Needlework, picture, 41.
Neville, Ralph, Earl of Westmorland,
  36.
Newbole, Henry de, 118.
Newlonde, Gloucester, 17.
Newenton, 22.
Newth, Charles, 268, 280.
Niblets Hill, 286.
Nicholls, Robert and Walter, 398.
Non-conformist Meetings, 274-5.
Norreys, Anne, 309.
  Henry, 289.
  Sir Lionel, 309.
Norman remains, 115.
Northampton, Earls of, 310.
Northfleet, Kent, 118-9.
Northwick, Worcs., 234, 329.
Notelyn, John, 276.
Notgrove, 246.
Nottingham, Sir William, 100, 289 (will)
  339.

Oak, John of the, 17.
Oaklands Grove, 56, 268.
Oakridge Church, 273.
Oatlands Wood, 334.
Oatridge, Margaret, 359.
Ohell, Edgeworth, 108.
Old House, Bussage, 343.
  Colcombe, 315.
Oldisworth, Arnold, 229.
Old Neighbouring, 317-8.
Olyffe, Agnes, 36, 276-7, 308.
  Robert, 276, 308.
  William, 308.
Olyvver, Thomas, vicar, 139.
Oppi, Robert, vicar, 139.
Orkeld, Jerome, 326.
Ormerod, Rev. G. T., 274.
Osbert, vicar, 115, 130.
Osborn, R. M., 324.

D3

Overcourt, 14, 24, 36.
    Indenture of sale and purchase, 46.
    Cottage, 47, 49.
Oxford, Corpus Christi College, 304, 309.

Pacy (or Peacey), Thomas, 274.
    Samuel, 270, 392.
Page, John, 16.
Pagenhill, 23, 81.
Pagenhull, Thomas de, 16.
    Walter de, 30, 305.
Pagett, James, 67, 267.
Paggonshill Farm, 335.
Paine, John, 295.
Painswick, 235, 367.
Palmer, Dr. F. C., 296.
Panting, John, 97, 271, 282, 340.
Paramour, Thomas, 228.
Parish registers, 186-7.
Parker, Thomas, 374.
Parry, John, 79.
Parsons, Alexander, 280.
Partridge, Charles, 292.
    Henry, 365.
    Rebecca, 291.
    Robert and William, 69.
Pate, Mary, and Thomas, 259.
Paulmead Cottage, 35.
Pauntley, Chapel of St. Gregory, 220.
Payne, John, 400.
Payton, Charles, 96.
Pear, The, 17, 228, 230-1.
Pearce, Anne, 108.
    George, 285.
    James, and Joan, 283.
    Robert, 288.
Peckitt, Henry, 50, 209.
Peers, Thomas, 378.
    Walter, 76, 378 (will).
Pegler, Mary, 272.
Pelly, Robert P., 318.
Pere, Robert de la, 17-8.
    William de la, 16-8, 84, 117, 230.
Perrin, John, 336.
    Richard, 144, 194, 384 (will).
Pers, Henry, 145, 277.
    John, 277.
    Walter, 71.
    Family, 278.
Pesthouse, 5, 211, 271.
Petifer, Roger, 389.
Pettit, Mary, 393 (will).
    Thomas, 103.
    William, 393
Petyl, Thomas, 221.
Phelps, Reuben, 274.
Philips, G. W., 300.
Phill, Elizabeth and Henry, 238.
Phillips, Charles Tayloe, 330.
    Stephen, vicar, 128, 155, 196, 319, 323,
        330 n.
Piedmont, 85.

Pillhouse, Painswick, 83.
Pinall, Henry, 358.
Pinbury, Richard, 253.
Pinchin, Henry and Thomas, 109.
Pincott, James, 270.
Piper, Rev. G. A., vicar, 160.
Piper, Mrs. 359.
Pitchcombe, 228, 236.
    Manor, 237.
Pitt, Joseph, 290.
    Rev. Wm., 50, 321.
Pitt-Eykyn, Rev., 299.
Plantagenet, Philippa, 33.
    Richard, Duke of York, 34.
Platt, Richard, 383.
Playne, George, 404.
Pleydell, Edward, 111.
Pole, John, clk., 139.
Poole, Arms of, 353.
    Rev. A., 349.
    Elizabeth, 45.
    Grace Anne, 352.
    Sir Henry, 37, 100, 126, 269, 365.
    Robert, 353.
    Thomas, 81, 353.
    William, 391.
Ponting, James, John, and William,
    200-1.
Pope Alexander VI., 141.
Pope, John, 85, 247, 340.
    Richard, 108, 339, 340.
    Thomas, 71, 77, 104, 152, 233, 339.
Porter, Arthur and Mabel, 101.
Powell, Alfred, 269.
    Thomas, 104, 145.
Powys, Lord of, 34.
Poyntz, Sir Nicholas, 101.
    Thomas, 37.
Prestbury, William of, rector of Minchin-
    hampton, 134.
Prevost, Rev. Sir George, 168, 324.
Pridie, John of, 131.
Priest, Family, 154 n.
    Martha, 152. ,
    Simon, vicar, 45, 153-4 (will).
Price, Mrs., 336.
Primrose Mount Cottage, murders at, 370.
Prinn, William Hunt, 314.
Prout, John, vicar, 138.
Proute, William, 131, 133.
Pirie, Robert de la, 18.
Pyddoke. Rev. E. W., 51, 169, 209,
    297-9.
Pye, Anthony, 79.
    Edward, 364.
Pyper, Thomas, clk, 192.

Query, Anne, 259.
    Arms of, 266.

Rack, Hill, 328, 333.
Radebrigg, William de, 27.

Radnor, Old, 116.
Raleigh, Sir Edward, 36, 269.
  George, 100, 269.
  Francis, 109.
  Sir William, 100.
Ram Inn, Bussage, 344.
Ramme, Elizabeth, 231.
Raymond-Barker, Rev. F. M., 63.
Randall, Ralph, 316.
  Wilfrid, 404.
Ratcliffe (or Ractcliffe) Charles, 334, 359.
  Elizabeth J., 263.
Rawlyns, Richard, vicar, 145, 167.
Reap, Emily, 302.
Rectory Farm, 129, 388.
  House, 126, 128-9, 314.
Reem (or Freame), Edward, 71, 255.
  John, 254.
  Roger, 23, 247, 254-5.
  Thomas, 254.
  William, 16, 23, 27, 30, 254.
Restall, Edward, 283, 378 (will).
  Henry, 283.
  Joan, 270.
  Mabel, 270.
  Matthias, 270.
  Nathaniel, 285.
  Richard, 377 (will).
  William, 200, 274.
Reynolds, Rev. J. W., 299.
Richards, Rev. K. K. E, 300.
Richmond, Professor, O. L., 69.
Ridler, Abraham, 272.
  Anne, 314.
  Francis, 110.
  George, 344.
  Hannah, 331.
  Jane, 405.
  Joan, 206.
  John, 44.
  Mary, 206, 331.
  Rev. Mr., 346.
  Mr. 45.
  Nathaniel, 328, 331, 361.
  Samuel, 272.
  Sara, 331.
  Thomas, 206.
  Robert, 263.
  Walter, 206.
  William, 110.
Road from London, 244.
Roberd, Thomas, 89.
Robert, vicar, 18.
Roberts, Arthur, 168.
  John, 233, 284, 330, 331 n
  Hester, 329.
Robbins, John, 406.
Robinson, Elizabeth, and William, 384.
Robyn, Adam, clk., 165, 218.
Roche, Stephen atte., clk., 123.
Rodburgh, Cecily of, 25-6, 115.
  Edward, 276.

Rodburgh, Philip, 246, 276.
  Thomas, 130, 204, 246.
  Feoffees of, 400.
Roderick, Owen de, 364.
Rodmarton, 223.
  Church, 220.
Rodney House, 297.
Roger, vicar, 134.
Rogers, Dr., 380.
Rogers, Elizabeth, 343.
  Henry, 165.
  George, 341.
  John, vicar, 139, 140, 142, 221.
  Joseph, 359.
  Mary, 340.
  Nathaniel, 209.
  Richard, 148, 340 (will), 343, 358, 361.
  Samuel, 341, 343.
  Thomas, 340-1 (will), 357.
  William, 310.
Rogers, Family, 400.
Rogers-Tillston, Dr. J. M., 296.
Rok, John de la, 165.
Rokwood, 18.
  Adam de, 389.
  Thomas de, 30.
Roman remains, 115.
Romney, Elizabeth, 292.
Roof of Church, 175.
Rookwoods, 282, 388-390.
Roos, Thomas, 219.
Roper, Miss Ida, 172-3.
Rose, Philip, D., 51.
Rothenstein, Albert, 394.
  Sir William, 392.
Rowles, Henry, 286.
  Marshall, 288.
  Oliver and William, 288.
Royatt, William, 56, 267.
Rundle, Ralph, 317.
Rushborne, Kent, 228.
Russell, Thomas, 292, 344.
Rutter, William, 86.
Rychman, John, 67.
Ryckman, Bauldwin, 60.
Rydings Farm, 285-6.
Sadleir, Michael, 73.
St. Gabriel, Fenchurch, 310.
St. Michael's Cottage, Bussage, 342.
Salisbury, Archdeacon of, 119.
Sampson, Rev. Gerald, 300.
Sancta Brigidia, Nicholas, 15.
Sandhurst, Berks, 22.
Sapperton, Church, 311.
Saunders, Catherine, 56, 268.
  Richard, 292.
Savell Family, 103-113.
  Richard, 104-5.
  William, 104, 248.
Sawyer, Rev. H., 351.
Saxon font, 52.
  Remains, 114.

Schobbeden, 25-6.
Scott, Roger, 41.
Sedgwick, John, vicar, 149.
  Katharine, 149, 186.
  Obadiah, 397.
Serche, Elizabeth, 61.
Selwyn, Robert, 27, 133, 357.
  William, 357.
Selwyn's Mill, 356.
Sered, John, 339.
  Walter, 305.
  William, 135.
Seredhouse, 132.
Sethcombe, 215.
  Thomas, clk, 304-5.
Sevill, Arms of, 86.
  Ann, 253.
  Frances, 331.
  Hester, 331.
  John, 302, 326.
  Mary, 326.
  Sarah, 401.
  Scholastice, 86.
  Samuel, 85-6, 110.
  Walter, 326.
  William, 85-6. 110, 253, 282, 326, 331,
    401.
Sewell, Agnes, 106.
  Alice, 109, 111.
  Anne, 109.
  Annes, 106.
  Edward, 111.
  Elizabeth, 106, 110.
  Giles, 107.
  Jane, 110.
  John, 102. 104, 107 (will), 108-9.
  Katherine, brass to, 103, 177.
  Richard, 104-5, 106. (I.P.M.)
  Robert, 110.
  Thomas, 85, 103-104 (will), 105, 107,
    109, 110.
  Walter, 106 (will), 107, 108 (will), 111.
  William, 104, 106-7, 109, 110, 111
    (will).
Seymour, Nicholas le, 131, 133.
  Sir Thomas, 37.
Shaw, Sir John, 166.
Sheephouse, 393.
Shefin, William, 101.
Shelford, Great, 153.
Shelley, Sir John, 59.
  Charles, 262.
Sheppard, Mrs. 324.
  Philip, 200, 262.
  Samuel, 200, 383.
Sherley, Mr., 230.
Sherman, Henry, 106.
  John, 85, 104.
  Walter, 309.
Shewell, 146.
  Elizabeth, 82, 310.
  Henry, 233.

Shewell, Jane, 82.
  John, 112 (will), 358, 404.
  Marjorie, 95.
  Robert, 86, 155.
  Thomas, 82, 358.
  Walter, 88, 340.
  William, 95, 358.
Shill, Thomas, 400.
Shirburn, Richard, clk., 120.
Short, Richard and Thomas, 48.
Shrewsbury, Edrich, Earl of, 25.
Sibree, John, 342.
Simkin, Rev. R. L., 274.
Siston Manor, 30.
Skaites Hill, 331-5.
  Farm, murder at, 332.
Skittermishe, James and Thomas, 258.
Skiveralls (see Corderries), 292-6.
  Wood, 393.
Skynner, John, 252.
  Thomas, vicar, 139.
Slad Farm, Steanbridge, 366.
Smalrugge, John, vicar, 138, 139.
Smart, Alice, 77 (will), 82.
  Andrew, 285-6.
  Edward, 78, 288.
  George, 108, 268.
  Henry, 45, 395.
  James, 75-6.
  Rev. 77.
  John, 80, 247-8.
  Joseph, 270.
  Judith, 285-6.
  Margaret, 67, 75-6.
  Richard, 71, 73, 79 (will), 82, 257,
    270, 357, 379, 394.
  Robert, 75.
  Thomas, 61 (will), 67, 69, 74-6, 78
    (will), 79, 83, 285 (will), 296.
  William, 67, 75 (will), 145.
Smart's Farm, 284-5.
Smith, builder, 98.
  C. W., 324.
  Henry, 339.
  Jocose, 339.
  Rev. John, 350.
  Thomas, 374.
Smyth, Rev. Christopher, 336, 350.
  Rt. Rev. Bishop Edmund, 297, 337.
  John, 219.
  Richard le, 35.
Snow. Alice, 41.
  Anthony, 356.
  Daniel, 361.
  Edward, 357.
  Ferdinando, 357, 402.
  John, 38, 357.
  Richard, 71, 357.
  Robert, 233.
  William, 82, 357, 385.
Snow's Mill, 356.
Sodynton, 34-5.

Sodynton, Thomas de, 364.
Solers, John, 139, 276, 308.
　Robert, 210.
　Thomas, 286.
Solomon's Court, 284.
Southam Delabere, 232, 239.
Southrop, 159.
Sparrow, Thomas, 45.
Spedour, John, clk., 193.
Speke, Capt., 241.
　Georgiana (Lady Dorington), 241.
Spelman, Nicholas, 246.
Spenser, Charles and Mary, 391.
Stafford, Henry, Lord, 249.
Stained glass at Lypiatt, 240.
Stancombe, 397-8.
　Robert, and Thomas, 397.
Standley, John, 373.
Stanton, Anis, 137.
　Rev. A. W., 263.
Steanbridge, 365-7.
　King Charles I. at, 367.
Stephens, Arms of, 237.
　Of Inner Temple, 103.
　Anne, 237.
　Edward, 42, 230, 235 (will).
　Farrington, 238-9.
　George, 288.
　Henry, 282.
　Hester, 237.
　John, 78, 102, 150, 231-3, 237-9.
　Jonathan, 341.
　Nathaniel, 228, 232.
　Richard, 249, 252.
　Thomas, 39, 42, 78, 227-9 (will), 230,
　　234, (will), 236-7, 357.
　William, 200.
　Vault, desecration of, 238-9.
Stephensbridge, 318 n, 325.
Starwell, or Sterwell, 111, 112 n, 372.
Stevens, Henry, 146.
　William, 401.
Stitchell, William, 384.
Stokes, Thomas, 117.
Stoke Clare, 14.
　College of, 104, 120-1, 125, 194.
Stokes, Capt., 87.
Stokesend, 14, 21, 27, 35.
Stone, Elizabeth and John, 228.
　William, 328.
Stone Coffin, 53.
Stonedge House, 111.
Stoneham, John, 34-5.
Stonehenge, John, 202.
　Robert, 16, 21, 89, 202, 304.
　Walter, 16, 30, 395.
　William, 165, 202.
Stonehing, Estate of, 202-5, 337.
Stow-in-the-Wold, 225.
Strangford, Lord, 240.
Stratford, Edward, 257.
　Elizabeth, 279 (will).

Strode, Robert de, clk., 19.
　Richard de, 19.
Stroud, Chapel, 221.
　Church, Chapel of the Assumption,
　　220.
　Curate of, 127.
　Thomas, 267.
Stroud, Thomas de, 67.
Stumpe, Sir James and William, 68.
Strudwick, Rev. C. H., 300.
Sturmy, Arms of, 87.
　Alice, 88 (will), 278.
　Edmund, 88.
　Henry, 87.
　John, 27, 30, 87, 133.
Sturmye's Court, 87-8, 199-202.
Suckling, Rev. Robert, 347.
　Mrs. Suckling, 342.
　Rev. R. A., 348-9.
Sudgrove, Thomas, 22.
Sunday Institution, 209.
Swayne, Rev. R. G., 349.
Swedenborgian Chapel, 319.
Swerde, Prebendary of, 118.
Swetenham, Matthew de, 33.
Syde, rectory, 148.
Sydenham, John, 85, 101.
　Walter of, 30.
　William of, 27, 84, 133.
Sydenhams, 18, 84-7, 331.

Tailo, Simon, vicar, 135, 138, 395.
Talbot, Sir Richard de, 22.
Tankard, Springs, 253.
Tanglewood, Brownshill, 202-3, 337.
Tanner, John and Isaac, 268.
Tarleton, 225-6, 260.
Taunton, John, 70.
Taverner, Edward, 17.
Tayloe (or Tailoe), Arms of, 49, 330.
　Alice, 405.
　Hester, 49, 154, 320-2 (will), 330 (will),
　　333.
　John, 317-8.
　Mary, 203, 286.
　Margerie, 327.
　Nathaniel, 44.
　Rebecca, 45.
　Richard, 85.
　Robert, 43, 45-6, 293 (will), 302, 391.
　Samuel, 44-5, 47-8.
　Sarah, 45, 327-8.
　Simon, 41.
　Thomas, 38, 41, 42-4 (will), 45, 47-8
　　(will), 49, 148, 233, 293, 327-8 (will),
　　360, 404-5.
　Walter, 330-1.
　William, 41, 85, 203, 205, 238, 286,
　　294-5 (will), 317-8, 327-330 (will),
　　331, 334.
Tayler, John, 207.
　Thomas, 54.

Tayler, Thomas, vicar, 75, 145.
Taylor (or Tayloe), Anne, 270, 292-3.
  Robert, 292-3.
Taylor, John, 167, 207.
  Richard, 108.
  Thomas, 252.
Teakle, Farmer, 290.
  William, 51.
Temple Church, London, 38.
Temple Guiting, 32.
Teste, Alice, 101.
  Giles, 91, 101.
  Lawrence, 91, 101.
  William, 91.
Tetbury, Church of, 220.
Tewkesbury, Abbot of, 247.
Teynham, Lord, 336.
Thames and Severn Canal, 97.
Theyer, John, 384.
Thirteenth century well cover, 170-1.
Thorp, Archdeacon, 348.
  John, clk., 121.
Thomas, pro-rector, 116.
  Benjamin, 295.
  John, 320.
Thoresby Bishop, 117.
Thour, John, 141-2.
Throckmorton (Throgmorton), George, 396.
  John, 94-5, 226-7, 231.
  Nicholas, 101.
  Thomas, 396.
  William, 222.
Througham, Reginald de, 19, 66.
  Richard de, 66.
Througham, 64-9.
  Chapel at, 66.
  Manor of, 67, 310, 312.
  Manor House, 72-3.
  Upper and Lower Farms at, 72-3.
Througham Slad, 71-2.
Tiler, Thomas, 340.
Timbercombe, 110, 312.
Timbull, Rachel, 391.
Tithe, Great, 125-8.
Tithes, Vicarial, 160-1.
Tocknell, James, 76, 289.
Tocwell, Richard, 105.
Todsmore, 42, 355-9.
  Common, 356.
  Fishpond, 213.
Toghill, William, 318, 324, 342, 344.
Tombs, Sarah, 294.
Tomlins, Robert, Dr., 54, 61, 148, 233, 384.
Tomson, John, clk., 378.
Tonleye, William de, 19, 305.
Totty, Richard, vicar 139.
Tower of Church, 183.,
Towesyer, Agnes, 377.
Townsend, Catherine, 384.
  Edward, 393 (will).

Townsend, Henry, 54.
  Joane, 42.
  Katherine, 149.
  Mary, 147.
  Poriander, 384.
  Richard, 365, 404.
  Theyer, 207.
  Thomas, 391.
  Widow, 45.
Trapp, Judith, 111.
  William, 396.
Trenhulle, William, 284, 306.
Trevylyon, John, clk., 144, 166, 224, 256.
Trinity Lodge, Bisley, 299.
Tristram, Anne, 96.
  Seth, 41, 395.
  Thomas, 96.
  Walter, 276, 306-7.
Troham, Hardwisia, 65.
  Reginald de, 305.
  Richard de, 65.
  William de, 389.
Trotman, Edward, 294.
  Elinor, 70.
  John, 319, 333.
  Mary, 45.
  Mrs. M., 322-3.
  Samuel, 294.
  Thomas, 46-7, 329, 360.
Trillies, 56, 68, 267.
Tunley, 88, 100.
  Farm, 97.
  William of, 27, 88, 133.
Turnbull, John, clk., 193.
Turner, 80-4.
  Arms of, 84.
  Rev. Charles, 159.
  Edward, 83 (will), 110.
Turner, Frances, 230.
  Henry, 68, 70, 80 (will), 110.
  John, 80-1 (will), 82-3 (will).
  Margaret, 68.
  Roger, 82.
  Samuel, 83.
  Thomas, 68, 70.
  William, 69-70 (will), 74.
Twissel or Tywssell, Alice, 93.
  Henry, 41, 148.
  John, 43.
  Robert, 277-9, 309.
  William, 278 (will).
Twissel family, brass to, 279.
Tydmarshe, John, 226.
Tyler, Esther, 282.
  Henry, 270.
  James, 341, 343.
  John, 270, 330.
  Martha, 330.
  Nathaniel, 282.
  Thomas, 341, 343.
  Walter, 270.
Tymberhulle, Henry, clk., 193.

Tymberhulle, Katherine, 306.
　William, 373.
Tyndall, Thomas, 55.
　William, 55.

Unwin, Maurice, clk., 194.
Uphaven, Henry de, clk., 192.
Upton-St.-Leonards, 207.

Vale, Oliver, clk., 166.
Vauce, William, 120, 139, 140, 193.
Verdun, Arms of, 31.
　John de, 30, 118.
　Theobald de, 20, 28-31, 118.
Vicarage of Bisley, Ordinance of, 136-7.
Vicarage House, 162.
Vines, Mr., 249.
Visitation of Bisley, 135.
Vizard, Mary, 55.

Wakeman, John, Bishop of Gloucester, 145.
　Thomas, 145.
Walbank, Abraham, 294, 316, 333.
Walker, T. A., 52.
Wall, John, 154.
　Richard, 76.
Wallis, Charles P., 163.
　John Edmund, bequest, 347.
　Katherine, 340.
　Mabel, 359.
　William T., 263.
Walwyn, Thomas, 22.
Wanborough, Wilts., 260.
Wansford, John, vicar, 139, 276, 308.
Wantage, Community of St. Mary the Virgin, 353.
Ward, Thomas, clk., 88, 108-9.
Ware, Daniel, 332.
Warneford, Rev. Dr., 322.
Warner, Thomas, 235.
Warren, iron artificer, 261, 263.
Warwick, Countess of, 229.
Washbourne, 198.
　Mary, 326.
Watercombe, House, 3, 4, 272.
Waterlane, 271-2.
Wathen, Sir Paul, als. Baghott, 240.
Watkins, Daniel, 49.
　Elizabeth, 51, 344.
　Giles, 154.
　James, 326.
　John, 167.
　Mary, 50.
　Sarah, 49.
　Thomas, 50-1.
　William, 326, 356, 358.
Wax for candles, 137.
Wear, James, 296.
Webb, Daniel, 292.
　Edmund, 196, 311-2.
　Elizabeth, 47, 332.

Webb, John, 47, 196, 295, 302, 390, 393.
　Katherine, 323.
　Samuel, 204, 233, 282 (will), 329.
　Thomas, 106, 252.
　William, 282 (will).
Webb's Court House, 282.
Weelock, Cheshire, 236.
Well House, Aveniss, 286.
West, William, 289 (will).
Westbury, St. Mary, College of, 195.
Western, Dr. G., 296.
Westley, Sir Robert, 262.
Westmacott, Theodore, 302.
　Thomas, 201.
Westwood Farm, 267.
Wetmore, Ann and Thomas, 294.
Wheeler, Dr. 301.
Whish, Evelyn, 344.
White, George, 154.
　Gilbert, clk., 299.
　Thomas, 249.
Whitehead, 294.
　Susan, 84.
Whithed, 289.
Whitntye, Sir James, 226.
Whitteneye, Giles, 337.
Whitt, Elizabeth, 105.
Whytington, Charles, 166.
　Guy, 219.
　John, 104, 221.
　Richard, 219, 220.
　Robert, 219.
　Thomas, 140, 220-1 (will), 255, 308-9.
　William, 71, 220, 308.
　Monument, 222.
Whything, John, 357.
Whytyng, John, 70, 75, 257, 274.
Wickham Grange, 329, 333.
Wigmore Abbey, 25-6, 28.
William, parson of Bisley, 12, 18, 26, 115-6.
Williams, Rev. Isaac, 51, 168-9, 348-9.
Willie or Wyllie, Anthony, 312, 396.
Willis, lay rector, 128.
Willoughby, Lord, 365.
Wills, List of, 407-415.
Wilson, Mrs., 344.
Winchcombe, John, 394.
　Mary, 105 n, 2.
Winchester, William, Bishop of, 33.
Windowe, Arms of, 260.
　Henry, Sarah, and William, 260.
Wine for peoples' Communion, 137.
Winn, John, 354.
　Mary, 354.
　William, 205, 295, 339.
Winstone, 32-4.
　Samuel, 392.
Winterbotham, Dr. A., 290.
Wishanger, 28, 69.
Witlesey, Bishop, 119.
Witt, Elizabeth, 354.

Witts, Daniel, 357-8.
  Thomas, 95.
Wittan Tree, 7, 111.
  Quars, 155.
Wodenorton, Roger, clk., 123.
Wolrugge, John, 138.
Wood, Charles, 109.
Wood, J. G., F.S.A., 6.
Woodall, Corbett W., 263.
  Elizabeth and Simon, 333.
Woodcock, Judge, 242.
Woodfield, Daniel, 57.
  Moses, 402.
Woodhouse, Gordon, 263.
Woodlands, Bussage, 342.
Woodruffe, Paul, 59.
Woodville, Elizabeth, 36.
Wool Industry, 380-2.
Worcester Cathedral, 220.
Workhouse, Bisley, 210-1.
Workman, Nathaniel, 361.
  Thomas, 146, 378 (will).
  William, 343.
Wright, Samuel, 334.
Wroth, Richard, 373.
Wyatt, Daniel, 290.
  Henry, 249.

Wybury, James and Richard, 224.
Wye, Arms of, 224.
  Elizabeth, 226.
  Johanna, 224.
  Juliana, 226.
  Robert, 103, 221-2 (will), 223-4, 255.
  Thomas, 222, 224-5 (will).
  William Master, 224.
Wyks, William de, 90.
Wymar, Thomas, 310, 312.
Wyndham, Frederick and James, 280.
Wyndle, Christopher, vicar, 106, 147-8.
  Mary, 148-9.
Wyresdell, Henry, vicar, 142-3.
Wyvelesford, John, vicar, 133.

Yale, John, 342.
Yaneworth, Walter de, vicar, 134.
Yates, Nathaniel, 148.
Yelloly. Anna Maria and Dr., 348.
York, Cecily, Duchess of, 24, 277, 308.
  Richard, Duke of, 24, 36, 121, 174, 195, 307.
Young, George, 69.
  James, 362.
  John, 361.
  Joseph, 279.

Thanet House,
Chalford,
Stroud.

May 1977.

Dear Reader.

I trust a word of explanation will be accepted as to the reasons for intruding into these pages after the lapse of forty years since the original publication of Miss Rudd's work.

Miss Mary Amelia Rudd of The Woodlands. Bussage. got in contact with me upon hearing that I possessed many notes upon the history of the locality. Meetings followed. both at Bussage and Chalford. together with the exchange of letters. Meetings usually took the form of questions by her. while it must be said her general manner was rather didactic. This is shown in that her first question was where I had worshipped on the previous Sunday?

When it was ascertained that she had already been engaged for some years upon this historical venture (for which I once had an ambition). most of the gathered notes with copies of Deeds and Wills were made available for her use.

As many things upon which further information could have been given were never sought, a number of corrections could have been effected before publication. When some items were volunteered it became clear that she was tiring of the task, and once confessed the "she had left it too late in life", and did not wish to pursue subjects which she obviously considered closed.

It will be understood throughout the following notes that Miss Rudd is referred to as "the author" or "she", while I have preferred to refer to myself as "the writer".

After this lapse of time I greatly cherish a number of her original notes, proferred by her and gratefully accepted. Letters also dated in 1936.

It is sincerely hoped that these invited corrections and explanations will not be interpreted as any reflection upon the author's ability or assiduity, but rather as a belated contribution to a good and useful pioneer work.

Frederick T. Hammond

CORRECTIONS AND ADDITIONS

Preface — 'Brimpsfield' should read 'Brimfield'.

p.57 — There is little reason to suppose that the early Jaynes mentioned were connected with Jaynes Court. Formerly known as Higgins Court, it came to the Jaynes by the devise of Walter Hancox.

p.75 — The date should be 1558 not 1588.

p.75 — The pedigree of the Througham Smarts is far from complete. Had she discovered a certain will the two parts could have joined. This was never discussed, but the writer has long been interested since his wife was of this name.

p.78 — The Smart monument refers to burials in the north aisle at Bisley, and Bigland gives an inscription upon a heraldic stone there. This was placed outside as a paving stone at the restoration, but to make it fit, part of the original inscription was cut away.

p.79   –   'buried at Stonehouse' should be "Duntisbourne House".

p.95   –   William Hancox died in 1672 not 1670. The brass plate to his memory bears the seemingly contradictory phrase "A Cavilier under Oliver Cromwell".

p.98   –   It would have been a feat of strength indeed if Thomas Hancox lifted any person over Daneway Bridge 'into the lock'. Locks were usually some yards from bridges, so that if any such event ever happened, the victim would have been dropped into the 'pound' below the lock.

p.185   –   Some pre-Reformation glass (a saint's head) has been seen built into the window of a back room (at Bussage) of a house built for himself by a foreman mason employed at the re-building of Bisley Church.

p.200   –   Samuel Shepherd should be "Sheppard".

p.236   –   Thomas Stephens had eight children, but two died young.

p.236   –   "whilst Katherine must have been born and baptised elsewhere" – the said Catherine was baptised at Stroud on November 16 1710.

p.281   –   Any reader interested in heraldry may be puzzled at the blazon of the Dorington arms, since they differ from those upon a mural in Bisley chancel and upon the Market House. The reason appears that other families were using this coat also (Sable, three bugle horns Argent). When Mr. J.E. Dorington was created a Baronet in 1886, the arms were modified to those given.

p.259   –   There seems to be confusion respecting the Freame monuments at Bisley and Stroud. There is record of a very ornate monument at Stroud now reduced to a tablet, but it may still be found in its original state high in the tower space; while other (at Bisley) formerly adorned with bust and general profusion profusion of ornament has been reduced to a slate tablet. As there are varying references to the Freame arms a false impression may be gained from one on the same page. The usual arms of this family were – "Argent, a chevron Sable, in chief a bar engrailed Gules", but they also used (see reference in 1623 Herald's Visitations as a second quartering)– "Argent, a cross patonce between four ears of wheat proper". Finally, the arms of the unidentified wife of the last male Freame of Nether Lypiatt, as shown as impalement at Stroud, but as a quartering upon a stone shield mentioned in a later note, were – "Gules, a dexter arm in plate mail, embowed Or". (See note for page 265.)

p.260   –   Charles Coxe the Judge who rebuilt Nether Lypiatt married only once, namely to Ann Chamberlayne. On their marriage licence issued in the Archbishop's Court, he is described as a bachelor aged 30. Miss Rudd has followed others in this second wife myth, which apparently arose from the loose wording of Atkyns of "Coxe marrying the Freame heiress". Whereas this is true, it was not to a Freame daughter but to a daughter's daughter.

p.261   –   It seems singular that a 12 ft. monument was erected to Coxe's horse yet there is no memorial to him. Whereas there are several monuments at Rodmarton, to his brother and to his own descendants, the only local note of his death is in the Rodmarton burial register which reads "1728 Oct. 22 – Charles Coxe Esq. of the parish of Stroud".

p.262   –   Miss Rudd seems uncertain of the date of the death of Sir Robert Westley, sometime Lord Mayor of London. A monument on the west wall at Kemple Church gives Sep. 24 1746 aged 75.

P.262   –   William Gardner died at Nether Lypiatt in 1812 aged 82 or 83 (the burial register and his obituary plate differing by a year). The Ridler family continued the tenancy of whom, George Ridler by his Will dated 1837 passed his interest in the lease between his son Robert (died 1845) and his daughter Jane who married Charles Ractliffe. The last names (who had previously farmed the Abnash) continued the lease. Their daughter Jane Elizabeth married William Thomas Wallis, and followed by his son Charles Pearson Wallis, who continued at Nether Lypiatt until 1915. Thus a connected tenancy of well over a century was broken.

p.262   –   A supplement to the record of later owners of Nether Lypiatt may be acceptable at this point.

1882–May 15 –   Deed of Gift by Anna Gordon to Philip Sheppard.
1883–May 23 –   Mortgage, Philip Sheppard (1) Edw. Fredk. Chadwick, Rev. Hayton Osborne Sheppard & Rev. Edmund Broome (2)
1898–Dec. 29 –   Death of Osborne Sheppard.
1914–July 14 –   Conveyance, the above E.F. Chadwick & G. Hayton (1) & Arthur W. Stanton (2)
1919–Sep. 19 –   Conveyance, A.W. Stanton to Corbett W. Woodall.

with the intention of restoring, but as seen above, the purchase was immediately before the First World War, during which much unessential building was suspended. In the same year Mr. Stanton's bachelor uncle Charles Holbrow Stanton died, and in due course A.W. Stanton moved to his late uncle's residence, Field Place, Paganhill. Incidentally there a further connection locally in that the wife of P. Morley Horder the architect was a daughter of Ebenezer Apperly, a brother of Sir Alfred Apperly of Rodborough Court & Dudbridge Mills.

p.263 –   The house presumably belonged to Mrs. Violet Gordon Woodhouse, as the writer recalls her assertion upon more than one occasion. She was an early broadcaster being a brilliant exponent of the Spinet or Harpsichord.

p.265 –   There is also some confusion of two separate items at Nether Lypiatt:– (1) an iron fire-back with raised initials I.C 1734 (for John Coxe) & – (2) an heraldic stone found during restoration, built face inwards & used as building material. This must have been a relic of the older house, and measured about 2 feet square & four inches thick. It bore a quartered shield with the arms of Freame and Biggs with those of Ann previously mentioned as the wife of the last direct Freame. (See 259 note.) As it contained this last coat, it suggests its erection as being soon after the marriage which was about 1631, but before the husband's death in 1664. When found, it was re-set centrally over the fireplace in the dining room, but soon removed to make room for panelling Mr. Woodall had acquired. During the process of extraction from the wall the stone became badly fractured. The last time the writer saw this interesting relic was in an outhouse, stoutly crated. This was during the Woodhouse-Barrington occupation. The note on p.266 is a shortened account furnished to Miss Rudd concerning the above.

p.265 –   Miss Rudd refers to the discovery of human skeletons. These were said to be seven in number and buried radially feet inwards. This was not verified, but when the writer visited the scene in a few days he was conducted by the tenant farmer to a heap of bones beneath a wall and covered by a sheet of corrugated iron. Nothing was whole, but an enquiry if a specimen could be taken evoked the reply "Take the lot if you like". A piece, about five-eights of a jawbone was finally selected. This was filled with teeth, all of which were worn flat, apparently by coarse food. After the lapse of some years this was passed to Stroud Museum.

p.284 –   More recent history of Lillyhorn House could have been given. Like so many other properties this came into the hands of the Driver family, one of whose daughters married Richard William Walter Nathaniel Hancox, descended from a younger branch of the Denway stock. After his wife's death he led a lonely and neglected life, said to be owing to alleged habits. He was finally removed to a Cirencester institution where he died.

p.287 –   The brass plates commemorating the Baker, Aldridge and Twissell families stood, not in the tower space at Bisley, but on the west wall of the south aisle. Since the author's death these have been moved to allow organ alterations.

p.294 –   Brillings Firth or Coppice Gate was not near the Corderries as supposed. It lies in Coppice Hill, Chalford at the entrance to the Barley Grounds. Edward Corderoy owned a weaving shed with a cottage there, which he sold for £70 to Nathaniel Overbury, a Tetbury Woolstapler in 1746. The purpose was for the latter to promote a Baptist Meeting; and the modified building is the present schoolroom of Chalford Tabernacle. There was a quantity of woodland near this spot as late as 1870.

p.295 - 'Arthur' Blackwell should read 'Archer' Blackwell. This unusual Christian name given to some owners of 'The Grove', Chalford arose by a mid 17th. century marriage of John Blackwell & Elizabeth Archer.

p.299 - Pitt Eykyn, Curate in Charge of France Lynch, subsequently became Vicar of Magor-with-Renwick.

p.314 - It seems strange that after the detailed records of the vicissitudes of the Chalford Estate in pre-Reformation days, Miss Rudd seemed unaware of the many post-Reformation leases, copies of which are in the fire-proof vaults of the library of Corpus Christi College, Oxford. Through the kindness of the Librarian the writer has been allowed to examine these which clearly shows that following the financial success of the Ridler family they regularly renewed the lease previously taken, and sub-let to clothiers — hence the families of Bliss, Ballinger and others. After the death of the last Ridler of the male direct line there were three co-heiresses, part of the fortune coming to the wife of Doddington Hunt, whose descendant William Hunt Prinn (mentioned p.314) represented the Ridler interest. The College dispersed much of its Chalford property in the 1870's.

p.319 - 'Conk' should read 'Monk'. Dr. Monk, Bishop of Gloucester was said to be the last bishop to wear a wig. His portrait is in the Church House, Gloucester.

p.321 - 'Mathew Blagden' should read 'Mathew Blagden Hale', Vicar of Stroud.

p.320 - 'Gobb' should read 'Gabb'.

p.322 - Reliance seems to have been placed on 'Glos. Notes & Queries' for the position of the Charity Boards in Chalford Church. These were formerly on the gallery which was taken down about 1880, when the said boards were removed to the belfry.

p.322 - Rev. Hamilton Kingsford was given temporary charge of Chalford during the extended illness and leave of absence by the Vicar Rev. Solomon Gompertz.

p.324 - 'Henry Bengh' should read 'Henry Burgh' the Stroud Attorney and Banker and sometime occupier of Stanley Park.

p.324 - If William Toghill was ever at Smart's Mill (now Arnold's Designs Ltd) he would have been a tenant which is unlikely. There has been a complete transcription of the 18th. & 19th. century of this property, with no mention of Toghill. In the Deeds of Thanet House, Toghill is described as of 'New Mill' and 'Two ponds of water'. This suggests one of the mills in Dark Lane with which William Toghill was associated at the time of his bankruptcy.

p.329 - It may be interesting to record that Wickham Grange became the property (after the Ballingers) of yet another branch of the Tayloe family. From legal correspondence at the time of purchase by William Dangerfield it appears that a William Tayloe (a co-lateral of the High Sheriff), by his Will created certain entails which were of necessity broken to achieve a sale. A Statuary Declaration by Edward Tayloe of South Lodge, Clapham, co. Middlesex, Surgeon, affirms his own baptism and the marriage of his parents. It is interesting to note that the copy of Rudder which was in the library at Stroud contained a bookplate with the arms of this family, together with the name "Mary Tayloe, South Lodge, Clapham".

p.332 - Charles Ballinger married Elizabeth daughter of John Webb of Howcombe, Clothier, and whose impaled shield is in France Congregational Church, Chalford Hill.

p.333 - A later Charles Ballinger married Sarah, daughter of Richard Jones of Kynaston, co. Hereford.

p.355 - The reference by Sir Robert Atkyns to the Roger Bacon tradition associated with St. Mary's, Chalford, was taken from William Camden's "Brittania" first published in 1586.